FREE DVD FREE FREE DVD

From Stress to Success **DVD** fron ......est Prep

Dear Customer,

Thank you for purchasing from Trivium Test Prep! Whether you're a new teacher or looking to advance your career, we're honored to be a part of your journey.

To show our appreciation (and to help you relieve a little of that test-prep stress), we're offering a **FREE *CLEP Social Sciences and History Test Tips DVD**** by Trivium Test Prep. Our DVD includes 35 test preparation strategies that will help keep you calm and collected before and during your big exam. All we ask is that you email us your feedback and describe your experience with our product. Amazing, awful, or just so-so: we want to hear what you have to say!

To receive your **FREE *CLEP Social Sciences and History Test Tips DVD***, please email us at 5star@triviumtestprep.com. Include "Free 5 Star" in the subject line and the following information in your email:

1. The title of the product you purchased.
2. Your rating from 1 – 5 (with 5 being the best).
3. Your feedback about the product, including how our materials helped you meet your goals and ways in which we can improve our products.
4. Your full name and shipping address so we can send your **FREE *CLEP Social Sciences and History Test Tips DVD***.

If you have any questions or concerns please feel free to contact us directly at 5star@triviumtestprep.com.

Thank you, and good luck with your studies!

* Please note that the free DVD is <u>not included</u> with this book. To receive the free DVD, please follow the instructions above.

CLEP Social Sciences and History Study Guide 2018-2019

CLEP Test Prep and Practice Test Questions for the Social Science & History Exam

TABLE OF CONTENTS

ONLINE RESOURCES

To help you fully prepare for your CLEP Social Sciences and History exam, Accepted includes online resources with the purchase of this study guide.

Practice Test

In addition to the practice test included in this book, we also offer an online exam. Since many exams today are computer based, getting to practice your test-taking skills on the computer is a great way to prepare.

Flash Cards

A convenient supplement to this study guide, Accepted's flash cards enable you to review important terms easily on your computer or smartphone.

Cheat Sheets

Review the core skills you need to master the exam with easy-to-read Cheat Sheets.

From Stress to Success

Watch From Stress to Success, a brief but insightful YouTube video that offers the tips, tricks, and secrets experts use to score higher on the exam.

Reviews

Leave a review, send us helpful feedback, or sign up for Accepted promotions—including free books!

Access these materials at:

www.acceptedinc.com/clep-social-studies-online-resources

INTRODUCTION

Congratulations on choosing to take the CLEP Social Sciences and History exam! By purchasing this book, you've taken an important step on your path to college.

This guide will provide you with a detailed overview of the CLEP Social Sciences and History exam, so you know exactly what to expect on test day. We'll take you through all the concepts covered on the test and give you the opportunity to test your knowledge with practice questions. Even if it's been a while since you last took a major test, don't worry; we'll make sure you're more than ready!

What is the CLEP?

The College-Level Examination Program, or CLEP, offers standardized tests in thirty-six subjects. The CLEP assesses college-level knowledge and allows students to demonstrate they have proficiency in a subject and bypass the coursework. If a student passes the exam, he or she earns college credit without having to take a single class. Anyone can take the CLEP, but it is designed specifically for people who have had experiences that have allowed them to obtain substantial expertise outside of the classroom: students who have been homeschooled or undertaken extensive independent study, students who studied outside of the United States, adults returning to school after being the workforce, and members of the military.

Approximately 2900 colleges and universities in the United States grant CLEP credit. Each college or university determines which exams to accept and sets their own passing score for each exam. Typically these range from fifty to sixty out of eighty points. Each college also decides how much credit an exam is worth. Typically, colleges will offer three credits for an exam, but some schools offer more (depending on the test), and some may offer only an exemption from the requirement, but no credit towards graduation. If credits are given, they are added to your transcript just like credits from your coursework would be. CLEP credits carry the same weight as any other earned credits.

What's on the CLEP Social Sciences and History Exam?

The CLEP Social Sciences and History exam gauges college-level content knowledge in history economics, political science, and geography. It also assesses important social science skills, including interpretation, analysis, and application of abstractions. Candidates are expected to demonstrate thorough conceptual knowledge, not related to a specific undergraduate course, but that which could be found in any introductory course in each of the focus areas. The CLEP Social Sciences and History exam is designed for non-history or social science majors.

You will have ninety minutes to answer 120 multiple-choice questions, including unscored pre-test questions.

CLEP Social Sciences and History Exam Content

PART I: HISTORY – 40% OF EXAM

CONTENT AREA	TOPICS	PERCENTAGE
United States History	◆ The colonial period, the American Revolution, the early republic ◆ Civil War and Reconstruction ◆ Industrialization, the Progressive Era ◆ World War I, the 1920s ◆ The Great Depression and the New Deal ◆ World War II ◆ The 1950s, the Cold War, social conflict—the 1960s and 1970s ◆ The late twentieth century, the early twenty-first century	13 – 15%
Western Civilization	◆ Ancient Western Asia, Egypt, Greece, and Rome ◆ Medieval Europe ◆ Modern Europe, including its expansion and outposts throughout the world ◆ Europe's imperial contraction and new economic and political forms	13 – 15%
World History	◆ Prehistory to present of: Africa, Asia, Australia, Europe, North America, and South America ◆ Focus on global themes and interactions	13 – 15%

PART II: Social Sciences – 60% of Exam

Content Area	Topics	Percentage
Economics	◆ Economic measurements ◆ International trade ◆ Major theorists and schools ◆ Monetary and fiscal policy ◆ Product markets ◆ Resource markets ◆ Scarcity, choice, and cost	20%

Content Area	Topics	Percentage
Geography	◆ Key geographic skills ◆ Cultural geography ◆ Physical geography ◆ Population ◆ Regional geography ◆ Rural and urban land use ◆ Spatial interaction	20%

Government/
Political Science
	◆ Comparative politics
	◆ International relations
	◆ Methods
	◆ United States
	  ❖ Civil rights and liberties
	  ❖ Constitution and its interpretation
	  ❖ Institutions
	  ❖ Parties, interest groups, and media
	  ❖ Voting and political behavior
		20%

Part I: History

The history section focuses on a general knowledge of each historical category. Test-takers are expected to demonstrate an understanding of the chronology and context of historical events. Test-takers should also be able to understand history through various lenses: political, diplomatic, social, economic, intellectual, and cultural.

Expect depth of knowledge to correlate with the length of the timeframe covered. So, for world history, the breadth of content is extensive: essentially all of the world's continents from pre-history to present. These questions generally will not require a significant depth of knowledge. The United States history questions, however, only cover about 400 years of history in one specific place. Because the breadth is so much narrower, greater depth of knowledge is expected.

Part II: Social Sciences

In each of the three social science sections, test-takers are expected to demonstrate both mastery of key concepts and of skills specific to the social science. For example, in economics not only should you be able to identify the major economic theories and apply them to real world circumstances, you also be able to properly use basic economic measures.

In geography, map, table, and chart reading are of particular importance, in addition to understanding measures and theories of population growth and economic development, land use, and the relationship between people and the land.

The government and political science questions can be organized into two types: those specific to the American system of government and those looking at government from an international or comparative perspective. Methods of analyzing and interpreting data especially important in these questions.

How is the CLEP Social Sciences and History Exam Scored?

Your CLEP Social Sciences and History exam is scored immediately upon completion. Before you see your scores, you will choose whether you want them reported. You must make this choice before you have seen your score. Once you have seen your score, you cannot choose to have it cancelled.

Your CLEP scores will automatically be added to your CLEP transcript. When you register, you can pre-select the college or employer you would like to receive your scores. If you are taking the exam before you have enrolled in school, you can request your CLEP transcript when you are ready. The first transcript request is free regardless of when it is requested.

Each multiple-choice question is worth one raw point. The total number of questions you answer correctly is added up to obtain your raw score. The raw score is then scaled to a score between twenty and eighty. Minimum passing scores vary by institution, so check with your college or university.

There is no guessing penalty on the CLEP Social Sciences and History exam, so you should always guess if you do not know the answer to a question.

How is the CLEP Social Sciences and History Exam Administered?

The CLEP Social Sciences and History exam is a computer-based test offered at over 1700 locations worldwide. There are four different types of test centers:

- ◆ Open test centers will test any student who has registered and paid the fee.
- ◆ Limited test centers are located at universities and colleges and will only test admitted or enrolled students.

- On-base test centers are located in military installations and only test eligible service members and civilians with authorized access to the installation.
- Fully funded test centers are also only for military service members, eligible civilians, and their spouses. These centers test DANTES-funded test-takers who are exempt from the administrative fee.

Regardless of the type of test center, you must contact the test center directly to make a reservation to take the exam.

Check https://clep.collegeboard.org/search/test-centers for more information.

You will need to print your registration ticket from your online account and bring it, along with your identification, to the testing site on test day. Some test centers will require other forms or documentation, so check with your test center in advance. Test centers may also require administrative fees in addition to the registration fee for the exam itself. No pens, pencils, erasers, printed or written materials, electronic devices or calculators are allowed. You also may not bring any kind of bag or wear headwear (unless for religious purposes). You may take the test once every three months. Please note that DANTES does not fund retesting.

About This Guide

This guide will help you to master the most important test topics and also develop critical test-taking skills. We have built features into our books to prepare you for your tests and increase your score. Along with a detailed summary of the test's format, content, and scoring, we offer an in-depth overview of the content knowledge required to pass the test. In the review you'll find sidebars that provide interesting information, highlight key concepts, and review content so that you can solidify your understanding of the exam's concepts. You can also test your knowledge with sample questions throughout the text and practice questions that reflect the content and format of the CLEP Social Sciences and History exam. We're pleased you've chosen Accepted, Inc. to be a part of your journey!

one

UNITED STATES HISTORY

North America Before European Contact

Northeastern Societies

Prior to European colonization, diverse Native American societies controlled the continent; they would later come into economic and diplomatic contact, and military conflict, with European colonizers and United States forces and settlers.

Major civilizations that would play an important and ongoing role in North American history included the **IROQUOIS** and **ALGONQUIN** in the Northeast; the Iroquois in particular were known for innovative agricultural and architectural techniques, including the construction of longhouses and the farming of maize. The Iroquois farmed according to the *three sisters* tradition, farming maize, beans, and squash; these plants complement each other, providing natural protection from pests and the elements, and increasing availability of nitrogen necessary for growth. Both of those tribes would also be important allies of the English and French, respectively, in future conflicts, in that part of the continent.

The Iroquois actually consisted of five tribes. According to tradition, before European contact, five tribes—the **MOHAWK**, **SENECA**, **CAYUGA**, **ONEIDA**, and **ONONDAGA**—made peace thanks to the leadership of the peacemaker **HIAWATHA**. Also known as the **FIVE NATIONS**, they organized into the regionally powerful **IROQUOIS CONFEDERACY**, bringing stability to the eastern Great Lakes region including Upstate New York, Southern Ontario, and parts of Quebec and the Midwest. Later, the Tuscarora tribe would join, and the union became known as the **SIX NATIONS**.

While many Native American, or First Nations, people speak variants of the Algonquin language, the **ALGONQUIN** people themselves have historically been a majority in what is today Quebec and the Great Lakes region. Active in the fur trade, the Algonquin developed important relationships with French colonizers and a rivalry with the Iroquois. Many Algonquin in French-controlled North America converted to Christianity.

The Midwest

Later, the young United States would come into conflict with the Shawnee, Lenape, Kickapoo, Miami, and other tribes in the Midwestern region of Ohio, Illinois, Indiana, and Michigan in early western expansion. These tribes formed the Northwest Confederacy to fight the United States, developments discussed in more detail in later sections.

The SHAWNEE were an Algonquin-speaking people based in the Ohio Valley; however their presence extended as far east and south as the present-day Carolinas and Georgia. While socially organized under a matrilineal system, the Shawnee had male kings and only men could inherit property. The Lenape, also a matrilineal society, originally lived in what is today southern New Jersey and the Delaware Valley (but were later driven west by colonization). Also Algonquin-speaking, the LENAPE were considered by the Shawnee to be their "grandfathers" and thus accorded respect. Another Algonquin-speaking tribe, the KICKAPOO were originally from the Great Lakes region but would move throughout present-day Indiana and Wisconsin. The MIAMI, also Algonquin-speaking, moved from Wisconsin to the Ohio Valley region forming settled societies and farming maize. They also took part in the fur trade as it developed during European colonial times.

The Southeast

In the South, major tribes included the CHICKASAW and CHOCTAW, the descendants of the MISSISSIPPI MOUND BUILDERS or Mississippian cultures, societies that built mounds from around 2,100 to 1,800 years ago as burial tombs or the bases for temples. Both tribes were organized in clans along matrilineal lines, and both spoke languages of the Muskogean family. The Chickasaw were a settled tribe originally based in what is today northern Mississippi and Alabama and western Kentucky and Tennessee, and like the Iroquois, they farmed in the sustainable three sisters tradition. The Choctaw, whose origins trace to Mississippi, Louisiana, Alabama, and Florida, spoke a similar language to the Chickasaw. These two tribes would later form alliances with the British and French, fighting proxy wars on their behalf.

Figure 1.1. Mississippi Mounds

The **Creek**, or **Muscogee**, also descended from the Mississippian peoples, originated in modern Alabama, Georgia, South Carolina, and Florida. Speaking a language similar to those of the Chickasaw and Choctaw, the Creek would later participate in an alliance with these and other tribes—the Muscogee Confederacy—to engage the United States, which threatened tribal sovereignty.

Unlike the Chickasaw, Choctaw, and Creek, the **Cherokee** spoke (and speak) a language of the Iroquoian family. It is thought that they migrated south to their homeland in present-day Georgia sometime long before European contact, where they remained until they were forcibly removed in 1832. Organized into seven clans, the Cherokee were also hunters and farmers like other tribes in the region, and would later come into contact—and conflict—with European colonizers and the United States of America.

Great Plains, Southwest, Pacific Northwest

Farther west, tribes of the Great Plains like the **Sioux**, **Cheyenne**, **Apache**, **Comanche**, and **Arapaho** would later come into conflict with American settlers as westward expansion continued. Traditionally nomadic or semi-nomadic, these tribes depended on the **buffalo** for food and materials to create clothing, tools, and domestic items; therefore they followed the herds. While widely known for their equestrian skill, horses were introduced by Europeans and so Native American tribes living on the Great Plains did not access them until after European contact. Horseback riding facilitated the hunt; previously, hunters surrounded buffalo or frightened them off of cliffs.

In the Southwest, the **Navajo** controlled territory in present-day Arizona, New Mexico, and Utah. The Navajo were descendants of the **Ancestral Pueblo** or **Anasazi**, who had settled in the Four Corners area, engaging in three sisters agriculture and stone construction, including cliff dwellings. The Navajo also practiced pastoralism, and lived in semi-permanent wooden homes called *hogans*, the doors of which face eastward to the rising sun. The Navajo had a less hierarchical structure than other Native American societies, and engaged in fewer raids than the Apache to the north.

Figure 1.2. Ancestral Pueblo Cliff Palace at Mesa Verde

In the Pacific Northwest, fishing was a major source of sustenance, and Native American peoples created and used canoes to engage in the practice. Totem poles depicted histories. The **COAST SALISH**, whose language was widely spoken throughout the region, dominated the Puget Sound and Olympic Peninsula area. Farther south, the **CHINOOK** controlled the coast at the Columbia River.

Ultimately, through both violent conflict and political means, Native American civilizations lost control of most of their territories and were forced onto reservations by the United States. Negotiations continue today over rights to land and opportunities and reparations for past injustices.

EXAMPLES

1) Which of the following best describes the political landscape of the Northeast before European contact?

   A. Many small, autonomous tribes scattered throughout the region fought over land and resources.

   B. Several organized tribes controlled the region, including a major confederation.

   C. A disorganized political landscape would facilitate European colonial domination.

   D. The land was largely uninhabited, allowing easy exploitation of resources.

   E. A dominant tribe organized the region into a decentralized empire of vassal states.

   Answers:

   A. Incorrect. While there were numerous tribes in the region besides the Iroquois and the Algonquin, and while the Iroquois themselves were made up of smaller tribes, regional political organization and alliances were strong before European contact.

   B. **Correct.** Powerful tribes controlled trade and territory; among these were the powerful Iroquois Confederacy.

   C. Incorrect. The political landscape was highly organized; European settlers would later have to form alliances and sign treaties with local regional powers.

   D. Incorrect. Many people inhabited the land and had done so for centuries.

   E. Incorrect. There were multiple powerful tribes in the region, as well as weaker tribes that maintained their independence.

2) How do the movements of the tribes of the Northwest (throughout present-day Indiana, Illinois, Ohio, Michigan, and Wisconsin) illustrate tribal interactions before European contact and during colonial times?

   A. Having been pushed westward by the Iroquois, the Lenape are just one example of forced migration in early North American history.

   B. The migration of the Miami from Ontario to the Ohio Valley illustrates the diffusion of the Algonquin language throughout the continent.

   C. Despite the wide geographic range of the Shawnee, Kickapoo, Miami and Lenape, all these peoples spoke variants of the Algonquin language; this shows the importance of this language for many Native American tribes whether or not they were Algonquin people.

    D.   Ongoing conflict between the Northwest Algonquin Confederacy, based in Ontario and the Upper Midwest, and the Iroquois Confederacy, based in the eastern Great Lakes region and present day Upstate New York, resulted in instability that forced tribes to move throughout the region.

    E.   Conflicting social traditions between the Shawnee and the Kickapoo eventually led to the migration of the Kickapoo to present-day Indiana.

Answers:

    A.   Incorrect. The Lenape were forced west by European colonization, not by conflict with the Iroquois.

    B.   Incorrect. While their experience was indeed illustrative of the wide range of the Algonquin language, the Miami moved from present-day Wisconsin, not Ontario.

    C.   **Correct.** While the Algonquin people were primarily located in what is today Quebec and southern Ontario, the Algonquin language was spoken widely throughout North America among both settled and semi-settled non-Algonquin peoples.

    D.   Incorrect. While many tribes did move throughout the region as a result of intertribal conflict, the Northwest Confederacy emerged later in response to the United States; furthermore, it was not rooted in a shared Algonquin experience.

    E.   Incorrect. The Kickapoo migrated into present-day Indiana and Wisconsin from the Great Lakes where they had no direct contact with the Shawnee.

3)   At the time of European contact, the Southeastern United States was mainly populated by

    A.   the Mississippi Mound Builders.

    B.   settled tribes who spoke Muskogean and Iroquoian languages.

    C.   nomadic tribes who spoke Muskogean and Iroquoian languages.

    D.   the Ancestral Pueblo cliff dwellers.

    E.   the peripheral vassal tribes of the Aztec empire.

Answers:

    A.   Incorrect. The Mississippi Mound Builders and their civilization had disappeared by European contact; the Chickasaw, Choctaw, Creek, and other tribes were their descendants.

    B.   **Correct.** The Choctaw, Creek, Chickasaw, and others were Muskogean-speaking peoples; the Cherokee spoke an Iroquoian language. Both tribes were settled.

    C.   Incorrect. While the tribes in the Southeast did speak languages from these families, they were not nomadic.

    D.   Incorrect. The Ancestral Pueblo, or Anasazi, lived in the Southwest.

    E.   Incorrect. The Aztec empire extended into the Southwestern United States, not the Southeastern.

4) Tribes living in the Great Plains region were dependent on which of the following for survival?

    A. food and resources seized from conquered tribes

    B. domesticated horses for hunting and warfare

    C. access to rivers to engage in the fur trade

    D. three sisters agriculture

    E. buffalo for nutrition and materials for daily necessities

Answers:

    A.   Incorrect. The tribes of the Great Plains were primarily hunter-gatherers and did not conquer other tribes.

    B.   Incorrect. Horses were not introduced to North America until European contact.

    C.   Incorrect. Great Plains tribes did not depend on the fur trade for survival before European contact or afterwards.

    D.   Incorrect. While three sisters agriculture was widely practiced throughout North America, most major tribes living on the Great Plains were hunter-gatherers and depended primarily on buffalo for food.

    E.   **Correct.** The Great Plains tribes depended on buffalo, which were plentiful before European contact and settlement, for food; they also used buffalo parts for clothing and to make necessary items.

5) How were the Navajo influenced by the Ancestral Pueblo, or Anasazi?

    A. The Navajo continued the practice of pastoralism, herding horses throughout the Southwest.

    B. The Navajo expanded control over land originally settled by the Ancestral Pueblo.

    C. The Navajo began building cliff dwellings, improving on the Anasazi practice of living in rounded homes built from wood.

    D. The Navajo developed a strictly hierarchical society, abandoning the looser organization of the Ancestral Pueblo.

    E. Like the Ancestral Pueblo The Navajo used warfare to dominate other tribes in the region.

Answers:

    A.   Incorrect. Horses were introduced to North America by Europeans; neither the Navajo nor the Ancestral Pueblo had access to them before contact.

    B.   **Correct.** The Ancestral Pueblo had settled in what is today the Four Corners region; the Navajo came to control land extending through present-day Arizona, New Mexico, and Utah.

    C.   Incorrect. The Anasazi or Ancestral Pueblo themselves had built cliff dwellings.

    D.   Incorrect. The Navajo did not have a strictly hierarchical society.

    E.   Incorrect. The Navajo were known for engaging in fewer raids and less warfare than other tribes like the Apache.

Colonial North America

The Americas were quickly colonized by Europeans after Christopher Columbus first laid claim to them for the Spanish, and the British, French, and Spanish all held territories in North America throughout the sixteenth, seventeenth, eighteenth, and nineteenth centuries.

Spain in the West and Southwest

Spanish *CONQUISTADORS* explored what is today the Southwestern United States, claiming land for Spain despite the presence of Southwestern tribes. Prominent *conquistadors* included **HERNANDO DE SOTO** and **FRANCISCO VASQUEZ DE CORONADO**; Spanish colonization not only included the control and settlement of land but also the mission to spread Christianity. Indeed, **MISSIONS** were established in the West and Southwest for this purpose, throughout Mexico and parts of what is today Texas, New Mexico, Arizona, and California. The Spanish Crown granted *ENCOMIENDAS*, land grants to individuals to establish settlements, allowing the holder to ranch or mine the land. *Encomiendas* allowed colonists to demand tribute and forced labor from local Native peoples, essentially enslaving them, to profit from the land. Spain's holdings ultimately extended through Mexico into Texas, the Southwest, and California, reaching as far north into what are today parts of Montana and Wyoming. Spain also controlled the Gulf Coast, including New Orleans and Florida.

Throughout this region, Spanish colonizers encountered resistance from Native Americans. In 1680, the **PUEBLO REVOLT**, led by the leader **POPÉ**, resulted in a two-year loss of land for Spain. Sometimes referred to as part of the ongoing **NAVAJO WARS**, this revolt included several Native American tribes. (In the literature and in some primary sources, *pueblo* is often used interchangeably with "Indian" to refer to Native Americans; here, the term refers to Navajo, Apache, and other tribes that came together to resist Spanish hegemony in the region.) Spain eventually reconquered the territory, subjugating the peoples living in the region to colonial rule.

The conflict led to friction among Spanish thinkers over the means, and even the notion, of colonization. The priest **BARTOLOMÉ DE LAS CASAS**, appalled at the oppression of colonization, argued for the rights and humanity of Native Americans. De las Casas lived in the Americas and had first-hand experience with the brutal consequences of colonization. On the other hand, **JUAN DE SEPULVEDA**, who never left Spain, argued that the Native Americans needed the rule and "civilization" brought by Spain, justifying their treatment at the hands of colonizers.

Despite ongoing conflict between Native Americans and Spanish colonizers, there was social mixing among the people. Intermarriage and fraternization resulted in a stratified society based on race, not only in North America but throughout Spanish and Portuguese holdings in the Americas. According to the *CASTA* system, an individual's place in societal hierarchy was determined by his or her race, with white people most privileged. The term *MESTIZO* referred to people of mixed white European and Native American, who were more privileged than the Native American peoples.

The Spanish also introduced African people to the Americas, and North America was no exception. Forced labor and diseases like **SMALLPOX** had decimated Native American populations in Mexico and the Southwest. Consequently, in order to exploit these resource-rich lands, Spanish colonizers took part in the European-driven TRANS-ATLANTIC SLAVE TRADE, kidnapping African people or purchasing them on the West African coast, bringing them to the Americas and forcing them into slavery in mines and plantations in the Western Hemisphere.

French Hegemony in the Midwest and Northeast

Unlike Spain, which sought not only profit but also to settle the land and convert Native Americans to Christianity, France was mainly focused on trade. French explorers like SAMUEL DE CHAMPLAIN reached what is today Quebec, Vermont, upstate New York, and the eastern Great Lakes region as early as the seventeenth century. While the explorer JACQUES CARTIER had claimed New France (present-day Quebec) for France in the sixteenth century, Champlain founded Quebec City and consolidated control of France's colonies in North America in 1608.

France prioritized trade; the FUR and beaver pelts from game plentiful in the Northeast were in great demand in Europe. French colonists were also more likely to establish agreements and intermarry with local Native Americans than other European powers; they did not establish settlements based on forced labor or arrive with families. The term *MÉTIS* described mixed-race persons; eventually France would control much of the Great Lakes and the Mississippi region through Louisiana and New Orleans, valuable trade routes.

England and the Thirteen Colonies

While the Spanish and French arrived generally as single men for trade, who would intermarry with local inhabitants, the English brought their families and settled in North America, with the goal of establishing agricultural settlements. In the sixteenth century, Sir Walter Raleigh established the Roanoke colony in present-day Virginia; while this settlement disappeared by 1590, interest in colonization reemerged as JOINT-STOCK COMPANIES sought royal charters to privately develop colonies on the North American Atlantic coast. The first established colony, JAMESTOWN, was also located in Virginia, which became so profitable that the Crown took it over as a colony in 1624.

The colonial leader JOHN ROLFE introduced TOBACCO to Virginia farmers, which became the primary cash crop. Requiring plantation farming, Virginia required INDENTURED SERVANTS, who were freed from servitude after a period of work. Some of these indentured servants were from Africa. However in 1660, the HOUSE OF BURGESSES, which governed Virginia, declared that all blacks would be lifelong slaves. The South became increasingly socially stratified, with enslaved persons, indentured servants, landowners, and other classes. The Carolinas and Georgia would also become important sources of tobacco and rice; South Carolina institutionalized slavery in North America for the next two centuries by adopting the slave codes from Barbados.

Slavery was not as widespread in the northern colonies as it was in the south, as the land and climate in the north did not support plantation agriculture; this led to far less demand for slaves than in the south, where unskilled labor was needed to harvest tobacco and later, cotton.

While Jamestown and Virginia were populated by diverse populations of settlers, businessmen, indentured servants, and slaves, the demographics were different farther north. In New England, SEPARATISTS, members of the Church of England who believed it had strayed too far from its theological roots, had come to North America seeking more religious freedom. The first group of Separatists, the Pilgrims, arrived on the *Mayflower* in 1620 and had drawn up the MAYFLOWER COMPACT, guaranteeing government by the consent of the governed. They were later joined by the PURITANS, who had been persecuted in England by King Charles I, whom many suspected of weakening the Church of England and even of plotting to restore Catholicism. The colonial Puritan leader JOHN WINTHROP envisioned the Massachusetts Bay Colony in the model of the Biblical *CITY UPON A HILL*, rooted in unity, peace, and what would be a free, democratic spirit; its capital was Boston. These philosophies would later inform the American Revolution.

Despite differences from the South, social stratification existed in New England as well: according to Puritan belief, wealth and success showed that one was a member of the ELECT, or privileged by God. Poorer farmers were generally tenant farmers; they did not own land and rarely made a profit.

The concepts of religious tolerance were not isolated to New England. The mid-Atlantic region was well-suited for agricultural crops and trade, with fertile lands and natural harbors. The settlement of New Amsterdam, an ideal port and trading post, came under English control in 1664 and was renamed New York; in 1682, the Quaker WILLIAM PENN founded the city of Philadelphia, based on tolerance. Penn had been given the land later called Pennsylvania by the Crown to settle a debt; Pennsylvania, New Jersey, and Delaware were founded in the Quaker spirit as part of Penn's HOLY EXPERIMENT to develop settlements based on tolerance.

Quakerism promotes equality, community, non-violence, conflict resolution, and tolerance. These tenets are at the root of the name of Philadelphia, the "City of Brotherly Love."

Earlier in the region, in 1649 the MARYLAND TOLERATION ACT had ensured the political rights of all Christians there, the first law of its kind in the colonies. This was due, in part, to the influence of LORD BALTIMORE, who had been charged by Charles I to found a part of Virginia (to be called Maryland) as a Catholic haven—helping him maintain power in an England divided between Catholics and Protestants.

The North American colonial economy was part of the ATLANTIC WORLD, taking part in the TRIANGULAR TRADE (pictured on the following page) between the Americas, Africa and Europe, where slaves were exchanged in the Americas for raw materials shipped to Europe to be processed into goods for the benefit of the colonial powers, and sometimes exchanged for slaves in Africa. In this way, North America was part of the COLUMBIAN EXCHANGE, the intersection of goods and people throughout the Atlantic World.

Exploitation of colonial resources and the dynamics of the Columbian Exchange supported MERCANTILISM, the prevailing economic system: European powers controlled their economies in order to increase global power. Ensuring a beneficial BALANCE OF TRADE is essential; the country must export more than it imports. An unlimited supply of desirable goods obtainable at a low cost made this possible, and the colonies offered just that. In this way, European powers would be able to maintain their reserves of gold and silver rather than spending them on imports. Furthermore, those countries that obtained access to more gold and silver—notably, Spain, which gained control of mines in Central America and Mexico—exponentially increased their wealth, dramatically changing the balance of economic power in Europe. Long-term consequences included the decline of feudalism and the rise of capitalism.

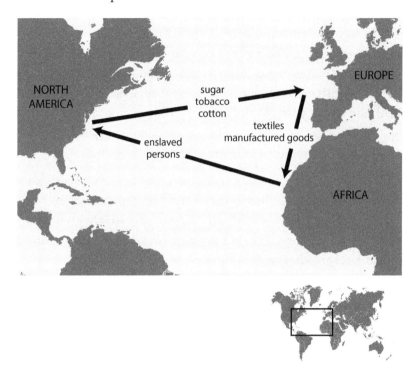

Figure 1.3. Triangular Trade

Colonial Conflict

Throughout the chaos in England during the ENGLISH CIVIL WAR, policy toward the Colonies had been one of SALUTARY NEGLECT, allowing them great autonomy. However, stability in England and an emerging culture of independence in the Thirteen Colonies caught the attention of the British Crown; to ensure that the British mercantilist system was not threatened, it passed the NAVIGATION ACTS in 1651 to prevent colonial trade with any other countries. An early sign of colonial discontent, BACON'S REBELLION in 1676 against Governor Berkeley of Virginia embodied the growing resentment of land-owners, who wanted to increase their own profit rather than redirect revenue to Britain. Following the 1688 Glorious Revolution in England, many colonists thought they might gain more autonomy; however, the new leadership under William and Mary continued to limit self-rule.

American colonists were also increasingly influenced by Enlightenment thought. John Locke's *SECOND TREATISE* was published in 1689; critical of absolute monarchy, it became popular in the Colonies. Locke's concepts of government by consent of the governed and the natural rights of persons became the bedrock of the United States government. Locke argued for REPUBLICANISM: that the people must come together to create a government for the protection of themselves and their property, thereby giving up some of their natural rights. However, should the government overstep its bounds, the people have the right to overthrow it and replace it.

In the mid-eighteenth century, a sense of religious fervor called the GREAT AWAKENING spread throughout the Colonies; people became devoted to God beyond the confines of tra-ditional Christianity, attracted to traveling preachers and convinced that they must confess sins publicly to avoid going to hell. Many universities, including some Ivy League schools, were founded during this time to train ministers; the Great Awakening helped develop a more singularly North American religious culture. It also created a divide between traditional European Christianity and emerging North American faiths.

Meanwhile, North America served also as a battleground for France and England, already in conflict in Europe and elsewhere. In the mid-seventeenth century, the Algonquin and Iroquois, allied with the French and Dutch, and English, respectively, fought the **BEAVER WARS** for control over the fur trade in the northeastern part of the continent. The Iroquois would ultimately push the Shawnee and other tribes associated with the Algonquin from the Northeast and Great Lakes area farther west to present-day Wisconsin. Given the British alliance with the Iroquois, England would also refer to the Beaver Wars and Iroquois control over the Northeast (today, the Ohio Valley and Great Lakes region) to assert their own claim over this area, which was called the **NORTHWEST TERRITORIES**.

France had come to control the vast **LOUISIANA TERRITORY**, from the Ohio Valley area through the Mississippi Valley, the area down the Mississippi River to its capital of New Orleans, and as far as the reaches of the Missouri River and the Arkansas/Red River stretching west. Not only did France clash with Britain in the northern part of the continent, but the two colonial powers came into conflict in the South as well. In 1736, French forces, allied with the Choctaw, attacked the English-allied Chickasaw as part of France's attempts to strengthen its hold on the southeastern part of North America in the **CHICKASAW WARS**.

Following another period of salutary neglect in the Colonies, in 1754, French and English conflict exploded once again in North America as fighting broke out in the Ohio Valley. The British government organized with North American colonial leaders to meet at Albany; **BENJAMIN FRANKLIN** helped organize the defensive Albany Plan of Union and argued for this plan in his newspaper, the *Pennsylvania Gazette*, using the famous illustration *Join, or Die*. However, the Crown worried that this plan allowed for too much colonial independence, adding to tensions between the Thirteen Colonies and England.

Figure 1.4. *Join or Die*

The Seven Years' War broke out in Europe in 1756; this conflict between the British and French in North America was known as the FRENCH AND INDIAN WAR. War efforts in North America accelerated under the British leader (essentially, Prime Minister) WILLIAM PITT THE ELDER, who invested heavily in defeating the French beyond Europe (see Chapter Two, "World History," for details). Ultimately, Britain emerged as the dominant power on the continent. France had allied with the Algonquin, traditional rivals of the British-allied Iroquois. However, following defeats by strong colonial military leaders like George Washington and despite its strong alliances and long-term presence on the continent, France eventually surrendered. Britain gained control of French territories in North America—as well as Spanish Florida—in the 1763 TREATY OF PARIS which ended the Seven Years' War.

EXAMPLES

1) How did Spanish and French colonization in North America differ?
   A. Both intermarried with Native Americans; however the Spanish took a more aggressive approach in spreading Christianity.
   B. Spain sought accord and agreement with Native Americans, while France forced marriages as part of settling the land, resulting in the mixed-race métis class.
   C. France colonized the Southwest; Spain colonized the Northeast and Midwest.
   D. France imported enslaved Africans as part of the Triangular Trade in order to support New France, while Spain mainly exploited local Native American tribes, forcing them to perform labor and essentially enslaving them.
   E. New France was dominated by individual large landowners while New Spain was comprised primarily of traders.

Answers:
   A. **Correct.** Spain established missions to spread Christianity, in addition to settling and exploiting the land; France worked to establish networks of trade and did not concentrate on religious conversion (although the Church was present and at work in its colonies). Both intermarried locally.
   B. Incorrect. Spanish encounters with tribes in the West and Southwest were frequently violent; *métis* were not the result of a campaign of forced marriages.
   C. Incorrect. France came to control Northeastern Canada (New France, what is today Quebec and other regions) and parts of the Midwest south through Louisiana. Spain did control some territory through the Gulf Coast, but primarily settled the Southwest.
   D. Incorrect. Spain brought African slaves to the Americas and, in North America, forced them to work in mines. Given the nature of the fur trade, which supported New France in the northern part of the continent, there was no real role for slaves; however, slavery was practiced in colonies in the southern parts of North America where plantation farming was profitable. France also practiced slavery widely in other colonies such as Haiti and throughout the Caribbean.
   E. Incorrect. Because the bulk of its profit came from the fur trade, most settlers in New France were traders. In New Spain, the *encomienda* system granted large swaths of land to individuals.

2) On the Atlantic coast of North America, which of the following contributed to demographic differences between North and South?

    A. a climate that supported plantation agriculture in the southern colonies, which resulted in high demand for African slaves

    B. geography favorable to ports in the Northeast, resulting in diverse and tolerant centers of commerce and trade in Boston, New York, and Philadelphia

    C. a climate that supported small-scale agriculture and family farms in the northern colonies, which resulted in a very low demand for African slaves

    D. a charter based on religious separatism led, in the northern colonies, to a social hierarchy based on religion

    E. all of the above

Answers:

    A. Incorrect. While it is true that the climate in the former colonies of Georgia, the Carolinas, and Virginia supported plantation agriculture, requiring large numbers of unskilled laborers to grow and harvest crops like tobacco and rice, this choice does not sufficiently answer the question.

    B. Incorrect. Indeed, geography in the Northeast lent itself to the establishment of ports and commercial centers in these areas, but this answer choice does not sufficiently respond to the question.

    C. Incorrect. It is true that the climate in the Northeast supported crops grown on small family farms rather than those grown on plantations; thus, there was very little demand for African slaves in that area and a preponderance of tenant farmers instead. However, this choice does not completely answer the question.

    D. Incorrect. It is true that Puritan belief impacted social standing. However, this choice does not completely answer the question.

    E. **Correct.** All of the above answer choices are true.

3) Upon what premise were Mid-Atlantic colonies like Pennsylvania, Delaware, and New Jersey founded?

    A. A beacon of unity and humanity, reminiscent of John Winthrop's *City Upon a Hill*.

    B. Tolerance, as part of William Penn's *Great Experiment*.

    C. Profit, in accordance with their roots in joint-stock companies seeking profit from the land through royal charters.

    D. Conquest and conversion, in order to take land from Native American tribes and convert those original inhabitants to Christianity.

    E. A second chance, as they served as safe havens for Britain's debtors and convicts.

Answers:

    A. Incorrect. Winthrop was a leader in Massachusetts and his philosophies applied to development in that region.

    B. **Correct.** William Penn founded these colonies in the spirit of his tolerant Quaker faith.

    C. Incorrect. Joint-stock companies sought profit in Virginia; profit was not Penn's primary motive in founding Pennsylvania, Delaware, and New Jersey.

D. Incorrect. While conquest was certainly an element of colonization, this was not Penn's primary motive, nor was Christian conversion. Furthermore, spreading Christianity was not a priority of the English as it was for the Spanish.

E. Incorrect. Georgia was the colony established to provide a second chance to debtors.

4) How did the British and French rivalry spill over into North America?

A. While Britain and France were often on opposite sides in European conflict, they found common ground against Native Americans in North America.

B. European conflicts between Catholics and Protestants affected Catholic French and Protestant English settlers; related violence from the Hundred Years' War broke out between them as a result.

C. These European powers engaged in proxy wars, supporting the Iroquois and Algonquin, respectively, as well as the Chickasaw and Choctaw, in jockeying for control of land in the Great Lakes and southeastern regions of North America.

D. France and Britain formed an alliance to prevent Spain from moving eastward on the continent.

E. French traders often raided British settlements in an attempt to extend France's territory.

Answers:

A. Incorrect. These colonial powers formed alliances with different North American tribes as part of ongoing rivalries on and off the continent in maneuvering for power and control of land.

B. Incorrect. The British colonies were not a religious battleground; furthermore, the Hundred Years' War had ended in Europe before the explorations of Columbus and the beginnings of settlement in the Western Hemisphere.

C. **Correct.** The Beaver Wars, the Chickasaw Wars, and later the French and Indian War, which was part of the Seven Years' War, are all examples of British-French conflict playing out in North America.

D. Incorrect. France and Britain never had a long-term alliance on North America.

E. Incorrect. There were no ongoing conflicts between French traders and British settlers.

5) Which of the following were factors in stirring up colonial discontent?

A. Locke's *Second Treatise*

B. trade restrictions like the Navigation Acts

C. the Great Awakening

D. limitations on self-rule

E. all of the above

Answers:

A. Incorrect. While Locke's *Second Treatise* criticized absolute monarchy and so became very popular in the Thirteen Colonies, where colonists sought more autonomy, it was only one of many factors; given the other answer choices, this choice is incomplete.

B. Incorrect. Restrictive measures like the Navigation Acts did limit colonial trade to Britain only, to the chagrin of colonial merchants who desired to broaden their commercial enterprises. Still, this choice does not completely answer this question.

C.   Incorrect. The Great Awakening was a religious revival that contributed to ongoing cultural differences between the Colonies and Europe in that it deepened divisions between Christian practices in Europe and newer religious thought in North America. However, this choice does not sufficiently answer the question, given the other options.

D.   Incorrect. While the colonists did desire greater autonomy, this answer is incomplete.

E.   **Correct.** All of the above are true.

Revolution and the Early United States

The American Revolution

Despite British victory in the French and Indian War, Britain had gone greatly into debt. Furthermore, there were concerns that the Colonies required a stronger military presence following **PONTIAC'S REBELLION** in 1763. The leader of the **OTTAWA** people, Pontiac, led a revolt that extended from the Great Lakes region through the Ohio Valley to Virginia. As this land had been ceded to England from France (lacking any consultation with the native inhabitants) the Ottawa people and other Native Americans resisted further British settlement and fought back against colonial oppression. **KING GEORGE III** signed the **PROCLAMATION OF 1763**, an agreement not to settle land west of the Appalachians, in an effort to make peace; however much settlement continued in practice.

As a result of the war and subsequent unrest, Britain once again discarded its colonial policy of salutary neglect; furthermore, in desperate need of cash, the Crown sought ways to increase its revenue from the Colonies.

King George III enforced heavy taxes and restrictive acts in the colonies to generate income for the Crown and punish disobedience. England expanded the **MOLASSES ACT** of 1733, passing the **SUGAR ACT** in 1764 to raise revenue by taxing sugar and molasses. Sugar was produced in the British West Indies and widely consumed in the Thirteen Colonies. In 1765, Britain enforced the **QUARTERING ACT**, requiring colonists to provide shelter to British troops stationed in the region.

The 1765 **STAMP ACT**, the first direct tax on the colonists, triggered more tensions. Any document required a costly stamp, the revenue reverting to the British government. **PATRICK HENRY** protested the Stamp Act in the Virginia House of Burgesses; the tax was seen as a violation of colonists' rights, given that they did not have direct representation in British Parliament. In Britain, it was argued that the colonists had **VIRTUAL REPRESENTATION** and so the Act—and others to follow—were justified.

As a result, colonists began boycotting British goods and engaging in violent protest. **SAMUEL ADAMS** led the **SONS AND DAUGHTERS OF LIBERTY** in violent acts against tax collectors. In response, the Chancellor of the Exchequer Charles Townshend enforced the punitive **TOWNSHEND ACTS** which imposed more taxes and restrictions on the colonies; customs officers were empowered to search colonists' homes for forbidden goods with **WRITS OF ASSISTANCE**. **JOHN DICKINSON'S** *LETTERS FROM A FARMER IN PENNSYLVANIA* and Samuel Adams' MASSACHUSETTS CIRCULAR LETTER argued for the repeal of the Townshend Acts (which were, indeed, repealed in 1770) and demanded *no taxation without representation*. Samuel Adams continued to stir up rebellion with his COMMITTEES OF CORRESPONDENCE, which distributed anti-British propaganda.

Protests against the Quartering Act in Boston led to the BOSTON MASSACRE in 1770, when British troops fired on a crowd of protesters. By 1773, in a climate of continued unrest driven by the Committees of Correspondence, colonists protested the latest taxes on tea levied by the TEA ACT in the famous BOSTON TEA PARTY by dressing as Native Americans and tossing tea off a ship in Boston Harbor. In response, the government passed the INTOLERABLE ACTS, closing Boston Harbor and bringing Massachusetts back under direct royal control.

In response to the Intolerable Acts, colonial leaders met in Philadelphia at the FIRST CONTINENTAL CONGRESS in 1774 and issued the *DECLARATION OF RIGHTS AND GRIEVANCES*, presenting colonial concerns to the King, who ignored it. However, violent conflict began in 1775 at LEXINGTON AND CONCORD, when American militiamen (MINUTEMEN) had gathered to resist British efforts to seize weapons and arrest rebels in Concord. On June 17, 1775, the Americans fought the British at the BATTLE OF BUNKER HILL; despite American losses, the number of casualties the rebels inflicted caused the king to declare that the colonies were in rebellion. Troops were deployed to the colonies; the Siege of Boston began.

King George III also hired Hessian mercenaries from Germany to supplement British troops; adding foreign fighters only increased resentment in the colonies and created a stronger sense of independence from Britain.

In May 1775, the SECOND CONTINENTAL CONGRESS met at Philadelphia to debate the way forward. Debate between the wisdom of continued efforts at compromise and negotiations and declaring independence continued. The king ignored the Congress' *DECLARATION OF THE CAUSES AND NECESSITIES OF TAKING UP ARMS*, which asked him to consider again the colonies' objections; he also ignored the OLIVE BRANCH PETITION which sought compromise and an end to hostilities. THOMAS PAINE published his pamphlet *COMMON SENSE*; taking Locke's concepts of natural rights and the obligation of a people to rebel against an oppressive government, it popularized the notion of rebellion against Britain.

By summer of 1776, the Continental Congress agreed on the need to break from Britain; on July 4, 1776, it declared the independence of the United States of America and issued the DECLARATION OF INDEPENDENCE, drafted mainly by THOMAS JEFFERSON and heavily influenced by Locke.

Americans were still divided over independence; PATRIOTS favored independence while those still loyal to Britain were known as TORIES. GEORGE WASHINGTON had been appointed head of the Continental Army and led a largely unpaid and unprofessional army; despite early losses, Washington gained ground due to strong leadership, superior knowledge of the land, and support from France (and to a lesser extent, Spain and the Netherlands). The tide turned in 1777 at VALLEY FORGE, when Washington and his army lived through the bitterly cold winter and managed to overcome British military forces. The British people did not favor the war and voted the Tories out of Parliament; the incoming Whig party sought to end the war. In the 1783 TREATY OF PARIS, the United States was recognized as a country, agreeing to repay debts to British merchants and provide safety to those British loyalists who wished to remain in North America. The American Revolution would go on to inspire revolution around the world.

Federalists and Democratic-Republicans

Joy in the victory over Great Britain was short-lived. Fearful of tyranny, the Second Continental Congress had provided for only a weak central government, adopting the **ARTICLES OF CONFEDERATION** to organize the Thirteen Colonies—now states—as a loosely united country. A unicameral central government had the power to wage war, negotiate treaties, and borrow money. It could not tax citizens, but could tax states. It also set parameters for westward expansion and establishing new states: the **NORTHWEST ORDINANCES** of 1787 forbade slavery north of the Ohio River. Areas with 60,000 people could apply for statehood. However, it soon became clear that the Articles of Confederation were not strong enough to keep the nation united.

The Northwest Ordinances also effectively nullified King George III's Proclamation of 1763, which promised Native Americans that white settlement would not continue in the Ohio Valley region. The United States did not recognize the Proclamation, and tensions would build.

The new country was heavily in debt. Currency was weak, and taxes were high: Daniel Shays led **SHAYS' REBELLION**, a revolt of indebted farmers who rose up to prevent courts from seizing property in Massachusetts and to protest debtor's prisons. Furthermore, debt and disorganization made the country appear weak and vulnerable to Great Britain and Spain. If the United States was to remain one country, it needed a stronger federal government.

ALEXANDER HAMILTON and **JAMES MADISON** called for a **CONSTITUTIONAL CONVENTION** to write a Constitution as the foundation of a stronger federal government. Madison and other **FEDERALISTS** like **JOHN ADAMS** believed in **SEPARATION OF POWERS**, republicanism, and a strong federal government.

To determine the exact structure of the government, delegates at the convention settled on what became known as the **GREAT COMPROMISE**, a **BICAMERAL LEGISLATURE**. Two plans had been presented: the **NEW JERSEY PLAN**, which proposed a legislature composed of an equal number of representatives from each state (which would benefit smaller states), and the **VIRGINIA PLAN**, which proposed a legislature composed of representatives proportional to the population of each state. States with large African American slave populations accounted for those persons with the **THREE-FIFTHS COMPROMISE**, which counted a slave as three-fifths of a person; while represented in a state's population to determine that state's number of representatives in Congress, enslaved persons had no place in the political process. The states adopted both plans, creating the **HOUSE OF REPRESENTATIVES** and the **SENATE**, to most fairly represent the large and small states at the federal level. (See Chapter Three, "Government," for more information.)

Despite the separation of powers provided for in the Constitution, **ANTI-FEDERALISTS** like **THOMAS JEFFERSON** called for even more limitations on the power of the federal government. The first ten amendments to the Constitution, or the **BILL OF RIGHTS**, a list of guarantees of American freedoms, was a concession to the anti-Federalists, who would later become the **DEMOCRATIC-REPUBLICAN PARTY** (eventually, the Democratic Party).

Federalists were generally from the North and were usually merchants or businessmen; Anti-Federalists were usually from the South or the rural west, and farmed the land.

In order to convince the states to ratify the Constitution, Hamilton, Madison, and John Jay wrote the *FEDERALIST PAPERS*, articulating the benefits of federalism. Likewise, the Bill of Rights helped convince the hesitant. In 1791, the Constitution was ratified. GEORGE WASHINGTON was elected president, with John Adams serving as vice president; Washington appointed Hamilton as Secretary of the Treasury and Jefferson as Secretary of State.

Hamilton prioritized currency stabilization and repayment of debts; he also believed in establishing a national bank—the BANK OF THE UNITED STATES (BUS), which Washington signed into law in 1791. He also favored tariffs and excise (sales) taxes, which Anti-Federalists—who became known as DEMOCRATIC-REPUBLICANS—vehemently opposed. in 1795, rebellion against the excise tax on whiskey broke out; the WHISKEY REBELLION indicated unrest in the young country and was put down by militia.

Meanwhile, the French Revolution had begun in Europe. However, President Washington issued the NEUTRALITY PROCLAMATION in 1793. Despite this action, British and French ships accosted American ships in the Atlantic and forced American sailors into naval service (IMPRESSMENTS). John Jay attempted to reinstate neutrality; JAY'S TREATY was unsuccessful and unpopular, only negotiating the removal of British forts in the western frontier. Furthermore, it concerned Spain, which feared changes in the balance of power on the continent. President Washington had Thomas Pickney negotiate a new treaty with Spain; providing for US rights on the Mississippi River and in the Port of New Orleans, PICKNEY'S TREATY was a diplomatic success, ratified by all thirteen states. The ongoing NORTHWEST INDIAN WARS continued conflict with the Shawnee, Lenape, Kickapoo, Miami, and other tribes in the Ohio region; the Americans gained more territory in Ohio and Indiana following the defeat of allied tribes at the BATTLE OF FALLEN TIMBERS in 1794.

In President Washington's FAREWELL ADDRESS, he recommended the United States follow a policy of neutrality in international affairs, setting a precedent for early American history. Vice President John Adams, a Federalist, became the second president. France continued to seize American ships, so Adams sent representatives to negotiate; however, in what became known as the XYZ AFFAIR, the Americans were asked for bribes in order to even meet with French officials. The insulted Americans began an undeclared conflict in the Caribbean until the CONVENTION OF 1800 negotiated a cessation of hostilities.

During the Adams administration, the Federalists passed the harsh ALIEN AND SEDITION ACTS. The Alien Act allowed the president to deport "enemy aliens"; it also increased the residency requirements for citizenship. The Sedition Act forbade criticism of the president or of Congress. Divisions between the Federalists and the Democratic-Republicans were deeper than ever and the presidential elections of 1800 were tense and controversial; nevertheless, Thomas Jefferson was elected to the presidency in 1801 in a non-violent transfer of power.

Jefferson shrank the federal government. The Alien and Sedition Acts were repealed. Economic policies favored small farmers and landowners, in contrast to Federalist policies, which supported big business and cities. However, Jefferson also oversaw the LOUISIANA PURCHASE, which nearly doubled the size of the United States. This troubled some Democratic-Republicans, who saw this as federal overreach, but the Louisiana Purchase would be a major step forward in westward expansion. MERIWETHER LEWIS and WILLIAM CLARK were dispatched to explore the western frontier of the territory: Jefferson hoped to find an all-water route to the Pacific Ocean (via the Missouri River). While this route did not exist, Lewis and Clark returned with a deeper knowledge of the territory the US had come to control.

Figure 1.5. Louisiana Purchase

Jefferson was also forced to manage chaotic international affairs. Britain and France, at war with each other in the **NAPOLEONIC WARS**, were attempting to blockade each other's international trade, threatening US ships, as the United States did business with both countries. In an attempt to avoid the conflict, Congress passed the **EMBARGO ACT** under the Jefferson administration in 1807, which limited US international trade; however the Embargo Act only damaged the US economy further. In addition, the United States was fighting North African pirates in the Mediterranean, who were seizing US ships. At the end of Jefferson's presidency, Congress passed the **NON-INTERCOURSE ACT**, which allowed trade with foreign countries besides Britain and France; under President **JAMES MADISON**, tensions would remain high.

Monroe Doctrine and Manifest Destiny

British provocation at sea and in the northwest led to the **WAR OF 1812**. Growing nationalism in the United States pressured Madison into pushing for war after the **BATTLE OF TIPPECANOE** in Indiana, when **GENERAL WILLIAM HENRY HARRISON** fought the **NORTHWEST CONFEDERACY**, a group of tribes led by the Shawnee leader **TECUMSEH**. The Shawnee, Lenape, Miami, Kickapoo, and others had come together not only out of common interest—to maintain independent territory at the northwest of the United States (present-day Indiana and region) but also because they followed Tecumseh's brother **TENSKWATAWA**, who was considered a prophet. Despite the Confederacy's alliance with Britain, the United States prevailed. Congress declared war under Madison with the intent to defend the United States, end chaotic trade practices and treatment of Americans on the high seas, and penetrate British Canada.

The war resulted in no real gains or losses for either the Americans or the British; however **Andrew Jackson** became a popular war hero following the Battle of New Orleans (fought two weeks after the **Treaty of Ghent** was signed, ending the war in 1814). Yet at the war's end, the United States had successfully defended itself as a country and reaffirmed its independence. Patriotism ran high.

The **Era of Good Feelings** began with the presidency of **James Monroe** as a strong sense of public identity and nationalism pervaded in the country. During this period, religious revival became popular and people turned from Puritanism and predestination to Baptist and Methodist faiths, among others, following revolutionary preachers and movements. This period was called the **Second Great Awakening**. In art and culture, romanticism and reform movements elevated the "common man," a trend that would continue into the presidency of Andrew Jackson.

However, not all was well. Federalists had strongly opposed the war. They had also opposed economic policies taken under Jefferson and Madison. At the **Hartford Convention**, Federalists developed an anti-Republican platform; however by the time they completed their discussions and were ready to head to Washington, the War of 1812 had already ended. The Federalists essentially collapsed afterwards.

From a financial perspective, the country would again struggle. Disagreement over the **Tariff of 1816** divided industrialists, who believed in nurturing American industry, from Southern landowners, who depended on exporting cotton and tobacco for profit. Later, following the establishment of the **Second Bank of the United States**, the **Panic of 1819** erupted when the government cut credit following overspeculation on western lands; the BUS wanted payment from state banks in hard currency, or **specie**. Western banks foreclosed on western farmers, and farmers lost their land.

With the Louisiana Purchase, the country had almost doubled in size. In the nineteenth century, the idea of **manifest destiny**, or the sense that it was the fate of the United States

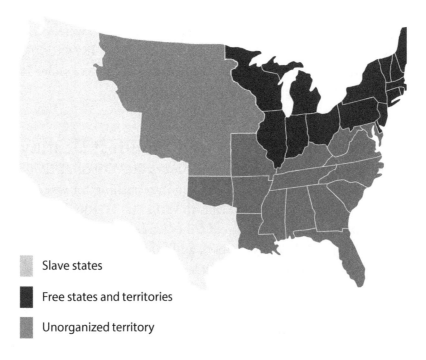

Slave states

Free states and territories

Unorganized territory

Figure 1.6. Missouri Compromise

to expand westward and settle the continent, pervaded. Also in 1819, the United States purchased Florida from Spain in the **ADAMS-ONIS TREATY**. The **MONROE DOCTRINE**, James Monroe's policy that the Western Hemisphere was "closed" to any further European colonization or exploration, asserted US hegemony in the region.

Westward expansion triggered questions about the expansion of slavery, a divisive issue. Slavery was profitable for the southern states which depended on the plantation economy, but increasingly condemned in the North. Furthermore, the Second Great Awakening had fueled the **ABOLITIONIST** movement. In debating the nature of westward expansion, the Kentucky senator **HENRY CLAY** worked out a compromise. The **MISSOURI COMPROMISE**, also known as the **COMPROMISE OF 1820**, allowed Missouri to join the union as a slave state, but provided that any other states north of the **THIRTY-SIXTH PARALLEL (36°30')** would be free. Maine would also join the nation as a free state. However, more tension and compromises over the nature of slavery in the West were to come.

Jacksonian Democracy

Demographics were changing throughout the early nineteenth century. Technological advances such as the **COTTON GIN** had allowed exponential increases in cotton; therefore, more persons were enslaved than ever before, bringing more urgency to the issue of slavery. In addition, **IMMIGRATION** from Europe to the United States was increasing—mainly Irish Catholics and Germans. Reactionary **NATIVIST** movements like the **KNOW-NOTHING PARTY** feared the influx of non-Anglo Europeans, particularly Catholics, and discrimination was widespread, especially against the Irish. Other technological advances like the **RAILROADS** and **STEAMSHIPS** were speeding up westward expansion and improving trade throughout the continent; a large-scale **MARKET ECONOMY** was emerging. With early industrialization and changing concepts following the Second Great Awakening, women were playing a larger role in society, even though they could not vote.

Most states had extended voting rights to white men who did not own land or substantial property: **UNIVERSAL MANHOOD SUFFRAGE**. Elected officials would increasingly come to better reflect the electorate, and the brash war hero Jackson was popular among the "common man."

During the election of 1824, Andrew Jackson ran against **JOHN QUINCY ADAMS**, Henry Clay, and William Crawford, all Republicans (from the Democratic Republican party); John Quincy Adams won. By 1828, divisions within the party had Jackson and his supporters known as Democrats, in favor of small farmers and inhabitants of rural areas, and states' rights. Clay and his supporters became known as **NATIONAL REPUBLICANS** and, later, **WHIGS**, a splinter group of the Democratic-Republicans which supported business and urbanization; they also had federalist leanings. Thus the **TWO-PARTY SYSTEM** emerged.

Jackson's popularity with the "common man," white, male farmers and workers who felt he identified with them, and the fact that owning property was no longer a requirement to vote, gave him the advantage and a two-term presidency. Jackson rewarded his supporters, appointing them to important positions as part of the **SPOILS SYSTEM**.

Opposed to the Bank of the United States, he issued the **SPECIE CIRCULAR**, devaluing paper money and instigating the financial **PANIC OF 1837**. Despite his opposition to such deep federal economic control, Jackson was forced to contend with controversial tariffs.

The **Tariff of 1828**, or **Tariff of Abominations**, benefitted Northern industry, but heavily affected Southern exports; Senator **John C. Calhoun** of South Carolina spoke out in favor of **nullification**, wherein he argued that a state had the right to declare a law null and void if it was harmful to that state.

Tensions increased with the **Tariff of 1832**; Calhoun and South Carolina threatened to secede if their economic interests were not protected. Jackson managed the **Nullification Crisis** without resorting to violence; paradoxically, he protected the federal government at the expense of states' rights, working out a compromise in 1833 that was more favorable to the South.

Socially and politically, white men of varying levels of economic success and education were able to have stronger political voices and more opportunities in civil society. However, women, African Americans, and Native Americans were oppressed. With continental expansion came conflict with Native Americans. Despite efforts by the Cherokee, who unsuccessfully argued for the right to their land in the Supreme Court in *Cherokee Nation v. Georgia* (1831), President Andrew Jackson enforced the 1830 **Indian Removal Act**, forcing Cherokee, Creek, Chickasaw, Choctaw, and others from their lands in the Southeast. Thousands of people were forced to travel mainly on foot, with all of their belongings, to Indian Territory (today, Oklahoma) on the infamous **Trail of Tears**, to make way for white settlers. Violent conflicts would continue on the Frontier farther west between the US and the Apache, Comanche, Sioux, Arapaho, Cheyenne, and other tribes throughout the nineteenth century.

EXAMPLES

1) How did the Quartering Act impact the colonists?
    A. Colonists were forced to take British soldiers into their homes; protests against the Act led to the Boston Tea Party.
    B. Colonists were forced to build quarters for British soldiers who were stationed locally.
    C. Colonists had to provide one-quarter of their earnings to support British soldiers stationed locally.
    D. Colonists were forced to take British soldiers into their homes; protests against the Act led to the Boston Massacre.
    E. Colonists were forced to pay taxes to support British soldiers, a quarter of which went to soldiers stationed locally.

Answers:
   A. Incorrect. While the Quartering Act did require colonists to provide housing for British soldiers, whose numbers were increasing in the Colonies with rising tensions, protests against it did not include the Boston Tea Party; this event protested the Tea Act.
   B. Incorrect. The Quartering Act required colonists to take British soldiers into their own homes to provide them with a place to stay, not to build them housing.
   C. Incorrect. The Quartering Act was not a tax.

D. Correct. Anger at being forced to provide shelter for British soldiers led to protests; in 1770, British soldiers fired on protests against the Quartering Act in what came to be called the Boston Massacre.

E. Incorrect. The Quartering Act did not tax people, nor did it address soldiers stationed outside of the colonies.

2) What was the impact of Shays' Rebellion?

A. It showed resistance to imposing excise taxes on whiskey and other consumer goods.

B. Its quick suppression showed the increased strength of the new government under the Constitution.

C. Inspired by *Letters from a Farmer in Pennsylvania*, Daniel Shays and other farmers rose up to protest taxes and the fiscal policies engineered by Alexander Hamilton during the Washington administration.

D. Shays, who was concerned about strengthened federal powers under the new Constitution, organized radical Democratic-Republicans to protest the fiscal measures espoused by Hamilton, particularly the Bank of the United States.

E. It showed the tenuous nature of governmental control in the young United States and illustrated the need for a stronger federal government.

Answers:

A. Incorrect. The Whiskey Rebellion erupted in response to the imposition of excise taxes (in addition to tariffs) under the Federalist Treasury Secretary Alexander Hamilton's fiscal policies, which reflected a stronger federal government.

B. Incorrect. Washington's quick and decisive response to the Whiskey Rebellion demonstrated the strength of the new federal government.

C. Incorrect. Shays and his allies—indebted farmers—revolted against seizures of land and debtors' prisons, consequences of post-revolution disorganization and the indebtedness of the new United States. Furthermore, Dickinson's *Letters from a Farmer in Pennsylvania* had stirred up pre-revolutionary protest against the Townshend Acts and the concept of being taxed without proper representation in Parliament; this document was not a factor in Shays' Rebellion.

D. Incorrect. Shays and his group were driven by personal interest, not politics; furthermore, Shays' Rebellion took place before the Constitution was written and before these fiscal policies were put into place.

E. Correct. Shays' Rebellion, in which Daniel Shays led a rebellion of indebted farmers shortly after the end of the Revolution, showed the need for a stronger federal government to ensure national stability and was a major factor in planning the Constitutional Convention.

3) Despite King George III's agreement with Native American tribes in the Northwest (Great Lakes and Ohio Valley region) in issuing the Proclamation of 1763, the United States did not recognize this deal. What was the impact of that diplomatic reversal?

A. A series of conflicts between the Americans and the Northwest tribes—the Shawnee, Lenape (who had been pushed west from the Atlantic coast by colonization), Kickapoo, Miami, and others—culminated in the Battle of Fallen Timbers; later, organized into the Northwest Confederacy under the Shawnee leader Tecumseh, inspired by his brother Tenskwatawa, and backed by the

British, the tribes once again came into conflict with the Americans, defending their land at the Battle of Tippecanoe and in the War of 1812. Ultimately, the US would control the land.

B. The French and British were able to form the Northwest Confederacy, allying against the United States in an effort to control more land in North America.

C. A series of conflicts between the Americans and the Northwest tribes—the Algonquin, Oneida, Mohawk, Onondaga, Cayuga, Seneca, and others—culminated in the Battle of Fallen Timbers; later, organized into the Northwest Confederacy under the Mohawk leader Tecumseh, inspired by his brother Tenskwatawa, and backed by the British, the tribes once again came into conflict with the Americans, defending their land at the Battle of Tippecanoe and in the War of 1812. Ultimately, the US would control the land.

D. The Northwest Confederacy of British and American soldiers united to drive Native American tribes from what is today the Midwest region of the United States, in order to allow whites to establish settlements in the region.

E. France allied with the Shawnee, Lenape, Miami, and Kickapoo to form the Northwest Confederacy in an effort to retake land lost in the French and Indian War.

Answers:

A. **Correct.** Despite efforts by the tribes to retain control over their land, they would eventually lose a series of conflicts and the United States would establish states in the Midwest and Ohio Valley region.

B. Incorrect. While Britain allied with the Shawnee-led Northwest Confederacy, Britain and France did not form an alliance during this time. By the turn of the century, France no longer had a presence at all in North America.

C. Incorrect. While most of these tribes were Algonquin-speaking, the ethnic Algonquin were not major participants; furthermore, Tecumseh was Shawnee, not Mohawk. In addition, the Mohawk, Seneca, Oneida, Onondaga, and Cayuga composed the Iroquois Confederacy, which did not take part in this conflict.

D. Incorrect. The British and Americans did not form an alliance in North America; they came into conflict in the region.

E. Incorrect. The Northwest Confederacy was an entirely tribal confederation led by the Shawnee leader, Tecumseh.

4) How did demographics play a part in democratic change during the early and mid-nineteenth century, particularly in the context of Jacksonian Democracy?

A. The rising strength of industry in the Northeast, coupled with the beginnings of railroads, strengthened support for pro-business politicians and the business class.

B. Wealthy European immigrants shifted the balance of power away from the "common man" to business owners and the elites, leading to the rise of the powerful Whig party.

C. Universal manhood suffrage shifted the balance of political power away from the elites; immigration accelerated westward expansion and began to power early industry and urban development.

D. Jackson's focus on strengthening the federal government dissatisfied the South, leading to the Nullification Crisis.

E. The influx of immigrants into Eastern cities led to nativism and a reversal of democratic change in the election process.

Answers:

A. Incorrect. While early industry and railroads were a feature of this era, universal manhood suffrage and the popular notion of the "common man" actually meant that more power went to working people and small rural farmers. Also, rising numbers of poor European immigrants tipped the balance of power away from the rich.

B. Incorrect. European immigrants were not wealthy; furthermore, their rapid influx led to nativist movements such as the Know-Nothing party. The Whigs emerged later as an offshoot of the Democratic-Republicans.

C. **Correct.** Universal manhood suffrage allowed all white males, whether or not they owned property, to vote; the "common man" had a voice in government, and Jackson enjoyed their support. Likewise, an influx of poor European immigrants changed the country's demographics, providing more workers for early industry, more settlers interested in populating the west, and a stronger voice in government against the wealthy.

D. Incorrect. Jackson did not favor a strong federal government. However, the series of tariffs passed during the early nineteenth century, which benefitted the North at the expense of the Southern economy, led to the Nullification Crisis in which John C. Calhoun of South Carolina argued that states could declare federal laws they judged harmful to their own interests null. Jackson managed to negotiate compromises to end the crisis.

E. Incorrect. While the increase in immigrants did lead to nativism, the democratic changes in the electoral process, including universal white manhood suffrage, were unaffected.

5) How did the Missouri Compromise reflect divisions over slavery?

A. It showed disagreement over the nature of westward expansion.

B. It showed the impact of the abolitionist movement on politics.

C. It showed how the Second Great Awakening had influenced society.

D. It showed that national unity was still of greater importance than ending or expanding slavery.

E. all of the above

Answers:

A. Incorrect. While the Missouri Compromise was indeed a compromise over how far west slavery would be permitted to extend, this choice does not fully answer the question, given the other answer choices available.

B. Incorrect. The abolitionist movement did indeed impact politics to the extent that permitting slavery was at the forefront of Congress' agenda. However, given these answer choices, this choice does not fully respond to the question.

C. Incorrect. The Second Great Awakening did indeed influence society by liberalizing thought, including popularizing humanism and the abolition of slavery. However, this answer choice is incomplete given the other options available.

D. Incorrect. While both sides chose to compromise rather than risk the Union, this answer is incomplete given the options available.

E. **Correct.** All of the answer choices are true.

Civil War, Expansion, and Industry

The Road to Conflict

The Civil War was rooted in ongoing conflict over slavery, states' rights, and the reach of the federal government. Reform movements of the mid-nineteenth century fueled the abolitionist movement. The Missouri Compromise and the Nullification Crisis foreshadowed worsening division to come.

In 1836, Texas, where there were a great number of white settlers, declared independence from Mexico; one reason was because Mexico abolished slavery, an institution white Texans wished to retain. In 1845, Texas joined the Union; this event, in addition to ongoing US hunger for land, triggered the **MEXICAN-AMERICAN WAR**. As a result of the **TREATY OF GUADALUPE HIDALGO**, which ended the war following the surrender of the Mexican General Santa Ana, the United States obtained territory in the Southwest: the Utah and New Mexico Territories, and gold-rich California. The population of California would grow rapidly with the **GOLD RUSH** as prospectors in search of gold headed west to try their fortunes. However, Latinos and Latinas who had lived in the region under Mexico lost their land and were denied many of the rights that whites enjoyed—even though they had been promised US citizenship and equal rights under the Treaty. They also suffered from racial and ethnic discrimination.

Meanwhile, social change in the Northeast and growing Midwest continued. As the market economy and early industry developed, so did an early **MIDDLE CLASS**. Social views on the role of **WOMEN** changed; extra income allowed them to stay at home. The **CULT OF DOMESTICITY**, a popular cultural movement, encouraged women to become homemakers and focus on domestic skills. However, women were also freed up to engage in social activism, and they were active in reform movements. Activists like **SUSAN B. ANTHONY** and **ELIZABETH CADY STANTON** worked for women's rights, including women's suffrage, culminating in the 1848 **SENECA FALLS CONVENTION** led by the **AMERICAN WOMAN SUFFRAGE ASSOCIATION**. Women were also active in the temperance movement. Organizations like the Woman's Christian Temperance Union advocated for the prohibition of alcohol, which was finally achieved with the Eighteenth Amendment, although it was later repealed with the Twenty-First.

Reform movements continued to include abolitionism, which ranged from moderate to radical. The American Colonization Society wanted to end slavery and send former slaves to Africa. The former slave **FREDERICK DOUGLASS** advocated for abolition. An activist leader and writer, Douglass publicized the movement along with the American Anti-Slavery Society and publications like Harriet Beecher Stowe's *Uncle Tom's Cabin*. The radical abolitionist **JOHN BROWN** led violent protests against slavery. Abolitionism became a key social and political issue in the mid-nineteenth century.

The industrial change in the North did not extend to the South, which continued to rely on plantations and cotton exports. Nor were the majority of demographic changes occurring in the South. Differences among the regions grew, and disputes over extending slavery into new southwestern territories obtained from Mexico continued. Another compromise was needed.

Anti-slavery factions in Congress had attempted to halt the extension of slavery to the new territories obtained from Mexico in the 1846 **Wilmot Proviso**, but these efforts were unsuccessful. The later **Compromise of 1850** admitted the populous California as a free state and Utah and New Mexico to the Union with slavery to be decided by **popular sovereignty**, or by the residents. It also reaffirmed the **Fugitive Slave Act**, which allowed slave owners to pursue escaped slaves to free states and recapture them. It would now be a federal crime to assist escaped slaves, an unacceptable provision to many abolitionists.

Shortly thereafter, Congress passed the **Kansas-Nebraska Act of 1854** Which allowed those two territories to decide slavery by popular sovereignty as well, effectively repealing the Missouri Compromise. A new party, the **Republican Party**, was formed by angered Democrats, Whigs, and others as a result; later, one of its members, Abraham Lincoln, would be elected to the presidency. Violence broke out in Kansas between pro- and anti-slavery factions in what became known as **Bleeding Kansas**.

In 1856, an escaped slave, **Dred Scott**, took his case to the Supreme Court to sue for freedom. Scott had escaped to the free state of Illinois and sought to stay there; his former "owner" had argued that he could him back regardless of the state he was in. The Court heard the case, ***Scott v. Sandford***, and ruled in favor of Sandford, upholding the Fugitive Slave Act, the Kansas-Nebraska Act, and nullifying the Missouri Compromise. The Court essentially decreed that African Americans were not entitled to rights under US citizenship.

In 1858, a series of debates between Illinois Senate candidates, Republican **Abraham Lincoln** and Democrat **Stephen Douglas**, showed the deep divides in the nation over slavery and states' rights. During the **Lincoln-Douglas Debates**, Lincoln spoke out against slavery, while Douglas supported the right of states to decide its legality on their own. In 1860, Lincoln was elected to the presidency. Given his outspoken stance against slavery, South Carolina seceded immediately thereafter, followed by Mississippi, Alabama, Florida, Louisiana, Georgia, and Texas. They formed the Confederate States of America, or the **Confederacy**, on February 1, 1861, under the leadership of **Jefferson Davis**, a senator from Mississippi.

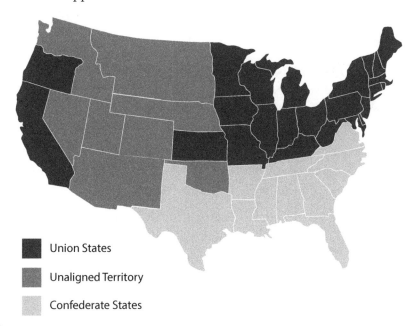

Union States

Unaligned Territory

Confederate States

Figure 1.7. Union and Confederacy

Shortly after the South's secession, Confederate forces attacked Union troops in Charleston Harbor, South Carolina; the **BATTLE OF FORT SUMTER** sparked the Civil War. As a result, Virginia, Tennessee, North Carolina, and Arkansas seceded and joined the Confederacy. West Virginia was formed when the western part of Virginia refused to join the Confederacy.

Both sides believed the conflict would be short-lived; however, after the First Battle of Bull Run when the Union failed to route the Confederacy, it became clear that the war would not end quickly. Realizing how difficult it would be to defeat the Confederacy, the Union developed the **ANACONDA PLAN**, a plan to "squeeze" the Confederacy, including a naval blockade and taking control of the Mississippi River. Since the South depended on international trade in cotton for much of its income, a naval blockade would have serious economic ramifications for the Confederacy.

However, the **SECOND BATTLE OF BULL RUN** was a tactical Confederate victory, led by **GENERAL ROBERT E. LEE** and **STONEWALL JACKSON**. The Union army remained intact, but the loss was a heavy blow to Union morale. The **BATTLE OF ANTIETAM** was the first battle to be fought on Union soil. Union General **GEORGE B. McCLELLAN** halted General Lee's invasion of Maryland, but failed to defeat Confederate forces. Undaunted, on January 1, 1863, President Lincoln decreed the end of slavery in the rebel states with the **EMANCIPATION PROCLAMATION**. The **BATTLE OF GETTYSBURG** was a major Union victory, led by General George Meade. It was the bloodiest battle in American history up to this point; the Confederate army would not recover.

President Lincoln later delivered the Gettysburg Address onsite, in which he framed the Civil War as a battle for human rights and equality.

Meanwhile, following the **SIEGE OF VICKSBURG**, Mississippi, Union forces led by **GENERAL ULYSSES S. GRANT** gained control over the Mississippi River, completing the Anaconda Plan. The **BATTLE OF ATLANTA**, was the final major battle of the Civil War; following the Union victory led by **GENERAL WILLIAM T. SHERMAN**, the Union proceeded into the South, and the Confederacy fell. One of the final conflicts of the war, the Battle of Appommatox Court House, resulted in Confederate surrender at Appommatox, Virginia, on April 9, 1865, where General Lee surrendered to General Grant and the war ended.

Aftermath and Reconstruction

Despite the strong leadership and vast territory of the Confederacy, a larger population (strengthened by immigration), stronger industrial capacity (including weapons-making capacity), the naval blockade of Southern trade, and superior leadership resulted in Union victory. Yet bitterness over Northern victory persisted, and President Lincoln was assassinated on April 15, 1865. Post-war **RECONSTRUCTION** would continue without his leadership.

Despite ratifying the amendments, Southern states instituted the Black Codes to continue oppression of freedmen, or freed African Americans, who faced ongoing violence.

Before his death, Lincoln had crafted the **TEN PERCENT PLAN**: if ten percent of a Southern state's population swore allegiance to the Union, that state would be readmitted into the Union. However Lincoln's vice president, Andrew Johnson, enforced Reconstruction weakly and the white supremacist **KU KLUX KLAN** emerged to intimidate and kill black people in the

South; likewise, states developed the oppressive BLACK CODES to limit the rights of African Americans.

As a result, the punitive Congress passed the CIVIL RIGHTS ACT in 1866, granting citizenship to African Americans and guaranteeing African American men the same rights as white men (later reaffirmed by the FOURTEENTH AMENDMENT). Eventually former Confederate states also had to ratify the 1865 THIRTEENTH AMENDMENT, which abolished slavery; the FOURTEENTH AMENDMENT, which upheld the provisions of the Civil Rights Act; and the FIFTEENTH AMENDMENT, which in 1870 granted African American men the right to vote. (No women, regardless of race, would receive the right to vote in federal elections until the ratification of the Nineteenth Amendment in 1920.)

Conflict over how harshly to treat the South persisted in Congress between Republicans and Democrats and in 1867, a Republican-led Congress passed the RECONSTRUCTION ACTS, placing former Confederate states under the control of the US Army, effectively declaring martial law. While tensions and bitterness existed between Northern authorities and Southern leaders, Reconstruction did provide for modernization of Southern education systems, tax collection, and infrastructure. The FREEDMEN'S BUREAU was tasked with assisting freed slaves (and poor whites) in the South.

While technically enslaved African Americans had been freed, many slaves were not aware of this; others still remained voluntarily or involuntarily on plantations. All slaves were eventually freed; however, few had education or skills. Furthermore, oppressive social structures remained: the JIM CROW LAWS enforced SEGREGATION in the South. Despite the Fourteenth Amendment, the rights of African Americans were regularly violated. In 1896, the Supreme Court upheld segregation in *PLESSY V. FERGUSON* when a mixed-race man, Homer Plessy, was forced off a whites-only train car. When Plessy challenged the law, the Court held that segregation was, indeed, constitutional; according to the Court, *separate but equal* did still ensure equality under the law. This would remain the law until *BROWN V. BOARD OF EDUCATION* in 1954.

Black leaders like BOOKER T. WASHINGTON and W.E.B. DuBOIS sought solutions. Washington believed in gradual desegregation and vocational education for African Americans, providing it at his TUSKEGEE INSTITUTE. DuBois, on the other hand, favored immediate desegregation and believed African Americans should aim for higher education and leadership positions in society. His stance was supported by the advocacy group, the NATIONAL ASSOCIATION FOR THE ADVANCEMENT OF COLORED PEOPLE (NAACP). These differing views reflected diverse positions within and beyond the African American community over its future. Furthermore, many blacks fled the South for greater opportunities in the North, in cities, and farther West, as part of a greater demographic movement known as the GREAT MIGRATION.

Resentment over the Reconstruction Acts never truly subsided, and military control of the South finally ended with the COMPROMISE OF 1877, which resolved the disputed presidential election of 1876, granting Rutherford B. Hayes the presidency, and removed troops from the South.

While the Civil War raged and during the chaotic post-war Reconstruction period, settlement of the West continued. California had already grown in population due to the gold rush. In the mid-nineteenth century, CHINESE IMMIGRANTS came in large numbers to California, in search of gold but arriving to racial discrimination instead. At the same time, however, the US was opening up trade with East Asia, thanks to CLIPPER SHIPS that made journeys across the Pacific Ocean faster and easier. Earlier in 1853, COMMODORE MATTHEW PERRY had used "gunboat diplomacy" to force trade agreements with Japan; even earlier, the United States had signed the TREATY OF WANGXIA, a trade agreement, with Qing Dynasty China.

Despite the racism faced by Chinese immigrants, Americans of European descent were encouraged to settle the Frontier. The HOMESTEAD ACT OF 1862 granted 160 acres of land in the West to any settler who promised to settle and work it for a number of years; frontier life was difficult, however, as the land of the Great Plains was difficult to farm. Meanwhile, ranching and herding cattle became popular and profitable. White settlers also hunted the buffalo; mass buffalo killings threatened Native American survival.

Meanwhile, the Great Plains and Rockies were already populated with the Sioux, Cheyenne, Apache, Comanche, Arapaho, Pawnee, and others. Conflict between Native American tribes and white settlers was ongoing; the 1864 SAND CREEK MASSACRE in Colorado, when US troops ambushed Cheyenne and Arapaho people, triggered even more violence. The United States came to an agreement with the Sioux in South Dakota, offering them land as part of the burgeoning RESERVATION system. However, by the late nineteenth century, gold was discovered in the Black Hills of South Dakota on the GREAT SIOUX RESERVATION. The US reneged on its promise, encouraging exploration and seeking control over that gold. The resulting SIOUX WARS culminated in the 1876 BATTLE OF LITTLE BIG HORN and General George Custer's famous "last stand." While the US was defeated in that battle, reinforcements would later defeat the Sioux and the reservation system continued. Conflict continued as well: the GHOST DANCE MOVEMENT united Plains tribes in a spiritual movement and in the belief that whites would eventually be driven from the land. In 1890, the military forced the Sioux to cease this ritual; the outcome was a massacre at WOUNDED KNEE and the death of the Sioux chief, SITTING BULL.

In 1887, the DAWES ACT ended federal recognition of tribes, withdrew tribal land rights, and forced the sale of reservations—tribal land. It also dissolved Native American families; children were sent to boarding schools, where they were forced to abandon their cultures and assimilate to the dominant American culture.

The Gilded Age and the Second Industrial Revolution

Back in the Northeast, the market economy and industry were flourishing. Following the war, the INDUSTRIAL REVOLUTION, accelerated in the United States. The Industrial Revolution had begun on the global level with textile production in Great Britain, had been fueled in great part by supplies of Southern cotton, and was evolving in the United States with the development of heavy industry—what would come to be called the SECOND INDUSTRIAL REVOLUTION.

The GILDED AGE saw an era of rapidly growing income inequality, justified by theories like SOCIAL DARWINISM and the GOSPEL OF WEALTH, which argued that the wealthy had been made rich by God and were socially more deserving of it. Much of this wealth was generated by heavy industry in what became known as the SECOND INDUSTRIAL REVOLUTION (the first being textile-driven and originating in Europe). Westward expansion required railroads; railroads required steel, and industrial production required oil: all these commodities spurred the rise of powerful companies like John D. Rockefeller's Standard Oil and Andrew Carnegie's US Steel.

The creation of MONOPOLIES and TRUSTS helped industrial leaders consolidate their control over the entire economy; a small elite grew to hold a huge percentage of income. Monopolies let the same business leaders control the market for their own products. Business leaders in varying industries (monopolies) organized into trusts, ensuring their control over each other's industries, buying and selling from each other, and resulting in the control of the economy by a select few. These processes were made possible thanks to VERTICAL and HORIZONTAL INTEGRATION of industries. One company would dominate each step in manufacturing a good, from obtaining raw materials to shipping finished product, through vertical integration. Horizontal integration describes the process of companies acquiring their competition, monopolizing their markets. With limited governmental controls or interference in the economy, American CAPITALISM—the free market system—was becoming dominated by the elite.

However, the elite were also powering industrial growth. Government corruption led only to weak restrictive legislation like the INTERSTATE COMMERCE ACT of 1887, which was to regulate the railroad industry, and the SHERMAN ANTITRUST ACT (1890), which was intended to break up monopolies and trusts, in order to allow for a fairer marketplace; however, these measures would remain largely toothless until President Theodore Roosevelt's "trust-busting" administration in 1901.

Not only were products from the US market economy available in the United States; in order to continue to fuel economic growth, the United States needed more markets abroad. NEW IMPERIALISM described the US approach to nineteenth and early twentieth century imperialism as practiced by the European powers. Rather than controlling territory, the US sought economic connections with countries around the world.

While the free markets and trade of the CAPITALIST economy spurred national economic and industrial growth, the WORKING CLASS, comprised largely of poor European and Chinese immigrants working in factories and building infrastructure, suffered from dangerous working conditions and other abuses. As the railroads expanded westward, white farmers suffered: they lost their land to corporate interests. In addition, Mexican Americans and Native Americans were harmed and lost land as westward expansion continued with little to no regulations on land use. African Americans in the South, though freed from slavery, were also struggling under SHARECROPPING, in which many worked the same land for the same landowners, leasing land and equipment at unreasonable rates, essentially trapped in the same conditions they had lived in before.

These harmful consequences led to the development of reform movements, social ideals, and change.

Populism and the Progressive Era

The PEOPLE'S (POPULIST) PARTY formed in response to corruption and industrialization injurious to farmers (later, it would also support reform in favor of the working class and oppressed groups like women and children). Farmers were suffering from crushing debt in the face of westward expansion, which destroyed their lands; they were also competing (and losing) against industrialized and mechanized farming. Groups like the NATIONAL GRANGE advocated for farmers. More extreme groups like LAS GORRAS BLANCAS disrupted the construction of railroads altogether in efforts to protect land from corporate interests.

Farmers were also concerned about fiscal policy. In order to reduce their debt, they believed that introducing a SILVER STANDARD would inflate crop prices by putting more money into national circulation. The GREENBACK-LABOR PARTY was formed in an effort to introduce a silver standard. Debate would continue until the passage of the SHERMAN SILVER PURCHASE ACT in 1890, which allowed Treasury notes to be backed in both gold and silver. However, political conflict and continuing economic troubles led to the PANIC OF 1893, the result of the silver standard and of the failure of a major railroad company. GROVER CLEVELAND, who had never been in favor of the silver standard, asked Congress to repeal the Act.

Meanwhile, the COLORED FARMERS' ALLIANCE formed to support sharecroppers and other African American farmers in the South. The Jim Crow laws remained in place in much of the South, reaffirmed by the Supreme Court case *PLESSY V. FERGUSON*. The NAACP was formed to advocate for African Americans nationwide and still functions today.

At the same time, the LABOR MOVEMENT emerged to support mistreated industrial workers in urban areas. SAMUEL GOMPERS led the AMERICAN FEDERATION OF LABOR (AFL), using STRIKES and COLLECTIVE BARGAINING to gain protections for the unskilled workers who had come to cities seeking industrial jobs. The KNIGHTS OF LABOR further empowered workers by integrating unskilled workers into actions. MOTHER JONES revolutionized labor by including women, children, and African Americans into labor actions.

Poor conditions led to philosophies of reform. Many workers were inspired by SOCIALISM, the philosophy developed in Europe that the workers should own the means of production and that wealth should be distributed equally, taking into account strong economic planning. Other radical movements included UTOPIANISM, whose adherents conceptualized establishing utopian settlements with egalitarian societies. More modern philosophies included the SOCIAL GOSPEL, the notion that it was society's obligation to ensure better treatment for workers and immigrants. With the continual rise of the MIDDLE CLASS, women took a more active role in advocating for the poor and for themselves. Women activists also aligned with labor and the emerging Progressive Movement.

With the Progressive THEODORE ROOSEVELT'S ascension to the presidency in 1901 following President William McKinley's assassination, the Progressive Era reached its apex. The *TRUST-BUSTER* Roosevelt enforced the Sherman Antitrust Act and prosecuted the NORTHERN SECURITIES railroad monopoly under the Interstate Commerce Act, breaking up trusts and creating a fairer market. He led government involvement in negotiations between unions and industrial powers, developing the *SQUARE DEAL* for fairer treatment of workers. The Progressive Era also saw a series of acts to protect workers, health, farmers, and children under Presidents Roosevelt and Taft.

Roosevelt continued overseas expansion following McKinley's SPANISH-AMERICAN WAR (1898 – 1901), in which the US gained control over Spanish territory in the Caribbean, Asia, and the South Pacific.

The Spanish-American War had been the first time the United States had engaged in overseas military occupation and conquest beyond North America, entirely contrary to George Washington's recommendations in his Farewell Address.

During this period, the US annexed Hawaii, Guam, Puerto Rico, and took over the Panama Canal; Cuba became a US protectorate; and the US annexed the Philippines, which would fight an ongoing guerrilla war for independence.

Spanish abuses in Cuba had concerned Americans; however, many events were sensationalized and exaggerated in the media—this YELLOW JOURNALISM aroused popular concern and interest in intervention in Cuba. The discovery of a letter from the Spanish minister de Lome, which insulted President McKinley, along with the mysterious explosion of the United States battleship USS Maine in Havana spurred the US into action.

Many Americans did not support intervention, however. According to the TELLER AMENDMENT, Cuba would revert to independence following the war. The US signed a peace treaty with Spain in 1898. As a result, it controlled Puerto Rico and Guam. Despite having promised independence to the Philippines, McKinley elected to keep it; furthermore, under the PLATT AMENDMENT, the United States effectively took over Cuba despite previous promises of independence.

The ROOSEVELT COROLLARY to the Monroe Doctrine, which promised US intervention in Latin America in case of European intervention there, essentially gave the US total dominance over Latin America. Under the HAY PAUNCEFOTE TREATY, Great Britain granted its claims to the area that would become the Panama Canal (at the time, in Colombia) to the US As Colombia refused to recognize the treaty, President Roosevelt engineered a revolution, creating the new country of Panama, and beginning construction of the canal. This NEW IMPERIALISM expanded US markets and increased US presence and prestige on the global stage.

EXAMPLES

1) Which of the following is true about the roots of the Civil War?
   A. John C. Calhoun used slavery as the reason behind his doctrine of nullification; indeed, disagreements over the institution of slavery precipitated the Nullification Crisis, an early example of Southern discontent with the federal government.
   B. The high numbers of immigrants moving to the North in the early nineteenth century represented a threat to the South, which had a smaller population in comparison, so it wanted to maintain control over the slaves.
   C. Lincoln and Douglas provoked anti-slavery sentiment in their debates around the country.
   D. The Missouri Compromise, the Compromise of 1850, and the Kansas-Nebraska Act all reflected dissent within the Union over the nature of the future of the country—whether slavery should be extended as the United States grew.
   E. As the Northern economy industrialized it became less dependent on the crops grown by slaves in the South.

Answers:
A. Incorrect. High tariffs were the impetus behind nullification.

B. Incorrect. Slavery was an essential part of the plantation economy of the South; its benefit lay in its role in supporting the cotton trade, not in balancing population relative to the North.

C. Incorrect. The Lincoln-Douglas debates reflected white Americans' conflicted views on slavery; furthermore, Douglas was not against outlawing the institution, believing instead it was an issue best left up to states.

D. **Correct.** These pieces of legislation represent ongoing efforts to bridge the gap between differences in views over slavery in determining the future of the country.

E. Incorrect. The textile industry was at the center of Northern industrialization, and it relied heavily on Southern cotton.

2) How did the Dawes Act impact Native Americans in the West?

  A. It forced them to move from their ancestral lands to what is today Oklahoma.

  B. It revoked tribal rights to land and federal recognition of tribes, forcing assimilation.

  C. It granted them land on reservations: for example, the Sioux received deeds to the Great Sioux Reservation in the Black Hills of South Dakota.

  D. It provided 160 acres of land to any settler willing to farm land on the Great Plains for at least five years, threatening Native American rights to land.

  E. It granted limited sovereignty to tribes and required all acquisition of Native lands to be done by treaty.

Answers:

  A. Incorrect. The Indian Removal Act was responsible for this.

  B. **Correct.** The punitive Dawes Act forced assimilation by revoking federal recognition of tribes, taking lands allotted to tribes and dissolving reservations, and forcing children into assimilationist schools (thereby dividing families).

  C. Incorrect. The Dawes Act actually dismantled the reservation system.

  D. Incorrect. The Homestead Act was responsible for this.

  E. Incorrect. Tribal sovereignty was not recognized in law until the 1930s.

3) How was a small elite of wealthy businesspersons able to dominate the economy during the Gilded Age?

  A. The Sherman Antitrust Act put a few expert business leaders in charge of economic policy.

  B. Monopolies and trusts, developed through horizontal and vertical integration, ensured that the same business leaders controlled the same markets.

  C. Industrialization was encouraging the United States to shift to a planned economy in keeping with philosophical changes in Europe.

  D. The silver standard allowed specific businesspeople holding large silver reserves to dominate the market.

  E. Due to shifting global resource needs, the United States economy was reduced to only a few key industries.

Answers:

  A. Incorrect. The Sherman Antitrust Act, though largely toothless until the Roosevelt administration, was intended to break up monopolies and avoid the concentration of economic power in the hands of a few.

B. **Correct.** Horizontal and vertical integration of industries allowed the same companies—and people—to control industries, or create monopolies. Those elites who monopolized specific markets organized trusts so that one group controlled entire sectors of the economy.

C. Incorrect. The United States was a capitalist economy (though imperfect, due to strong monopolies). A planned economy would be a socialist economy.

D. Incorrect. The silver standard affected government fiscal policy and backed currency; it did not directly affect class organization.

E. Industrialization and innovation led to the birth of many new industries during the Gilded Age.

4) How did the Progressive Movement change the United States during the Second Industrial Revolution?

A. Trade unions fought for workers' rights and safety; the Social Gospel, an early philosophy of charity and philanthropy, developed to support the poor and urban disadvantaged.

B. The Seneca Falls Convention drew attention to the question of women's suffrage.

C. Progressives argued to extend rights and protections to Native Americans, particularly those displaced by settlement on the Great Plains.

D. The Supreme Court ruled segregation unconstitutional in *Plessy v. Ferguson*.

E. The federal government developed new social programs intended to provide a safety net for the nation's poor.

Answers:

A. **Correct.** Unions improved conditions for industrial workers; the Social Gospel imparted a sense of social responsibility that eventually manifested in laws and regulations protecting the rights and safety of workers, farmers, the poor, and others.

B. Incorrect. While women's suffrage continued to be an important issue during the Progressive Era and while women continued to advocate for their rights, the Seneca Falls Convention took place several decades before.

C. Incorrect. Protection of Native Americans was not a central part of the Progressive platform.

D. Incorrect. The Supreme Court maintained that segregation was constitutional in *Plessy v. Ferguson*.

E. Incorrect. Substantive federally directed social programs were not created until the New Deal. Aid to the poor during the Progressive movement came from private organizations.

5) How did the Spanish-American War change perceptions of the United States?

A. It was clear to Europe and Latin America that the United States had military and territorial, in addition to economic, aspirations as an imperial power.

B. The United States had begun to prove itself as a military power on the global stage, with strong naval capabilities.

C. It was clear that nationalism was strong among the American people.

D. It was clear to Europe and Latin America that the United States had abandoned the foreign policy principles established in Washington's Farewell Address.

E. all of the above

Answers:

A. Incorrect. Given the failure of the United States to follow through on its promises of independence for Cuba and the Philippines, it was clear that the country had interests in gaining territory. However, this choice does not completely answer the question.

B. Incorrect. The United States had indeed demonstrated formidable naval powers, fighting a war in both the Pacific Ocean and Caribbean Sea. However, this choice does not completely answer the question.

C. Incorrect. While a strong sense of nationalism drove public opinion to favor the war, this choice does not completely answer the question.

D. Incorrect. America's aggressive imperialism in Cuba, and especially in the Philippines (which lay outside the Americas) was a break from the non-interventionist foreign policy established by Washington. However, given the other options, this answer is not complete.

E. **Correct.** All of the above answer choices satisfy the question.

The United States Becomes a Global Power

Socioeconomic Change and World War I

Social change led by the Progressives in the early twentieth century resulted in better conditions for workers, increased attention toward child labor, and calls for more livable cities.

The Roosevelt administration focused its attention on economic change at the corporate level. The SHERMAN ANTITRUST ACT, despite its intended purpose—to prosecute and dissolve large trusts and create a fairer market place—had actually been used against unions and farmers' alliances. Under Roosevelt, the Act was used to prosecute enormous trusts like the NORTHERN SECURITIES COMPANY, which controlled much of the railroad industry, and STANDARD OIL. Actions like this earned Roosevelt his reputation as a trust-buster.

Jacob Riis' groundbreaking book and photo essay *How the Other Half Lives* revealed the squalor and poverty the poor urban classes—often impoverished immigrants—endured, leading to more public calls for reform.

Continuing economic instability also triggered top-down reform. Banks restricting credit and overspeculating on the value of land and interests, coupled with a conservative gold standard, led to the PANIC OF 1907. To stabilize the economy and rein in the banks, Congress passed the FEDERAL RESERVE ACT in 1913 to protect the banking system. Federal Reserve banks were established to cover twelve regions of the country; commercial banks had to take part in the system, allowing "the Fed" to control interest rates and avoid a similar crisis.

During the Progressive Era, while the United States became increasingly prosperous and stable, Europe was becoming increasingly unstable. Americans were divided over how to respond. Following the Spanish-American War, debate had arisen within the US between INTERVENTIONISM and ISOLATIONISM—whether the US should intervene in international matters or not. Interventionists believed in spreading US-style democracy, while isolationists believed in focusing on development at home. This debate became more pronounced with the outbreak of World War I in Europe.

Inflammatory events like German SUBMARINE WARFARE (U-boats) in the Atlantic Ocean, the sinking of the *LUSITANIA*, which resulted in many American civilian deaths, the embarrassing ZIMMERMAN TELEGRAM (in which Germany promised to help Mexico in an attack on the US), and growing American NATIONALISM, or pride in and identification with one's country, triggered US intervention in the war. On December 7, 1917, the US declared war. With victory in 1918, the US had proven itself a superior military and industrial power. Interventionist PRESIDENT WOODROW WILSON played an important role in negotiating the peace; his FOURTEEN POINTS laid out an idealistic international vision, including an international security organization. However, European powers negotiated and won the harsh TREATY OF VERSAILLES, which placed the blame for the war entirely on Germany and demanded crippling REPARATIONS from it, one contributing factor to WORLD WAR II later in the twentieth century. The LEAGUE OF NATIONS, a collective security organization, was formed, but a divided US Congress refused to ratify the Treaty, so the US did not join it. Consequently, the League was weak and largely ineffective.

Divisions between interventionists and isolationists continued. Following the Japanese invasion of Manchuria in 1932, the STIMSON DOCTRINE determined US neutrality in Asia. Congress also passed the NEUTRALITY ACTS of 1930s in face of conflict in Asia and ongoing tensions in Europe.

For more information on the First World War, please see Chapter Two, "World History."

On the home front, fear of homegrown radicals—particularly of communists and anarchists—and xenophobia against immigrants led to the RED SCARE in 1919 and a series of anti-immigration laws. Attorney-General Palmer authorized J. EDGAR HOOVER (who would later head the FBI) to lead a series of raids (the PALMER RAIDS) on suspected radicals, precipitating the hysteria of the Red Scare; Palmer was later discredited. In response to widespread xenophobia and a sentiment of isolationism following the First World War, Congress limited immigration specifically from Asia, Eastern Europe, and Southern Europe with the racist EMERGENCY QUOTA ACT of 1921 and NATIONAL ORIGINS ACT of 1924.

The ongoing Great Migration of African Americans to the North led to differing views on black empowerment. Leaders like MARCUS GARVEY believed in self-sufficiency for blacks, who were settling in urban areas and facing racial discrimination and isolation. Garvey's UNITED NEGRO IMPROVEMENT ASSOCIATION would go on to inspire movements like the Black Panthers and the Nation of Islam; however, those radical philosophies of separation were at odds with the NAACP, which believed in integration. Tensions increased with 1919 race riots. In the South, the Ku Klux Klan was growing in power, and blacks faced intimidation, violence, and death; LYNCHINGS, in which African Americans were kidnapped and killed, sometimes publicly, occurred frequently.

Despite race riots and discrimination in northern cities, African American culture did flourish and become an integral part of growing American popular culture. The HARLEM RENAISSANCE, the development and popularity of African American-dominated music (especially JAZZ), literature, and art, was extremely popular nationwide and contributed to the development of American pop culture. So did the evolution of early technology like radio, motion pictures, and automobiles—products which were available to the middle class through credit. Furthermore, the women's rights movement was empowered by the heightened visibility of women in the public sphere; the NINETEENTH AMENDMENT, giving all women the right to vote, was ratified in 1920. However, the ROARING TWENTIES, a seemingly trouble-free period of isolation from chaotic world events, would come to an end.

Great Depression

Following WWI, the United States had experienced an era of consumerism and corruption. The government sponsored LAISSEZ-FAIRE policies and supported MANUFACTURING, flooding markets with cheap consumer goods. Union membership suffered; so did farmers, due to falling crop prices. While mass-production helped the emerging middle class afford more consumer goods and improve their living standards, many families resorted to CREDIT to fuel consumer spending. These risky consumer loans, OVERSPECULATION on crops and the value of farmland, and weak banking protections helped bring about the GREAT DEPRESSION, commonly dated from October 29, 1929, or *BLACK TUESDAY*, when the stock market collapsed. During the same time period, a major drought occurred in the Great Plains, affecting farmers throughout the region. Millions of Americans faced unemployment and poverty.

Figure 1.8. Soup Kitchen During the Great Depression

Speculation, or margin-buying, meant that speculators borrowed money to buy stock, selling it as soon as its price rose. However, since the price of stocks fluctuated, when buyers lost confidence in the market and began selling their shares, the value of stocks fell. Borrowers could not repay their loans; as a result, banks failed.

Following weak responses by the Hoover administration, FRANKLIN DELANO ROOSEVELT was elected to the presidency in 1932. FDR offered Americans a *NEW DEAL*:

a plan to bring the country out of the Depression. During the *FIRST HUNDRED DAYS* of FDR's administration, a series of emergency acts (known as an *ALPHABET SOUP* of acts due to their many acronyms) was passed for the immediate repair of the banking system. Perhaps most notable was the **GLASS-STEAGAL ACT**, which established the **FEDERAL DEPOSIT INSURANCE CORPORATION (FDIC)** to insure customer deposits in the wake of bank failures. (Later, to monitor stock trading, the **SECURITIES AND EXCHANGE COMMISSION (SEC)** was established; it also has the power to punish violators of the law.) To address the effects of overspeculation on land, the **AGRICULTURAL ADJUSTMENT ACT (AAA)** reduced farm prices by subsidizing farmers to reduce production of commodities. The **HOME OWNERS LOAN CORPORATION (HOLC)** refinanced mortgages to protect homeowners from losing their homes, and the **FEDERAL HOUSING ADMINISTRATION (FHA)** was created for the long term to insure low-cost mortgages.

The **TENNESSEE VALLEY AUTHORITY (TVA)**, was the first large-scale attempt at regional public planning; despite being part of the First Hundred Days, it was a long-term project. While intended to create jobs and bring electricity to the impoverished, rural inhabitants of the Tennessee Valley area, one of its true objectives was to accurately measure the cost of electric power, which had been supplied by private companies. The TVA was the first public power company and still operates today.

FDR did not only address economic issues; a number of acts provided relief to the poor and unemployed. The federal government allotted aid to states to be distributed directly to the poor through the **FEDERAL EMERGENCY RELIEF ACT**. The New Deal especially generated jobs. The federal government distributed funding to states through the **PUBLIC WORKS ADMINISTRATION (PWA)** for the purpose of developing infrastructure and to provide construction jobs for the unemployed. Likewise, the **CIVILIAN CONSERVATION CORPS (CCC)** offered employment in environmental conservation and management projects. Later, during the **SECOND NEW DEAL**, the **WORKS PROGRESS ADMINISTRATION (WPA)** was established. The WPA was a long-term project that generated construction jobs and built infrastructure throughout the country. It also employed writers and artists: the **FEDERAL WRITERS' PROJECT** and the **FEDERAL ART PROJECT** created jobs for writers and artists, who wrote histories, created guidebooks, developed public art for public buildings, and made other contributions.

The New Deal addressed labor issues as well. The **WAGNER ACT** ensured the right to unionize and established the **NATIONAL LABOR RELATIONS BOARD (NLRB)**. Strengthening unions guaranteed collective bargaining rights and protected workers.

FDR was a Democrat in the Progressive tradition; the Progressive legacy of social improvement was apparent throughout the New Deal and his administration. The New Deal and its positive impact on the poor, the working class, unions, and immigrants led these groups to support the Democratic Party, a trend that continues to this day.

International Affairs and World War II

The entire world suffered from the Great Depression, and Europe became increasingly unstable. With the rise of the radical Nazi Party in Germany, the Nazi leader Adolf Hitler led German takeovers of several European countries and became a threat to US allies, bombing Britain. However, the United States, weakened by the Great Depression and reluctant to engage in international affairs due to continuing public and political support for isolationism, reinforced by the Neutrality Acts, remained militarily uncommitted in the war. However, the Neutrality Act of 1939 allowed cash-and-carry arms sales to combat participants; in this way, the United States could militarily support its allies (namely, Great Britain).

FDR was increasingly concerned about the rise of fascism in Europe, seeing it as a global threat. To ally with and support Great Britain without technically declaring war on Germany, FDR convinced Congress to enact the **LEND-LEASE ACT**, directly supplying Britain with military aid, in place of cash-and-carry. FDR and the British Prime Minister **WINSTON CHURCHILL** met in response to the non-aggression pact between Hitler and Stalin to sign the **ATLANTIC CHARTER**, which laid out the anti-fascist agenda of free trade and self-determination. To garner support for his position, FDR spoke publicly about the **FOUR FREEDOMS**: freedom of speech, freedom of religion, freedom from want, and freedom from fear.

However, after the Japanese attack on **PEARL HARBOR** on December 7, 1941, the US entered the war. While directly attacked by Japan, allied with the fascist Axis powers of Italy and Germany, the United States focused first on the European theater, having agreed with the other Allied powers (Great Britain and the Soviet Union) that Hitler was the primary global threat. The United States focused on eliminating the Nazi threat in the air and at sea, destroying Nazi U-boats (submarines) that threatened the Allies throughout the Atlantic. The US also engaged Germany in North Africa, defeating its troops to approach the fascist Italy from the Mediterranean. On June 6, 1944, or **D-DAY**, the US led the invasion of Normandy, invading German-controlled Europe. After months of fighting, following the deadly and drawn-out **BATTLE OF THE BULGE** when the Allies faced fierce German resistance, the Allies were able to enter Germany and end the war in Europe.

The United States was then able to focus more effectively on the war in the Pacific. The United States had been able to break the Japanese code; at the same time, Japan had been unable to crack US code thanks to the **NAVAJO CODE TALKERS**, who used the Navajo language, which Japan was unable to decipher. The US strategy of **ISLAND HOPPING** allowed it to take control of Japanese-held Pacific islands, proceeding closer to Japan itself despite **KAMIKAZE** attacks on US ships, in which Japanese fighter pilots intentionally crashed their planes into US ships. President **HARRY TRUMAN** had taken power following FDR's death in 1945. Rather than force a US invasion of Japan, which would have resulted in huge numbers of casualties, he authorized the bombing of **HIROSHIMA** and **NAGASAKI** in Japan, the only times that **NUCLEAR WEAPONS** have been used in conflict. The war ended with Japanese surrender on September 2, 1945.

Japanese-Americans faced oppression and discrimination at home simply due to their race. Forced into internment camps, Japanese-Americans challenged this violation of their rights in *Korematsu v. US*; however, the Supreme Court ruled that this forced displacement was constitutional.

The **UNITED NATIONS** was formed in the wake of the Second World War, modeled after the failed League of Nations. Unlike the League, however, it included a **SECURITY COUNCIL** comprised of major world powers, with the power to militarily intervene for peacekeeping purposes in unstable global situations. With most of Europe destroyed, the victorious US and the Soviet Union emerged as the two global **SUPERPOWERS**.

In 1945, Stalin, Churchill, and Roosevelt had met at the **YALTA CONFERENCE** to determine the future of Europe. The

Allies had agreed on free elections for European countries following the fall of the fascist regimes. However, following the war, the USSR occupied Eastern Europe, preventing free elections. The United States saw this as a betrayal of the agreement at Yalta. Furthermore, while the US-led MARSHALL PLAN began a program to rebuild Europe, the USSR consolidated its presence and power in eastern European countries, forcing them to reject aid from the Marshall Plan. This division would destroy the alliance between the Soviets and the West, leading to the COLD WAR between the two superpowers and the emergence of a BIPOLAR WORLD.

Cold War at Home and Abroad

With the collapse of the relationship between the USSR and the US, distrust and fear of COMMUNISM grew. Accusations of communist sympathies against public figures ran rampant during the MCCARTHY ERA in the 1950s, reflecting domestic anxieties.

President Harry S. Truman's TRUMAN DOCTRINE stated that the US would support any country threatened by authoritarianism (communism), leading to the KOREAN WAR (1950 – 1953), a conflict between the US and Soviet-backed North Korean forces, which ended in a stalemate. The policy of CONTAINMENT, to contain Soviet (communist) expansion, defined US foreign policy; according to DOMINO THEORY, once one country fell to communism, others would quickly follow. Other incidents included the BAY OF PIGS invasion in Cuba (1961), a failed effort to topple the communist government of Fidel Castro, and the CUBAN MISSILE CRISIS (1962), when Soviet missiles were discovered in Cuba and military crisis was narrowly averted, both under the administration of the popular President JOHN F. KENNEDY.

Meanwhile, in Southeast Asia, communist forces in North Vietnam were gaining power. Congress never formally declared war in Vietnam but gave the president authority to intervene militarily there through the GULF OF TONKIN RESOLUTION (1964). However, this protracted conflict—the VIETNAM WAR—also led to widespread domestic social unrest, which only increased with US deaths there, especially after the Vietnamese-led TET OFFENSIVE (1968). The US ultimately withdrew from Vietnam and the North Vietnamese forces, or VIET CONG, led by HO CHI MINH, took over the country.

For more detailed information, please see Chapter Two, "World History."

EXAMPLES

1) Which of the following precipitated US entry into the First World War?
   A. the sinking of the *Lusitania*
   B. anger stirred up by the Zimmerman telegram
   C. the threat of German U-boats in the Atlantic
   D. growing American nationalism
   E. all of the above

   Answers:
   A. Incorrect. The sinking of the *Lusitania* had a strong impact on public opinion in the United States, as many American civilians died on board. However, this event alone did not cause the US to enter into the war.

B. Incorrect. The Zimmerman telegram eliminated any remaining feelings of neutrality in the United States. However, despite its embarrassing nature, it was not the only factor that pushed the US to join the war.

C. Incorrect. German U-boats threatened American activity and shipping in the North Atlantic Ocean, but this threat was not the only reason the United States was compelled to join hostilities against Germany.

D. Incorrect: Nationalism was growing in the United States, fueled in part by the legacy of the Spanish-American War and anti-immigrant xenophobia.

E. Correct. All of the above events together precipitated US entry into the First World War.

2) How did the United States change in the 1920s?
   A. The Great Migration ceased.
   B. Popular culture was shaped, in large part, by an African American arts movement centered in Harlem.
   C. The Great Depression caused high unemployment.
   D. Thanks to the New Deal, millions of Americans found jobs.
   E. The migration of people from rural communities into cities slowed considerably.

Answers:
   A. Incorrect. The Great Migration was an ongoing phenomenon; furthermore, discrimination and violence against African Americans in the South continued to drive black people to northern cities.
   B. Correct. The Harlem Renaissance was an explosion of African American art, literature, and movement that represented the first significant crossover of African-American culture into white popular culture.
   C. Incorrect. The Great Depression began in 1929, and mass unemployment followed; it was not a major feature of the 1920s.
   D. Incorrect. The New Deal was a consequence of the Great Depression and a feature of the 1930s.
   E. Incorrect: Urbanization increased during the 1920s, and for the first time, more Americans lived in cities than in rural areas.

3) How did the New Deal repair the damage of the Great Depression and help the United States rebuild?
   A. Immediate economic reforms stabilized the economy during the First Hundred Days; later, longer-term public works programs provided jobs to relieve unemployment and develop infrastructure.
   B. Social programs put into effect during the First Hundred Days provided jobs for Americans; measures to protect homeowners, landholders, and bank deposits followed to guarantee financial security.
   C. Programs like the Tennessee Valley Authority helped the government determine proper pricing and institute price controls for important public goods.
   D. FDR proposed supporting banks and big business with federal money in order to reinvigorate the market by limiting government intervention.
   E. A government call for voluntary restraint in wage reductions and layoffs by companies and strikes by unions stabilized companies and curbed unemployment.

Answers:

A. **Correct.** FDR focused on immediate economic stabilization upon taking office, then attacked poverty and unemployment on a sustainable basis.

B. Incorrect. While some social programs were initiated during the First Hundred Days, emergency financial measures like the Glass-Steagal Act, the HOLC, and the AAA were the hallmark of the First Hundred Days, when FDR prioritized immediate economic stabilization.

C. Incorrect. While one purpose of the TVA was indeed to determine the true cost of providing electricity, the government did not enforce price controls on public goods in the long term or on a widespread basis. Furthermore, the TVA was mainly an exercise in regional planning and poverty relief.

D. Incorrect. FDR's focus was on limiting the power of large banks and dramatically increasing government intervention in the market.

E. Incorrect. This was a tactic used by Hoover that ultimately proved unsuccessful as the economy worsened.

4) Why did the former allies, the United States and the Soviet Union, turn against each other following the end of the Second World War?

A. Stalin felt that the Marshall Plan should have been extended to the Soviet Union.

B. Because of the fear of communism in the United States, the US had considered invading the USSR following the occupation of Nazi Germany.

C. Despite assurances to the contrary, the USSR occupied Eastern European countries, preventing free elections in those countries.

D. The Soviet Union was concerned that the United States would use the nuclear bomb again.

E. The Soviet Union viewed the continued presence of American troops in Germany and Japan as a threat to their national security.

Answers:

A. Incorrect. The Marshall Plan was not intended for the USSR; it was part of an effort to create a post-war Europe in the model of the Atlantic Charter, espousing free trade and democracy.

B. Incorrect. During WWII, the US and Soviet Union were allies (despite mutual suspicion), and the US did not plan to invade the USSR.

C. **Correct.** Stalin's refusal to permit free elections or democracy in the countries of Eastern Europe were seen as a betrayal of the agreement reached by the Allies at Yalta, and a major reason for the collapse of the US-Soviet relationship.

D. Incorrect. While this was a major concern of the Soviet Union, it was not the precipitating reason for the collapse of the relationship.

E. Incorrect. All of the major powers agreed to the importance of maintaining a strong military presence in the aggressor nations.

GO ON

5) What was the purpose of the United Nations Security Council?

   A. to provide a means for international military intervention in case of conflict that could threaten global safety, in order to avoid another world war

   B. to provide a forum for the superpowers to maintain a dialogue

   C. to provide a means for countries to counter the power of the US and USSR in an effort to limit the reach of the superpowers

   D. to develop a plan to rebuild Europe and Japan

   E. to prevent the spread of communism throughout Asia and Europe

Answers:

   A. **Correct.** While the UN was modeled in part after the League of Nations, the Security Council was (and is) able to militarily intervene in cases of armed conflict that could pose a global threat, an ability the League of Nations did not have.

   B. Incorrect. While both the US and the USSR had permanent seats on the Security Council, the purpose of the Council was not to facilitate their relationship, nor did it.

   C. Incorrect. The Security Council was formed before the Cold War and did not necessarily envision the development of a bipolar world; furthermore, it was not intended as a forum for global dialogue (that is the role of the UN General Assembly).

   D. Incorrect. The Security Council was not involved in post-war development; its purpose was (and is) to safeguard international security.

   E. Incorrect. The Security Council is an international body that is neutral to forms of government as long as they do not threaten world peace. In addition, the USSR was one of the original permanent members.

Postwar and Contemporary United States

Civil Rights and Social Change

During the 1960s, the US experienced social and political change, starting with the election of the young and charismatic John F. Kennedy in 1960. Following JFK's assassination in 1963, President **Lyndon B. Johnson**'s administration saw the passage of liberal legislation in support of the poor and of civil rights. The **Civil Rights Movement**, led by activists like the **Rev. Dr. Martin Luther King, Jr.** and **Malcolm X**, fought for African American rights in the South, including the abolition of segregation, and also for better living standards for Blacks in northern cities.

Civil rights came to the forefront with the 1954 Supreme Court case *Brown v. Board of Education*, when the Warren Court (so-called after Chief Justice Earl Warren) found segregation unconstitutional, overturning its decision in *Plessy v. Ferguson*. *Brown* took place shortly after the desegregation of the armed forces, and public support for civil rights and racial equality was growing.

The **Southern Christian Leadership Conference (SCLC)** and Dr. King, a religious leader from Georgia, believed in civil disobedience, non-violent protest. In Montgomery, Alabama, **Rosa Parks**, an African American woman, was arrested for refusing to give up her seat to a white man on a bus. Buses were segregated at the time, and leaders including Dr. King organized the **Montgomery Bus Boycott** to challenge segregation; the effort was ultimately successful. Building on their success, civil rights activists, now including many students and the **Student Nonviolent Coordinating Committee (SNCC)**, led peaceful protests and boycotts to protest segregation at lunch counters, in stores, at public pools, and other public places.

The movement grew to include voter registration campaigns organized by CORE, the Congress of Racial Equality, supported by students and other activists (both black and white) from around the country—the **Freedom Riders**, so-called because they rode buses from around the country to join the movement in the Deep South. SNCC and activists organized to protest segregation at government and public facilities and on university campuses. The movement continued to gain visibility as non-violent protesters were met with violence by the police and state authorities, including attacks by water cannons and police dogs in Alabama. Undaunted, activists continue to fight against segregation and unfair voting restrictions on African Americans.

The Civil Rights Movement had national public attention, and had become a major domestic political issue. Civil rights workers organized the **March on Washington** in 1963, when Dr. King delivered his famous *I Have a Dream* speech. Widespread public support for civil rights legislation was impossible for the government to ignore. In 1964, Congress passed the **Civil Rights Act**, which outlawed segregation.

Figure 1.9. March on Washington

However, African Americans' voting rights were still not sufficiently protected. According to the Fifteenth and the Nineteenth Amendments, all African Americans—men and women—had the right to vote, but many Southern states had voting restrictions in place such as literacy tests and poll taxes, which disproportionately affected African Americans. Dr. King and civil rights workers organized a march from Selma to Montgomery, Alabama, to draw attention to this issue; however it ended in violence as marchers were attacked by police. In 1965, led by President Lyndon B. Johnson, Congress passed the **VOTING RIGHTS ACT**, which forbade restrictions impeding the ability of African Americans to vote, including literacy tests. Separately, the **TWENTY-FOURTH AMENDMENT** made poll taxes unconstitutional.

Today, some states have instituted voter identification laws similar to literacy tests and poll taxes, which disproportionately affect minorities.

Meanwhile, **MALCOLM X** was an outspoken proponent of **BLACK EMPOWERMENT**, particularly for African Americans in urban areas. Unlike Martin Luther King Jr., who believed in integration, Malcolm X and other activists, including groups like the **BLACK PANTHERS**, believed that African Americans should stay separate from whites to develop stronger communities.

The Civil Rights Movement extended beyond the Deep South. **CESAR CHAVEZ** founded the **UNITED FARM WORKERS (UFW)**, which organized Hispanic and migrant farm workers in California and the Southwest to advocate for unionizing and collective bargaining. Farm workers were underpaid and faced racial discrimination. The UFW used boycotts and non-violent tactics similar to those used by civil rights activists in the South; Cesar Chavez also used hunger strikes to raise awareness of the problems faced by farm workers.

The Civil Rights Movement also included **FEMINIST** activists who fought for fairer treatment of women in the workplace and for women's reproductive rights. The **NATIONAL ORGANIZATION FOR WOMEN** and feminist leaders like **GLORIA STEINEM** led the movement for equal pay for women in the workplace. The landmark case of *ROE V. WADE* struck down federal restrictions on abortion.

The **AMERICAN INDIAN MOVEMENT (AIM)** brought attention to injustices and discrimination suffered by Native Americans nationwide. Ultimately it was able to achieve more tribal autonomy and address problems facing Native American communities throughout the United States.

In New York City in 1969, the **STONEWALL RIOTS** occurred in response to police repression of the gay community. These riots and subsequent organized activism are seen as the beginning of the LGBT rights movement.

President Kennedy had envisioned a liberal United States in the tradition of the Progressives. His youth and charisma were inspiring to many Americans, and his assassination in 1963 was a shock. Kennedy's vice president Lyndon B. Johnson continued the liberal vision with the **GREAT SOCIETY**. LBJ embraced **LIBERALISM**, believing that government should fight poverty at home, and play an interventionist role abroad (in this era, by fighting communism).

Johnson launched a **WAR ON POVERTY**, passing reform legislation to support the poor. The **MEDICARE ACT** provided medical care to elderly Americans; the creation of the

DEPARTMENT OF HOUSING AND URBAN DEVELOPMENT increased the federal role in housing and urban issues. Johnson's HEAD START program provided early intervention for disadvantaged children before elementary school (and still does today); the ELEMENTARY AND SECONDARY EDUCATION ACT increased funding for primary and secondary education. Additionally, the IMMIGRATION ACT OF 1965 overturned the provisions of the Emergency Quota Act, ending the racist limitations on immigrants to the US.

At the same time, LBJ's overseas agenda was increasingly unpopular. Adhering to containment and domino theory—US policy toward communism in an effort to stop its spread—Johnson drew the United States deeper into conflict in Southeast Asia. The VIETNAM WAR was extremely unpopular in the US due to high casualties, the unpopular draft (which forced young American males to fight overseas) and what seemed to many to be the purposelessness of the war. Student activists, organizing in the mold of the Civil Rights Movement, engaged in non-violent (and, at times, violent) protest against the Vietnam War. The rise of a COUNTERCULTURE among the youth—the development and popularity of ROCK AND ROLL MUSIC, the culture of HIPPIES, and changing concepts of drug use and sexuality—added to a sense of rebellion among Americans, usurping government authority and challenging traditional values.

For more information on the Vietnam War, please see Chapter Two, "World History."

The Rise of Conservatism

Radical social change in the 1960s, coupled with the toll of the Vietnam War on the American public, many of whom had lost loved ones in the war, or served themselves in combat, led to backlash against liberalism. CONSERVATISM strengthened in response to the heavy role of government in public life throughout the 1960s, high rates of government spending, and social challenges to traditional values. Due in great part to the escalation of the Vietnam War, LBJ announced his intention not to run for another term, and the conservative RICHARD NIXON became president in 1970.

During the administration of the conservative President Richard Nixon, the conflict in Vietnam ended and a diplomatic relationship with China began. Nixon also oversaw economic reforms—he lifted the gold standard in an effort to stop STAGFLATION, a phenomenon when both unemployment and inflation are high at the same time. Ending the gold standard reduced the value of the dollar in relation to other global currencies, and foreign investment in the United States increased. However, the Nixon administration was found to have engaged in corrupt practices. A burglary at the Democratic National Headquarters, based at the Watergate Hotel, was found to have been connected to the Oval Office. The WATERGATE SCANDAL eventually forced Nixon to resign, and Vice President GERALD FORD took office for one term. Nixon's resignation further destroyed many Americans' faith in their government.

During the 1970s, the economy suffered due to US involvement in the Middle East. US support for Israel in the Six Day War and 1973 Yom Kippur War caused **OPEC** (the Organization of Petroleum Exporting Countries), led by Saudi Arabia and other allies of Arab foes of Israel, to boycott the US As a result, oil prices skyrocketed. In the 1979 Iranian Revolution and the resulting HOSTAGE CRISIS, when the US Embassy in Teheran was taken over by anti-American activists, the economy suffered from another oil shock. (For more information on these events, please see Chapter Two, "World History.") While President Jimmy Carter had been able to negotiate peace between Israel and Egypt in the CAMP DAVID ACCORDS, he was widely perceived as ineffective. Carter lost the presidency in 1980 to the conservative Republican RONALD REAGAN.

OPEC COUNTRIES

Algeria	Kuwait	United Arab
Ecuador	Libya	Emirates
Indonesia	Nigeria	Venezuela
Iran	Quatar	
Iraq	Saudi Arabia	

Figure 1.10. OPEC

Reagan championed domestic tax cuts and an aggressive foreign policy against the Soviet Union. The Reagan Revolution revamped the economic system, cutting taxes and government spending. According to supply-side economics (popularly known as *Reaganomics*), cutting taxes on the wealthy and providing investment incentives, wealth would "trickle down" to the middle and working classes and the poor. However, tax cuts forced Congress to cut or eliminate social programs that benefitted millions of those same Americans. Later, the TAX REFORM ACT of 1986 ended progressive income taxation.

Despite promises to lower government spending, the Reagan administration invested huge sums of money in the military. This investment in military technology—the ARMS RACE with the Soviet Union—helped bring about the end of the Cold War with the 1991 fall of the USSR and later, a new era of globalization. In addition to funding a general arms buildup and supporting measures to strengthen the military, the Reagan administration funded and developed advanced military technology to intimidate the Soviets, despite having signed the STRATEGIC ARMS LIMITATION TREATIES (SALT I AND II) limiting nuclear weapons and other strategic armaments in the 1970s. Ultimately, the US would outspend the USSR militarily, a precipitating factor to the fall of the Soviet Union. (For more information on the fall of the USSR, please see Chapter Two, "World History.")

The Reagan Revolution also ushered in an era of conservative values in the public sphere. After the Civil Rights Era, whose victories had occurred under the auspices of the Democratic Johnson administration, many Southern Democrats switched loyalties to the Republican Party. At the same time, the Democrats gained the support of African Americans and other minority groups who benefitted from civil rights and liberal legislation. During the Reagan Era, conservative Republicans espoused a return to "traditional" values.

CHRISTIAN FUNDAMENTALISM became popular, particularly among white conservatives. Groups like FOCUS ON THE FAMILY lobbied against civil rights reform for women and advocated for traditional, two-parent, heterosexual families.

The End of the Cold War and Globalization

The administration of GEORGE H. W. BUSH signed the Strategic Arms Reduction, or START, TREATY with the Soviet Union in 1991, shortly before the dissolution of the USSR.; later, it would enter into force in 1994 between the US and the Russian Federation as an agreement to limit the large arsenals of strategic weapons possessed by both countries.

With the collapse of the Soviet Union, the balance of international power changed. The bipolar world became a unipolar world, and the United States was the sole superpower. The first major crisis occurred in the Middle East when Iraq, led by SADDAM HUSSEIN, invaded oil-rich Kuwait. The US intervened—with the blessing of the United Nations, and the support of other countries. The resulting GULF WAR, or OPERATION DESERT STORM (1991)—cemented its status as the world's sole superpower; Saddam's forces were driven from Kuwait, and Iraq was restrained by sanctions and no-fly zones.

With the election of President BILL CLINTON in 1992, the US took an active role in international diplomacy, helping broker peace deals in the former Yugoslavia, Northern Ireland, and the Middle East. Clinton's election also indicated a more liberal era in American society: while conservative elements remained a strong force in politics and sectors of society, changing attitudes toward minorities in the public sphere and increased global communication (especially with the advent of the Internet) were a hallmark of the 1990s.

As part of GLOBALIZATION, the facilitation of global commerce and communication, the Clinton administration prioritized free trade. Encouraging open borders, the United States signed the NORTH AMERICAN FREE TRADE AGREEMENT (NAFTA) with Mexico and Canada, creating a free trade zone throughout North America, removing trade restrictions. The Clinton administration also eased financial restrictions in the United States,

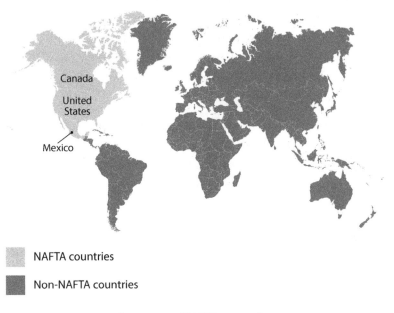

Figure 1.11. NAFTA countries

rolling back some of the limitations provided for under Glass-Steagal. These changes were controversial: many American jobs went overseas, especially manufacturing jobs, where labor was cheaper. Furthermore, globalization began facilitating the movement of people, particularly undocumented immigrants from Latin America seeking a better life in the United States. IMMIGRATION REFORM would be a major issue into the twenty-first century.

Clinton faced dissent in the mid-1990s with a conservative resurgence. A movement of young conservatives elected to Congress in 1994 promised a CONTRACT WITH AMERICA, a conservative platform promising a return to lower taxes and traditional values. Clinton also came under fire for personal scandals: allegations of corrupt real estate investments in the Whitewater scandal and inappropriate personal behavior in the White House. These scandals fueled social conservatives and Christian fundamentalists who favored a return to the conservative era of the 1980s. Despite these controversies and political division, society became increasingly liberal. Technology like the INTERNET facilitated national and global communication, media, and business; minority groups like the LGBT community engaged in more advocacy; and environmental issues became more visible.

The Twenty-First Century

By the end of the twentieth century, the United States had established itself as the dominant global economic, military, and political power. Due to its role in global conflict from the Spanish-American War onwards, the US had established military bases and a military presence worldwide, in Europe, Asia, the Pacific, and the Middle East. The US dominated global trade: American corporations established themselves globally, taking advantage of free trade to exploit cheap labor pools and less restrictive manufacturing environments (at the expense of American workers). American culture was widely popular: since the early twentieth century, American pop culture like music, movies, television shows, and fashion was enjoyed by millions of people around the world.

However, globalization also facilitated global conflict. While terrorism had been a feature of the twentieth century, the United States had been relatively untouched by large-scale terrorist attacks. That changed on SEPTEMBER 11, 2001, when the terrorist group AL QAEDA hijacked airplanes, attacking New York and Washington, D.C. in the largest attack on US soil since the Japanese bombing of Pearl Harbor. The 9/11 attacks triggered an aggressive military and foreign policy under the administration of President GEORGE W. BUSH, who declared a *WAR ON TERROR*, an open-ended global conflict against terror organizations and their supporters.

Following the attacks, the US struck suspected al Qaeda bases in Afghanistan, beginning the AFGHANISTAN WAR, during which time the US occupied the country. Suspected terrorist fighters captured there and elsewhere during the War on Terror were held in a prison in GUANTANAMO BAY, Cuba, which was controversial because it did not initially offer any protections afforded to prisoners of war under the Geneva Conventions.

President Bush believed in the doctrine of PREEMPTION, that if the US was aware of a threat, it should preemptively attack the source of that threat. Preemption would drive the invasion of Iraq in 2003. In 2003, the US attacked Iraq, believing that Iraq held WEAPONS OF MASS DESTRUCTION that could threaten the safety of the United States. This assumption was later revealed to be false; however, the United States promulgated the IRAQ WAR, deposing Saddam Hussein and supporting a series of governments until it withdrew its troops in 2011, leaving the country in a state of chaos.

At home, Congress passed the **USA PATRIOT ACT** to respond to fears of more terrorist attacks on US soil; this legislation gave the federal government unprecedented—and, some argued, unconstitutional—powers of surveillance over the American public.

Despite the tense climate, social liberalization continued in the US Following the Bush administration, during which tax cuts and heavy reliance on credit (especially in the housing market—the **SUBPRIME MORTGAGE CRISIS**) helped push the country into the **GREAT RECESSION**, the first African American president, **BARACK OBAMA**, was elected in 2008. Under his presidency, the US emerged from the recession, ended its occupations of Iraq and Afghanistan, passed the Affordable Care Act, which reformed the healthcare system, and legalized same-sex marriage. The Obama administration also oversaw the passage of consumer protection acts, increased support for students, and safety nets for homeowners.

EXAMPLES

1) Why did the Civil Rights Movement continue to push for legislative change even after the passage of the 1964 Civil Rights Act?

   A. While the Civil Rights Act provided legal protections to African Americans and other groups, many believed it did not go far enough as it did not outlaw segregation.

   B. Leaders like Malcolm X believed further legislative reform would ensure better living conditions for blacks in cities.

   C. Civil rights leaders wanted legislation to punish white authorities in the South that had oppressed African Americans.

   D. Legal restrictions like literacy tests, poll taxes, and voter registration issues inhibited African Americans from exercising their right to vote, especially in the South.

   E. Civil rights leaders wanted legislation to ensure equal representation of African Americans in local, state and federal governments.

Answers:

   A.   Incorrect. The Civil Rights Act of 1965 was the *de jure* end to segregation, even though discrimination was still widespread.

   B.   Incorrect. Black empowerment focused on strengthening black communities from within and at the grassroots level, not working for legislative reform from the outside.

   C.   Incorrect. Prosecution and punishment was not the goal of the mainstream Civil Rights Movement.

   D.   Correct. Despite the end to legal segregation, discrimination was deeply entrenched, and laws still existed to prevent African Americans from voting. Civil rights activists worked to ensure the passage of the Voting Rights Act in 1965.

   E.   Incorrect. There was never a call for legislation setting quotas for elected representatives or appointed government officials.

2) Which of the following best describes liberalism under LBJ?

   A. Liberalism was the philosophy that the government should be deeply involved in improving society at home, and work on fighting communism abroad.

   B. According to liberalism, the US should devote its resources to improving life at home for the disadvantaged, but refrain from direct intervention in international conflict.

   C. Liberals believed in moderate social programs, but that spending should be limited.

   D. Liberalism frowns upon conflict intervention, as shown by the mass demonstrations against the Vietnam War in the 1960s.

   E. Liberalism emphasized reducing government regulations of the economy as a way to improve society overall.

   Answers:

   A. **Correct.** LBJ believed in forming a Great Society and launched a War on Poverty, initiating federal government-sponsored social programs to support the disadvantaged; he also actively waged a war against the spread of communism in Southeast Asia, ultimately unsuccessfully.

   B. Incorrect. Liberals believe that the federal government should devote resources both to social programs domestically and to fighting communism (or, today, to humanitarian intervention) internationally.

   C. Incorrect. Liberals favored government spending.

   D. Incorrect. LBJ's liberalism favored overseas intervention; furthermore, demonstrations against the Vietnam War were organized by diverse groups of students and other activists who did not necessarily share all of LBJ's liberal philosophies.

   E. Incorrect. Liberals argued for regulations of business to ensure fair workplace policies and promote environmental responsibility.

3) How did Reagan's economic policies affect working class and poor Americans?

   A. They had little effect on these classes because the United States has a free market economy.

   B. They increased taxes by eliminating the progressive income tax and cut social programs needed by many disadvantaged people.

   C. They benefitted the working and middle classes by cutting taxes and increasing investment opportunities.

   D. Despite Reagan's tax cuts, the government was able to fund all social programs, so lower income Americans who used them were unaffected by changes in revenue.

   E. The decreased tax cuts for the wealthy led to a growth in business which ultimately increased wages and employment for the working class.

   Answers:

   A. Incorrect. While the US espouses capitalism, it is in practice a mixed economy; the federal government does intervene in the economy to an extent (although in a more limited way than in other economies around the world).

   B. **Correct.** Supply-side economics theorized that low taxes on the wealthy would encourage investment in the economy; as a result, wealth would "trickle down" to the middle and working classes and the poor. However, in practice, lower taxes meant less government revenue and many social programs that were needed by poor Americans were cut.

C. Incorrect. These policies benefitted the wealthy more than the working and middle classes.

D. Incorrect. Tax cuts forced the federal government to cut many social programs, harming low-income Americans.

E. Incorrect. This was the theory behind Reagan's "trickle-down" economics, however the actual result was a concentration of wealth.

4) Which of the following best describes globalization?

A. the free movement of goods and services across borders

B. easier communication worldwide thanks to technology like the Internet

C. facilitated movement of persons from one country to another

D. increasing influence of disparate cultures on each other

E. all of the above

Answers:

A. Incorrect. While commercial activity without restrictions or tariffs is a core element of economic globalization, globalization is more than just an economic phenomenon.

B. Incorrect. The Internet, improved telephone and television technology, and other improved communications technology are indeed a part of globalization; however, better global communication is not its only feature.

C. Incorrect. While globalization can include both open borders and socioeconomic structures that facilitate the movement of persons (for example, improved communication can strengthen family ties across borders, and free trade agreements may help migrant workers establish roots in a foreign country, even if temporarily), globalization is more than just international migration.

D. Incorrect. Cultures increasingly mix as people from different parts of the world interact more. However, this is not the only feature of globalism listed in the options.

E. Correct. Globalization is a multifaceted phenomenon that takes into account all the factors listed above.

5) How did the Bush doctrine of preemption affect US foreign policy in the early twenty-first century?

A. The US believed that in order to contain terrorism, it had to occupy countries that might harbor terrorists.

B. Fearing that the entire Middle East would succumb to terrorists, the Bush administration established a presence in the centrally located country of Iraq to avoid a "domino effect" of regime collapse.

C. The US engaged diplomatically and economically with countries at risk of harboring terrorist groups.

D. The US held prisoners captured during the War on Terror at Guantanamo Bay, where they were not given the protections and privileges entitled to prisoners of war under the Geneva Conventions.

E. The Bush administration justified international intervention and foreign invasion without previous provocation in order to preempt possible terrorist attacks.

Answers:

A. Incorrect. This describes the concept of containment theory, a Cold War philosophy.

B. Incorrect. This describes domino theory, part of US policy during the Cold War.

C. Incorrect. The Bush Doctrine was a doctrine about use of American military force, not economic or diplomatic strategies.

D. Incorrect. While this did occur, it was not part of the Bush doctrine of preemption.

E. **Correct.** Preemption was used to justify the 2003 invasion of Iraq, on the assumption that Iraq had weapons of mass destruction it intended to use or to provide for terrorist attacks against the United States.

two

WORLD HISTORY

Early Civilizations and the Great Empires

Paleolithic and Neolithic Eras

The earliest humans were hunter-gatherers until the development of agriculture in about 11,000 B.C.E. 60,000 – 70,000 years ago, early humans began migrating from Africa, gradually spreading out across the continents in several waves of migration throughout Europe and Asia, eventually into Australia, the Pacific Islands, and the Americas.

Early human history begins with the **PALEOLITHIC ERA**, the period before agricultural development and settled communities. During this period, early **HOMINIDS** exhibited the use of tools, up to and including our ancestors, *Homo sapiens sapiens*. Other early hominids included *Australopithecus*, from which *Homo habilis*, *Homo neanderthalensis*, *Homo erectus*, and others descended. In fact, evidence suggests that *Homo sapiens sapiens* and *Homo neanderthalensis* coexisted. All are now extinct, save for us, *Homo sapiens*.

During the Paleolithic Era, human technology was rudimentary, based on stone; hence, the term *STONE AGE* describes this period before metalworking was invented. Between approximately 11,000 – 10,500 B.C.E., humans began changing their behavior; they started settled communities, developed agricultural practices, and began domesticating animals. Notable technological developments occurred: humans began to create tools, weapons, and other objects made of metal. Furthermore, all species of humans except *Homo sapiens sapiens* became extinct. This transition marked the beginning of the **NEOLITHIC** period, characterized by behavioral and technological change like the invention of the wheel. During the **BRONZE AGE**, humans began working with copper and tin, creating stronger tools and weapons.

Middle East and Egypt

Beginning in the Near East, settled societies organized into larger centralized communities characterized by early social stratification and rule of law; the earliest known examples of these were in the **FERTILE CRESCENT**, the area in North Africa and Southwest Asia stretching from Egypt through the Levant and into Mesopotamia.

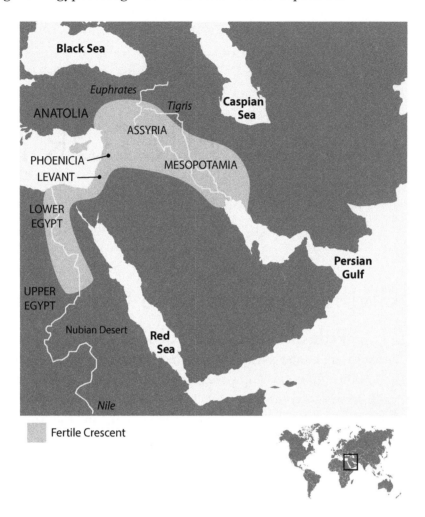

Figure 2.1. Fertile Crescent

Around 2500 B.C.E. (or possibly earlier) the **SUMERIANS** emerged in the Near East (eventually expanding into parts of Mesopotamia); developing irrigation and advanced agriculture, they were able to support settled areas that developed into city-states and eventually major cities like Uruk.

They also developed **CUNEIFORM**, the earliest known example of writing to use characters to form words; early education, and literary and artistic developments resulted such as the early poetry of *The Epic of Gilgamesh* and architectural achievements like ziggurats. Sumer featured city-states, the potter's wheel, early astronomy and mathematics, and religious thought. More advanced governance and administration were facilitated by the written language of cuneiform.

Eventually the Sumerians were overcome by Semitic-speaking, nomadic peoples in the Fertile Crescent: the result was the **AKKADIAN EMPIRE**, which grew to encompass much of the Levant, Mesopotamia, and parts of Persia. One of its major legacies was the Semitic Akkadian language, which adopted cuneiform.

Around the eighteenth century B.C.E., the Akkadians had given way to **BABYLONIA** in Southern Mesopotamia and **ASSYRIA** in the north. These two civilizations would develop roughly concurrently and remain at odds, with Babylonia eventually coming under Assyrian domination until the final defeat of Assyria by Babylonia in 612 B.C.E. in the battle of **NINEVEH**, the Assyrian capital.

Before its defeat, Assyria had developed as a powerful city-state in northern Mesopotamia. The Assyrians had based much of their culture on the Sumerian and Akkadian legacies, contributing unique sculpture and jewelry, establishing military dominance, and playing an important role in regional trade. At odds with Babylonia over the centuries, the Assyrian Empire had grown to encompass most of the Fertile Crescent. The Assyrian identity persists to this day among the (widely persecuted) Assyrian people in Iraq, Syria, Turkey, and Iran.

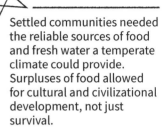 Settled communities needed the reliable sources of food and fresh water a temperate climate could provide. Surpluses of food allowed for cultural and civilizational development, not just survival.

Around 1200 B.C.E. during a time of instability in Mesopotamia, the region became vulnerable to the **HITTITES** from Anatolia. The Hittites had developed in the Bronze Age but flourished in the **IRON AGE**, developing expertise in metallurgy to create strong weapons; they also mastered horsemanship and invented chariots. These technological developments made the Hittites a strong military power and a threat to both the Assyrians and later the Egyptians (see below); not only did these empires risk losing land but they also lost control of trade routes throughout the Fertile Crescent. Eventually Assyria grew strong enough to overcome the Hittites.

Like Assyria, Babylonia inherited the Akkadian language and used the Sumerian language in religious settings; it also inherited other elements of Sumerian civilization and developed them further. In the eighteenth century B.C.E., King Hammurabi in Babylonia had developed courts and an early codified rule of law—THE **CODE OF HAMMURABI**—which meted out justice on an equal basis: "an eye for an eye, a tooth for a tooth."

Babylonia continued settled, urban development supported by organized agriculture, warfare, administration, and justice; **BABYLON** became a major ancient city. Babylonia developed more advanced astronomy, medicine, mathematics, philosophy, and art (particularly in working with clay, building bricks, and bas relief).

Furthermore, Babylonian civilization featured literature, developing the Sumerian poetry that was the basis for the *Epic of Gilgamesh* into the extended work we know today. (In fact, according to the Smithsonian, more lines from the epic have been discovered in stone fragments in Iraq as recently as 2011.) After the fall of Nineveh, Babylonia would control Mesopotamia until the fall of Babylon to the Persian Achaemenid Empire in Persia in 539 B.C.E. (see below).

Meanwhile, development had been under way in the **NILE VALLEY** in ancient **EGYPT**. Known for their pyramids, art, and pictorial writing (**HIEROGLYPHS**), the ancient Egyptians emerged as early as 5000 B.C.E.; evidence of Egyptian unity under one monarch, or **PHARAOH**, dates to the First Dynasty, around 3000 B.C.E.

Despite the surrounding Sahara Desert, the fertile land on the banks of the Nile River lent itself to agriculture, and the early Egyptians were able to develop settled communities thanks to agriculture and irrigation. Civilizations developed on the Upper and Lower Nile, unifying under the early dynasties, which established the Egyptian capital at **MEMPHIS**. By the Fourth Dynasty, Egypt's civilizational institutions, written language, art, and architecture were well developed. It was during this period that the famous **PYRAMIDS** were erected at Giza; these structures were actually burial tombs for the Pharaohs Khufu, Khafre, and Menkaure circa 2400 – 2500 B.C.E. In addition, the religious framework of ancient Egypt had become established, with a complex mythology of various gods.

Following this period, around 2200 B.C.E. Egypt became increasingly unstable; eventually fighters from the city of Thebes took over, establishing the Eleventh Dynasty. The subsequent Twelfth Dynasty took control of Nubia (now Sudan), an area rich in gold and other materials. Egypt grew in power; it reached its apex during the Eighteenth Dynasty, between 1550 and 1290 B.C.E. Led by the powerful Pharaoh **THUTMOSE III**, Egypt expanded into the Levant.

What were the contributions of the early Middle Eastern civilizations? List several.

Later, **KING AKHENATEN (AMENHOTEP IV)** abolished the Egyptian religion, establishing a cult of the sun—Aten—linked to himself. During this period Egypt saw a surge of iconoclastic art and sculpture. However, Akhenaten's successors, particularly Ramesses I and Ramesses II, founded the Nineteenth Dynasty and returned to traditional values. Under **RAMESSES II**, Egypt battled the aggressive Hittites in the Levant, reaching a stalemate. Egypt eventually fell into decline, losing control of the Levant and eventually falling to Assyria.

India

Meanwhile, early civilizations also developed farther east. The **INDUS VALLEY CIVILIZATIONS** flourished in the Indian Subcontinent and the Indus and Ganges river basins. The **HARAPPAN** civilization was based in Punjab from around 3000 B.C.E. The major cities of **HARAPPA** and **MOHENJO-DARO** featured grid systems indicative of detailed urban planning; they may be the earliest planned cities in the world. In addition, Harappan objects found in Mesopotamia reveal trade links between the civilizations.

Centuries later, concurrent with the Roman Empire, the **GUPTA EMPIRE** emerged in India. During this period, known as the Golden Age of India, the region was economically strong; there was active trade by sea with China, East Africa, and the Middle East in spices, ivory, silk, cotton, and iron, which was highly profitable as an export.

The Guptas encouraged music, art, architecture, and Sanskrit literature and philosophy. While practitioners of Hinduism, the empire was tolerant of Buddhists and Jains. Organized administration and rule of law made it possible for **CHANDRAGUPTA II** to govern a large territory throughout the Subcontinent. However, by 550, invasions from the north by the Huns and internal conflicts within the Subcontinent led to imperial decline.

China

In China, the **SHANG DYNASTY**, the first known dynasty, ruled the **HUANG HE** or **YELLOW RIVER** area around the second millennium B.C.E. and developed the earliest known Chinese writing, which helped unite Chinese-speaking people throughout the region.

Like the early civilizations in the Middle East, the Shang Dynasty featured the use of bronze technology, horses, wheeled technology, walled cities, and other advances beyond the Neolithic societies.

Around 1056 B.C.E. the ZHOU Dynasty emerged. It succeeded the Shang and expanded Chinese civilization to the CHIANG JIANG (Yangtze River) region. Under the Zhou Dynasty, China developed a social and political infrastructure in which family aristocracies controlled the country, with the capital at HAO (near XI'AN). Ancestral cults controlled tracts of land throughout the country in a hierarchy similar to later European feudalism, setting the foundation for hierarchical rule and social stratification.

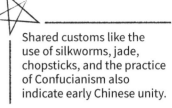

Shared customs like the use of silkworms, jade, chopsticks, and the practice of Confucianism also indicate early Chinese unity.

The concept of the MANDATE OF HEAVEN, in which the emperor had a divine mandate to rule, emerged from the understanding that land was divinely inherited. The unstable period toward the end of the Zhou Dynasty was known as the SPRING AND AUTUMN PERIOD; during this time CONFUCIUS lived (c. 551 – 479 B.C.E.). His teachings would be the basis for Confucianism, the foundational Chinese philosophy emphasizing harmony and respect for hierarchy.

Following the chaotic WARRING STATES PERIOD (c. 475 – 221 B.C.E.) the short-lived but influential QIN DYNASTY emerged, unifying disparate Chinese civilizations and regions under the first Emperor, QIN SHIHUANGDI. This dynasty (221 – 206 B.C.E.) was characterized by a centralized administration, expanded infrastructure, standardization in weights and measures, standardized writing, a standardized currency, and strict imperial control. The administrative BUREAUCRACY established by the emperor was the foundation of Chinese administration until the twentieth century. In addition, the Emperor constructed the GREAT WALL OF CHINA; Emperor Qin Shihuangdi's tomb is guarded by the famous TERRACOTTA FIGURINES. During the Qin Dynasty, China expanded as far south as Vietnam.

Figure 2.2. Great Wall of China

Despite the short length of the Qin Dynasty, it had a lasting impact on Chinese organization. The **HAN DYNASTY** took over in 206 for the next 300 years (206 B.C.E. – 220 C.E.), retaining Qin administrative organization and adding Confucian ideals of hierarchy and harmony. The Han prized education in the Confucian tradition and the idea that educated men should control administrative government began to take root in China. Women were not included in politics or administration.

The Americas

Prehistoric peoples migrated to the Americas from Asia during the Paleolithic period, and evidence of their presence dates to 13,000 years ago; remnants of the **CLOVIS** people dating to this time have been found in New Mexico. Recent findings in Canada suggest, however, that prehistoric peoples may have come to North America even earlier, about 13,300 years ago. Migration from Asia was gradual, probably occurring over hundreds or thousands of years; early humans likely crossed by land from Siberia to Alaska, while some may even have had naval capabilities and arrived by boat. Gradually, humans spread throughout the hemisphere.

From around 1200 B.C.E., the **OLMEC** civilization developed on the Mexican Gulf Coast. Its massive sculptures reflect complex religious and spiritual beliefs. Later civilizations in Mexico included the **ZAPOTECS**, **MIXTECS**, **TOLTECS**, and **MAYAS** in the Yucatán peninsula. Throughout Mesoamerica, civilizations had developed irrigation to expand and enrich agriculture, similar to developments in the Fertile Crescent.

Meanwhile, in South America, artistic evidence remains of the **CHAVIN**, **MOCHE**, and **NAZCA** peoples, who preceded the later Inca civilization and empire. The complex Chavin style, which focused on animals, went on to influence Andean art, while the Moche have left behind complicated ceramics comparable to Hellenic artifacts. The construction of the famous Nazca lines, enormous sketches in the ground only visible from the air, remains a mystery.

In North America, the remains of mounds in the Mississippi Valley region may be ancient spiritual structures. For more discussion of precolonial North American peoples, please see Chapter One, "United States History."

Persia and Greece

The **PERSIAN** emperor **CYRUS**, founder of the **ACHAEMENID EMPIRE**, conquered the Babylonians in the sixth century B.C.E. His son **DARIUS** extended Persian rule from the Indus Valley to Egypt, and north to **ANATOLIA** by about 400 B.C.E., where the Persians encountered the ancient **GREEKS**. Known for its fundamental impact on Western civilization to this day, neighboring Greek or **HELLENIC CIVILIZATION** included political, philosophical, and mathematical thought; art and architecture; and poetry and theater.

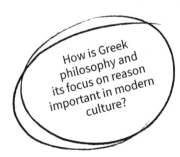
How is Greek philosophy and its focus on reason important in modern culture?

Greece was comprised of **CITY-STATES** like **ATHENS**, the first known **DEMOCRACY**, and the military state **SPARTA**. Historically these city-states had been rivals; however, they temporarily united to come to the aid of Ionian Greeks in Anatolia under Persian rule and drive Persia from Greece. In Anatolia, the Persian king XERXES led two campaigns against Greek forces. The Greeks held the Persians at bay, and much of Greece became unified under Athens following the war. It was during this period, the GOLDEN AGE of Greek civilization that much of the Hellenic art, architecture, and philosophy known today emerged.

The term *democracy* comes from the Greek word *DEMOKRATIA*—"people power." It was participatory rather than representative; officials were chosen by groups rather than elected. Athens was the strongest of the many small political bodies (in fact, the word *political* comes from the Greek word *POLIS* meaning "city-state" or "community"). The Persians had been decisively defeated at the battles of MARATHON (490 B.C.E.) and SALAMIS (480 B.C.E.) around 460 B.C.E. Athens became a revolutionary democracy controlled by the poor and working classes under the Athenian leaders PERICLES and EPHIALTES.

In this period and into the fourth century B.C.E., the PARTHENON was built, as were other masterpieces of ancient Greek sculpture and architecture. SOCRATES began teaching philosophy, influencing later philosophers like PLATO who founded the Academy where figures like ARISTOTLE emerged, establishing the basis for modern western philosophical and political thought. Playwrights like SOPHOCLES, EURIPIDES, and AESCHYLUS emerged; their work influenced later western literature.

Despite its status as a democracy, Athens was not fully democratic: women did not have a place in politics, and Athenians practiced slavery. Furthermore, those men eligible to participate in political life had to prove that both of their parents were Athenian (the criterion of double descent).

Toward the end of the fifth century B.C.E., Athens and Sparta were at odds once again during the PELOPONNESIAN WAR (431 – 404 B.C.E.), which involved most of the Hellenic world and ultimately crippled the Athenian democracy permanently. Instability permitted the rise of the northern state of Macedon; later in the fourth century B.C.E., Philip II of Macedonia was able to take over most of Greece. His son ALEXANDER (later known as Alexander the Great) would go on to conquer Persia, spreading Greek civilization throughout much of Western and Central Asia.

Rome

Meanwhile, in Italy, the ancient Romans had begun consolidating their power. The city of ROME was founded as early as the eighth century B.C.E.; it became strong thanks to its importance as a trade route for the Greeks and other Mediterranean peoples. Early Roman culture drew from the ETRUSCANS, native inhabitants of the Italian peninsula, and the Greeks, from whom it borrowed elements of architecture, art, language, and even religion.

Originally a kingdom, Rome became a republic under LUCIUS JUNIUS BRUTUS in 509 B.C.E. As a REPUBLIC, Rome elected lawmakers (senators) to the Senate. The Romans developed highly advanced infrastructure, including aqueducts and roads, some still in use today. Economically powerful Rome began conquering areas around the Mediterranean with its increasingly powerful military, expanding westward to North Africa in the PUNIC WARS (264 – 146 B.C.E.) against its rival Carthage (in present-day Tunisia). With conquest of territory and expansion of trade came increased slavery, and working class Romans (PLEBEIANS) were displaced; at the same time, the wealthy ruling class

(PATRICIANS) became more powerful and corrupt. Resulting protest movements led by the tribunes GAIUS and TIBERIUS led to legislative reform and republican stabilization, strengthening the republic by the first century B.C.E.

The increasingly diversified republic, while militarily and economically strong, was still divided between the wealthy ruling class (the OPTIMATES, or "the best") and the working, the poor, and the military (now calling themselves POPULARE, "the people," still favoring more democratization). As the Senate weakened due to its own corruption, the FIRST TRIUMVIRATE of the military leaders GAIUS JULIUS CAESAR and GNAEUS POMPEIUS MAGNUS (POMPEY THE GREAT), and the wealthy citizen MARCUS LICINIUS CRASSUS consolidated their rule of the republic. Pompey and Crassus belonged to the Optimate class, while Julius Caesar, a popular military leader, was firmly of the Populare.

Caesar had proven himself in the widely chronicled conquest of GAUL (today, France), and was respected and beloved by the military for his personal devotion to his troops. Meanwhile, Crassus was the wealthiest man in Rome, controlling most of the political class; despite his wealth, he was not popular among the Populare and was not regarded as a military leader on the level of Caesar, though he had played a role in the defeat of the widespread slave rebellion led by the gladiator SPARTACUS. Pompey had led successful missions conquering territory for Rome in Syria and elsewhere in the Levant; he also took credit for defeating Spartacus, though he played less of a role than Crassus, causing a rift between the two.

With resentment between Crassus and Pompey over credit for the defeat of Spartacus, Crassus' insecurity over his perception as a military leader, and Caesar's popularity among the Populare, the Triumvirate was short-lived. Crassus was killed fighting the Parthians in Turkey in 53 B.C.E., at which point Pompey and Caesar declared war upon each other; the two fought in Greece where Pompey was defeated, fled to Egypt, and was assassinated.

Forcing the corrupt Senate to give him control, Caesar began to transition Rome from a republic (if, at that point, in name only) to what would become an empire. Caesar was assassinated by a group of senators led by BRUTUS and CASSIUS in 44 B.C.E.; however, in that short time he had been able to consolidate and centralize imperial control. His cousin, MARCUS ANTONIUS (MARK ANTONY), his friend MARCUS AEMILIUS LEPIDUS, and his nephew GAIUS OCTAVIUS THURINUS (OCTAVIAN) defeated Brutus and Cassius two years later at the Battle of Philippi, forming the SECOND TRIUMVIRATE.

Lepidus was sent from Rome to Hispania (Spain) and Africa while Mark Antony and Octavian split control of Rome between east and west, respectively. However, the two went to war after Antony became involved with the Egyptian queen CLEOPATRA, upsetting the balance of power; Octavian defeated Antony and Cleopatra, taking control of Rome in 31 B.C.E. He took the name AUGUSTUS CAESAR when the Senate gave him supreme power in 27 B.C.E., becoming the first Roman emperor and effectively starting the Roman Empire.

At this time, Rome reached the height of its power, and the Mediterranean region enjoyed a period of stability known as the *PAX ROMANA*. Rome controlled the entire Mediterranean region and lands stretching as far north as Germany and Britain, territory into the Balkans, far into the Middle East, Egypt, North Africa, and Iberia. In this time of relative peace and prosperity, Latin literature flourished, as did art, architecture, philosophy, mathematics, science, and international trade throughout Rome and beyond into Asia and Africa. A series of emperors would follow and Rome remained a major world power, but it would never again reach the height of prosperity and stability that it did under Augustus.

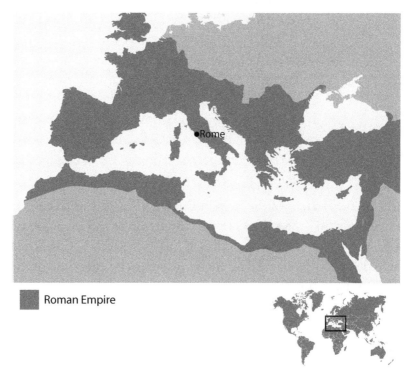

Figure 2.3. Pax Romana

It was during the time of Augustus that a Jewish carpenter named Jesus in Palestine began teaching that he was the son of the Jewish God, and that his death would provide salvation for all of humanity. Jesus was eventually crucified; followers of **JESUS CHRIST**, called Christians, preached his teachings throughout Rome. Despite the persecution of Christians, the concept of forgiveness of sin became popular and **CHRISTIANITY** would eventually become the official religion of Rome. Christianity's universal appeal and applicability to people of diverse backgrounds would allow it to spread quickly.

By 300 C.E., Rome was in decline. Following a series of unstable administrations, **DIOCLETIAN** (284 – 305 C.E.) took over as Emperor, effectively dividing the empire into two: the Western Roman Empire and the Eastern Roman Empire. Diocletian reestablished some stability and more effective administration, creating a loose power-sharing agreement throughout the empire. The Christian **CONSTANTINE** took over the eastern half of the empire, establishing a new capital at **CONSTANTINOPLE**, and Christianity as an official religion. However, the ambitious Constantine reconquered the Western Roman Empire and reunited the empire in 324 C.E.; the capital remained at Constantinople, and the balance of power and stability shifted to the east.

This political shift enabled the western (later, Catholic) Church to gain power in Rome. One of Jesus Christ's followers, Peter, was considered to be the first **POPE**, or leader of Christian ministry. He had been executed in Rome in 67 C.E. after a lifetime of spreading the religion; ever since, the city has been a base of Christianity and home to the **VATICAN**, the seat of the Catholic Church. Over time, the Catholic Church would become one of the most powerful political entities in the world; even today, following several schisms in Christianity, there are around one billion Catholics worldwide.

The western part of the Roman Empire gradually fell into disarray: a weakening Rome had created security agreements with different European clans like the **ANGLO-SAXONS**, the **FRANKS**, the **VISIGOTHS**, the **OSTROGOTHS**, and the **SLAVS**, among others, to protect its western and northern borders. Eventually, these groups rebelled against the government and what was left of the Roman Empire in the west finally fell. In Western Europe, the last Roman emperor was killed in **476 C.E.**, marking the end of the empire. The west dissolved into territories controlled by these and other tribes.

These clans and others from Central Asia were able to defeat the Romans in the north and settle in Europe, thanks to their equestrian skills, superior wheels, and iron technology.

Meanwhile the eastern part of the Roman Empire, with its capital at Constantinople, evolved into the unified **BYZANTINE EMPIRE**. The Byzantine emperor **JUSTINIAN** (527 – 565 C.E.) re-conquered parts of North Africa, Egypt, and Greece, established rule of law, reinvigorated trade with China, and built the **HAGIA SOPHIA**, the cathedral and center of orthodox Christianity. Ultimately, the Byzantines would control varying amounts of land in Anatolia, the Levant, and North Africa until the conquest of Constantinople by the Ottoman Turks in 1453.

Figure 2.4. Hagia Sophia

He also continued the establishment of Christianity, rebuilding the Hagia Sophia, and eliminating the last vestiges of the Greco-Roman religion and competing Christian sects. However, over time, differences in doctrine between the church in Rome and Christians in Constantinople would give way to a schism, creating the Roman Catholic Church and the Greek Orthodox Church, as discussed.

During the early Middle Ages in Europe and the Byzantine Empire, the roots of another civilization were developing in the Arabian Peninsula. In the seventh century, the Prophet **MUHAMMAD** began teaching **ISLAM**. Based on the teachings of Judaism and Christianity, Islam presented as the final version of these two religions, evolving its own set of laws and philosophical teachings. Like Christianity, it held universal appeal.

Conversion was (and is) simple, as is practicing the faith; the religion transcends national and ethnic differences; and it offers the possibility of redemption, forgiveness of sins, and a pleasant afterlife. Furthermore, due to ideological similarities, Muslims were willing to accept Jews and Christians as **PEOPLE OF THE BOOK** rather than forcing their conversion, enabling their later conquest of Southwest Asia and facilitating relationships in the region. Leading a small group of followers out of the desert to conquer the Arabian cities of Mecca and Medina, where they would establish the beginnings of the **CALIPHATE**, the political embodiment of the society envisioned in Islam, Muhammad's followers would later come to control Southwest Asia and North Africa.

EXAMPLES

1) What is required for a settled community?

- **A.** domesticated animals
- **B.** a source of fresh water
- **C.** technology
- **D.** weapons
- **E.** sacred sites

Answers:

A. Incorrect. While domesticated animals can be a food source or facilitate production, they are not absolutely necessary for food production or surplus.

B. Correct. Fresh water permits a reliable food source, which allows for settlement; people need not travel in search of food.

C. Incorrect. While technology is useful and can improve quality of life, it is not absolutely necessary for a settled society.

D. Incorrect. While weapons are useful for ensuring safety, they are not essential for establishing a settled society.

E. Incorrect. While most civilizations did develop systems of religion, this is a byproduct of a settled community rather than a contributing factor.

2) The earliest known form of writing to use characters to create words was

- **A.** akkadian developed by the Babylonians.
- **B.** cuneiform, developed by the Sumerians.
- **C.** hieroglyphs, developed by the Egyptians.
- **D.** hieroglyphs developed by the Babylonians.
- **E.** akkadian developed by the Sumerians.

Answers:

A. Incorrect. Akkadian was a spoken language used in Babylonia after the development of the first writing system.

B. Correct. The Sumerians developed cuneiform.

C. Incorrect. While the Egyptians did develop hieroglyphs, this system emerged later than cuneiform.

D. Incorrect. The Babylonians did not develop hieroglyphs.

E. Incorrect. The Sumerians did not develop Akkadian.

3) The Shang and Zhou Dynasties are particularly relevant in Chinese history for their contributions in

A. developing Chinese administration.

B. centralizing Chinese imperial power as symbolized through the terracotta figurines in the imperial tombs.

C. forming a Chinese identity through the development of written language, the Emperor's Mandate of Heaven, and fostering Confucianism.

D. ensuring China's safety by building the Great Wall of China.

E. promoting education and incorporating Confucian ideals of hierarchy and harmony into the bureaucracy.

Answers:

A. Incorrect. These developments occurred under the Qin Dynasty.

B. Incorrect. The terracotta figurines are found in the tomb of the Qin Emperor Shihuangdi.

C. Correct. Written Chinese developed under the Shang Dynasty, and the Mandate of Heaven emerged under the Zhou Dynasty; furthermore, traditions like the use of chopsticks also came about during these periods.

D. Incorrect. Again, construction of the Great Wall of China began during the Qin Dynasty.

E. Incorrect. The Han dynasty added Confucian ideals of hierarchy and harmony, as well as the emphasis on education.

4) The Athenian concept of democracy embraced

A. participatory democracy, in which local groups made decisions directly by vote, permitting the poor to dominate the process rather than the elites.

B. an anonymous electoral process similar to that of the United States in which officials were elected.

C. people of all backgrounds, so that all residents of Athens had a stake in the political process.

D. an educated electorate in order to ensure the best possible decision-making.

E. consensus for all matters pertaining to social issues, but not economic or military.

Answers:

A. Correct. The Athenian notion of *demokratia*, or people power, was participatory rather than representative.

B. Incorrect. Voting was not anonymous in Athens.

C. Incorrect. Only free male Athenians, who could prove Athenian parentage, could take part in the process.

D. Incorrect. Education was not required to participate.

E. In Athens, all matters of law were decided by majority rule.

5) How did Julius Caesar rise to and retain power?

A. He invaded Rome with his armies from Gaul, and used his military resources to control the Empire.

B. He was elected president of the Senate by the people thanks to political support throughout the Republic.

World Religions

Judaism

Judaism was the first MONOTHEISTIC religion; its adherents believe in only *one* god. It is believed that God came to the Hebrew Abraham and that the Hebrews—the Jew—were to be God's *chosen people*, to serve as an example to the world. Later, MOSES would lead the Jews out of slavery in Egypt, and God gave him TEN COMMANDMENTS or laws, the basis of what would become Judeo-Christian and Islamic moral codes. Notably, these moral codes applied to all people, including slaves. In addition to confirming the singular nature of God, the Ten Commandments laid out social rules for an organized society under that one god: to refrain from theft and murder and to honor one's parents, among others. Judaism's holy texts are the TORAH and the TALMUD (religious and civil law). There are different branches of Judaism with varying teachings, including Orthodox, Conservative, and Reform Judaism, among others.

Christianity

In Roman Palestine, the Jewish carpenter JESUS taught that he was the son of the singular, Jewish God. Christians believe that Jesus came to suffer and die for the sins of mankind so that all mankind may be forgiven for sin. He gained many followers for his teaching; ultimately, he was crucified. Christians believe that Jesus rose from the dead three days later (the RESURRECTION) and ascended to heaven. Christians believe that Jesus was miraculously born from a virgin mother (the VIRGIN MARY) and believe in the HOLY TRINITY, that God is made up of the Father, the Son, and the Holy Spirit, all parts of one God. The CATHOLIC CHURCH is led by the Pope and descended from the early western

Church that followed the **Schism of 1054**, when theological disagreement divided the Church into the western Catholic Church and **Eastern Orthodox** Christianity. Later in Western Europe, the **Protestant Reformation** gave rise to other forms of Protestant, or non-Catholic, Christianity.

Islam

Islam is rooted in the Arabian Peninsula. Muslims believe that the angel Gabriel spoke to the **Prophet Muhammad**, transmitting the literal word of **Allah** (God), which was

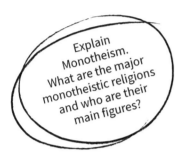
Explain Monotheism. What are the major monotheistic religions and who are their main figures?

later written down as the **Qur'an**. Muhammad is considered by Muslims to be the final prophet of the god of the Jews and Christians, and Islam shares similar moral teachings. Islam recognizes leaders like Abraham, Moses, and Jesus, but unlike Christianity, views Jesus as a prophet, not as the son of God. The Prophet Muhammad was a religious, military, and political leader; in conquering the Arabian Peninsula and later other parts of the Middle East, he protected the **People of the Book**, or Jews and Christians. After his death, discord among his followers resulted in the **Sunni-Shi'a Schism** over his succession and some teachings; to this day, deep divisions remain between many Sunnis and Shi'ites. Like Judaism, Islam also has a book of legal teachings called the **Hadith**.

Hinduism

Major tenets of Hindu belief include **reincarnation**, or that the universe and its beings undergo endless cycles of rebirth and **karma**, that one creates one's own destiny. The soul is reincarnated until it has resolved all karmas, at which point it attains **moksha**, or liberation from the cycle. Hindus believe in multiple divine beings. Religion is based in the **Vedic scriptures**; other important texts include the **Upanishads**, the **Mahabharata**, and the **Bhagavad Gita**. Hinduism is the primary religion in India and is intertwined with the **caste system**, the hierarchical societal structure.

Buddhism

In Buddhism, the Prince **Siddhartha Gautama** is said to have renounced worldly goods and lived as an ascetic in what is today northern India, seeking **enlightenment** around

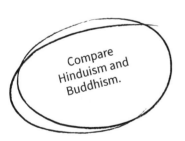
Compare Hinduism and Buddhism.

the third century B.C.E. Buddhism teaches that desire—the ego, or self—is the root of suffering, and that giving up or **transcending** material obsessions will lead to freedom, or **nirvana**—enlightenment. While Buddhism originated in India, it is practiced throughout Asia and the world. The main Buddhist schools of theology are the **Mahayana**, which is prevalent in northern and eastern Asia (Korea, parts of China, Mongolia), and **Theravada**, dominant in Southeast Asia and Indian Ocean regions. **Vajrayana** Buddhism is central to Tibetan Buddhism.

Confucianism

Confucianism teaches obedience and adherence to tradition in order to maintain a harmonious society. Ideally, practicing integrity and respecting wisdom would ensure that authority would be used for beneficial purposes. Confucius himself was a Chinese scholar in the sixth century B.C.E.; his philosophy would go on to inform Chinese culture for centuries.

Feudalism through the Era of Expansion

The Middle Ages in Europe

The Byzantine Empire remained a strong civilization and a place of learning. Constantinople was a commercial center, strategically located at the Dardanelles, connecting Asian trade routes with Europe. Later, missionaries traveled north to Slav-controlled Russia, spreading Christianity and literacy. The ninth-century missionaries Saints Cyril and Methodius are credited with developing what would become the **CYRILLIC** alphabet used in many Slavic languages. In 988 C.E., the Russian Grand Prince of Kiev, **VLADIMIR I**, converted to Christianity and ordered his subjects to do so as well. Russian Christianity was influenced by the Byzantine doctrine, what would become Greek Orthodox Christianity.

Despite the chaos in Western Europe, the Church in Rome remained strong, becoming a stabilizing influence. However, differences in doctrine between Rome and Constantinople became too wide to overcome. Beginning in 1054, a series of **SCHISMS** developed in the now-widespread Christian religion between the **ROMAN CATHOLIC CHURCH** and the **GREEK ORTHODOX CHURCH** over matters of doctrine such as the role of the Pope and papal authority, the use of leavened versus unleavened bread in religious services, and some theological concepts. Eventually the two would become entirely separate churches.

In Europe, the early Middle Ages (or *DARK AGES*) from the fall of Rome to about the tenth century, were a chaotic, unstable, and unsafe time. What protection and stability existed were represented and maintained by the Catholic Church and the feudal system.

Society and economics were characterized by decentralized, local governance, or **FEUDALISM**, a hierarchy where land and protection were offered in exchange for loyalty. Feudalism was the dominant social, economic, and political hierarchy of the European middle ages from the time of Charlemagne (discussed further below).

In exchange for protection, **VASSALS** would pledge **FEALTY**, or **PAY HOMAGE TO LORDS**, landowners who would reward their vassals' loyalty with land, or fiefs. Economic and social organization consisted of **MANORS**, self-sustaining areas possessed by lords but worked by peasants. The peasants were **SERFS**, not slaves but not entirely free. Tied to the land, they worked for the lord in exchange for protection; however they were not obligated to fight. Usually they were also granted some land for their own use. While not true slaves, their lives were effectively controlled by the lord.

Warriors who fought for lords, called **KNIGHTS**, were rewarded with land and could become minor lords in their own right. Lords themselves could be vassals of other lords; that hierarchy extended upward to kings or the Catholic Church. The Catholic Church itself was a major landowner and political power. In a Europe not yet dominated by sovereign states, the **Pope** was not only a religious leader, but also a military and political one.

Small kingdoms and alliances extended throughout Europe, and stable trade was difficult to maintain. The **Celts** controlled Britain and Ireland until the invasion of the **Saxons**; around 600 C.E., the Saxons conquered Britain while the Celts were pushed to Ireland, Scotland, and Brittany in northwest France. While the Church was gaining power, it was insecure in Italy as the **Germanic tribes** vied for control in Germany and France. Monasteries in Ireland and England retained and protected classical documentation in the wake of the fall of Rome and insecurity in Italy. The Germanic tribes themselves were threatened by Asian invaders like the **Huns**, increasing instability in central and eastern parts of Europe, where **Slavs** also fought for supremacy north of Byzantium.

There were limits on sovereign power, however. In 1215, long before the revolution, English barons forced King John to sign the Magna Carta, which protected their property and rights from the king and was the basis for today's parliamentary system in that country.

One exception to the chaos was the Scandinavian **Viking** civilization. From the end of the eighth century until around 1100, the Vikings expanded their influence from Scandinavia, ranging from the Baltic Sea to the East to the North Sea through the North Atlantic, thanks to their extraordinary seafaring skills and technology. The Vikings traded with the Byzantine Empire and European powers; Byzantine and Middle Eastern artifacts have been found among Viking excavations in Scandinavia. They traveled to and sometimes raided parts of Britain, Ireland, France, and Russia.

The Icelandic **Erik the Red** established a settlement in Greenland, and his son **Leif Erikson** may have traveled as far as North America. In addition to military prowess and advanced shipbuilding technology, the Vikings had a complex religion with a pantheon of gods and well-developed mythology; they also developed a literary canon of sagas in Old Norse, the basis of some Scandinavian languages today. Viking achievements have been documented in literature from other European cultures like the Anglo-Saxons, as well as the Arab historian Ibn Fadlan.

Meanwhile, by the eighth century the North African **Moors**, part of the expanding Islamic civilization, had penetrated Iberia and were a threat to Christian Europe. **Charles Martel**, leader of the **Franks** in what is today France, defeated the Moors at the **Battle of Tours (or Poitiers)** in 732 C.E., effectively stopping any further Islamic incursion into Europe. The Christian Martel had previously consolidated his control of France, leading the Franks in victory over the Bavarians, Frisians, and other tribes and supporting their conversion to Christianity. Instability followed Charles Martel's death, however, and **Charlemagne**, the son of a court official, eventually took over the Merovingian kingdom following disputes over succession, complicated by the Merovingian traditions.

Charlemagne was able to maintain Frankish unity and consolidate his rule, extending Frankish control into Central Europe and defending the **Papal States** in central Italy. In what is considered the reemergence of centralized power in Europe, parts of Western and Central Europe were organized under Charlemagne, who was crowned emperor of the Roman Empire by Pope Leo III in **800 C.E.** While in retrospect this seems long after the end of Rome, at the time many

Europeans still perceived themselves as somehow still part of a Roman Empire. Today Charlemagne's rule is referred to as the CAROLINGIAN EMPIRE.

Charlemagne brought stability to Western and Central Europe during a period when two powerful, non-Christian, organized civilizations—the Vikings in the north and the Islamic powers in the south—threatened what was left of western Christendom, and when insecurity was growing to the east with the decline of the Byzantines and the emergence of the Umayyad Caliphate based in Damascus. His reign strengthened the Roman Catholic Church and enabled the reemergence of Roman and Christian scholarship that had been hidden in English and Irish monasteries.

It was also under Charlemagne that the feudal system became truly organized, bringing more stability to Western Europe. The Catholic Church would dominate Europe from Ireland towards Eastern Europe—an area of locally controlled duchies, kingdoms, and alliances. In **962 C.E.**, **OTTO I** became emperor of the **HOLY ROMAN EMPIRE** in Central Europe, a confederation of small states which remained an important European power until its dissolution in **1806**.

While the Holy Roman Empire remained intact, the Carolingian Empire did not. Spain and Portugal remained under Muslim control, and France dissolved into small fiefdoms and territories. Meanwhile, England and Scotland were controlled by Norsemen (Vikings), especially Danish settlers, and various local Anglo-Saxon rulers, the remnants of the Germanic tribes that had come to rule Europe and led to the fall of Rome.

In 1066, **WILLIAM THE CONQUEROR** left Normandy in northwest France. The **NORMANS** established organization in England, including a more consolidated economy and kingdom supported by feudalism. They also consolidated Christianity as the local religion. English possessions included parts of France, nominally a kingdom but consisting of smaller territories with some level of independence. Intermarriage and conquest resulted in English control of Anjou and Bordeaux in France; William had brought control of French Brittany with him when he arrived on the island of Britain. Conflict between Britain and France would continue for several centuries, while rulers in Scandinavia and Northwest Europe consolidated power.

The Islamic World

Meanwhile, in the wake of the decline of the Byzantine Empire, ARAB-ISLAMIC EMPIRES characterized by brisk commerce, advancements in technology and learning, and urban development arose in the Middle East.

Before the rise of Islam in the seventh century, the Arabian Peninsula was located at the intersection of the Byzantine Empire, a diverse collection of ethnicities, ruled by Greek Orthodox Christians, and the SASANIANS (Persians), who practiced ZOROASTRIANISM. Both of these empires sought to control trade with Central and eastern Asia along the Silk Road; they also sought to establish trade ties with Christian AXUM (Ethiopia).

In Arabia itself, Judaism, Christianity, and animist religions were practiced by the Arab majority. The Prophet MUHAMMAD was born in Mecca around 570; he began receiving messages from God (Allah), preaching them around 613 as the last affirmations of the monotheistic religions, and writing them as the QUR'AN, the Islamic holy book. Driven from **MECCA** to Medina in 622, Muhammad and his followers were able to recapture the city and other major Arabian towns by the time of his death, establishing Islam and Arab rule in the region.

After Muhammad's death in **632 C.E.**, his followers, led by the first caliph **ABU BAKR**, went on to conquer land beyond Arabia north into the weakening Byzantine Empire. The well-organized Muslim Arabs, based in Arabia, led incursions into Syria, the Levant, and Mesopotamia, taking over these territories. Thanks to military, bureaucratic, and organizational skill as well as their ability to win over dissatisfied minorities, the Arabs eventually isolated the Byzantines to parts of Anatolia and Constantinople and crushed the Persian Sasanians.

Muhammad's cousin and son-in-law **ALI**, his wife **FATIMA** (Muhammad's eldest daughter), and their followers, had always believed that the leader of the Muslim Arabs should be a blood relative of Muhammad. Since Muhammad had no sons, the logical choice was Ali. However, the Meccan elites had felt differently, and the popular Abu Bakr was chosen as the first caliph.

A caliph was considered both a political and a religious leader.

Abu Bakr was succeeded by the second caliph Umar; upon his death the third caliph Uthman took over. Widely accused of corruption, Uthman was murdered in 656. The Islamic leadership finally settled on Ali to take over as the fourth caliph (the first four caliphs are known as the *Rashidun*, or rightly-guided ones). However, others in power felt differently. **MUAWIYA**, based in Damascus, led the opposition to Ali; this conflict is at the heart of the **SUNNI-SHI'A SCHISM**.

Ali's followers called themselves the *party of Ali* or, in Arabic, the *shiat Ali*, which is the origin of the word *Shia* or *Shi'ite* Muslims.

Ali and Fatima established their base in Kufa, in Mesopotamia. Unable to come to an agreement, the Arabs became embroiled in the First Civil War (656 – 661) over leadership; the conflict ended when Ali was murdered in 661. Unrest continued, and the bloody massacre of Ali's son Hussein and his family in 680 in Karbala triggered the Second Civil War (680 – 692).

The violence of these years cemented divisions in Islam, and **SHI'ITE ISLAM** emerged in Mesopotamia. The Shi'ites believed that Ali was the rightful heir to Muhammad's early Islamic empire, and maintained a focus on martyrdom, especially that of Ali and Hussein. The followers of the Meccan elites became known as **SUNNIS**, "orthodox" Muslims with a focus on community rather than genealogy. Over the centuries, other differences in theology and history would develop.

Muawiya is considered the first caliph of the **UMAYYAD CALIPHATE** (empire), named for the leading Meccan tribe that had supported Muhammad from the beginning. The Arabs already controlled Arabia; by 750, they would control parts of Iberia, North Africa, Egypt, Arabia, the Levant, Mesopotamia, Persia, Armenia, and parts of Central Asia into Transoxiana (Uzbekistan) and the Indus River Valley (parts of Pakistan). Spain, or **AL-ANDALUS**, was settled as early as 711.

Ongoing conflict among Arab elites resulted in the **ABBASID CALIPHATE** in 750 C.E., based in Baghdad. The Umayyad were overthrown by the Arab-Muslim Abbasid family, which established a new capital in Baghdad. The caliph **AL-MUTASIM** professionalized the military, creating professional soldiers called **MAMLUKS**, freed slaves usually of Turkish origin. It was thought they would be more loyal with no family or national ties. The mamluks helped al-Mutasim consolidate imperial control and improve tax collection. Abbasid administration was also highly organized, allowing efficient taxation.

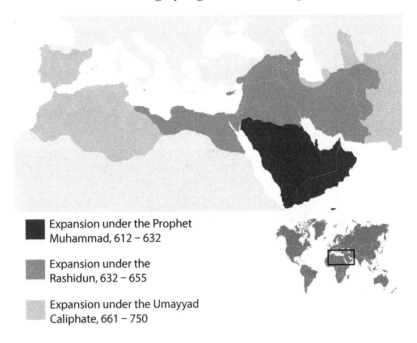

Expansion under the Prophet Muhammad, 612 – 632

Expansion under the Rashidun, 632 – 655

Expansion under the Umayyad Caliphate, 661 – 750

Figure 2.5. Islamic Expansion

The administration and stability provided by the caliphates fostered an Arabic literary culture. Stability permitted open trade routes, economic development, and cultural interaction throughout Asia, the Middle East, North Africa, and parts of Europe. Furthermore, the Abbasid ruler **AL-MAMUN** fostered cultural and scientific study.

Thanks to the universality of the Arabic language, scientific and medical texts from varying civilizations—Greek, Persian, Indian—could be translated into Arabic and shared throughout the Islamic world. Arab thinkers studied Greek and Persian astronomy and engaged in further research. Arabs studied mathematics from around the world and developed algebra, enabling engineering, technological, and architectural achievements. Finally, Islamic art is well known for its geometric designs.

Around this time, the **SONG DYNASTY (960 – 1276)** controlled most of China. Under the Song, China experienced tremendous development and economic growth. Characterized by increasing urbanization, the Song featured complex administrative rule, including the difficult competitive written examinations required to obtain prestigious bureaucratic positions in government. Most traditions recognized as Chinese emerged under the Song, including the consumption of tea and rice and common Chinese architecture. The Song engaged not only in overland trade along the Silk Road, exporting silk, tea, ceramics, jade, and other goods, but also sea trade with Korea, Japan, Southeast Asia, India, Arabia and even East Africa.

Conflict and Cultural Exchange

Cultural exchange was not limited to interactions between Christian Europeans, Egyptians, and Levantine Muslims. Indeed, international commerce was vigorous along the **SILK**

ROAD, trading routes which stretched from the Arab-controlled Eastern Mediterranean to Song Dynasty China, where science and learning also blossomed. The Silk Road reflected the transnational nature of Central Asia: the nomadic culture of Central Asia lent itself to trade between the major civilizations of China, Persia, the Near East, and Europe. Buddhism and Islam spread into China. Chinese, Islamic, and European art, pottery, and goods were interchanged between the three civilizations—early globalization. The Islamic tradition of the HAJJ, or the pilgrimage to Mecca, also spurred cultural interaction. Islam had spread from Spain throughout North Africa, the Sahel, the Middle East, Persia, Central Asia, India, and China; peoples from all these regions traveled and met in Arabia as part of their religious pilgrimage.

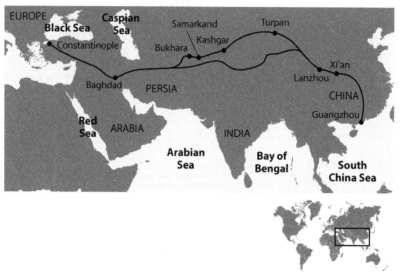

Figure 2.6. The Silk Road

How did the Silk Road and Islam both contribute to global cultural exchange?

Islam also spread along trans-Saharan trade routes into West Africa and the Sahel. Brisk trade between the gold-rich **KINGDOM OF GHANA** and Muslim traders based in Morocco brought Islam to the region around the eleventh century. The Islamic **MALI EMPIRE** (1235 – 1500), based farther south in **TIMBUKTU**, eventually extended beyond the original Ghanaian boundaries all the way to the West African coast, and controlled the valuable gold and salt trades. It became a center of learning and commerce. At the empire's peak, the ruler **MANSA MUSA** made a pilgrimage to Mecca in 1324. However, by 1500, the **SONGHAI EMPIRE** had overcome Mali and eventually dominated the Niger River area.

Loss of Byzantine territory to the Islamic empires meant loss of Christian lands in the Levant—including Jerusalem and Bethlehem—to Muslims. In **1095 C.E.**, the Byzantine Emperor asked **POPE URBAN II** for help to defend Jerusalem and protect Christians. With a history of Muslim incursions into Spain and France, anti-Muslim sentiment was strong in Europe and Christians there were easily inspired to fight them in the Levant, or **HOLY LAND**; the Pope offered lords and knights the chance to keep lands and bounty they won from conquered Muslims (and Jews) in this **CRUSADE**. He also offered Crusaders **INDULGENCES**—forgiveness for sins committed in war and guarantees they would enter heaven.

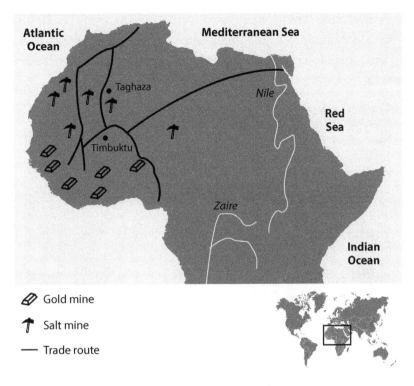

Figure 2.7. Trans-Saharan Trade Routes

Meanwhile, towards the end of the tenth century, the Abbasid Caliphate was in decline. The Shi'ite **FATIMIDS** took control of Syria and Egypt, addressing the Shi'ite claim to the caliphate. Other groups took control of provinces in Mesopotamia, Arabia, and Central Asia. In Spain, **ABD AL-RAHMAN III** (891 – 961) had defied the Abbasids and the Fatimids, taking over **AL-ANDALUS** (Spain) himself and fostering a unique Hispano-Arabic culture where intellectual pursuits bloomed. Based in Cordoba, Rahman was responsible for the Great Mosque. In Muslim Spain, the famous Muslim philosopher **AVERROES** developed his commentary on Aristotle; likewise, the Jewish **MAIMONIDES** developed religious and philosophical thought. Conflict persisted with the Carolingians and with smaller Christian kingdoms in northern Spain, however.

In Western Europe, instability had been ongoing as control over continental territories passed between England and France. France never regained the strength it had under Charlemagne; while the French monarchy existed, smaller states remained powerful and power was decentralized. In England, despite internal divisions, organization accelerated upon William's 1066 conquest. The two civilizations were at odds.

Despite conflict in Europe, Christians found they had more in common with each other than with Muslims, and were able to unite to follow the Pope's call to arms to fight in the Middle East. The decline of the Abbasids had left the Levant vulnerable, and Christian Crusaders were able to establish settlements and small kingdoms in Syria and on the Eastern Mediterranean coast, conquering major cities and capturing Jerusalem by 1099 in the **FIRST CRUSADE** as called for by Pope Urban II (see above).

The Crusades continued over several centuries. In 1171, the Kurdish military leader **SALAH AL-DIN** (Saladin) abolished the Fatimid Caliphate; in 1187 he reconquered Jerusalem, driving European Christians out for good. Following Salah al-Din's death and a succession of rulers, elite slave troops took power. The MAMLUKS (1250 – 1517), whose roots traced back to Abbasid Caliph al-Mutasim's fighting force, controlled Egypt; later they would defeat the Mongols in 1260, protecting Egypt and North Africa from the Mongol invasions.

Figure 2.8. Great Mosque Cordoba

While the ongoing Crusades never resulted in permanent European control over the Holy Land, they did open up trade routes between Europe and the Middle East, stretching all the way along the Silk Road to China. This increasing interdependence led to the European Renaissance.

During the Hundred Years' War, Joan of Arc led the French in the 1429 Battle of Orléans, reinvigorating French resistance to English incursions.

Ongoing interactions between Europeans and Muslims exposed Europeans, who could now afford them thanks to international trade, to improved education and goods. However, the BUBONIC (BLACK) PLAGUE also spread to Europe as a result of global exchange, killing off a third of its population from 1347-1351. The plague had a worldwide impact: empires fell in its wake.

Back in Europe, conflict reached its height throughout the thirteenth and fourteenth centuries known as the HUNDRED YEARS' WAR (1337 – 1453). France was in political chaos during the mid-fourteenth century, decentralized and at times without a king; suffering the effects of the Black Plague; vulnerable to English attack; and periodically under English rule. While conflict would continue, England lost its last territory in France, Bordeaux, in 1453 to the French **KING CHARLES VII**.

In AL-ANDALUS (Spain), despite some coexistence between Christians and Muslims under Muslim rule, raids and conflict were ongoing during the lengthy period of the **RECONQUISTA**, which did not end until 1492 when Christian powers took Grenada. From the zenith of Muslim rule under **ABD AL-RAHMAN**, Christian raids continued, as did shifting alliances between the small kingdoms of Christian Spain and Portugal. By the second half of the thirteenth century, the only remaining Muslim power in Iberia was Grenada. By the fifteenth century, small Christian Spanish kingdoms were vying for dominance. The marriage of **FERDINAND** of Castilla and **ISABELLA** of Aragon in 1479 connected those two kingdoms, and the monarchs were able to complete the Reconquista by taking Grenada and uniting Spain.

Ferdinand and Isabella launched the Inquisition, an extended persecution of Jews and Jewish converts to Christianity who continued to practice Judaism in secret. Jews were tortured, killed, and exiled; their belongings and property were confiscated. Muslims were also persecuted and forced to convert to Christianity or be exiled.

Empires in Transition

Beyond Egypt and the Levant, the collapse of the Abbasid Caliphate led to instability and decentralization of power in Mesopotamia, Persia, and Central Asia; smaller sultanates (territories ruled by sultans, regional leaders) emerged, and production and economic development declined. **TANG DYNASTY CHINA** closed its borders and trade on the Silk Road declined. In the eleventh century, the nomadic Seljuks, Turks from Central Asia, nominally took over the region from Central Asia through parts of the Levant. However, the Seljuks lacked effective administration or central authority.

Despite the lack of political cohesion, Islam remained a unifying force throughout the region, and political instability and decentralization paradoxically allowed local culture to develop, particularly Persian art and literature. Furthermore, Islam was able to thrive during this period: local religious leaders (*ULAMA*) had taken up community leadership positions following the loss of any powerful central authority, and Islam became a guiding force in law, justice, and social organization throughout the region. Yet political decentralization ultimately left the region vulnerable to the Mongol invasions of the twelfth and thirteenth centuries.

During this period, Persian-influenced Sufi (mystical) Islam and poetry developed; Shi'ite theology and jurisprudence also developed as part of a strengthening independent Shi'ite identity.

In the Near East, the **MONGOL INVASIONS** destroyed agriculture, city life and planning, economic patterns and trade routes, and social stability. After some time, new patterns of trade emerged, new cities rose to prominence, and stability allowed for prosperity, but the Mongol invasions dealt a blow to the concept that Islam was inherently favored by God.

The **MONGOL EMPIRE** was based in Central Asia; led by **GENGHIS KHAN**, the Mongols expanded throughout Asia thanks to their abilities in horsemanship and archery. Despite the rich history of transnational activity across Asia, the continent was vulnerable. Central

Asia lacked one dominant culture or imperial power; Southwest Asia was fragmented following the decline of the Abbasids. These weaknesses, along with the disorganization of the Seljuks and the remnants of the Byzantines, allowed the Mongols to take over most of Eurasia—ultimately they controlled Pannonia (Hungary) through the Middle East, Persia, Central Asia, Northern and Western China, and Southeast Asia.

Likewise, in China, the Mongols destroyed local infrastructure, including the foundation of Chinese society and administration—the civil service examinations. However, in order to govern the vast territory effectively, the Mongols in China took a different approach. Genghis Khan's grandson **KUBLAI KHAN** conquered China and founded the Mongol **YUAN DYNASTY** in 1271.

Despite abolishing the examinations until 1315, the Yuan Dynasty maintained most of the administrative policy of the preceding Song Dynasty, including the Six Ministries, the Secretariat, and provincial administrative structure. Additionally, in spite of Mongol distrust of Confucianism and Confucian administrator-scholars, Kublai Khan educated his son in the Confucian tradition. The Yuan did, however, upend Chinese social hierarchy, placing Mongols at the top, followed by non-ethnic Han Chinese, and then Han Chinese.

Mongol attempts at imperial expansion in China into Japan and Southeast Asia, coupled with threats from the Black Plague, financial problems, and flooding, led to the decline of the Yuan Dynasty and the rise of the native Chinese **MING DYNASTY** in 1368. **ZHU YUANZHANG** led the Chinese to victory and ruled as the first Ming emperor from Nanjing; the capital later moved to Beijing in 1421. Ming China controlled land throughout Asia, accepting tribute from rulers in Burma, Siam (Thailand), Annam (Vietnam), Mongolia, Korea, and Central Asia.

The Ming reasserted Chinese control and continued traditional methods of administration; however the construction of the **FORBIDDEN CITY**, the home of the Emperor in Beijing, helped consolidate imperial rule. The Ming also emphasized international trade; demand for ceramics in particular, in addition to silk and tea, was high abroad, and contact with seafaring traders like the Portuguese and Dutch in the sixteenth century was strong. The Ming also encouraged trade and exploration by sea; the Chinese explorer **ZHENG HE** traveled to India, Sri Lanka, and Asia.

Despite some decline in Mongol hegemony throughout Asia, the military leader **TIMUR** (also known as **TAMERLANE**), a Mongol descendant from Transoxania (now Uzbekistan) began conquering land in the area around 1364. By 1383, he occupied Moscow and turned toward Persia. Up to the turn of the century he had conquered Persia, Mesopotamia, much of the Caucasus, and Delhi. In the early fifteenth century, Timur took Syria, invaded Anatolia, and extracted tribute from Egypt. He died in 1405 on an expedition to China.

While rarely spending too much time in one place, Timur had contributed to the development of the capital of his empire, **SAMARKAND**, enriching Central Asia culturally.

Mongol decline was not only isolated to China; in Russia, **IVAN THE GREAT** brought Moscow from Mongol to Slavic Russian control. In the late fifteenth century, Ivan had consolidated Russian power over neighboring Slavic regions. Despite Muscovy's status as a vassal state, Ivan, through both military force and diplomacy, achieved Moscow's independence in 1480. Turning Russian attention toward Europe, he set out to bring other neighboring Slavic and Baltic lands, including Poland-Lithuania and later, parts of

Ukraine, under Russian rule. Ivan achieved a centralized, consolidated Russia that was the foundation for an empire and a sovereign nation that sought diplomatic status with Europe.

A century later, IVAN THE TERRIBLE set out to expand Russia further, to integrate it into Europe, and to strengthen Russian Orthodox Christianity. Named the first TSAR, or emperor, Ivan reformed government, strengthening centralization and administrative bureaucracy and disempowering the nobility. He led the affirmation of orthodox Christianity, calling councils to organize the church and to canonize Russian saints. Ivan also reorganized the military, including promoting officials based on merit rather than status. However, overextension of resources and his oppressive entourage, the OPRICHNINA, depopulated the state and gave him the reputation as a despotic ruler. However, despite his weaknesses, Ivan's reforms strengthened the apparatus of the Russian state; he also expanded and improved foreign policy and relations, and developed Russian culture and religion.

Farther south in Central Asia, one of Timur's descendants, BABUR, laid claim to Timur's dominions and would found the MUGHAL EMPIRE of India. Despite his Mongol roots, Babur identified as Turkic due to his tribal origins, and enjoyed support from the powerful Ottoman Empire in Turkey (see below). In 1525, Babur set out for India. By 1529, he had secured land from Kandahar in the west to Bengal in the east; his grandson, AKBAR, would consolidate the empire, which at the time consisted of small kingdoms. The Mughals would rule India until the eighteenth century and nominally control parts of the country until British takeover in the nineteenth century.

The Mughal emperor Shah Jahan built the Taj Mahal in 1631.

During Mughal rule in India, the Ming Dynasty fell in China and the Qing took over. In 1644, the Ming fell to a peasant revolt; the MANCHU, a non-Han group from the north, took the opportunity to seize Beijing and take the country. Despite their status as non-Han Chinese, the Manchu were accepted; thus began the QING DYNASTY. They would also be China's last imperial rulers, losing power in 1911.

The first Qing emperor, the KANGXI EMPEROR, promoted the arts and education. Under the reign of the QIANLONG EMPEROR (1736 – 1796), China grew to its largest size, including Tibet, Mongolia, Xinjiang, and parts of Russia. It became the dominant power in East Asia and a successful multi-ethnic state. Like the Kangxi Emperor, the Qianlong Emperor was a patron of the arts.

Meanwhile, in Persia, the SAFAVIDS emerged in 1501 in the wake of the Timurid Empire. This dynasty would rule from Azerbaijan in the west through to modern-day Pakistan and Afghanistan. A major rival of the Ottoman Empire, the Safavids were a stabilizing force in Asia. Following Sufism, the Safavids supported art, literature, architecture, and other learning. Their organized administration brought order and stability to Persia throughout their rule, which lasted until 1736, when the QAJAR DYNASTY took over.

Despite the instability inland, Indian Ocean trade routes had continued to function since at least the seventh century. These oceanic routes connected the Horn of Africa, the East African Coast, the Arabian Peninsula, Southern Persia, India, Southeast Asia, and China. The ocean acted as a unifying force throughout the region, and the MONSOON

WINDS permitted Arab, Persian, Indian, and Chinese merchants to travel to East Africa in search of goods such as ivory and gold—and slaves.

Despite the civilizational achievements of the Islamic empires, Tang and later Ming Dynasty China, and the Central Asian and Indian empires that would emerge from the Mongols, the EAST AFRICAN SLAVE TRADE remained vigorous until the nineteenth century. Arabs, Asians and other Africans kidnapped African people and sent them to lives of slavery throughout the Arab world and South Asia. Later, Europeans would take part in the trade, forcing Africans into slavery in colonies throughout South and Southeast Asia, and on plantations in Indian Ocean islands such as Madagascar.

The major East African port was ZANZIBAR, from which slaves, gold, coconut oil, ivory, and other African exports made their way to Asia and the Middle East. However, enslaved persons from Sub-Saharan Africa were also forced north overland to markets in CAIRO, where they were sold and dispersed throughout the Arab-Islamic, Fatimid, and Ottoman empires.

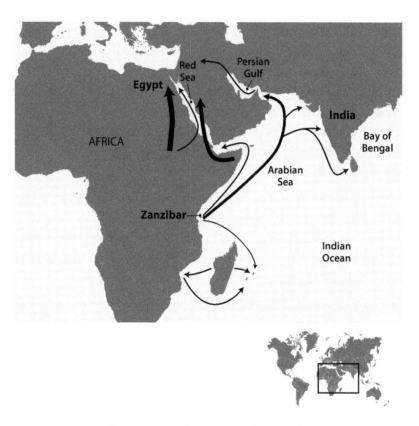

Figure 2.9. Indian Ocean Slave Trade

Islam also spread throughout the African coast and inland; given the cosmopolitan nature of the coastline, the SWAHILI language adopted aspects of Arabic and other Asian languages.

Further north, the Ottoman Turks represented a threat to Central Europe. Controlling most of Anatolia from the late thirteenth century, the Ottomans spread west into the Balkans, consolidating their rule in 1389 at the BATTLE OF KOSOVO. In 1453 they captured Istanbul, from which the OTTOMAN EMPIRE would come to rule much of the Mediterranean world.

Under the leadership of **MEHMED THE CONQUEROR** in the fifteenth century and his successors, the Ottomans would conquer Pannonia (Hungary), North Africa, the Caucasus, the Levant and Mesopotamian regions, western Arabia, and Egypt. Under **SULEIMAN THE MAGNIFICENT** (1520 – 1566), the **OTTOMAN EMPIRE** consolidated control over the Balkans, the Middle East, and North Africa and would hold that land until the nineteenth century.

The capture of Istanbul (Constantinople) had represented the true end of the Byzantine Empire; the remaining Christian Byzantines, mainly isolated to coastal Anatolia, Constantinople, and parts of Greece, fled to Italy, bringing Greek, Middle Eastern, and Asian learning with them and enriching the emerging European Renaissance.

The European Renaissance

The **RENAISSANCE**, or *rebirth*, included the revival of ancient Greek and Roman learning, art, and architecture. However, the roots of the Renaissance stretched farther back to earlier interactions between Christendom, the Islamic World, and even China, during the Crusades and through Silk Road trade. Not only did the Renaissance inspire new learning and prosperity in Europe, enabling exploration, colonization, profit, and later imperialism, but it also led to scientific and religious questioning and rebellion against the Catholic Church and, later, monarchical governments.

It is important to note that Russia would not experience these cultural changes until the eighteenth century, when **PETER THE GREAT** and **CATHERINE THE GREAT** copied modern European culture, modernized the military, and updated technology, including building the new capital city of **ST. PETERSBURG**, a cultural center.

Reinvigoration of classical knowledge was triggered in part by Byzantine refugees from the Ottoman conquest of Constantinople, including scholars who brought Greek and Roman texts to Italy and Western Europe. The fall of Constantinople precipitated the development of **HUMANISM** in Europe, a mode of thought emphasizing human nature, creativity, and an overarching concept of truth in all philosophical systems (the concept of **SYNCRETISM**). Emerging in Italy, the seat of the Catholic Church, humanism was supported by some popes, including Leo X. However in the long term it represented a threat to religious, especially Catholic, orthodoxy, however, as it allowed for the questioning of religious teaching. Figures associated with humanism included Dante, Petrarch, and Erasmus. Ultimately humanism would be at the root of the **REFORMATION** of the sixteenth century.

Art, considered not just a form of expression but also a science in itself, flourished in fifteenth century Italy, particularly in **FLORENCE**. Major figures who explored anatomy in sculpture, design and perspective, and innovation in architecture included Leonardo da Vinci, Bramante, Michelangelo, Rafael, and Donatello. Leonardo is particularly known for his scientific pursuits in addition to his artistic achievement. While artists worked throughout Italy and found patrons in the Vatican among other places, the Florentine **MEDICI FAMILY** funded extensive civic projects, construction, décor, and public sculpture throughout Florence, supporting Renaissance art in that city.

Meanwhile, scholars like Galileo, Isaac Newton, and Copernicus made discoveries in what became known as the **SCIENTIFIC REVOLUTION**, rooted in the scientific knowledge of the Islamic empires, which had been imported through economic and social contact initiated centuries prior in the Crusades. Scientific study and discovery threatened the power of the Church, whose theological teachings were often at odds with scientific findings and logical reasoning.

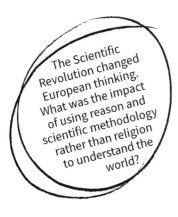

The Scientific Revolution changed European thinking. What was the impact of using reason and scientific methodology rather than religion to understand the world?

Also in the mid-fifteenth century, in Northern Europe, **JOHANN GUTENBERG** invented the **PRINTING PRESS**; the first book to be published would be the Bible. With the advent of printing, texts could be more widely and rapidly distributed, and people had more access to information beyond what their leaders told them. Combined with humanism and increased emphasis on secular thought, the power of the Church and of monarchs who ruled by divine right was under threat. Here lay the roots of the **ENLIGHTENMENT**, the basis for reinvigorated European culture and political thought that would drive its development for the next several centuries—and inspire revolution.

Transnational cultural exchange had also resulted in the transmission of technology to Europe. During the sixteenth century, European seafaring knowledge, navigation, and technology benefitted from Islamic and Asian expertise; European explorers and traders could now venture beyond the Mediterranean. Portuguese and Dutch sailors eventually reached India and China, where they established ties with the Ming Dynasty. Trade was no longer dependent on the Silk Road. Improved technology also empowered Europeans to explore overseas, eventually landing in the Western Hemisphere, heretofore unknown to the peoples of Eurasia and Africa.

Mesoamerican and Andean Civilizations

In the Americas, the **MAYA**, who preceded the Aztecs in Mesoamerica, came to dominate the Yucatan peninsula around 300. They developed a complex spiritual belief system accompanied by relief art, and built pyramidal temples that still stand today. In addition, they developed a detailed calendar and a written language using pictographs similar to Egyptian hieroglyphs; they studied astronomy and mathematics. Maya political administration was organized under monarchical city-states from around 300 until around 900, when the civilization began to decline.

Throughout Mayan history there is evidence of interaction with the Mesoamerican city-state of **TEOTIHUACAN**, a major city likely comprised of various Mesoamerican peoples such as Toltecs, Mixtecs, Zapotecs, some Mayans, and other peoples. By around 1400, two major empires dominated Central and South America: the Incas and the Aztecs. These two empires would be the last indigenous civilizations to dominate the Americas before European colonization of the Western Hemisphere.

As smaller Mesoamerican civilizations had weakened and collapsed, the **AZTECS** had come to dominate Mexico and much of Mesoamerica. Their military power and militaristic culture allowed the Aztecs to dominate the region and regional trade in precious objects like quetzal bird feathers. The main city of the Aztec empire, **TENOCHTITLAN**, was founded in 1325 and, at its height, was a major world city home to several million people.

Aztec civilization was militaristic in nature and divided on a class basis: it included slaves, indentured servants, serfs, an independent priestly class, military, and ruling classes. However, it did allow for upward mobility, especially for those who had proven themselves in battle. The Aztecs shared many beliefs with the Mayans; throughout Mesoamerica the same calendar was used. Central in the Aztec religion was worship of the god QUETZAL-COATL, a feathered snake.

Meanwhile, in the Andes, the INCAS had emerged. Based in CUZCO, the Incas had consolidated their power and strengthened in the area, likely due to a surplus of their staple crop maize, around 1300. They were able to conquer local lords and, later, peoples further south, thanks in part to domesticated llamas and alpacas which allowed the military to transport supplies through the mountains.

Figure 2.10. Quetzalcoatl

Inca engineers built the citadel of MACHU PICCHU and imperial infrastructure, including roads throughout the Andes. Thanks to highly developed mountain agriculture, they were able to grow crops at high altitudes and maintain waystations on the highways stocked with supplies, keeping track of them through a system called *QUIPUS*, knotted cords. In order to subdue local peoples, they moved conquered groups elsewhere in the empire and repopulated conquered areas with Incas.

Colonization of the Western Hemisphere

Interest in exploration grew in Europe during the Renaissance period. Technological advancements made complex navigation and long-term sea voyages possible, and economic growth resulting from international trade drove interest in market expansion. Global interdependence got a big push from Spain when King Ferdinand and Queen Isabella agreed to sponsor CHRISTOPHER COLUMBUS' exploratory voyage in 1492 to find a sea route to Asia, in order to speed up commercial trade there. Instead, he stumbled upon the Western Hemisphere, which was unknown to Europeans, Asians, and Africans to this point.

Columbus landed in the Caribbean; he and later explorers would claim the Caribbean islands and eventually Central and South America for Spain and Portugal. However, those areas were already populated by the major American civilizations (discussed above).

The Aztec ruler **MONTEZUMA II** led the Aztecs during their first encounter with Spain; explorer **HERNAN CORTÉS** met with him in Tenochtitlan after invading other areas of Mexico in 1519. Due to Spanish superiority in military technology, Montezuma attempted to compromise with Cortés; however, Cortés, seeking wealth and prestige in Mexico, had unlawfully left the Spanish stronghold of Cuba, disobeying Spanish colonial authorities. Thus in no position to compromise with the Aztecs, a few days later Cortés arrested Montezuma and took over the city. Spain was especially interested in subduing the Aztec religion, which included ceremonies with human blood and human sacrifice, and in controlling Mexican and Mesoamerican gold. Spain then began the process of colonizing Mexico and Central America, and the Aztec Empire collapsed.

In South America, as in Mexico and Central America, the Spanish were interested in economic exploitation and spreading Christianity, accessing the continent in the early sixteenth century. In 1533, the Spanish conquistador **FRANCISCO PIZZARO** defeated the Inca king **ATAHUALPA** and installed a puppet ruler, marking the decline of the Inca Empire. While the empire remained nominally intact for several years, the Spanish desecrated important religious artefacts—like mummies important for ancestor worship—installed Christianity, and took economic and political control of the region.

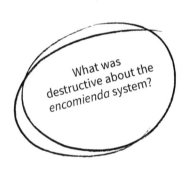
What was destructive about the encomienda system?

Spain took over the silver- and gold-rich Mesoamerican and Andean territories, and the Caribbean islands where sugar became an important cash crop. Thus developed **MERCANTILISM**, whereby the colonizing or *MOTHER COUNTRY* took raw materials from the territories they controlled for the colonizers' own benefit. Governments amassed wealth through protectionism and increasing exports at the expense of other rising colonial powers. This eventually involved developing goods and then selling them back to those colonized lands at an inflated price. The *ENCOMIENDA* system granted European landowners the "right" to hold lands in the Americas and demand labor and tribute from the local inhabitants. Spreading Christianity was another important reason for European expansion. Local civilizations and resources were exploited and destroyed.

The **COLUMBIAN EXCHANGE** enabled mercantilism to flourish. Conflict and illness brought by the Europeans—especially **SMALLPOX**—decimated the Native Americans, and the Europeans were left without labor to mine the silver and gold or to work the land. **AFRICAN SLAVERY** was their solution.

Slavery was an ancient institution in many societies worldwide; however, with the Columbian Exchange slavery came to be practiced on a mass scale the likes of which the world had never seen. Throughout Africa and especially on the West African coast, Europeans traded for slaves with some African kingdoms and also raided the land, kidnapping people. European slavers took captured Africans in horrific conditions to the Americas; those who survived were enslaved and forced to work in mining or agriculture for the benefit of expanding European imperial powers.

The Columbian Exchange described the TRIANGULAR TRADE (Figure 1.3) across the Atlantic: European slavers took kidnapped African people from Africa to the Americas, sold them at auction and exchanged them for sugar and raw materials; these materials were traded in Europe for consumer goods, which were then exchanged in Africa for slaves, and so on.

Enslaved Africans suffered greatly, forced to endure ocean voyages crammed on unsafe, unhygienic ships, sometimes among the dead bodies of other kidnapped people, only to arrive in the Americas to a life of slavery in mines or on plantations. Throughout this period, Africans did resist both on ships and later, in the Americas; MAROON COMMUNITIES of escaped slaves formed throughout the Western Hemisphere, the UNDERGROUND RAILROAD in the nineteenth-century United States helped enslaved persons escape the South, and TOUSSAINT L'OUVERTURE led a successful slave rebellion in Haiti, winning independence from the French for that country in 1791.

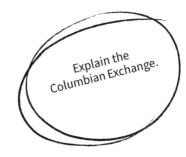

Explain the Columbian Exchange.

However, the slave trade continued for centuries. The colonies and later independent countries of the Western Hemisphere continued to practice slavery until the nineteenth century; oppressive legal and social restrictions based on race continue to affect the descendants of slaves to this day throughout the hemisphere.

During the eighteenth century, Spain and Portugal were preeminent powers in global trade thanks to colonization and IMPERIALISM, the possession and exploitation of land overseas. However, Great Britain became an important presence on the seas; it would later dominate the oceans throughout the nineteenth century.

Though Britain would lose its territories in North America after the American Revolution, it maintained control of the resource-rich West Indies. The kingdom went on to dominate strategic areas in South Africa, New South Wales in Australia, Mauritius in the Indian Ocean, and Madras and Bengal in the Indian Subcontinent, among other places. Later, in the nineteenth century, Britain would expand its empire further. Likewise, France gained territory in North America and in the West Indies; despite losses to Britain in the eighteenth century, that country would also expand its own global empire in the nineteenth century.

EXAMPLES

1) Which of the following explains why the Eastern Roman Empire remained stable and transitioned to the Byzantine Empire while Rome in Western Europe collapsed?

   A. Feudalism contributed to instability in Western Europe, and so that part of the continent disintegrated into a series of small states.

   B. The schism between the Catholic and Greek Orthodox Churches tore the empire apart.

   C. Muslims entered Constantinople and took it from Christian Roman control.

   D. Imprudent alliances in the West led to Roman collapse, while strong leadership and centralization in the East developed a new empire.

   E. When Constantine reconquered the Western Roman Empire, he used its resources to support the East.

Answers:

A. Incorrect. Feudalism actually helped stabilize Western Europe.

B. Incorrect. The divisions between the Catholic and Greek Orthodox Churches were not integral to the collapse of Rome.

C. Incorrect. Islam had not yet appeared as a religious movement.

D. **Correct.** Security alliances with Germanic and Gothic tribes left Western Rome vulnerable to their attack; meanwhile in the east, centralized power in Constantinople and strong leadership, particularly under Justinian, led to the rise of the powerful Byzantine Empire.

E. Incorrect. While power did shift east, this was not due to anti-Western policies.

2) Following the death of Muhammad, Muslim leadership became so divided that the religious movement eventually split into Sunnis and Shi'ites. This was due to

A. disagreement over secession to his place as leader.

B. disagreement over the legitimacy of Abraham, Moses and Jesus.

C. disagreement over the theological nature of Islam.

D. disagreement over whether to accept Christians and Jews as People of the Book.

E. disagreement about the importance of conquest.

Answers:

A. **Correct.** The Meccan elites believed that they should take over leadership of Islam and continue the movement beyond the Arabian Peninsula; however Ali and Fatima, Muhammad's cousin and daughter, believed Ali was Muhammad's rightful successor as his closest living male relative.

B. Incorrect. All Muslims accept Abraham, Moses, and Jesus as important prophets of God.

C. Incorrect. While the sides had some differences and while major theological differences eventually did develop between Sunni and Shia Islam, the original break was mainly based on the dispute over succession.

D. Incorrect. Accepting the People of the Book was not at issue.

E. Incorrect. All the Muslim leadership believed that they were called to spread Islam beyond the Arabian Peninsula.

3) Despite the violence of the Crusades, they were also beneficial for Europe in that they

A. resulted in substantial, long-term land gains for European leaders in the Middle East.

B. introduced European powers to the concept of nation-states, the dominant form of political organization in the Middle East.

C. exposed Europe to Islamic and Asian science, technology, and medicine.

D. enhanced tolerance of Islam throughout Europe.

E. The development of trade routes between Europe, Asia, the Middle East and Africa.

Answers:

A. Incorrect. While Europeans retained some territory in the Middle East, this was temporary.

B. Incorrect. Nation-states did not become a form of governance in Europe for several centuries; furthermore, they were not a form of political organization in the Middle East.

C. **Correct.** Europeans who traveled to the Levant to fight returned home with beneficial knowledge and technology.

D. Incorrect. Christian Europe was not tolerant of Islam.

E. Incorrect. These trade routes were well established before the Crusades.

4) Which of the following was a result of the rise of the Ottoman Turks?

A. Christian Byzantines left Constantinople for Western Europe, bringing classical learning with them.

B. The Ottomans were able to conquer the Balkans, the Levant, and eventually North Africa and the Middle East, establishing a large Islamic empire.

C. The Ottomans represented an Islamic threat to European Christendom, given their grip on the Balkan Peninsula.

D. The establishment of a unified Mediterranean empire that would last almost 300 years.

E. all of the above.

Answers:

A. Incorrect. Byzantine scholars did leave Constantinople and bring classical learning to Europe, especially Rome; this reintroduction of the classics would go on to influence the Renaissance. However, the other answer choices also apply, so this answer is incomplete.

B. Incorrect. At its height under Suleiman the Magnificent, the Ottoman Empire stretched from Morocco through Anatolia and the Levant to Persia. However, the other answer choices also apply, so this answer is incomplete.

C. Incorrect. The Ottomans represented a serious threat to Europe for centuries, as they controlled the Balkans and much of Pannonia; they even besieged Vienna twice. However, the other answer choices also apply, so this answer is incomplete.

D. Incorrect. While the Ottoman Empire did last until the 1800s, this is not a complete answer to the question.

E. **Correct.** All of the answer choices apply.

5) Which of the following best explains the Atlantic Triangular Trade?

A. American raw materials were transported to Africa, where they were exchanged for enslaved persons; enslaved persons were taken to the Americas, where they turned raw materials to consumer goods for sale in Europe.

B. Africa was not a major source of raw materials for Europe until the nineteenth century.

C. European raw materials were sent to the Americas to be transformed into consumer goods by people who had been kidnapped from Africa and enslaved. These consumer goods were then traded in Africa for more slaves.

D. Enslaved African people were traded in the Americas for raw materials; raw materials harvested by slaves went to Europe where they were utilized and turned to consumer goods; European consumer goods were exchanged in Africa for enslaved people.

E. African raw materials were transported along with slaves to Europe to produce consumer goods that were then sold in the Americas.

Answers:

A. Incorrect. American raw materials were transported to Europe where they were turned to consumer goods, not to Africa. Furthermore, American raw materials were converted into consumer goods in Europe.

B. Incorrect. European consumer goods were sold in Africa (and within Europe); the Americas were initially a source of raw materials, though this would later change. Furthermore, Africa was not a major source of raw materials for Europe until the nineteenth century.

C. Incorrect. Raw materials in the Triangular Trade came from the Americas; they were converted to consumer goods in Europe.

D. Correct. American raw materials (like sugar and tobacco) were used in Europe and also turned into consumer goods there. European goods (as well as gold extracted from the Americas) were exchanged in Africa for enslaved persons, who were forced to harvest the raw materials in the Americas.

E. Incorrect. Colonizing countries placed restrictions on manufacturing in the Americas to ensure all consumer goods were purchased from Europe.

Armed Conflicts

Reformation and New Europe

While Spain and Portugal consolidated their hold over territories in the Americas, conflict ensued in Europe. With the cultural changes of the Renaissance, the power of the Catholic Church was threatened; new scientific discoveries and secular Renaissance thought were at odds with many teachings of the Church. The Catholic monk **MARTIN LUTHER** wrote a letter of protest to the Pope in 1517 known as the **NINETY-FIVE THESES**, outlining ways he believed the Church should reform; his ideas gained support, especially among rulers who wanted more power from the Church. Triggering the **REFORMATION**, or movement for reform of the Church, Luther's ideas led to offshoots of new versions of Christianity in Western Europe, separate from the Orthodox Churches in Russia and Greece. Protestant thinkers like Luther and **JOHN CALVIN** addressed particular grievances, condemning the INFALLIBILITY of the Pope (its teaching that the Pope was without fault) and the selling of INDULGENCES, or guarantees of entry into heaven.

The English **KING HENRY VIII** developed the Protestant **CHURCH OF ENGLAND**, further consolidating his own power, famously allowing divorce and marrying several times himself. The reign of Henry VIII, of the **HOUSE OF TUDOR**, initiated a chain of events leading to the consolidation of Protestantism in England, and eventually civil war and the empowerment of Parliament.

In Britain, religious and ethnic diversity between Protestant England and Scotland, and Catholic Ireland, made the kingdom unstable. The Catholic **MARY QUEEN OF SCOTS**, who was the daughter of the Scottish King James V and half French, had been betrothed to Henry VIII's son Edward. However her guardians canceled the arrangement, causing conflict with England. She temporarily married Francis of France, uniting Scotland with that Catholic country; however he quickly died from illness. Mary then married her Protestant cousin the Earl of Darnley, with whom she had a son, JAMES. Darnley forced her to abdicate the Scottish throne in 1567 and she fled to England, seeking safety with her Protestant cousin ELIZABETH I, daughter of Henry VIII and queen of England. Her son, still a baby, became KING JAMES VI of Scotland.

The Tudor Queen Elizabeth imprisoned the Catholic Mary in England as she—and her son—represented a threat to her power. Not only was James' male sex a liability for Elizabeth's inheritance to the throne, but their religious identities as Catholics threatened Elizabeth's hold over the Catholics of England and Scotland, as well as her tenuous grip on Catholic Ireland. In 1587, Elizabeth had Mary executed following revelations of a Catholic plot to overthrow Elizabeth. Yet on Elizabeth's death in 1603, James succeeded Elizabeth as KING JAMES I of England and Ireland, ushering in the HOUSE OF STUART.

James I attempted to balance the diverse ethnic and religious groups in England, Scotland, and Ireland, including the Catholic majority in Ireland and the Calvinist Scots, who disagreed on many points with the more liberal Church of England (Anglicans). Despite his efforts at maintaining a delicate political balance, instability grew. In fact, despite James' roots in Catholicism, his mother having been the Catholic Mary, oppression of Catholics continued.

Furthermore, James' daughter married into the Bohemian royal family, forcing English involvement in the Thirty Years' War as that family lost power to Catholics in Central Europe—foreign involvement James was loath to initiate. His son CHARLES I continued the anti-Catholic conflict in 1625 upon his succession to the throne; however, upon his withdrawal in 1630, conservative Protestants in England and Scotland (PURITANS) began to suspect a royal movement to weaken Protestantism and even restore Catholicism in the kingdom. Many began moving to North America as a result.

The Gunpowder Plot to blow up the House of Lords and execute King James in the process was planned by Catholic fighters for the fifth of November, 1605. This plot was conceived by a group including the famous Guy Fawkes, who represents rebellion to this day.

Conflict between Protestants and Catholics was fierce on the Continent as well. The THIRTY YEARS' WAR (1618 – 1648) began in Central Europe between Protestant nobles in the Holy Roman Empire who disagreed with the strict Catholic FERDINAND II, king of Bohemia and eventually archduke of Austria and king of Hungary (what was not under Ottoman domination). Elected Holy Roman Emperor in 1619, Ferdinand II was a leader of the COUNTER-REFORMATION, attempts at reinforcing Catholic dominance throughout Europe during and after the Reformation in the wake of the Renaissance and related social change. Ferdinand was also closely allied with the Catholic HAPSBURG Dynasty, which ruled Austria and Spain.

Later interference in 1625 by Protestant Denmark and Sweden in Poland and Germany stirred further anti-Catholic discontent among local nobles in Germany, who yearned for independence from the imperial Holy Roman Empire. Despite Danish, Dutch, Swedish, and British support, the imperial military leader ALBRECHT VON WALLENSTEIN took control of most Protestant German states and Denmark. Ferdinand II issued the EDICT OF RESTITUTION, restoring rebellious Protestant German territory to imperial, Catholic control. 1629 also marked the defeat of Denmark as an important European power at that point in history.

Protestant Sweden engaged in further conflict with Catholic Poland. Polish political ambition drove it to take advantage of instability throughout the region, venturing east into Russia until the 1634 PEACE OF POLYANOV; it then battled Sweden for control over Baltic territory.

Meanwhile, farther west, Sweden had quickly reemerged in 1630 to reignite the Protestant cause. Allied with the Netherlands, Sweden reestablished a Protestant revival throughout Germany, driving imperial forces south. Ferdinand sought aid from the Catholic Spanish Hapsburgs and the Papacy; Sweden was defeated at NORDLINGEN in 1634 and Catholicism was reestablished in the south.

At the same time, despite France's status as a Catholic country, it came into conflict with its neighbors—Hapsburg-ruled Spain and Austria. Spain's victory in Central Europe in 1634 cemented its power in the region; Hapsburg dominance to France's south and east represented a threat to that country, which was now surrounded by a strong military power. As a result, despite their religious commonalities, France declared war on Spain in 1635 and shortly after on the Hapsburg-supported Holy Roman Empire. This political tactic represented a break from the prioritization of religious alliances and a movement toward emphasis on state sovereignty.

The tangled alliances between European powers resulted in war between not only France and Spain, but also Sweden and Austria, with the small states of the weakening Holy Roman Empire caught in the middle. The war had been centered on alliances and concerns about the nature of Christianity within different European countries. However, upon signing the 1648 TREATY OF WESTPHALIA, the European powers agreed to recognize STATE SOVEREIGNTY and practice NON-INTERFERENCE in each other's matters—at the expense of family and religious allegiance. 1648 marked a transition into modern international relations when politics and religion would no longer be inexorably intertwined.

The end of the Thirty Years' War represented the end of the notion of the domination of the Catholic Church over Europe and the concept of religious regional dominance, rather than ethnic state divisions. Over the next several centuries, the Church—and religious empires like the Ottomans—would eventually lose control over ethnic groups and their lands, later giving way to smaller NATION-STATES.

As state sovereignty became entrenched in European notions of politics, so too did conflict between states. Upon the death of the Hapsburg Holy Roman Emperor CHARLES VI in 1740, the WAR OF THE AUSTRIAN SUCCESSION began, a series of Continental wars over who would take over control of the Hapsburg territories. These conflicts would lead to the Seven Years' War.

Nominally, there was dispute over whether a woman, Charles' daughter MARIA THERESA, could inherit the Austrian throne; however, it is more likely that FREDERICK II (or FREDERICK THE GREAT) of Prussia took advantage of the instability in 1740 following Charles' death to capture the resource-rich province of Silesia from Hapsburg Austria. Prussia allied with France, Bavaria, and Spain; Maria Theresa sought help from Britain, which would be threatened by French dominance of Europe. Britain and Spain had been in conflict over territory beyond Europe for decades; Britain and France were rivals on the North American continent, in Asia, and in the West Indies. Thus conflict in Europe reflected overseas competition.

Fighting dragged on; forced by dwindling finances to the negotiating table, the European powers signed the Treaty of Aix la Chappelle in 1748, which granted Maria Theresa most Austrian possessions and gave Silesia to Prussia.

However, it was clear that Austria intended to regain Silesia. In an effort to protect its allies in Hannover during Continental instability, Britain formed a pragmatic alliance with Prussia, despite its traditional friendship with Austria. As a result, Austria allied with its former enemy France, in a development known as the *Diplomatic Revolution*.

In 1756, Austria was set to attack Prussia, but Frederick the Great attacked first, launching the **SEVEN YEARS' WAR**. In Europe, this war further cemented concepts of state sovereignty and delineated rivalries between European powers engaged in colonial adventure and overseas imperialism—especially Britain and France. It would kick-start British dominance in Asia and also lead to Britain's loss of its North American colonies, nearly bankrupting the Crown (as discussed below).

On the European front, Frederick the Great invaded Silesia and then Bohemia in 1787; however he was repelled by Austria. Meanwhile, while the English led a Hannoverian army against the French in the west, they too were defeated and the French marched on Prussia. Sweden attacked from the north, and Russia attacked from the east. So Frederick called on Britain for more support. **WILLIAM PITT THE ELDER**, the British political leader (essentially Prime Minister) authorized enormous financial contributions to Prussia; he also began focusing the war overseas against France on imperial possessions in the Western Hemisphere and Asia.

Fortunately for the Anglo-Prussian alliance in Europe, changes in Russian leadership led to Catherine the Great's takeover; she ended hostilities with Prussia and focused on development in Russia instead. Hostilities died down in Europe, but the conflict overseas set the stage for the building of empire (see below).

This time of change in Europe would affect Asia. European concepts of social and political organization became constructed around national sovereignty and nation-states. European economies had become dependent upon colonies and were starting to industrialize, enriching Europe at the expense of its imperial possessions in the Americas, in Africa, and increasingly in Asia.

Industrialization and political organization allowed improved militaries, which put Asian governments at a disadvantage. The major Asian powers—Mughal India, Qing China, the Ottoman Empire, and Safavid (and later, Qajar) Persia—would eventually succumb to European influence or come under direct European control.

The Age of Revolutions

Monarchies in Europe had been weakened by the conflicts between Catholicism and Protestant faiths; despite European presence and increasing power overseas, as well as its dominance in the Americas, instability on the continent and in the British Isles made the old order vulnerable. Enlightenment ideals like democracy and republicanism, coupled with political instability, would trigger revolution against **ABSOLUTE MONARCHY**. Revolutionary actors drew on the philosophies of enlightenment thinkers like JOHN LOCKE, JEAN-JACQUES ROUSSEAU, and MONTESQUIEU, whose beliefs, such as REPUBLICANISM, the SOCIAL CONTRACT, the SEPARATION OF POWERS, and the RIGHTS OF MAN would drive the Age of Revolutions.

In England, Puritans and Separatists—strict, conservative Protestants—were suspicious of King Charles I, believing he was weakening Protestantism and even possibly supporting Catholic plots. At the same time, more moderate Protestant leaders, including the weak Parliament and aristocratic class, were upset by Charles' dictatorial reign.

The period marked the early days of the AGE OF REVOLUTIONS, influenced especially by Enlightenment thinkers like Locke and Rousseau, who believed in the natural rights of man and the social contract between the people and government. Charles I was despotic and sidelined Parliament, causing political and military unrest. Conflict between England and Scotland in the late 1630s and an Irish uprising in 1641 weakened Charles further, as disgruntled English aristocracy, who felt that Charles had become a tyrannical ruler, withdrew support and began consolidating their own power. In 1642, the ENGLISH CIVIL WAR broke out between the ROYALISTS, who supported the monarchy, and the PARLIA- MENTARIANS, who wanted a republic.

Eventually, the Royalists succumbed to the Parliamentarians, and Charles was executed in 1649. Meanwhile, England had lost control over Ireland, and the Parliamentarian military leader OLIVER CROMWELL was sent to reestablish control over the island. Charles II, son of Charles I, had established control as king of Scotland; Cromwell defeated him and England took back control of Scotland in 1651. By 1653, England once again controlled Britain and Ireland; Cromwell was installed as Lord Protector.

Following Cromwell's death, Charles II restored the Stuart monarchy. However, stability was short lived once his Catholic brother James II succeeded him in 1685. By 1688, English Protestants asked the Dutch William of Orange, husband of James II's daughter Mary, to help restore Protestantism in Britain. WILLIAM AND MARY defeated James and consolidated Protestant control over England, Scotland, and Ireland under a Protestant constitutional monarchy in the GLORIOUS REVOLUTION. The 1689 ENGLISH BILL OF RIGHTS established constitutional monarchy, in the spirit of the MAGNA CARTA.

The AMERICAN REVOLUTION heavily influenced by Locke, broke out a century later. Please refer to Chapter One, "United States History," for details.

The French Revolution was the precursor to the end of the feudal order in most of Europe. KING LOUIS XIV, the *Sun King* (1643-1715), had consolidated the monarchy in France, taking true political and military power from the nobility. Meanwhile, French Enlighten- ment thinkers like JEAN-JACQUES ROUSSEAU, MONTESQUIEU, and VOLTAIRE criticized absolute monarchy and the repression of freedom of speech and thought; in 1789, the French Revolution broke out.

Louis XIV built the palace of Versailles, to centralize the monarchy—and also to contain and monitor the nobility.

The power of the Catholic Church had weakened and the Scientific Revolution and the Enlightenment had fostered social and intellectual change. Colonialism and mercantilism were fueling the growth of an early middle class: people who were not traditionally nobility or landowners under the feudal system were becoming wealthier and more powerful thanks to early capitalism. This class, the BOURGEOISIE, chafed under the rule of the nobility, which had generally inherited land and wealth (while the bourgeoisie earned their wealth in business).

In France, the problem was most acute as France had the largest population in Europe at the time. At the same time, France had one of the most centralized monarchies in Europe and entrenched nobilities. With a growing bourgeoisie and peasant class paying increasingly higher taxes to the nobility, resentment was brewing.

Louis XIV had strengthened the monarchy by weakening the nobility's control over their land and centralizing power under the king. However, his successors had failed to govern effectively or win the loyalty of the people; both the nobility and the monarch were widely resented. Furthermore, the bourgeoisie resented their lack of standing in government and society. Moreover, advances in medicine had permitted unprecedented population growth, further empowering the peasantry and bourgeoisie.

The French government was struggling financially, having supported the American Revolution; in desperation, the controller-general of finances suggested reforms that would tax the nobility. An unwilling council of nobles instead called for the ESTATES-GENERAL to be convened in 1787; this toothless body had not come together since 1614.

The Estates-General, a weak representative assembly, reflected French society: the clergy, the nobility, and the THIRD ESTATE—the middle class and the poor peasants, or *commoners*. The burden of taxation traditionally fell on the Third Estate. In fact, peasants had to TITHE, paying ten percent of their earnings to the nobles.

After a poor harvest in 1788, unrest spread throughout the country. King Louis XVI permitted elections to the Estates-General and some free speech; momentum against the elites grew. Once the Estates-General convened at Versailles in 1789, disagreement between the nobility and the elite clergy, on the one hand, and the Third Estate and lower-level parish priests, on the other, erupted. The two sides came to terms and formed the NATIONAL CONSTITUENT ASSEMBLY; still, the king and nobility were suspicious of the other side and Louis XVI planned to dissolve it.

At the same time, panic over dwindling food supplies and suspicion over a conspiracy against the Third Estate triggered the GREAT FEAR among the peasants in July 1789. Suspicion turned to action when the king sent troops to Paris, and on July 16 the people stormed the BASTILLE prison in an event still celebrated in France symbolic of the overthrow of tyranny. The peasantry then revolted in the countryside; consequently the National Constituent Assembly officially abolished the feudal system and tithing. Furthermore, the Assembly issued the DECLARATION OF THE RIGHTS OF MAN AND THE CITIZEN, the precursor to the French constitution assuring liberty and equality, in the model of Enlightenment thought.

Louis XVI refused to accept these developments; as a result, the people marched on Versailles and brought the royals back to Paris, effectively putting the Assembly in charge. Members of the JACOBINS, revolutionary political clubs, became members of the Assembly; the more extreme of these political figures would play key roles in the immediate future of the country.

Charles Dickens' *A Tale of Two Cities* features a fictional account of the storming of the Bastille. Contrary to popular belief, Victor Hugo's *Les Misérables* takes place several decades after the French Revolution.

The Assembly continued reforms, including nationalizing the lands of the Catholic Church to pay off debt, disempowering the Church. It also reorganized the administration of the ANCIEN *régime* (the old government) which allowed the election of judges. When Louis XVI attempted to escape France, he was detained.

An important tenet of the revolutionary ethos in France was the concept of self-determination, or the right of a people to rule themselves, which threatened rulers fearing revolution in their own countries.

The French Revolution inspired revolutionary movements throughout Europe and beyond; indeed, the revolutionary principle of self-determination drove revolutionary France to support its ideals abroad. The country declared war on Austria in 1792, but following severe defeats by joint Austrian-Prussian forces, the people became suspicious of the unpopular queen MARIE ANTOINETTE. Marie Antoinette was originally from Austria and had, in fact, encouraged an invasion, hoping to suppress the revolution. The people imprisoned the royal family; the Jacobins abolished the monarchy, establishing the republic later that year.

War in Europe dragged on into 1793, with considerable French losses against an alliance between Austria, Prussia, and Great Britain. Within France, the Jacobins—essentially, the government of the Republic—were breaking into two main factions: the more moderate GIRONDINS, who favored concentrating power in the hands of the bourgeoisie, and the more extreme MONTAGNARDS, led by ROBESPIERRE, who favored radical social policy empowering the poor.

Fearful of counterrevolutionaries in France and instability abroad, the republican government created the COMMITTEE OF PUBLIC SAFETY in 1793. Robespierre led the Committee and the REIGN OF TERROR began in France, during which time thousands of people were executed by GUILLOTINE, including Louis XVI and Marie Antoinette. Robespierre himself was executed a year later.

Ongoing war in Europe and tensions in France between republicans and royalists continued to weaken the revolution, but France had military successes in Europe. France had continued its effort to spread the revolution throughout the continent, led by NAPOLEON BONAPARTE, who even occupied Egypt in an attempt to threaten British power abroad. In 1799, Napoleon took power in France: the revolution was over.

In 1804 NAPOLEON BONAPARTE emerged as emperor of France, and proceeded to conquer much of Europe throughout the NAPOLEONIC WARS, changing the face of Europe. French occupation of Spain weakened that country enough that revolutionary movements in its colonies strengthened; eventually Latin American colonies, inspired by the Enlightenment and revolution in Europe, won their freedom.

Napoleon's movement eastward also triggered the collapse of the Holy Roman Empire. However, the powerful state of PRUSSIA emerged in its wake, and a strong sense of militarism and Germanic nationalism took root in the face of opposition to seemingly unstoppable France. (Prussia would later go on to unify the small kingdoms of Central Europe that had made up the Holy Roman Empire, forming Germany, as discussed below.)

Napoleon was finally defeated in Russia in 1812 and was forced by the European powers to abdicate in 1813. He escaped from prison on the Mediterranean island of Elba and raised an army again, overthrowing the restored monarch Louis XVIII. Defeated at

Waterloo by the British, he was once again exiled, this time to St. Helena in the southern Atlantic Ocean.

By 1815, other European powers had managed to halt his expansion; at the CONGRESS OF VIENNA in 1815, European powers including the unified Prussia, the AUSTRO-HUNGARIAN EMPIRE, RUSSIA, and BRITAIN agreed on a BALANCE OF POWER in Europe. Despite Napoleon's brief reemergence, the Congress of Vienna was the first real international peace conference and set the precedent for European political organization.

Latin American countries joined Haiti and the United States in revolution against colonial European powers. Inspired by the American and French Revolutions, SIMÓN BOLIVAR led or influenced independence movements in VENEZUELA, COLOMBIA (including what is today PANAMA), ECUADOR, PERU, and BOLIVIA in the early part of the nineteenth century.

Figure 2.11. Gran Colombia

European Division

The nineteenth century was a period of change and conflict, and the roots of the major twentieth century conflicts—world war and decolonization—are found in it. Modern European social and political structures and norms, including NATIONALISM and the NATION-STATE, would begin to emerge. Economic theories based in the Industrial Revolution like SOCIALISM and eventually COMMUNISM gained traction with the stark class divisions brought on by URBANIZATION and industry.

Following the Napoleonic Wars, Prussia had come to dominate the German-speaking states that once comprised the Holy Roman Empire. Prussia, a distinct kingdom within the Holy Roman Empire since the thirteenth century, had become a powerful Central European state by the eighteenth century. It had become the main rival of Austria for influence in the Germanic lands of Central Europe. By the nineteenth century and due in part to emphasis on military prowess, Prussia became an important military power and a key ally in the efforts against Napoleon.

Prussia had a particular rivalry with France, having lost several key territories during the Napoleonic Wars. In 1870, the militarily powerful kingdom went to war against France in the FRANCO-PRUSSIAN WAR, during which Prussia took control of ALSACE-LORRAINE, mineral rich and later essential for industrial development.

Following the Franco-Prussian War, OTTO VON BISMARCK unified those linguistically and culturally German states of Central Europe. Prussian power had been growing, fueled by NATIONALISM and the NATION-STATE, or the idea that individuals with shared experience (including ethnicity, language, religion, and cultural practices) should be unified under one government. In 1871, the GERMAN EMPIRE became a united state. Bismarck encouraged economic cooperation, instituted army reforms and, perhaps most importantly, created an image of Prussia as a defender of German culture and nationhood, portraying other European states in opposition to that.

Nationalism also led to ITALIAN UNIFICATION. As a region of small independent states, toward the end of the eighteenth century Italy was occupied by France and then Austria. Later invaded and occupied by Napoleon, the Italian peninsula was divided into three regions. Napoleonic concepts of nationalism, freedom, equality, and justice under the law spread throughout the peninsula, and what was left of feudalism faded.

Despite re-fragmentation throughout the nineteenth century following the fall of Napoleon, a secret movement for reorganization—the *RISORGIMENTO*—began working toward Italian unification. Following the 1859 FRANCO-AUSTRIAN WAR, Austria's loss of territorial control in northern Italy allowed Italian states to unite via elections. GIUSEPPE GARIBALDI led the Northern Italian overthrow of Southern Italian monarchies, uniting the Peninsula with the exception of Rome and Venice. The Kingdom of Italy was declared in 1861, under VICTOR EMMANUEL II. Thanks to an Italian alliance with Prussia during the AUSTRO-PRUSSIAN WAR in 1866, in which Austria lost even more territory, Italy took control of Venice. Finally, the Kingdom of Italy entered Rome and incorporated that city and the Papal States during the Franco-Prussian War.

Conflict in the Balkans

Farther east, as European kingdoms and empires consolidated their power, the Ottoman Empire was in decline. The Ottoman Empire had long been a major force in Europe, controlling the bulk of the Balkans. However, the empire had lost land in Europe to the Austrians and in Africa to British and French imperialists. In the Balkans, rebellion among small nations supported by European puppet masters would put an end to Ottoman power in Europe for good.

Despite previous conflict between some of these powers, deeper rivalries throughout the continent inspired Russia, Germany, and Austria-Hungary to form the THREE EMPERORS' LEAGUE in 1873. If one country went to war, the others would remain neutral, and the powers would consult each other on matters of war. However, the FIRST BALKAN CRISIS in 1874 would put an end to this alliance.

In 1874, Bosnia Herzegovina rebelled against Ottoman rule. Christian peasants in Herzegovina were unwilling to submit to Muslim landlords; neither regional Christians nor Bosnian Muslims were willing any longer to submit to rule by the ethnically-different Turks. Thus began the First Balkan Crisis.

Two years later, the Ottoman autonomous principality of Serbia, joined by Montenegro, rebelled in support of Bosnia. Having come under Russian influence thanks to PAN-SLAVISM—the concept that Slavic ethnic groups throughout Eastern and Southeastern Europe should embrace their Slavic heritage and turn toward Russia for support—Serbian rebellion attracted Russian attention. When the Ottoman SULTAN HAMID II refused to institute reforms to protect Balkan Christians, Russia declared war.

The RUSSO-TURKISH WAR ended in 1878 with the TREATY OF SAN STEFANO, which favored Russian territorial gains. However, Austro-Hungarian and British objections to the treaty, which threatened their influence in the region, led to the 1878 CONGRESS OF BERLIN, hosted by Otto von Bismarck. Unfortunately for Russia, which was the militarily and financially weaker power, Britain and Austria-Hungary changed the outcome of the war with the TREATY OF BERLIN. While the independence of Serbia and Montenegro was decided, Russia lost influence in Bulgaria as well as territorial gains in Asia. These insults would not be forgotten.

Germany and Austria-Hungary secretly formed the Dual Alliance to respond to fears of pan-Slavism, given developments in the Balkans. In 1882, Italy asked these countries for assistance against France, which had upset Italian imperial ambition in North Africa; thus formed the Triple Alliance, a secret political and military alliance. The 1885 Second Balkan Crisis, in which Bulgaria declared unification and independence, violating the Treaty of Berlin and Russian interests, further threatened stability in the Balkans and among the great powers. Serbia went to war against Bulgaria, requiring Austro-Hungarian support.

Eventually tension between Russia and Austria-Hungary—which was supported by Germany—led to the breakdown of Russian relationships with those countries, and improvement in Russian relations with Great Britain and France. In 1894, Russia and France became allies. This alliance would culminate in the 1907 TRIPLE ENTENTE, setting the stage for the system of alliances at the heart of the First World War.

> List some important European alliances in the nineteenth century.

Continued European involvement in the Balkans accelerated the ongoing loss of Ottoman influence there due to phenomena like nationalism, ethnocentrism (Pan-Slavism), military and political power, and religious influence. The small Balkan nations were empowered to continue rebellion against Ottoman rule, and European powers proceeded into the area.

In 1908, Austria-Hungary annexed Bosnia-Herzegovina, disregarding Russian objections. Russia helped form the BALKAN LEAGUE, comprised of Serbia, Montenegro, Greece, and Bulgaria, which went to war with the Ottomans in the 1912 FIRST BALKAN WAR. The Ottomans were defeated and lost nearly all their European possessions; however, disagreement over the division of land led to the SECOND BALKAN WAR the following year between Bulgaria and a Serbian-Greek alliance. Serbia wanted to keep Albanian territory, which Austria-Hungary insisted remain independent; Bulgaria wanted control over more land in Macedonia (which had come mainly under Greek and Serbian rule). Eventually, this instability would lead to the First World War which was triggered by the assassination of the Austro-Hungarian **ARCHDUKE FRANZ FERDINAND** by the Serbian nationalist **GAVRILO PRINCIP** in Bosnia-Herzegovina in 1914.

Imperialism

As colonialism in the fifteenth and sixteenth centuries had been driven by mercantilism, conquest, and Christian conversion, so was seventeenth, eighteenth and nineteenth century imperialism driven by capitalism, European competition, and conceptions of racial superiority.

Britain and France, historic rivals on the European continent, were also at odds colonizing North America and in overseas trade. During the **SEVEN YEARS' WAR** (1756 – 1763), considered by many historians to be the first truly global conflict, these two powers fought in Europe and in overseas colonies and interests in North America and Asia.

As discussed previously, while the Seven Years' War in Europe was the result of tangled alliances between Britain, Prussia, and Hanover on one side, and France, Austria, Sweden, and Russia on the other, that war's extension into the imperial realm made it a global conflict.

In North America, Britain and France had explored the region and controlled tremendous amounts of territory in what later would become Canada and the United States. Britain controlled the wealthy **THIRTEEN COLONIES** on the Atlantic coast, which were rich in tobacco, rice, vegetables, and other crops. It also controlled major ports like Boston, New York, and Philadelphia.

Meanwhile, the French controlled **QUEBEC** and northeastern territories rich in natural resources like beaver pelts, valuable in Europe for their water-repellant properties. They also controlled the ports of Montreal and Quebec City, on the St. Lawrence River (leading to the Atlantic Ocean). France also controlled considerable strategic territory in the Midwestern portions of the continent, which allowed products from the interior to reach the oceans. These routes included much of the **GREAT LAKES** region including the Detroit River (leading to the St. Lawrence and the Atlantic Ocean), and the Mississippi River and the Port of New Orleans (leading to the Gulf of Mexico).

The **FRENCH AND INDIAN WAR**, as the Seven Years' War is called in North America, resulted in net gains for Britain. France formed an important alliance with the powerful Algonquin in the northeast, while Britain was allied with the Iroquois. Thanks to strong military leaders like **GEORGE WASHINGTON**, Britain eventually took control of French Canada. However, financially exhausted from the costly conflict in Europe, Britain ceded control of the Northwest Territories (Michigan, Ohio, Indiana) to various tribes in the **TREATY OF PARIS IN 1763** (agreements later not honored by the United States). In addition, the financial and military strain suffered by Britain in the Seven Years' War made it particularly vulnerable to later rebellion in the Colonies, helping the Americans win the Revolutionary War there.

According to Pitt the Elder's plan, Britain went to war with France in Asia as well. In India, with the decline of the **MUGHAL EMPIRE** and the rising power of colonial companies specializing in exporting valuable resources like spices and tea, smaller Indian kingdoms were forming alliances with those increasingly influential corporations.

By the mid-eighteenth century, violence broke out between the **BRITISH EAST INDIA COMPANY** and the **FRENCH EAST INDIA COMPANY** and their allies among the small Indian states in a series of wars known as the **CARNATIC WARS** (1746 – 1763). With the end of the Seven Years' War, the Treaty of Paris established British dominance in the Subcontinent as France was allowed some trading posts in the region, but forced to recognize British power there. By 1803, British interests effectively took control of the Subcontinent and the Mughals were pushed to the north.

The Netherlands was already coming to dominate Indonesia (at the time, the Dutch East Indies) thanks to similar actions by the **DUTCH EAST INDIA COMPANY**.

Despite its loss of the Thirteen Colonies, at the dawn of the nineteenth century Britain retained control of Canada, rich in natural resources like beaver pelts and timber. In addition, it controlled the resource-rich and strategically important Indian Subcontinent. Britain would become the strongest naval power in the world and continue to expand its empire, especially in the search for new markets for its manufactured goods to support its industrial economy.

In 1837, **QUEEN VICTORIA** ascended to the throne. During her reign (1837 – 1901) the British Empire would expand to heretofore unseen lengths. In 1788, Britain had begun sending convicts to the penal colony of **AUSTRALIA**; however in 1851, when gold was discovered there British subjects began to voluntarily settle Australia and the Pacific. In 1857, the **INDIAN MUTINY** against private British troops controlled by the East India Company caused the British government to intervene, sending in military and eventually resulting in Victoria taking the title of **EMPRESS OF INDIA**, cementing the imperial nature of government and the **RAJ** (imperial administration).

In 1877, the British annexed **SOUTH AFRICA**; following the Boer Wars, Britain would retain control of diamond- and gold-rich South Africa (see below). The imperialist **CECIL RHODES** and his company, the British South Africa Company (BSAC), were chartered by Victoria to explore north from South Africa to mine the land. This was despite of conflicting European claims to the land, despite claims by the **AFRIKAANERS**, (see below) and despite the residence of the **MATABELE**, who had lived there for centuries. Rhodes and the BSAC forcefully took over Northern Rhodesia (**ZAMBIA**), Rhodesia (**ZIMBABWE**), Nyasaland (**MALAWI**) and Bechuanaland (**BOTSWANA**) using treaties, diplomacy, and violence. These territories were under English rule.

In East Africa, the British explorer **DAVID LIVINGSTONE** had been working in Kenya; the government had influence over the Sultan of Zanzibar. However, secret German agreements with coastal leaders and the establishment of the German colony of **TANGANYIKA** forced the British into more activity in the region. In an agreement with the Germans, the British took control over what would become **KENYA** and **UGANDA**, while Germany maintained Tanganyika. Borders were drawn without regard for the **KIKUYU**, **MASAI**, **LUO**, and other tribes living in the area.

The concept of the *WHITE MAN'S BURDEN*, wherein white Europeans were "obligated" to bring their "superior" culture to other civilizations around the globe, also drove imperialist adventure, popularizing it at home in Britain and elsewhere in Europe.

Despite its small size, **BELGIUM** controlled the **CONGO**, along with its vast resources in Central Africa. Coming into conflict with Rhodes at its southern edges, the Belgian Congo, which reached its heights under **KING LEOPOLD II**, was rich in rubber, timber, minerals, and diamonds. Furthermore, this territory was strategically important; controlling the Congo meant controlling the Congo River basin, allowing for the extraction of materials from the interior to the Atlantic Coast.

List some of the European powers' justifications for imperialism.

To gain access to closed **CHINESE** markets, Britain forced China to buy Indian opium; the **OPIUM WARS** ended with the **TREATY OF NANKING (1842)**, signed between the British and the increasingly impotent Qing government. As a consequence, China lost great power to Britain and later, other European countries, which gained **SPHERES OF INFLUENCE**, or areas of China they effectively controlled, and **EXTRATERRITORIALITY**, or privileges in which their citizens were not subject to Chinese law.

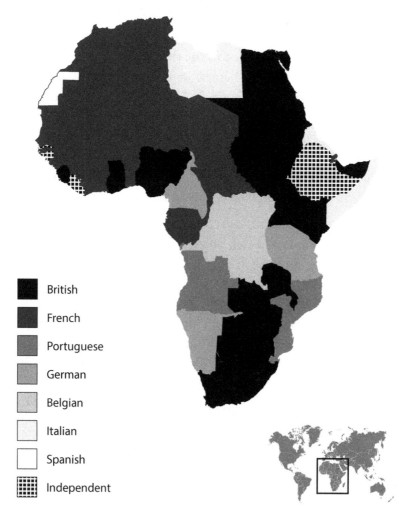

British
French
Portuguese
German
Belgian
Italian
Spanish
Independent

Figure 2.12. Imperial Africa

Discontent with the Qing Dynasty was growing as Chinese people perceived that their country was coming under control of European imperialists, even though nominally Chinese leadership still governed. Coupled with economic hardship and huge casualties in the Opium Wars and in the **SINO-JAPANESE WAR OF 1896** (see below), a violent uprising was inevitable. In 1900, the **BOXER REBELLION**, an uprising led by a Chinese society against the Emperor, was only put down with Western (including American) help. The Qing were humiliated further by being forced to pay the West enormous reparations for their assistance; meanwhile, living conditions for Chinese people continued to deteriorate.

The European powers were immersed in what became known as the *SCRAMBLE FOR AFRICA*; the industrial economies of Europe would profit from the natural resources abundant in that continent, and the white man's burden continued to fuel colonization. At the **1884 BERLIN CONFERENCE**, control over Africa was divided among European powers (Africans were not consulted in this process). Following the **BOER WAR (1899-1902)** between Afrikaaners of Dutch origin and the English, Britain officially gained control of South Africa, and whites would rule the country until the end of **APARTHEID** in the early 1990s. France controlled West Africa and eventually North Africa, especially Algeria, Mali, Niger, Chad, Cameroon, and what has become the Republic of the Congo (not to be confused with Belgian Congo, now the Democratic Republic of the Congo).

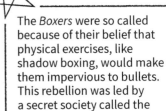

The *Boxers* were so called because of their belief that physical exercises, like shadow boxing, would make them impervious to bullets. This rebellion was led by a secret society called the *Yihequan*, or *The Society of Righteous and Harmonious Fists*.

However, not all non-European countries fell to European imperialism. During the **MEIJI RESTORATION** in Japan in 1868, the Emperor Meiji promoted modernization of technology, especially the military. Japan proved itself a world power when it defeated Russia in the **RUSSO-JAPANESE WAR** in 1905, and would play a central role in twentieth century conflict.

Industrial Revolution

Throughout this entire period, raw goods from the Americas fueled European economic growth and development, leading to the **INDUSTRIAL REVOLUTION** in the nineteenth century. This economic revolution began with textile production in Britain, fueled by cotton from its overseas territories in North America, and later India and Egypt. The first factories were in Manchester, where **URBANIZATION** began as poor people from rural areas flocked to cities in search of higher-paying unskilled jobs in factories.

Early industrial technology sped up the harvesting and transport of crops and their conversion to textiles. This accelerated manufacturing was based on **CAPITALISM**, the *LAISSEZ-FAIRE* (or **FREE MARKET**) theory developed by **ADAM SMITH**, who believed that an *INVISIBLE HAND* should guide the marketplace—that government should stay out of the economy regardless of abuses, as the economy would eventually automatically correct for inequalities, price problems, and any other problematic issues.

Technology like the **SPINNING JENNY** and **FLYING SHUTTLE** exponentially increased the amount of cotton that workers could process into yarn and thread. The **STEAM ENGINE** efficiently powered mills and ironworks; factories no longer had to be built near running water to access power. Advances in **IRON** technology allowed for stronger machinery and would support the later **SECOND INDUSTRIAL REVOLUTION** in the late nineteenth and early twentieth century, which was based on **HEAVY INDUSTRY**, railroads, and weapons.

To access the raw materials needed to produce manufactured goods, Britain and other industrializing countries in Western Europe needed resources—hence the drive for imperialism as discussed above. Cotton was harvested in India and Egypt for textile mills, minerals mined in South Africa and the Congo to power metallurgy. Furthermore, as industrialization and urbanization led to the development of early middle classes in Europe and North America, imports of luxury goods like tea, spices, silk, precious metals, and other items from Asia increased to meet consumer demand. Colonial powers also gained by selling manufactured goods back to the colonies from which they had harvested raw materials in the first place, for considerable profit.

Largely unbridled capitalism had led to the conditions of the early Industrial Revolution; workers suffered from abusive treatment, overly long hours, low wages or none at all, and unsafe conditions, including pollution. The German philosophers **KARL MARX** and **FRIEDRICH ENGELS**, horrified by conditions suffered by industrial workers, developed **SOCIALISM**, the philosophy that workers, or the **PROLETARIAT**, should own the means of production and reap the profits, rather than the **BOURGEOISIE**, who had no interest in the rights of the workers at the expense of profit and who did not experience the same conditions.

In his work *DAS KAPITAL*, Marx argued for the abolition of the class system, wages, and private property. He argued instead for collective ownership of both the means of production and products, with equal distribution of income to satisfy the needs of all. Later, Marx and Engels wrote the *COMMUNIST MANIFESTO*, a pamphlet laying out their ideas and calling for revolution. It inspired the formation of socialist groups worldwide.

The Communist Manifesto contained the famous words *Workers of the world, unite!*

A different version of socialism would later help Russia become a major world power. The Russian intellectuals **VLADIMIR LENIN** and **LEON TROTSKY** would take Marx and Engels' theories further, developing **MARXISM-LENINISM**. They embraced socialist ideals and believed in revolution; however they felt that **COMMUNISM** could not be maintained under a democratic governing structure. Lenin supported dictatorship, more precisely the *DICTATORSHIP OF THE PROLETARIAT*, paving the way for the political and economic organization of the Soviet Union.

EXAMPLES

1) The Treaty of Westphalia
   A. laid out the final borders of Europe, setting the stage for modern foreign policy.
   B. established the notion of state sovereignty, in which states recognized each other as independent and agreed not to interfere in each other's affairs.
   C. gave the Catholic Church more power in the affairs of Catholic-majority countries.
   D. established the notion of the nation-state, in which culturally and ethnically similar groups would control their own territory as sovereign countries.
   E. Officially recognized the existence of different legitimate sects of Christianity in different countries, laying the groundwork for religious tolerance.

Answers:

A. Incorrect. Europe's modern borders have only very recently been drawn, and they may continue to change over the course of history.

B. **Correct.** The Treaty of Westphalia was based on state sovereignty and non-interference, the core principles of modern international relations.

C. Incorrect. The political power of the Church had been weakening; the principles of state sovereignty weakened it further.

D. Incorrect. The notion of the nation-state would more fully develop in the nineteenth century and was not established by a treaty.

E. Incorrect. The Treaty of Westphalia did not address the nature of religion.

2) An important factor leading to the French Revolution was

   A. the corruption of Louis XIV.

   B. the strong organization of the Estates-General.

   C. support from the United States of America.

   D. the anti-monarchical philosophies of Enlightenment thinkers like Rousseau and Voltaire.

   E. increasing tensions between the bourgeoisie and the peasantry.

Answers:

A. Incorrect. Louis XIV strengthened the monarchy several decades before the revolution.

B. Incorrect. The Estates-General was weak and poorly organized, actually facilitating revolution.

C. Incorrect. While there was support for the revolutionaries, the United States maintained a cautious stance on the revolution given its hesitance to become embroiled in European conflict.

D. **Correct.** Enlightenment thinking fueled the Age of Revolutions, and revolutionary French thinkers and writers like Rousseau, Voltaire, and others influenced revolutionary French leaders.

E. Incorrect. The bourgeoisie and the peasantry both chafed under the rule of the nobility and elite clergy.

3) How did Pan-Slavism affect the crises in the Balkans?

   A. Pan-Slavism led Russia to directly intervene militarily throughout the nineteenth century in the Balkans, leading to violent conflict.

   B. Pan-Slavism generally ensured Russian support for Slavic ethnic groups in the Balkans, which contributed to ongoing tensions there already fueled by competing European and Ottoman interests and diverse nationalities.

   C. Russian interests in Slavic groups in the Balkans strengthened its alliance with Turkey.

   D. Pan-Slavism did not have a major effect on the Balkans, as the major Slavic cultures are located farther north in Europe.

   E. Pan-slavism increased Christian leadership in the Ottoman Empire, destablizing Muslim traditions.

Answers:

A. Incorrect. While Russia was very much involved in the Balkans (and continues to be), it was not always necessarily involved in a military capacity.

B. Correct. Russian support for Slavic ethnic groups in the Balkans—especially Serbia—helped fuel nineteenth century tensions in the region (and continued to do so throughout the twentieth century).

C. Incorrect. Russia and Ottoman Turkey were not allies; in fact they went to war in the Russo-Turkish War after the First Balkan Crisis.

D. Incorrect. Pan-Slavism had a tremendous effect on the dynamics of the nineteenth century Balkans, as several Slavic ethnic groups live in Southeast Europe and had alliances with Russia.

E. Incorrect. While Pan-Slavism did relate to a divide between Christians and Muslims, Christians did not gain greater power in the government of the Ottoman Empire.

4) Which of the following is NOT a way that the white man's burden influenced imperialism?

A. It inspired Europeans to settle overseas in order to improve what they believed to be "backward" places.

B. Europeans believed in imperialism as in the best interest of native people, who would benefit from adopting European languages and cultural practices.

C. Europeans believed it burdensome to be forced to tutor non-Europeans in their languages and customs.

D. Many Europeans supported the construction of schools for colonial subjects and even the development of scholarships for them to study in Europe.

E. Europeans created colonial governments modeled in theory after those in Europe but gave native populations the same rights as children in Europe.

Answers:

A. Incorrect. White Europeans approved of settled colonies; part of the rationale of settlement was the idea that a white European presence was helping "civilize" the area.

B. Incorrect. According to the idea of the white man's burden, the lives of non-Europeans would improve by adopting European customs and traditions.

C. Correct. The idea of the white man's burden was not meant to suggest a literal burden; it was a paternalistic concept of responsibility used to justify imperial dominance.

D. Incorrect. Schools were built throughout many colonies (though not all were of high quality, nor were they accessible to all people); furthermore, many colonial subjects moved to England, France, Belgium, and elsewhere in Europe to study.

E. Incorrect. Colonial governments excluded native individuals from participation and severely limited their rights.

5) Marx and Engels believed

A. that the proletariat must control the means of production to ensure a wageless, classless society to meet the needs of all equitably.

B. in the dictatorship of the proletariat, in which the workers would control the means of production in a non-democratic society.

C. that an organized revolution directed by a small group of leaders was necessary to bring about social change and a socialist society.

D. that the bourgeoisie would willingly give up control of the means of production to the proletariat.

E. that industrialization fostered inequity and an agrarian society could be truly classless.

Answers:

A. **Correct.** Marx and Engels believed in abolishing wages and the class structure in exchange for a socialist society where the means of production were commonly held and in which income was equally distributed.

B. Incorrect. The dictatorship of the proletariat was a Leninist concept.

C. Incorrect. While Marx and Engels believed in revolution, they believed that the workers would be able to bring it about; Lenin would later argue that the proletariat needed direction in revolution.

D. Incorrect. Marx and Engels believed that a socialist society could only be achieved through revolution.

E. Incorrect. Marx and Engels believed control of the means of production was the key issue, not the basis of the economy.

Global Conflicts

Pre-Revolutionary Russia

Russia had gone to war with Japan in 1904 to secure access to the Pacific and secure its interests in Asia. **Tsar Nicholas II**, unpopular at home, also believed that a victory would improve his security as a ruler. Japan, concerned about losing influence in Korea and seeking influence in China, attacked Russia; the **Russo-Japanese War** quickly ended in 1905 due to superior Japanese military technology, including naval technology, training, and leadership.

Russia's loss to Japan in the 1905 Russo-Japanese War was just another example of its difference from other European powers. While technically a European country, Russia had been slow to industrialize, due in part to its size and terrain. A largely agrarian country at the turn of the century, **serfdom**, the practice of "tying" peasants to the land and the last vestiges of feudalism, had only been abolished in 1861. Most Russians were still poor, rural farmers, and industrialization brought wretched conditions to workers in the cities. Russia also continued to have an absolute monarchy, unlike many European powers whose governments had shifted during the Age of Revolution.

Tsar Nicholas faced dissent at home due to the humiliating defeat by the Japanese; discontent was fueled by longer-term economic hardship in the face of a strengthening European industrial economy and limited freedoms in comparison to those enjoyed elsewhere in Europe. Unlawful trade unions appeared; workers began striking; and peasants rose up in protest of oppressive taxation.

Still, many Russians blamed the Tsar's advisors and minor officials for conditions, believing that the Tsar himself would act to improve conditions for Russians. These ideas were shattered in 1905 when a peaceful protest of working conditions in St. Petersburg ended in a bloody massacre of civilians by the Tsar's troops. **BLOODY SUNDAY**, as the event came to be called, resulted in the **REVOLUTION OF 1905**, during which the Tsar temporarily lost control of Russia and was discredited.

Following the Revolution of 1905, the Tsar made some reforms in Russia, including the establishment of a **DUMA**, or Parliament. However, economic hardship and social discontent continued in Russia.

While not directly involved with the failed Revolution of 1905, the Marxist Social Democrats, made up of the **BOLSHEVIKS**, led by **LENIN**, and the **MENSHEVIKS**, would gain power. They would eventually take over the country in 1917.

World War I

Instability in the Balkans and increasing tensions in Europe culminated with the assassination of the Austro-Hungarian Archduke **FRANZ FERDINAND** by the Serbian nationalist **GAVRILO PRINCIP** in Sarajevo on June 28, 1914. In protest of continuing Austro-Hungarian control over Serbia, Princip's action kicked off the **SYSTEM OF ALLIANCES** that had been in place among European powers.

Austria-Hungary declared war on Serbia, and Russia came to Serbia's aid. As an ally of Austria-Hungary as part of the Triple Alliance, Germany declared war on Russia. Russia's ally France prepared for war; as Germany traversed Belgium to invade France, Belgium pleaded for aid from other European countries and so Britain declared war on Germany.

Germany had been emphasizing military growth since the consolidation and militarization of the empire under Bismarck in the mid-nineteenth century. Now, under **KAISER WILHELM II**, who sought expanded territories in Europe and overseas for Germany (including the potential capture of overseas British and French colonies), Germany was a militarized state an important European power in its own right.

Figure 2.13. WWI Alliances

Wilhelm, the grandson of Frederick II on his father's side and of Queen Victoria, took over the German Empire in 1888. He had focused on improving naval power and expanding German territory overseas. Despite his connections to Britain, Germany's threat to British overseas power brought the war beyond Europe to Africa and Asia. In TOGO, Britain and France took over an important German communications point. In CHINA, Japan allied with Britain and France, taking control of the German settlement of Tsingtao and of German colonies in the PACIFIC ISLANDS.

Britain's imperial power allowed it to call on troops from all over the globe—Indians, Canadians, Australians, South Africans, and New Zealanders all fought in Europe. France, too, imported colonial fighters from North Africa.

The first international war to use industrialized weaponry, WWI was called "the Great War" because battle on such a scale had never before been seen.

In Europe, the 1914 BATTLE OF THE MARNE between Germany and French and British forces defending France resulted in trench warfare that would continue for years, marking the Western Front. At GALLIPOLI in 1915, Australian and New Zealander troops fought the OTTOMAN EMPIRE, allies of Germany, near Istanbul. Later that year, a German submarine, or U-BOAT, sank the *LUSITANIA*, a passenger ship in the Atlantic, killing many American civilians. In 1916, the BATTLE OF VERDUN, the longest battle of the war, ended in the failure of the Germans to defeat the French army. In 1916, the British navy pushed back the German navy in the BATTLE OF JUTLAND; despite heavy losses, Britain was able to ensure that German naval power was diminished for the rest of the war. On July 1, 1916, the BATTLE OF THE SOMME became part of an allied effort to repel Germany using artillery to end the stalemate on the Western Front; after four months, however, the front moved only five miles.

Finally, in 1917, the United States caught the ZIMMERMAN TELEGRAM, in which Germany secretly proposed an alliance with Mexico to attack the US This finally spurred US intervention in the war; despite Russian withdrawal after the Bolshevik Revolution in October 1917, Germany was forced to surrender in the face of invasion by the US-supported allies.

According to the SCHLIEFFEN PLAN, Germany had planned to fight a war on two fronts against both Russia and France. However, Russia's unexpectedly rapid mobilization stretched the German army too thin on the Eastern Front, while it became bogged down in TRENCH WARFARE on the Western Front against the British, French, and later the Americans. Germany lost the war and was punished with the harsh TREATY OF VERSAILLES, which held it accountable for the entirety of the war. The Treaty brought economic hardship on the country by forcing it to pay REPARATIONS. Wilhelm was forced to abdicate and never again regained power in Germany. German military failure and consequent economic collapse due to the Treaty of Versailles and later worldwide economic depression set the stage for the rise of fascism and Adolf Hitler.

The Treaty also created the LEAGUE OF NATIONS, an international organization designed to prevent future outbreaks of international war; however, it was largely toothless, especially because the powerful United States did not join.

Change in the Middle East

The end of WWI also marked the end of the Ottoman Empire, which was officially dissolved in 1923. From the end of the nineteenth century, the British had been increasing their influence throughout Ottoman territory in Egypt and the Persian Gulf, seeking control over the Suez Canal and petroleum resources in the Gulf. The Ottomans had already lost their North African provinces to France in the mid-nineteenth century.

In 1908, the **YOUNG TURKS**, a military government, had effectively taken over the empire in an effort to modernize it. They were especially concerned with nationalism and promoting *Turkishness*, a focus on Turkish ethnicity and culture, throughout the diverse empire. An ally of Germany, the Ottoman Empire had been defeated in the war; tremendous losses led to the collapse of many Ottoman institutions. Poor organization and refugee movements led to starvation and chaos throughout the region.

> In 1915, the Ottoman Empire launched a genocide against the Christian Armenian people, part of a campaign to control ethnic groups it believed threatened the Turkish nature of the empire. An estimated 1.5 million Armenians were forcibly removed from their homes and killed. To this day, the Turkish government denies the Armenian Genocide.

In 1916, France and Britain concluded the **SYKES-PICOT AGREEMENT**, which secretly planned for the Middle East following the defeat of the Ottoman Empire. The Agreement divided up the region now considered the Middle East into spheres of influence to be controlled by each power; Palestine would be governed internationally. In 1917, the secret **BALFOUR DECLARATION** promised the Jews an independent state in Palestine, but Western powers did not honor this agreement; in fact it conflicted directly with the Sykes-Picot Agreement. The state of Israel was not established until 1948.

At the end of the war the area was indeed divided into **MANDATES**, areas nominally independent but effectively controlled by Britain and France. The borders drawn are essentially those national borders that divide the Middle East today. After the First World War, the nationalist **MUSTAFA ATATURK**, one of the Young Turks who pushed a secular, nationalist agenda, kept European powers out of Anatolia and abolished the Caliphate in 1924, establishing modern Turkey.

After the dissolution of the Ottoman Empire, the future of the Middle East was uncertain. Despite its weaknesses, the Ottoman Empire had been the symbolic center of Islam, controlling Mecca and Medina. The Ottoman sultan held the title of Caliph, or the one entrusted with the leadership of those two holy cities. With the region broken up into European-controlled protectorates and an independent, nationalist, secular Turkey turned toward Europe, the social and political fabric of the region was becoming undone.

There was no more Caliph. Refugees and migrants had traveled throughout the Ottoman Empire over the course of the war, stopping in areas that were now suddenly restricted by international borders from their places of origin. People lacked identification papers. Ethnic and religious groups were divided by what would become the borders of the modern Middle East.

France and Britain backed different political factions in their mandates. While nominally autonomous, Egypt and its ruler, **KING FUAD**, were close allies of the British, having essentially been under their control. At the same time, **HUSAYN IBN ALI (KING HUSSEIN)**, the Sherif of Mecca, claimed the title of Caliph, but was eventually driven out of Mecca and granted the title of king of Jordan by the British (his family controls the monarchy to this day). The rest of the Arabian Peninsula, where oil had not yet been discovered, was taken by the **SAUDIS**, a tribe from the desert which followed an extreme form of Islam, the **WAHHABI MOVEMENT**; King Saud would eventually conquer Mecca and Medina but never take the title of Caliph.

The roots of two competing ideologies, **PAN-ARABISM** and **ISLAMISM**, developed in this context. According to Pan-Arabism, Arabs and Arabic speakers should be aligned regardless of international borders. Similar to Pan-Slavism, Pan-Arabism eventually became an international movement espousing Arab unity in response to European and US influence and presence later in the twentieth century.

Islamism began as a social and political movement. The **MUSLIM BROTHERHOOD** was established in Egypt in the 1920s, filling social roles that the state had abandoned or could not fill. Eventually taking a political role, the Muslim Brotherhood's model later inspired groups like Hamas and Hezbollah.

Russian Revolution

By 1917, Russia was suffering from widespread food shortages and economic crisis; morale was low due to conscription and as the military suffered enormous losses and humiliating defeats under the command of Nicholas II. During WWI, this combination of failures at home and on the front only added to widespread dissatisfaction with the rule of the Tsar. An enormous strike in Petrograd in January 1917 commemorating Bloody Sunday ended in revolt; soldiers refused to fire on protesters and the people formed the elected **PETROGRAD SOVIET** (Council) instead in the **FEBRUARY REVOLUTION**. The Tsar was forced to abdicate; the revolutionary movement resulted in the fall of his family, the Romanovs.

A weak provisional government was formed until elections could be held; however, it was widely regarded as working in the interests of the elite, making unpopular decisions like continuing to engage in WWI and putting off land reform. Meanwhile, other Soviets formed beyond Petrograd. The Provisional Government was ineffective in solving economic problems; however, the elected Soviets seemed to better represent the interests of the workers and peasants who suffered the most, and so they became more powerful. At the same time, the Soviets appealed to discontented soldiers fighting in the unpopular war.

The Bolsheviks, unlike the Mensheviks, believed that revolution must be planned and instigated at the right moment, not a phenomenon meant to occur naturally. The Bolsheviks, led by Lenin, consequently were not involved in the February Revolution. Lenin believed that revolution must be planned and that the proletariat needed direction in beginning and pursuing a revolution. However, later in 1917, the Bolsheviks had become a stronger force, and Lenin believed that the time was right to trigger revolution in Russia.

Lenin and the Bolsheviks proposed that power be concentrated in the Soviets, not in the Duma; that Russia would make peace and withdraw from European hostilities; that land would be redistributed among the peasants; and that economic crises in the cities would be solved. Lenin's plan was to take control of the Petrograd Soviet, of which **LEON TROTSKY** had become chairman. In the **OCTOBER REVOLUTION** Lenin, Trotsky, and the Bolsheviks took control of Russia, defeating the Provisional Government in a coup.

In 1918, despite withdrawal from WWI, the **Russian Civil War** was underway; the **White Armies**, former supporters of the Tsar, were in conflict with the Bolshevik **Red Army**. During the war, the communists consolidated their power by nationalizing industry, developing and distributing propaganda portraying themselves as the defenders of Russia against imperialism, and forcefully eliminating dissent. For many, it was more appealing to fight for a new Russia with hope for an improved standard of living than to return to the old times under the Tsar; furthermore, many Russians feared the specter of imperialism or interference by foreign powers. By 1921, the Bolsheviks were victorious and formed the **Soviet Union** or **Union of Soviet Socialist Republics (USSR)**.

Following Lenin's death in 1924, Trotsky and the Secretary of the Communist Party, **Josef Stalin**, struggled for power. Stalin ultimately outmaneuvered Trotsky, who was exiled and assassinated. Under Stalin's totalitarian dictatorship, the USSR became socially and politically repressive; the Communist Party and the military underwent **purges** where any persons who were a potential threat to Stalin's power were imprisoned or executed. This paranoia and oppression extended to the general population: Russians suffered under the **Great Terror** throughout the 1920s. Any hint of dissent was to be reported to the secret police—the **NKVD**—and usually resulted in imprisonment for life.

In the 1920s, around twenty million Russians were sent to the gulags, or prison labor camps, usually in Siberia, thousands of miles from their homes. Millions died.

Stalin also enforced **Russification** policies, persecuting ethnic groups. People throughout the USSR were forced to speak Russian and limit or hide their own cultural practices. Religious practices were restricted or forbidden.

In 1931, Stalin enforced the **collectivization** of land and agriculture in an attempt to consolidate control over the countryside and improve food security. He had the *kulaks*, or landowning peasants, sent to the *gulags*, enabling the government to confiscate their land. By 1939, most farming and land was controlled by the government, and most peasants lived on collective land. Collectivizing the farms enabled Stalin to encourage more peasants to leave the country and become industrial workers, to produce agricultural surpluses to sell overseas, and to eliminate the *kulaks*. However, systemic disorganization in the 1920s and early 1930s did result in famine and food shortages.

As part of modernizing Russia, Stalin focused on accelerating industrial development. Targeting heavy industry, these **Five Year Plans** increased production in industrial materials and staples like electricity, petroleum, coal, and iron; they also resulted in the construction of major infrastructure throughout the country from 1929 – 1938. These developments provided opportunities for women, but conditions for the workers were dismal. The USSR quickly became an industrial power, but at the expense of millions of Russians, Ukrainians, and other groups who lost their lives in purges, forced labor camps, and famine.

Change in East Asia

Following its victory in the Russo-Japanese War, Japan had become more visible internationally in the early part of the twentieth century. That country had undergone rapid modernization after being closed off from 1600 until the mid-nineteenth century under the TOKUGAWA SHOGUNATE; now, recognized as a military power for defeating Russia, Japan had joined a world focused on industry and imperialism.

Japan, having already embraced industrialization and modern militarization, turned towards imperialism throughout Asia. From 1894 – 1895, Japan had fought the FIRST SINO-JAPANESE WAR with Qing Dynasty China, establishing trading rights there, gaining influence over China's vassal KOREA, and controlling TAIWAN in the TREATY OF SHIMONOSEKI. This conflict revealed Chinese military and organizational limitations and showed Japanese military superiority.

The Russo-Japanese War had been important not only to solidify Japanese influence in Korea and Manchuria, but also to confirm Japan's status in the eyes of European empires as a world power. In 1910, Japan annexed Korea. After WWI, Japan was granted Germany's PACIFIC ISLANDS by the League of Nations.

Following the First World War, despite having provided assistance to the French and British in Asia, Japan began its own imperialist adventure in East and Southeast Asia not only to gain power and access to raw materials, but also to limit and eventually expel European rule in what Japan considered its *SPHERE OF INFLUENCE*. In 1931, Japan invaded MANCHURIA, creating the puppet state *MANCHUKUO*.

While Japan was building its global reputation and military and economic strength in Asia, China was undergoing political change. The XINHAI REVOLUTION broke out in 1911, resulting in the overthrow of the Qing and the end of dynastic Chinese rule, establishing the short-lived REPUBLIC OF CHINA. Led by SUN YAT-SEN, the revolutionaries not only had the support of the disaffected Chinese people; they also had the financial support of millions of Chinese living abroad.

However, despite Republican recognition by major international powers, the power vacuum left by the end of imperial China allowed the rise of warlords throughout the enormous country, and the government was unable to establish total control. The KUOMINTANG (KMT), or Nationalist Party of the revolutionary government worked to consolidate government power; following Sun Yat-sen's death in 1925, the KMT leader CHIANG KAI-SHEK (or JIANG JIESHI) went on to take control of much of China back from the warlords.

At the same time, communism was emerging in China. The country felt betrayed by European powers, which had awarded German possessions in China to Japan in the Treaty of Versailles. China refused to sign the treaty, and communism became popular among some Chinese leaders; thus emerged the CHINESE COMMUNIST PARTY. Temporarily working together, the KMT and CCP were able to bring Chinese territory back under Republican control. However, Chiang turned against the CCP in 1927, driving it south.

The CCP focused its organizing activities in the countryside on the peasants, becoming powerful in southern China. However, KMT attacks on the CCP in the south in 1934 forced the CCP to retreat on the LONG MARCH north. During this time of hardship, MAO ZEDONG emerged as the leader of the movement.

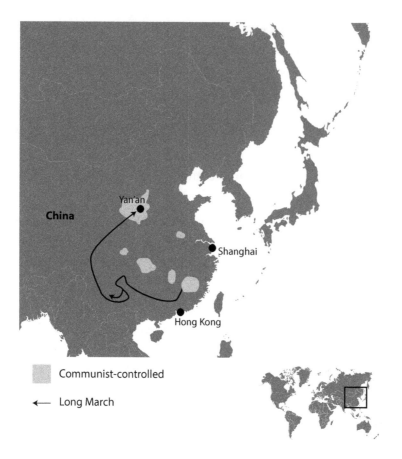

Figure 2.14. The Long March

World War II

Meanwhile, Germany suffered under the provisions of the Treaty of Versailles. In 1919, a democratic government was established at Weimar—the **WEIMAR REPUBLIC**. Germany was in chaos; the Kaiser had fled and the country was torn apart by war. However, the new government could not bring stability.

Blamed for WWI, Germany owed huge **REPARATIONS** according to the treaty to pay for the cost of the war, setting off **HYPERINFLATION** and impoverishing the country and its people. The rise of communists and a workers' party that came to be known as the National Socialist Party, or **NAZI PARTY**, led to further political instability. Following the crash of the stock market in 1929, German unemployment reached six million; furthermore, the United States had called in its foreign loans. Consequently, unemployed workers began supporting communism. On the other hand, the Nazis, led by **ADOLF HITLER**, gained support from business interests, which feared communist power in government. Thus, the Nazis became an important force in the Weimar Republic at the beginning of the 1930s.

Hitler maneuvered into the role of chancellor by 1933. His charisma and popular platform—to cancel the Treaty of Versailles—allowed him to rise. Enjoying the support of the wealthy and big business, which feared communism (especially with the development of Soviet Russia), Nazi ideals appealed strongly to both industry and the workers in the face of global economic depression. Finally, the Nazi Minister of Propaganda **JOSEPH GOEBBELS** executed an effective propaganda campaign, and would do so throughout Hitler's rule, known as the **THIRD REICH**.

The following year, Hitler became the *FÜHRER*, or *leader*, of Germany. A series of chaotic events followed: a fire in the Reichstag (German Parliament), which allowed Hitler to arrest communist leaders; the rise of the GESTAPO, or secret police (which violently enforced Nazi rule among the people); and the banning of political parties and trade unions. As a result, Hitler and the Nazis consolidated total control. They also set into motion their agenda of racism and genocide against "non-Aryan" (non-Germanic) or "racially impure" people.

Jewish people were particularly targeted. Germany had a considerable Jewish population; so did the other Central and Eastern European countries that Germany would come to control. Throughout the 1930s, the Nazis passed a series of laws limiting Jewish rights, including jobs that Jewish people could hold, rights to citizenship, places they could go, public facilities they could use, whom they could marry, even the names they could have. KRISTALLNACHT took place in 1938, an organized series of attacks on Jewish businesses, homes, and places of worship, so called because the windows of these places were smashed.

In 1939, Jews were forced from their homes into GHETTOES, isolated and overcrowded urban neighborhoods; in 1941, they were forced to wear YELLOW STARS identifying them as Jewish. Millions of Jewish people were sent to CONCENTRATION CAMPS; the Nazis decided on the FINAL SOLUTION to the "Jewish Question": to murder Jewish people by systematically gassing them at death camps. At least six million European Jews were murdered by the Nazis in the HOLOCAUST.

Roma, Slavic people, homosexuals, disabled people, people of color, prisoners of war, communists, and others not considered "Aryan" were also forced into slave labor in concentration camps and murdered there. Later, this concept of torturing and killing people based on their ethnicity in order to exterminate them would become defined as GENOCIDE.

Hitler was a FASCIST, believing in a mostly free market accompanied by a dictatorial government with a strong military. He sought to restore Germany's power and expand its reach by annexing AUSTRIA (the *ANSCHLUSS*, or *union*) and the SUDETENLAND, German-majority areas in part of what is today the Czech Republic.

With the collapse of the Weimar Republic and the League of Nations at its weakest state, France and Britain granted the Sudetenland to Hitler in 1938 in a policy called APPEASEMENT in an effort to maintain stability in Europe and avoid another war. In fact, given the threat posed by the new Soviet Union, Britain and France actually believed that a stronger Germany would be in their interests.

However, appeasement failed when Hitler invaded the rest of CZECHOSLOVAKIA and formed an alliance with ITALY the next year.

The Soviet Union made a pact with Germany in 1939: Germany would not invade the USSR, and the two countries would divide Poland. Germany then invaded POLAND; its 1939 invasion is commonly considered the beginning of the SECOND WORLD WAR (though some historians actually consider the Japanese invasion of Manchuria in 1931 to be the beginning of the war).

War exploded in Europe in 1939 as Hitler gained control of more land than any European power since Napoleon. In 1940, Germany had taken Paris. The BATTLE OF BRITAIN began in July of that year; however Germany suffered its first defeat and was unable to take Britain. Despite staying out of combat, in 1941 the UNITED STATES enforced the LEND-LEASE ACT which provided support and military aid to Britain. The two also released the ATLANTIC CHARTER, outlining common goals.

When Japan joined the AXIS powers of Germany and Italy, the SECOND SINO-JAPANESE WAR OF 1937 would also be subsumed under the Second World War, ending in 1945. The CHINESE CIVIL WAR between communists led by Mao Zedong and nationalists led by Chiang Kai-shek was interrupted by the Second Sino-Japanese War, when Japan tried to extend its imperial reach deeper into China, resulting in atrocities like the RAPE OF NANKING (1937 – 1938).

The Atlantic Charter described values shared by the US and Britain, including restoring self-governance in occupied Europe and liberalizing international trade.

At this time, Chiang was forced to form an alliance with Mao and the two forces worked together against Japan. By the end of the war, the CCP was stronger than ever, with widespread support from many sectors of Chinese society, while the KMT was demoralized and had little popular support.

Figure 2.15. Japanese Expansion in Asia

In June of 1941, Japan, now part of the AXIS along with Germany and Italy, attacked the United States at Pearl Harbor. Consequently, the US joined the war in Europe and in the Pacific, deploying thousands of troops in both theaters.

Meanwhile, in Asia, Japan continued its imperialist policies. In the early 1940s, it took advantage of chaos in Europe and the weakened European colonial powers to invade and occupy FRENCH INDOCHINA, INDONESIA, and BURMA; it also occupied the PHIL-IPPINES. Controlling these strategic areas meant the Axis was a direct threat to British India, Australia, and the eastern Soviet Union, not to mention European imperial and economic interests.

Back in Europe, having broken his promise to the Soviet Union, Hitler invaded Russia. But in 1942, the USSR defeated Germany at the BATTLE OF STALINGRAD, a turning point in the war during which the Nazis were forced to turn from the Eastern Front. In 1943, Churchill, Roosevelt, and Stalin all met in Teheran to discuss the invasion of Italy; the Allies took Rome later that year.

In 1944, the Allies invaded France on D-DAY. While they liberated Paris in August, the costly BATTLE OF THE BULGE extended into 1945. Despite thousands of American casualties, Hitler's forces were pushed back. In the spring of 1945, the US crossed the Rhine while the USSR invaded Berlin; Hitler killed himself and the Allies accepted German surrender.

The war in the Pacific would continue, however. Strategic battles were fought in SAIPAN and IWO JIMA to secure landing strips for American bombers. At LEYTE, the US destroyed most of the Japanese Navy. Despite casualties of up to 400,000, Japan continued to fight the US for territory in the PHILIPPINES. Finally, even after the war in Europe had ended, the US and Japan fought over OKINAWA, which the US planned to use as a staging point for an invasion of Japan in order to force Japanese surrender.

An American invasion of Japan would have likely resulted in hundreds of thousands of casualties. PRESIDENT TRUMAN, who had succeeded Roosevelt, elected to use the nuclear bomb on Japan instead to force surrender. In 1945, the US bombed the Japanese cities of HIROSHIMA and NAGASAKI. The tremendous civilian casualties did force the Emperor to surrender; at that point, the Second World War came to an end.

That year in China, the Chinese Civil War recommenced; by 1949 the communists had emerged victorious. The KMT withdrew to Taiwan, while Mao and the CCP took over China, which became a communist country.

WWII and the period immediately preceding it saw horrific violations of human rights in Europe and Asia, including the atrocities committed during the Japanese invasions of China, Korea, and Southeast Asia, and the European Holocaust of Jews and other groups like Roma and homosexuals. The war finally ended with the US atomic bombings of Hiroshima and Nagasaki in 1945, ending years of firebombing civilians in Germany and Japan; devastating ground and naval warfare throughout Europe, Asia, the South Pacific, and Africa; and the deaths of millions of soldiers and civilians all around the world.

The extreme horrors of WWII helped develop the concept of GENOCIDE, or the effort to extinguish an entire group of people because of their ethnicity, and the idea of HUMAN RIGHTS. The UNITED NATIONS was formed, based on the League of Nations, as a body to champion human rights and uphold international security. Its SECURITY COUNCIL is made up of permanent member states which can intervene militarily in the interests of international stability.

Allied forces took the lead in rebuilding efforts: the US occupied areas in East Asia and Germany, while the Soviet Union remained in Eastern Europe. The Allies had planned to rebuild Europe according to the MARSHALL PLAN; however, Stalin broke his promise made at the 1945 YALTA CONFERENCE to adhere to that plan and allow Eastern European countries to hold free elections. Instead, the USSR occupied these countries and they came under communist control. The COLD WAR had begun.

The Cold War

At the Yalta Conference in February 1945, Stalin, Churchill, and Roosevelt had agreed upon the division of Germany, the free nature of government in Poland, and free elections in Eastern Europe. However, at the POTSDAM CONFERENCE in July 1945, things had changed. Harry Truman had replaced Franklin D. Roosevelt, who had died in office, and Clement Atlee had replaced Winston Churchill. Stalin felt betrayed by the US use of the nuclear bomb; likewise, the US and the British felt that Stalin had violated the agreement at Yalta regarding democracy in Eastern Europe.

Stalin ensured that communists came to power in Eastern Europe, setting up satellite states at the Soviet perimeter in violation of the Yalta agreement. The Soviet rationale was to establish a buffer zone following its extraordinarily heavy casualties in WWII—around twenty million. With Stalin's betrayal of the Allies' agreement, in the words of the British Prime Minister WINSTON CHURCHILL, an *IRON CURTAIN* had come down across Europe, dividing east from west.

Consequently, western states organized the North Atlantic Treaty Organization or **NATO**, an agreement wherein an attack on one was an attack on all; this treaty provided for **COLLECTIVE SECURITY** in the face of the Soviet expansionist threat. The United States

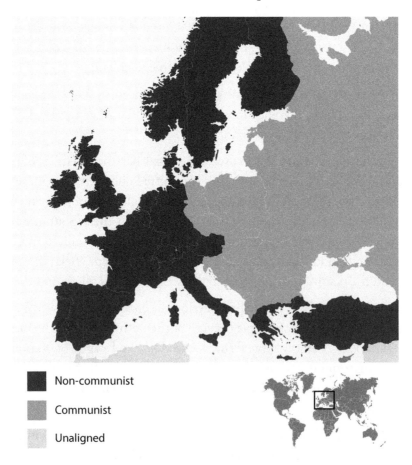

Figure 2.16. Cold War Europe

adopted a policy of CONTAINMENT, the idea that communism should be *contained*, as part of the TRUMAN DOCTRINE of foreign policy. The United States also sponsored the MARSHALL PLAN, which provided aid to European countries in an effort to restart the European economy and rebuild the continent. Stalin did not permit Soviet-controlled countries to take Marshall aid.

In response, the Soviet Union created the WARSAW PACT, a similar organization consisting of Eastern European communist countries. NUCLEAR WEAPONS, especially the development of the extremely powerful HYDROGEN BOMB, raised the stakes of the conflict. The concept of MUTUALLY-ASSURED DESTRUCTION, or the understanding that a nuclear strike by one country would result in a response by the other, ultimately destroying the entire world, may have prevented the outbreak of active violence.

How did the Cold War erupt between the Allies and the Soviet Union?

Germany itself had been divided into four zones, controlled by Britain, France, the US, and the USSR. Berlin had been divided the same way. Once Britain, France, and the US united their zones into West Germany in 1948 and introduced a new currency, the USSR cut off West Berlin in the BERLIN BLOCKADE. Viewing this as an aggressive attempt to capture the entire city, for nearly a year western powers provided supplies to West Berlin by air in the BERLIN AIRLIFT.

Berlin continued to be a problem for the USSR. Until 1961, refugees from the Eastern Bloc came to West Berlin, seeking better living conditions in the West. Furthermore, West Berlin was a center for Western espionage. In 1961, the USSR, now led by NIKITA KHRUSHCHEV, closed the border and constructed the BERLIN WALL.

Following the Second World War, Korea had also been divided. In the northern part of the country, the communist KIM IL SUNG controlled territory. South of the THIRTY-EIGHTH PARALLEL, the non-communist Syngman Rhee controlled the rest of the country. In 1950, Kim il Sung invaded the south with Russian and Chinese support, intending to create a communist Korea.

According to the Truman Doctrine, communism needed to be contained. Furthermore, according to DOMINO THEORY, if one country became communist, then more would, too, like a row of dominoes falling. Therefore, the United States, by way of the United Nations, became involved in the KOREAN WAR (1950 – 1953).

UN troops dominated and led by the US came to the aid of the nearly defeated South Koreans, pushing back Kim il Sung's troops. China supported Kim il Sung, and war on the peninsula continued until 1953, when US President Eisenhower threatened to use the nuclear bomb, ending the war in a stalemate.

Later, in CUBA, the revolutionary FIDEL CASTRO took over in 1959. Allied with the Soviet Union, he allowed missile bases to be constructed in Cuba, which threatened the United States. During the CUBAN MISSILE CRISIS in 1962, the world came closer than ever to nuclear war when the USSR sent missiles to Cuba. Cuba ships faced an American blockade and tension grew as the US considered invading Cuba. President Kennedy and Premier Khrushchev were able to come to an agreement in which the USSR promised to dismantle its Cuban bases as long as the US ended the blockade and secretly dismantled its own missile bases in Turkey. Nuclear war was averted.

Despite this success, the United States engaged in a lengthy violent conflict in Southeast Asia. Supporting anti-communist fighters in Vietnam in keeping with containment and Domino Theory, the United States pursued the **Vietnam War** for almost a decade. The **Gulf of Tonkin Resolution** authorized the US president to manage the ongoing conflict without consulting Congress, so for a period of years troops continued to be deployed to the region, fueling the conflict.

The US had become involved in the war after coming to the aid of Vietnam's old colonial master, France. **Ho Chi Minh**, the revolutionary Vietnamese leader, had actually originally approached the Americans for assistance in asserting Vietnamese independence. He led the North Vietnamese forces (**Viet Cong**) in a guerrilla war for independence throughout the 1960s.

Despite being outnumbered, Viet Cong familiarity with the difficult terrain, support from Russia and China, and determination eventually resulted in victory. Bloody guerrilla warfare demoralized the American military, but the 1968 **Tet Offensive** was a turning point. Despite enormous losses, the North Vietnamese won a strategic victory in this coordinated, surprise offensive. Extreme objection to the war within the United States, high casualties, and demoralization eventually resulted in US withdrawal in 1975.

Toward the end of the 1960s and into the 1970s, the Cold War reached a period of **détente**, or a warming of relations. The US and USSR signed the **Nuclear Non-Proliferation Treaty**, in which they and other nuclear power signatories agreed not to further spread nuclear weapons technology. Later, the USSR and the US signed the **SALT I Treaty** (Strategic Arms Limitation Treaty), limiting strategic weaponry. Some cultural exchanges and partnerships in outer space took place.

■ Communist countries

Figure 2.17. The Communist World

At the same time, the United States began making diplomatic overtures toward communist China. This was however, part of a different Cold War strategy. Despite its status as a communist country, China and the USSR had difficult relations due to their differing views on the nature of communism. While Khrushchev was taking a more moderate approach to world communism, Mao believed in more aggressive policies. Following the SINO-SOVIET SPLIT of the 1960s, China had lost much Soviet support for its modernization programs and despite advances in agriculture and some industrialization, Mao's programs like the GREAT LEAP FORWARD had taken a toll on the people.

In 1972, President Nixon visited China, establishing relations between the communist government and the United States. Communist China was permitted to join the UN (previously, China had been represented by the KMT, which was isolated to Taiwan).

The climate would change again, however, in the 1970s and 1980s. The US and USSR found themselves on opposite sides in proxy wars throughout the world (see below). In addition, and the ARMS RACE was underway. PRESIDENT RONALD REAGAN pursued a militaristic policy, prioritizing weapons development with the goal of outspending the USSR on weapons technology.

Perhaps the most famous proposal in weapons technology during this time was the Strategic Defense Initiative; popularly known as *Star Wars*, this outer-space based system would have intercepted Soviet intercontinental ballistic missiles.

Decolonization

Meanwhile, the former colonies of the fallen European colonial powers had won or were in the process of gaining their independence. One role of the United Nations was to help manage the DECOLONIZATION process. Already, the leader MOHANDAS GANDHI had led a peaceful independence movement in INDIA against the British, winning Indian independence in 1949. His assassination by Hindu radicals led to conflict between HINDUS and MUSLIMS in the SUBCONTINENT, resulting in PARTITION, the bloody division of India: Hindus fled into what is today India, while Muslims fled to EAST PAKISTAN (now BANGLADESH and WEST PAKISTAN). Instability is ongoing on the Subcontinent.

Bloody conflict in Africa like the ALGERIAN WAR against France (1954 – 1962), the MAU MAU REBELLION against the British in Kenya in the 1950s, and violent movements against Belgium in the CONGO ultimately resulted in African independence for many countries in the 1950s, 1960s, and 1970s; likewise, so did strong leadership by African nationalist leaders and thinkers like JOMO KENYATTA, JULIUS NYERERE, and KWAME NKRUMAH. The apartheid regime in South Africa, where segregation between races was legal and people of color lived in oppressive conditions, was not lifted until the 1990s; NELSON MANDELA led the country in a peaceful transition process.

In the Middle East, following the fall of the Ottoman Empire after WWI, European powers had taken over much of the area; these *PROTECTORATES* became independent states with arbitrary borders drawn and rulers installed by the Europeans. The creation of the state of ISRAEL was especially contentious: in the 1917 BALFOUR DECLARATION, the British had promised the ZIONIST movement of European Jews that they would be given a homeland in the British-controlled protectorate of Palestine; however, the US assured the Arabs in 1945 that a Jewish state would not be founded there. Israel emerged from diplomatic confusion, chaos, and tragedy after the murder of millions of Jews in Europe, and violence on the ground in Palestine carried out by both Jews and Arabs. This legacy of conflict lasts to this day in the Middle East.

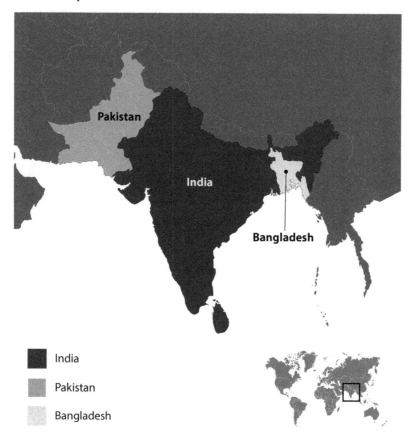

FIgure 2.18. Partition

While the Middle East had been divided into protectorates or into nominally independent states like Egypt that were still under strong European influence, these areas had become independent after the Second World War. Liberal activists against monarchical and dictatorial regimes and popular movements like Pan-Arabism and Islamism put pressure on Middle Eastern monarchies. Countries created by artificial borders based on the Sykes-Picot Agreement and comprised of divided and diverse ethnic and religious groups were already vulnerable to political instability; with added unrest, Middle Eastern governments fell. Furthermore, the Middle East became a Cold War battleground, with regimes courting the support of the Cold War powers.

In Egypt, **GAMAL ABDUL NASSER** led the Pan-Arabist movement in the region, which included creating an Arab alliance against Israel. In 1967, Arab allies launched a war against Israel; they were badly beaten, however, in the **SIX DAY WAR**, an embarrassing defeat for the Arab states and one from which Nasser never truly recovered. Furthermore, Israel took control of the Sinai Peninsula, the Golan Heights, and the West Bank of the Jordan River.

During the 1973 **YOM KIPPUR WAR**, while the US supported **ISRAEL**, the USSR supported **SYRIA** and **EGYPT**. Syria and Egypt had launched a surprise attack on Israel on the holiest day of the Jewish year in an attempt to gain back territory lost years prior. However, Israel was able to maintain its defenses.

In 1978, the American president Jimmy Carter was able to broker a peace agreement between the Egyptian leader **ANWAR SADAT** and the Israeli leader **MENACHEM BEGIN** known as the **CAMP DAVID ACCORDS**. However, other Arab countries, aside from Jordan, did not make peace with Israel. By the 1970s, Pan-Arabism was no longer the popular, unifying movement it had once been.

The **NON-ALIGNED MOVEMENT** arose in response to the Cold War. Instead of the bipolar world of the Cold War (one democratic, led by the US, the other communist, led by the USSR), the Non-Aligned Movement sought an alternative: the **THIRD WORLD**. Non-Aligned or Third World countries wanted to avoid succumbing to the influence of either of the superpowers, and many found a forum in the United Nations in which to strengthen their international profiles.

However, throughout the Cold War, PROXY WARS between the US and the USSR were fought around the world. In the 1980s, the United States began supporting the anti-communist **CONTRAS** in **NICARAGUA**, who were fighting the communist **SANDINISTA** government. In 1979, the USSR invaded **AFGHANISTAN**, an event which would contribute to the Soviet collapse; in response, the US began supporting anti-Soviet *MUJAHIDEEN* forces (some of whose patrons would later attack the US as part of international terrorist groups). Other examples include the **ANGOLAN CIVIL WAR**, the **MOZAMBICAN CIVIL WAR**, and the **NICARAGUAN REVOLUTION**.

In the **HORN OF AFRICA**, Somalia was formed when the Italian-administered UN trust territory of Somalia united with the British protectorate of Somaliland in 1960. Initially supported by the USSR for its socialist leanings, Somalia and its leader, Mohamed Siad Barre, initated a war against Ethiopia in 1977. Ultimately the USSR supported Ethiopia, and the United States supported Somalia.

While never officially colonized, **IRAN** had been under the oppressive regime of the western-supported **SHAH REZA PAHLAVI** for decades. During its imperial era, Britain had begun exploring petroleum interests in what was then Persia, and western oil companies had remained powerful in that country. The **PAHLAVI DYNASTY** had taken over Persia in 1920 from the Qajars, who had ruled since 1785, and who themselves had been important in administration under the Safavids since the sixteenth century.

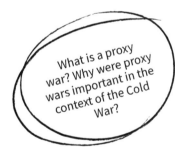
What is a proxy war? Why were proxy wars important in the context of the Cold War?

By the 1970s, the Shah's corrupt, oppressive regime was extremely unpopular in Iran, but it was propped up by the West. Several underground movements worked against the Shah, including communists and Islamic revolutionaries inspired by the Islamism of the early twentieth century. In the 1979 **IRANIAN REVOLUTION**, these forces overthrew the Shah; shortly afterward, Islamist revolutionaries took over the country. The new theocracy was led by a group of clerics led by the Supreme Leader **AYATOLLAH KHOMEINI**. The Ayatollah became Supreme Leader and instituted political and social reforms, including stricter interpretations of Islamic laws and traditions and

The revolutionary Iranian government would go on to support Shi'a militants (the *Hezbollah*, or the *Party of God*) in the **LEBANESE CIVIL WAR** throughout the 1980s; this group is also inspired by Islamism.

enforcing those throughout the country as national and local law. Later that year, radical students who supported the revolution stormed the US Embassy and held a number of staff hostage for over a year; the IRAN HOSTAGE CRISIS would humiliate the United States.

Following the Iranian Revolution, the Iraqi leader SADDAM HUSSEIN, an ally of the United States, declared war against Iran. While governed by Sunnis, Iraq was actually a Shi'ite-majority country, and Saddam feared Iran would trigger a similar revolution there. Iraq also sought control over the strategic Shatt al-Arab waterway and some oil-rich territories inland. The war raged from 1980 – 1990.

EXAMPLES

1) Which of the following was a weakness of the Schlieffen Plan?

A. It overstretched the German army.

B. It failed to anticipate a stronger resistance in France.

C. It underestimated Russia's ability to mobilize its troops.

D. It did not account for the difficulties of trench warfare.

E. all of the above

Answers:

A. Incorrect. While the German army was stretched too thin, the answer is incomplete as the other answer choices are also true.

B. Incorrect. While the Schlieffen Plan did indeed underestimate resistance on the Western Front, this answer choice is also incomplete as the other answer choices are also true.

C. Incorrect. While the Schlieffen Plan did fail to anticipate rapid Russian mobilization, this answer choice is incomplete given the other options.

D. Incorrect. While the Schlieffen Plan did not account for the realities of trench warfare, this answer choice is incomplete given the other options.

E. **Correct.** All of the answer choices are true.

2) According to the Sykes-Picot Agreement,

A. Israel would become an independent state.

B. Husayn ibn Ali would become Caliph.

C. Ataturk would lead an independent Turkey.

D. Palestine would be under international supervision.

E. The countries of the Middle East would be self-governing.

Answers:

A. Incorrect. Sykes-Picot made no promises of an independent Jewish state.

B. Incorrect. Husayn ibn Ali, while taken into account in the Agreement in determining positions of power, was never offered the title of Caliph.

C. Incorrect. Ataturk himself took control of Turkey, having been part of its leadership for some time and having held off European interference.

D. **Correct.** Sykes-Picot put Palestine under the supervision of various international powers.

E. Incorrect. Sykes-Picot established spheres of influence controlled by each power.

3) Which of the following led to the rise of the Nazis in early 1930s Germany?

A. the impact of reparations and the support of German industrialists

B. the impact of the Great Depression and the support of the workers

C. support from the international communist movement and the impact of reparations on the German economy

D. support from German industrialists and strong backing from other political factions in the Reichstag

E. support from Germany's national communist movement and support of the workers

Answers:

A. **Correct.** The Nazis planned to cease paying reparations, so their nationalist approach appealed to many Germans suffering from the hyperinflation that reparations had triggered. Furthermore, the Nazis had the support of German industrialists, who feared the rise of communism among the working classes.

B. Incorrect. While the economic suffering brought on by the Great Depression made the Nazis' promises appealing to many, they did not have the support of the majority of German workers, who mostly supported communists at the time.

C. Incorrect. The Nazis were against communism.

D. Incorrect. While they had support from German industrialists, the Nazis did not have widespread support in government: they were elected by popular vote.

E. Incorrect. The Nazis opposed communism which alienated most of the workers during that time.

4) Which of the following did NOT escalate tensions between the West and the Soviet Union immediately following World War II?

A. disagreement over the control of Berlin

B. Stalin's installation of pro-Soviet regimes in Eastern Europe

C. Western European and American resistance to communism

D. the development of nuclear weapons in both the US and the Soviet Union

E. the erection of the Berlin Wall

Answers:

A. Incorrect. When Germany was divided into four regions, the Soviet Union believed it should have full control of Berlin because Berlin was in their quadrant. The Western powers wanted refused to relinquish control of their sections.

B. Incorrect. At Yalta, Stalin agreed to free elections in eastern Europe after the war, however he did not abide by this and installed leaders friendly to his government instead.

C. Incorrect. The wartime alliance of the Soviet Union with the United States and Great Britain was one of convenience. When the war ended, their previous animosities based on government re-emerged.

D. Incorrect. The Soviet Union felt threatened by the U.S.'s atomic bomb. The U.S. felt equally threatened when the Soviet Union detonated their own in 1949.

    E.   **Correct.** While the division of Berlin was an immediate issue, the Berlin Wall was not built until 1961.

5) Which of the following precipitated the end of the Cold War?
    A.   the Iran Hostage Crisis
    B.   the Soviet War in Afghanistan
    C.   the Iran-Iraq War
    D.   the Yom Kippur War
    E.   the Camp David Accords

Answers:

    A.   Incorrect. While the Iran Hostage Crisis was an embarrassment for the United States, it did not significantly alter its role in the Cold War nor did it contribute to the collapse of the USSR.

    B.   **Correct.** The Soviet invasion of Afghanistan and the subsequent ten-year war sapped Soviet financial and military resources—and morale. This draining war, plus the high price of the arms race with the United States, contributed significantly to the fall of the Soviet Union.

    C.   Incorrect. While the Cold War powers had strong interests and some involvement in this war—particularly the United States, an enemy of the revolutionary Iranian government—it did not significantly affect the balance of power between the US and the USSR. Furthermore, both superpowers supported Iraq.

    D.   Incorrect. Arguably, the Yom Kippur War was indeed a proxy war: the Soviet Union supported Syria and Egypt, so the United States came to Israel's aid. However this war did not significantly change the balance of power between the superpowers, although it did significantly affect the Middle East.

    E.   Incorrect. The Camp David Accords was peace agreement between Anwar Sadat of Egypt and Menachem Begin of Israel.

Post-Cold War World

In 1991, the Soviet Union fell when Soviet Premier **MIKHAIL GORBACHEV**, who had implemented reforms like *GLASNOST* and *PERESTROIKA* (or *openness* and *transparency*), was nearly overthrown in a coup; a movement led by **BORIS YELTSIN**, who had been elected president of Russia, stopped the coup. The USSR was dissolved later that year and Yeltsin became president of the Russian Federation. The war in Afghanistan and military over-spending in an effort to keep up with American military spending had weakened the USSR to the point of collapse, and the Cold War ended.

Cold War Consequences

That same year, Saddam Hussein, the leader of Iraq, invaded Kuwait and took over its oil reserves and production facilities. In response, the United States and other countries went to war—with a UN mandate—to expel Iraq from Kuwait and to defend Saudi Arabia in order to regain control of the world's petroleum reserves in the **GULF WAR**. This event cemented the US status as the sole world superpower; the global balance of power had changed.

Despite stability throughout most of Europe, the changes following the fall of the Iron Curtain led to instability in the Balkans. In 1992, Bosnia declared its independence from the collapsing state of Yugoslavia, following Croatia and Slovenia. Violence broke out in Bosnia between Bosnian Serbs on one side, and Bosnian Muslims (Bosniaks) and Croatians on the other. The **Bosnian War** raged from 1992 to 1995, resulting in the deaths of thousands of civilians and another European genocide—this time, of Bosnian Muslims.

Also following the Cold War, proxy wars throughout the world and instability in former colonies continued. In 1994, conflict in Central Africa resulted in the **Rwandan Genocide**. Hutus massacred Tutsis, and violence continued on both sides. In **Zaire**, the country descended into instability following the fall of **Mobutu Sese Seko**, the US-supported dictator, in 1997. Renamed the **Democratic Republic of the Congo**, parts of this country and others in Central Africa would remain wracked by poverty and torn by violence for decades.

In the 1980s, drought in the Horn of Africa led to widespread famine; humanitarian affairs and issues came into the public eye and the general public, especially in wealthier families, became more concerned about providing foreign aid to the suffering.

The Somali leader Mohamed Siad Barre was overthrown in 1991 and **Somalia** was broken up under the control of various warlords and clans. The people suffered from starvation with the breakdown of social order. The United States intervened as part of a UN peacekeeping mission in an attempt to provide humanitarian aid; however, strong military resistance from the warlord Muhammad Aideed impacted US public opinion and the effort failed. To this day there is no central government in Somalia, and much of the country is still dependent on aid; however, autonomous areas function independently.

Cooperation and Conflict

Following the end of the Cold War and post-decolonization, the balance of economic and political power began to change. The **G-20**, the world's twenty most important economic and political powers, includes many former colonies and non-European countries. The **BRICS**—Brazil, Russia, India, China, and South Africa—are recognized as world economic and political leaders. With the exception of Russia, all these countries were only recently classified as developing countries. While still wrestling with considerable social, economic, and political challenges, the BRICS are world powers in their own right as independent nations—unthinkable developments a century ago.

Steps toward European unification had begun as early as the 1950s; the **European Union**, as it is known today, was formed after the **Maastricht Treaty** was signed in 1992. As the former Soviet satellite states moved from communism to more democratic societies and capitalistic economies, more countries partnered with the EU and eventually joined it; as of 2015, twenty-eight countries are members, with more on the path to membership.

European Union countries remain independent, but they cooperate in international affairs, justice, security and foreign policy, environmental matters, and economic policy.

Many also share a common currency, the EURO. According to the SCHENGEN AGREEMENT, some EU countries even have open borders.

Continental integration exists beyond Europe. In Africa, the AFRICAN UNION, originally the Organization of African Unity, has become a stronger political force in its own right, organizing peacekeeping missions throughout the continent. An organization similar to the EU, the AU is a forum for African countries to organize and align political, military, economic, and other policies.

> While benefits of international trade include lower prices and more consumer choice, unemployment often increases in more developed countries and labor and environmental violations are more likely in developing countries.

In this era of GLOBALIZATION, international markets became increasingly open through free-trade agreements like NAFTA (the North American Free Trade Agreement), MERCOSUR (the South American free-trade zone), and the TRANS-PACIFIC PARTNERSHIP, a proposed free-trade zone between nine countries on the Pacific Ocean. The WORLD TRADE ORGANIZATION oversees international trade. Technological advances like improvements in transportation infrastructure and the INTERNET made international communication faster, easier and cheaper.

However, more open borders, reliable international transportation, and faster, easier worldwide communication brought risks, too. In the early twenty-first century, the United States was attacked by terrorists on SEPTEMBER 11, 2001, resulting in thousands of civilian casualties. Consequently, the US launched a major land war in Afghanistan and another later in Iraq.

Following the attacks on 9/11, the United States attacked Afghanistan as part of the WAR ON TERROR. Afghanistan's radical Islamist TALIBAN government was providing shelter to the group that took responsibility for the attacks, AL QAEDA. Led by OSAMA BIN LADEN, al Qaeda was inspired by Islamism and also by the radical Wahhabism of the remote Arabian desert followed by the Saudis. Bin Laden had fought the Soviets with the US-supported Afghan *mujahideen* during the 1980s; despite that alliance, bin Laden and his followers were angered by US involvement in the Middle East throughout the 1990s and its support of Israel. While bin Laden was killed by the United States in 2011, and while control of Afghan security was turned over from the US to the US-backed government in 2014, the US still maintains a strong military presence in the country.

The Iraq War began in 2003 when the US invaded that country under the faulty premises that Saddam Hussein's regime was involved with al Qaeda, supported international terrorism, and possessed weapons of mass destruction that it intended to use in pursuit of terrorism. Iraq descended into chaos, with thousands of civilian and military casualties, Iraqi and American alike. While the country technically and legally remains intact under a US-supported government, the ethnically and religiously diverse country is de facto divided as a result of the disintegration of central power.

Elsewhere in the Middle East, reform movements began via the 2011 ARAB SPRING in Tunisia, Egypt, Bahrain, and Syria. Some dictatorial regimes have been replaced with democratic governments; other countries still enjoy limited freedoms or even civil unrest. In Syria, unrest erupted into civil war between BASHAR AL ASSAD, who inherited leadership from his father, and opposition fighters. One consequence has been enormous movements of refugees into Europe.

Today, a new group known as the Islamic State of Iraq and al Sham (**ISIS**) referring to Iraq and Syria (or Islamic State of Iraq and the Levant—ISIL) has filled the vacuum in parts of northern and western Iraq and eastern Syria. ISIS has established a de facto state in Iraq and Syria with extremist Islamist policies and presents a global terror threat.

Uprisings in Israeli-occupied West Bank and Gaza have continued sporadically. Israel passed control of **GAZA** to the Palestinian Authority in 2005; however following political divisions within Palestinian factions, Gaza is controlled by Hamas while the Palestinian Authority represents Palestinian interests abroad and in the **WEST BANK**. In 1999, US President Clinton attempted to broker a final peace deal between the Israelis and Palestinians delineating borders as part of a two-state solution, but these efforts failed and conflict continues.

EXAMPLES

1) While immediately after the fall of the Soviet Union the US emerged as the sole superpower, in the twenty-first century, which phenomenon has so far characterized global governance?

   A. international terrorism

   B. international economic and political organizations

   C. international conflict

   D. the European Union

   E. increasing isolationism

   Answers:

   A. Incorrect. While international terrorism has been a major feature of the past fifteen years, it is not a form of governance or political order.

   B. Correct. While the United States remains a leading world power, the emergence of international organizations like the BRICS, the EU, the G-20, and the AU has empowered other countries; furthermore, international trade agreements are helping mold the international balance of power.

   C. Incorrect. While international conflict has unfortunately been a major feature of the past fifteen years, there has been sufficient political global order to confidently state that the world has not fully descended into chaos.

   D. Incorrect. The European Union is an important world power as an international organization, but is not the dominant global superpower.

   E. Incorrect. In the twenty-first century, the world has become increasingly interconnected.

2) What was one reason for the Bosnian War?

   A. attacks by Bosniak Islamic extremists

   B. the dissolution of Yugoslavia

   C. the separation of Yugoslavia from the USSR

   D. attacks by Middle Eastern Islamic extremists

   E. US intervention in the Bosnian electoral process

Answers:

A. Incorrect. Bosniak Muslims were primarily the victims of genocide during the Bosnian War. Furthermore, while some mujahideen from the Soviet war in Afghanistan did go to the Balkans to fight, Islamic extremism is not traditionally a feature of Balkan Islam.

B. **Correct.** One reason for the Bosnian War was the Yugoslav government's attempt to force the country to stay together; following the end of the Cold War and the collapse of communism, the formerly communist Yugoslavia had started to break up.

C. Incorrect. Yugoslavia was never part of the USSR.

D. Incorrect. No actors from the Middle East triggered the Bosnian War.

E. Incorrect. The United States was not involved in the Balkans before the Bosnian War.

3) What is one major role that the African Union plays?

A. The AU is a free trade area.

B. The AU manages a single currency.

C. The AU manages several peacekeeping forces.

D. The AU represents individual African countries in international diplomacy.

E. The AU represents the majority of African countries in the United Nations.

Answers:

A. Incorrect. The AU is not a free trade zone; it is an organization of fifty-four African countries to convene and act in their common interests. While they may align trade policies, the entire continent is not a free trade zone.

B. Incorrect. There is no single African currency.

C. **Correct.** The AU organizes and manages peacekeeping forces in Africa; it also cooperates with the United Nations in peacekeeping.

D. Incorrect. Individual African countries are sovereign and manage their own international relations.

E. Incorrect. Countries represent themselves in the United Nations; they are not represented by other organizations.

24) Which of the following is NOT a reason that the Soviet Union collapsed?

A. glasnost

B. perestroika

C. the war in Afghanistan

D. the rise of the Taliban

E. American military dominance

Answers:

A. Incorrect. Glasnost, or openness, was one of Gorbachev's policies of reform, allowing for more free speech in the USSR; this arguably helped weaken the regime.

B. Incorrect. Perestroika, or transparency, was one of Gorbachev's policies of reform, providing a more transparent and democratic government under communism; this arguably helped weaken the regime.

C. Incorrect. The Soviet war in Afghanistan was financially ruinous for the USSR and cost the country much in morale.

D. **Correct.** The Taliban did not emerge in Afghanistan until well after Soviet withdrawal from the country.

E. Incorrect. The Soviet Union and the United States continually traded off military superiority. The Soviet Union was not intimidated by the U.S. military.

25) Despite his alliance with the US-supported *mujahideen* in the war in Afghanistan against the Soviets, Osama bin Laden sponsored attacks against the United States because

A. he opposed a US military presence in Saudi Arabia.

B. he opposed US support of Israel.

C. he wanted to destabilize the global capitalist system.

D. A and B

E. A, B, and C

Answers:

A. Incorrect. While this is true, it is incomplete as it is not the only correct answer choice.

B. Incorrect. While bin Laden opposed the US-Israeli alliance, this answer is incomplete as it is not the only correct answer choice.

C. Incorrect. bin Laden's goals were religious in nature, not economic.

D. **Correct.** He opposed U.S. intervention in the Middle East, particularly because he believed it furthered a Jewish agenda against Muslims.

E. Incorrect. While bin Laden did cite opposition to U.S. intervention, he did not express anti-capitalist ideology.

three

GOVERNMENT

Political Theory

Political theory is the study of the principles and ideas used to describe, explain, and analyze political events and institutions. At its core, political theory explores the purpose of government. There are two basic reasons for government: to provide law and order, and to protect people from conflicts. The first arises out of the second: in order to prevent and settle disputes between individuals, concrete rules of governance must be established. These goals are deceptively complicated, however, and lead to more questions. What kind of conflicts? How should conflict be prevented or managed? Who creates and enforces the rules that manage it? How far does that authority extend? To what extent should government intercede? What is the relationship between the government and the people? Political theorists have grappled with these questions throughout history.

Fundamental Concepts in Political Theory

Regardless of how they respond to these questions, all formal governments require recognition of their authority in order to exist. This recognition must come from both internal and external forces.

Recognition from outside governments comes in the form of sovereignty, the right of a group to be free of outside interference. A group is sovereign when others outside of the group recognize and respect that group's right to govern its own affairs and manage its own conflicts. Sovereignty can exist at different levels and to different degrees. For example, the United States has complete national sovereignty because other nations recognize the US government's right to rule its own people and manage its own affairs. Any attempt by another country to impose rules or regulate internal conflict would be viewed as a violation. Many wars have begun based on conflicts over sovereignty.

An organization like the National Rifle Association, on the other hand, has very limited sovereignty. It is subject to state and federal laws and oversight. It has the right to make some rules regarding its own internal organization and affairs; however, that level of sovereignty exists only to the extent that those rules do not interfere with those of the larger society. The sovereignty of groups—and more specifically of states—is an ongoing question within the United States.

Internal recognition of a government's authority is called its LEGITIMACY. This is the extent to which the people accept their government's authority. While it is important for other countries (or groups) to respect a government's right to handle its own affairs, if the people within the group do not believe in the government's right to power, it still cannot function. This legitimacy can be derived from a number of places: from God in a theocracy, from military might in a dictatorship, or from the people themselves in a democracy or a republic. Regardless of its source, however, once legitimacy is lost, a government cannot continue.

For example, during the Age of Reason rationality undermined popular belief in divine right (the idea that the king was chosen by God), destroying the legitimacy of the French monarchy. This allowed for the unrest brewing in France to erupt in the French Revolution. Similarly, the Confederate states in the US South broke away from the Union at the outbreak of the Civil War because they believed the federal government no longer represented their issues and was therefore an illegitimate government. A loss of legitimacy is at the center of every failed government and state.

EXAMPLES

1) Which of the following is NOT an example of the US protecting its national sovereignty?

    A. declaration of war after the bombing of Pearl Harbor

    B. signing of the Treaty of Paris at the end of the Revolutionary War

    C. President Eisenhower sending troops to Little Rock, Arkansas to integrate the schools

    D. patrolling of the US-Mexico border

    E. deployment of troops into Iraq to locate weapons of mass destruction

Answers:

A. Incorrect. The bombing of Pearl Harbor was viewed as a direct violation of American sovereignty. The US declared war to send a message to Japan that such a violation would not be tolerated.

B. Incorrect. The Treaty of Paris of 1783 established the United States as a sovereign nation independent of Great Britain. It protected the new country from interference from other nations, specifically Great Britain.

C. **Correct.** In Little Rock, the governor of Arkansas, Orval Faubus, refused to enforce the Supreme Court-ordered integration of the public schools. President Eisenhower sent troops to Little Rock to enforce national authority over a noncompliant state. This was an internal matter, not a matter of state sovereignty.

D. Incorrect. Controlling who enters into the United States is a prime example of national sovereignty.

E. Incorrect. Protecting the nation from outside attack is an example national sovereignty.

2) Which of the following is an example of a legitimate government?

    A. the German Federal Republic in the 1990s

    B. the Dole government in Hawaii in the 1890s

    C. Mexican rule of Texas in the 1830s

    D. the rule of Maximilian I in Mexico in the 1860s

    E. the Directory government in France in the 1790s

Answers:

A. **Correct.** Both former West and East German citizens recognized the newly unified German Federal Republic as the legal and political authority over both territories. Bringing the national capital back to Berlin legitimized the government in the eyes of the East, while maintaining the western currency and many western laws did so in the West.

B. Incorrect. While Sanford Dole and his group declared themselves rulers of Hawaii, the Hawaiian people maintained a belief in the legitimacy (based on divine right) of the Hawaiian monarchy. They did not acknowledge any of the laws the sugar magnates tried to put into place.

C. Incorrect. Although Texas was technically a Mexican state, the predominately American population blatantly ignored Mexican law, particularly in regard to slavery and religion. This ultimately led to the Texas War for Independence and the establishment of the Republic of Texas.

D. Incorrect. Created with the help of Napoleon III of France, Maximilian I's monarchy in Mexico was never recognized as legitimate by the majority of the people. Because there was no precedent for divine right in Mexico, and because of the authority invested in Mexican President Benito Juarez, he was never able to establish genuine rule.

E. Incorrect. The Directory government aimed to be a government of the people, however it never had general support and ultimately relied on the military until it was overthrown by Napoleon.

Major Political Theorists

Our understanding of government today is based upon the ideas of key political theorists. Each questioned the purpose of government and came to different conclusions. While there are many significant theorists, the most important to note follow below.

Niccolo Machiavelli (1469 – 1527) is best known for his work *The Prince*, a book of political advice for a new prince seeking power. In it, Machiavelli takes on the question of how government's purpose should be fulfilled. He argues that public morality and private or personal morality are two very different ideas. According to Machiavelli, a good ruler understands that sometimes immoral acts must be done to ensure the public good. He also argued that legitimacy derived from power; therefore maintenance of power was the most important priority for any leader. While some later readers have argued that *The Prince* was written as a satire, or at least with exaggerated ruthlessness, the ideas within it guided politics throughout the Western world for the next four hundred years.

John Locke (1632 – 1704) was one of the most influential of the Enlightenment thinkers, and his philosophical writings strongly influenced the central figures of the American and French Revolutions. He is responsible for several of the foundational ideas of the American government. Locke argued that, by nature, all men (women were not widely considered until later in history) are free and equal and endowed with certain natural rights: life, liberty, and property. In this, he challenged the traditional view that men were bound by

God to obey the monarchy, and instead argued that government was a natural outgrowth of the desire of individuals to protect their natural rights. Because of this desire, men turn over certain individual sovereignty to a neutral party (a government) which holds the responsibility to maximize the individual enjoyment of rights as well as the public good. As a result, a government's legitimacy derives from the consent of the people. This also means that when a government is no longer fulfilling its purpose and loses the people's consent, revolution is an appropriate and justified response.

A government's authority comes from the consent of the people it governs. Originally conceived by Thomas Hobbes, it is John Locke's version that most influenced the founders.

John Locke was not the first to consider this idea, also known as the SOCIAL CONTRACT, but his conception of it strongly impacted later thinkers and is fundamental to the modern republic.

Like John Locke, Baron de Montesquieu (1689 – 1755) is best known for his philosophical contributions to the political structure of the United States. Although a member of the French upper class, Montesquieu was a strong proponent of republican government. Much of his philosophy was in line with other Enlightenment thinkers; however, he wrote about the importance of balance of power in the success of a republic. Montesquieu advocated for DIVIDED GOVERNMENT: THE SEPARATION OF POWERS. Using Britain as his model, he argued that the most effective governments divided power between three different bodies or branches. He believed that powers should be equal, but differ in nature, saying, "When the [law making] and [law enforcing] powers are in the same person, there can be no liberty." Separation of powers, using a three-branch structure, is the central organizing principle of the American government.

Born eight years after John Locke's death, Jean-Jacques Rousseau (1712 – 1778) extended the idea of the social contract in his writing entitled *The Social Contract*. Much like Locke, Rousseau believed that government was a natural extension of the individual's desire to protect and best enjoy his (and her) natural rights. Locke, however, observed that the government that grew out of this desire would inevitably be imbalanced and class-based, as those with more resources structured the government to best protect their own rights at the expense of others. Eventually, this government would be overturned in revolution as the imbalance would lead to a loss of consent by those at the bottom. Rousseau, instead, argued for government built on the RULE OF LAW. Rousseau argued that a general will exists, a good common to everyone, and that this general will should be the basis of all laws. As a result, these laws would apply to all equally and would equally benefit all. By allowing these laws, rather than an individual or group of individuals, to govern society, make decisions and settle disputes, the inequities Locke feared could be avoided. The rule of law was another Enlightenment idea which became a central tenet of the new United States government.

An avid proponent of liberty and democracy, Alexis de Tocqueville (1805 – 1859) is best known for his work *Democracy in America*. Published in 1835, it detailed his travels throughout the United States, and chronicled his political analysis of what he saw. He celebrated the democratic underpinnings he saw in America—the emphasis on hard work and merit—and saw it as unique from the European experience. De Tocqueville had more complicated views on equality. He believed that inequality drove economic growth and that "radical equality" led to mediocrity. De Tocqueville's writings are often referenced as an accurate and detailed analysis of the early stages of American democracy.

EXAMPLES

1) Which political theorist argued for the separation of powers?

  A. Jean-Jacques Rousseau

  B. Baron de Montesquieu

  C. John Locke

  D. Alexis de Tocqueville

  E. Niccolo Machiavelli

Answers:

  A. Incorrect. Rousseau is best known for his writings on the social contract and natural rights. While deeply interested in the philosophical underpinnings of government, he did not particularly delve into its structure.

  B. Correct. Montesquieu believed that the separation of powers into three branches of government was essential to the success of a republic.

  C. Incorrect. Much like Rousseau, Locke's political writings focused on outlining natural rights and the nature of the social contract. He was more interested in the "why" of government than the "how."

  D. Incorrect. While de Tocqueville admired much about the American system of government, including the separation of powers, his focus was more on the actual functioning of an existing democracy, rather than the theory of an ideal republic.

  E. Incorrect. Machiavelli's writing focused on how government should fulfill its purpose, not the distribution of power.

2) The Declaration of Independence was most greatly influenced by which political theorist?

  A. John Locke

  B. Jean-Jacques Rousseau

  C. Niccolo Machiavelli

  D. Alexis de Tocqueville

  E. Baron de Montesquieu

Answers:

  A. Correct. The inalienable rights described in the Declaration of Independence, "life, liberty, and the pursuit of happiness," are a direct reference to the natural rights described by John Locke. The only variation: "pursuit of happiness" rather than "property," is seen as an expansion by Thomas Jefferson on Locke's original theory.

  B. Incorrect. Writing after Locke, Rousseau also acknowledges the existence of natural rights. However, it is Locke who names them. Rousseau's focus is more on how society best protects those rights.

C.   Incorrect. Machiavelli wrote about the nature of power, not the rights of man. His perspective on government can be seen as top-down, rather than Locke's more bottom-to-top view.

D.   Incorrect. De Tocqueville wrote almost sixty years after the writing of the Declaration of Independence. Therefore, his writing could not possibly have influenced it.

E.   Incorrect. The ideas of Montesquieu featured heavily in the writing of the Constitution, but not the Declaration of Independence.

3) Which best describes social contract theory?

A.   Government is a necessary evil to provide order for the people.

B.   Government is an agreement between a ruler and his or her subjects.

C.   Government exists as a promise to the people.

D.   Government exists at the will of the people.

E.   Government is a binding state that cannot be legitimately broken by either party.

Answers:

A.   Incorrect. Social contract theory does view government as a necessary element of a civilized society, but it does not believe that government is harmful or evil. Instead, social contract theory argues that government exists to serve the people and best provide for the common good.

B.   Incorrect. While social contract theory does allow for a governing body separate from the individual and with a greater degree of sovereignty, the contract does not exist between that body and the people. The contract is what itself creates the governing body.

C.   Incorrect. From a social contract perspective, government is not a promise by an outside ruler, but the result of consensus among a group of individuals living in a common society.

D.   **Correct.** Social contract theory argues that government is the natural consequence of individuals' attempts to protect their natural rights. As a result, individuals agree to turn over some of their sovereignty to a governing body in order to best enjoy those rights. Central to social contract theory is the idea that the people ultimately hold the power and can either allow a government to exist or remove it if it does not serve its purpose.

E.   Incorrect. According to social contract theory, if the leaders fail to fulfill the expectations of the people, the people are within their rights to end the government.

4) Which of the following is NOT true or consistent with Machiavelli's argument in *The Prince*?

A.   For a ruler to maintain power, the ends always justify the means.

B.   Divine right is essential for a monarch to maintain legitimacy.

C.   *The Prince* provides a blueprint for gaining and keeping power.

D.   Rulers should not be judged by moral standards.

E.   Power is derived from the people.

Political Orientations

In modern government, political ideology can be sorted into two main categories: liberal and conservative. What these terms mean vary slightly from state to state; however, liberals generally have a more expansive view of government, whereas conservatives have a more restrictive view. In the United States, the ideological views of each are as follows.

LIBERALS (also known as the left) believe in the power and responsibility of government to effect positive change. They see the government as essentially effective, and view it as a protector of and provider for its citizens. As a result, liberals generally support a government that actively regulates the economy and implements extensive social programs; for example, liberals would advocate for a national health care system. They support decreasing military spending and committing troops abroad, although often make exceptions for humanitarian or human rights purposes. They believe the government should not curtail the rights of its citizens, and support the existence of implied rights like the right to privacy. They do, however, believe the government should intervene to control economic factors that impede equality.

CONSERVATIVES (also known as the right), on the other hand, believe in the individual's (and private sector's) power and responsibility to effect positive change. They see the government as essentially ineffective at solving society's problems, and believe its reach should be limited. They believe that the government should only interfere to the extent that it makes it easier for the individual or private entity to better operate. They support free-market solutions to economic problems and a decrease in the regulation of business. Because they think private citizens and organizations can operate more effectively than the government, they generally oppose government-run social programs and believe a national healthcare system would lead to a decrease in the quality of care. They believe military power is necessary to maintain national sovereignty, so they advocate increased military spending and tend to be quicker to commit troops abroad.

The terms *left* and *right* were used to denote political orientation during the French Revolution. Those who supported the king sat on the right side of the Assembly, and those who supported revolution sat on the left. The terms were adopted in Great Britain and the United States in the 1930s.

While the liberal-conservative dichotomy generally covers opposing political ideologies in American politics, it is simplistic. Many American politicians are MODERATES and fall in between these two camps. Moderates hold some views from each side of the spectrum. For example, a moderate might support increased military spending, but also support some social programs.

There are also more extreme ideologies on each side of the spectrum. On the far left, SOCIALISTS advocate for a complete overhaul of the American economic and political system. They believe that the free market creates inequality, and that the market should be closely controlled by government to eliminate that inequality. They also advocate far-reaching government-run programs from healthcare to schools to utilities.

LIBERTARIANS, on the far right, support an extremely limited government, economically and socially. They do not support government programs of any kind, and believe a completely unfettered market is most efficient and effective. They also believe the government should not intervene to curtail or protect individual rights. Their ideal government would maintain only the most basic functions in order to ensure the functioning of the nation.

EXAMPLES

1) Which of the following would most likely be supported by liberals?
   A. an open trade agreement with China
   B. funding a new stealth bomber
   C. a law restricting the use of national forests
   D. vouchers for students to attend private schools
   E. law defining marriage as between a man and a woman

Answers:

A. Incorrect. Free trade agreements remove restrictions on the free market, allowing goods, labor, and resources to move more freely across borders. Liberals argue that free trade leads to decreased wages and the loss of American jobs.

B. Incorrect. Increased military spending is generally not supported by liberals. Because a new stealth bomber serves no immediate purpose but serves the more general national defense, it is even more likely to be rejected by this group, which would prefer that the money be put toward government social programs.

C. **Correct.** Protection of the environment is a central liberal goal. Because liberals view government as a vehicle for the improvement of society, they believe the government has a duty to actively protect nature for its citizens.

D. Incorrect. School vouchers would be supported by conservatives; they are based on the belief that a private organization—a school in this case—is more capable of providing a quality service than its public counterpart. Liberals, on the other hand, would advocate increased spending in public schools.

E. Incorrect. Liberals believe that the government should not be involved in regulated personal issues like sexual orientation.

2) Which of the following would a libertarian vote for, but not a liberal?

A. regulation of business

B. abortion rights

C. criminal rights

D. lower taxes

E. abortion access rights

Answers:

A. Incorrect. A liberal would most certainly vote for the regulation of business, as liberals feel that an unregulated economy has unfair negative impact on many citizens. A libertarian, on the other hand, is adamantly opposed to any government interference in the economy.

B. Incorrect. A libertarian would support a woman's right to an abortion, viewing any government attempt to limit it as an unfair overreach. A liberal, believing in the importance of individual rights, would vote to protect this as well.

C. Incorrect. A liberal is very much in support of individual rights, even those afforded to criminals. Liberals believe that the government, in its role as protector, has an obligation to protect all members of society. A libertarian, however, would argue the government has no right to intercede on behalf of criminals further than basic imprisonment for the sake of maintaining fundamental law and order. This action would extend beyond the necessary functions of government. Some libertarians might not even support the ability of a government to imprison, rendering the question moot.

D. **Correct.** A libertarian would certainly support lower taxes. In fact, a libertarian would likely argue for a complete repeal of taxes. Taxes are collected in order to support government activity, most of which is opposed by libertarians. In their view, lowering taxes returns the money to the hands of the individual where it belongs. A liberal, however, would oppose lowering taxes. The money collected from taxes is used to support social programs which they believe are the responsibility of the government and are necessary for a stronger, more effective country.

E. Incorrect. Both libertarians and liberals believe in a right to privacy protected from the government. Both oppose laws restricting access to abortions.

Constitutional Underpinnings of the US Government

Any study of the United States government must begin with its founding document: the Constitution. It was written as both an expression of ideals and as a practical framework for the functioning of the country. Designed to be a "living document." the Constitution and how it is interpreted has changed in the almost 230 years since it was written. However, its core principles have not. They continue to serve as the foundation and guiding light of American government and politics.

While it is tempting to view the Constitution as a timeless document, it is important to understand that it was actually very much a product of the time in which it was written. The ideals that inform it grew directly out of the Enlightenment, and the governing structure it created was in direct response to both colonial discontent under Britain and problems faced by the new republic. In order to understand the government that emerged, it is necessary to understand this context.

Historical Context of the Constitution

While influenced by philosophy, the Constitution is actually a very practical document. It lays out the overarching structure of the government without excessive detail, explanation, or justification. However, each decision made about the structure of the government was an attempt to either prevent the re-emergence of tyranny or fix the mistakes of the first, failed government.

In 1781, when it was all but assured that the colonies would win the Revolution, the Second Continental Congress had convened to organize a government for the emerging nation. The colonies had broken away from Britain, in short, because of what they viewed as the oppressive rule of an over-bearing central government. As a result, the first government they created, whose framework was called the Articles of Confederation, was intentionally weak. Called a "firm league of friendship," it was designed to create a loose confederation between the colonies (now states) while allowing them to retain much of their individual sovereignty.

As a result, the Articles established a political system which consisted of a UNICAMERAL LEGISLATURE (only one house) with extremely limited authority. The Congress of the Confederation, as it was called, did not have the power to levy taxes or raise an army. Any laws had to be passed by a two-thirds vote, and any changes to the Articles had to be passed unanimously—essentially an impossible feat. The legislature was intentionally and clearly subordinate to the states. Representatives were selected and paid by state legislatures.

It quickly became clear that this government was too weak to be effective, and by 1787, the new government of the United States, only six years old, was already in crisis. Without the power to levy taxes, the federal government had no way to alleviate its debt burden from the war. In addition, without an organizing authority, states began issuing their own currencies and crafting their own, competing trade agreements with foreign nations, halting trade and sending inflation through the roof. Without a national judicial system, there was no mechanism to solve the inevitable economic disputes.

Discontent was particularly strong among farmers, who were losing their property at devastating rates. Their unhappiness exploded into violence in 1786 when Daniel Shays led a rebellion against Massachusetts tax collectors and banks. Unable to raise an army, the Congress of the Confederation was powerless to intervene. The rebellion was finally suppressed when citizens of Boston contributed funds to raise a state militia. SHAYS' REBELLION made it clear that the new government was unable to maintain order.

EXAMPLES

1) Why did the framers of the Articles of Confederation create a decentralized political system?

   A. to cancel the debts the states owed from the Revolution

   B. to ensure that abuses of power like those that existed under British rule did not exist

   C. to delay the question of slavery

   D. to promote national sovereignty

   E. to promote an agrarian versus industrial economy

   Answers:

   A. Incorrect. The decentralized government created under the Articles of Confederation impeded the ability of both the national government and the state governments to pay off their debts.

   B. **Correct.** The perceived tyranny of Britain's rule was fresh on the minds of the framers. Their primary goal was to prevent it from re-emerging.

   C. Incorrect. While this would later become an area of great concern under the Constitution, slavery was not one of the key issues discussed when forming the original government.

   D. Incorrect. The decentralized political system was designed to promote state sovereignty over national sovereignty.

   E. Incorrect. The Articles of Confederation were designed to allow each state to determine its own course, not to make a national decision about the economy.

2) Which of the following ideas most influenced the framers of the Articles of Confederation?

   A. In order to have the consent of the people, all people must be allowed to vote.

   B. Three separate and balanced branches of government are essential for the protection of liberty.

   C. The central government's primary authority should be in monitoring trade.

   D. A strong central government threatens the liberty of the people.

   E. A legitimate government must be able to arbitrate disputes between its citizens.

   Answers:

   A. Incorrect. Only representatives voted on laws, and those representatives were selected by the state legislatures. There was no direct voting at the national level under the Articles of Confederation.

   B. Incorrect. The Articles of Confederation provided for one branch of government only: a legislature.

   C. Incorrect. The legislature had no authority to legislate trade under the Articles of Confederation. Even international trade was regulated between individual states and the countries with which they traded.

   D. **Correct.** Fear of an overpowering central government was the primary factor considered in writing the Articles of Confederation.

   E. Incorrect. There was no judicial branch under the Articles of Confederation.

3) Shays' Rebellion was considered a crisis of government because
    A.   people were previously unaware of the amount of debt that remained from the Revolution.
    B.   it illustrated the national government's inability to maintain order.
    C.   it allowed foreign intervention in American affairs.
    D.   civil liberties were once again threatened as they had been under British rule.
    E.   the central government was unable to keep the states from taking up arms against each other

Answers:
    A.   Incorrect. While it was Massachusetts' attempt to deal with its war debt that led to the rebellion, the debt was no secret.
    B.   **Correct.** The inability of the federal government to suppress the rebellion showed a major weakness in the new government.
    C.   Incorrect. No foreign nations involved themselves in this affair. However, many were afraid that the military weakness it demonstrated would inspire foreign nations to attempt to gain control of American territory, if not the whole country.
    D.   Incorrect. While the farmers rebelled because they did feel that they were being unjustly taxed—similar to the situation under British rule—this fear in no way threatened the stability of the federal government.
    E.   Incorrect. Shays' Rebellion was not a conflict between states. A group of farmers took up arms against the Massachusetts government.

4) Which of the following groups had the most to gain from a revision of the Articles of Confederation?
    A.   small farmers
    B.   members of state legislatures
    C.   women
    D.   immigrants
    E.   merchants

Answers:
    A.   Incorrect. Because small farmers primarily raised crops and livestock for their own consumption or local trade, they had little interaction with government at the federal level.
    B.   Incorrect. While they understood its weaknesses, members of the state legislatures enjoyed the level of sovereignty the Articles of Confederation gave them.
    C.   Incorrect. Women were not a part of the political landscape, and were not addressed in the Articles of Confederation. There was also no sense that they would be addressed in any revision.
    D.   Incorrect. There was no significant changes related to immigration in the Constitution.
    E.   **Correct.** Merchants' income relied on trade, which disintegrated under the Articles of Confederation. They required strong trade relationships with other countries, as well as clear laws governing trade between the various states.

Enlightenment Ideas

The founders of the United States were all very learned men who were educated in the philosophy of the Enlightenment. Several key elements of this philosophy are reflected in the Constitution.

RULE OF LAW: The very desire for a written constitution—a law above all others—reflected Enlightenment thinking, as it ensures a rule of law, rather than a rule of man. In a nation ruled by man, governance is at the whim of an individual or small group of individuals. Decisions are arbitrary based on the interests and needs of those in authority. In a nation ruled by law, governance is based on a body of written, or otherwise codified, law (such as the Constitution). No individual can make a governing decision in conflict with those laws.

REASON: The Constitution is a document based on reason, and is therefore relatively simple and straightforward. It lays out the structure of government without detailing every single function of that government. Rather than simply empowering authority, the Constitution aims to limit government while still allowing it to fulfill its function. It also insists that governing decisions are made outside the scope of religion, by actively separating the two.

SOCIAL CONTRACT: The document begins "We the People..." because the founders believed that government was a social contract, legitimized only by the consent of the people. This is also known as POPULAR SOVEREIGNTY. The Constitution protects individual liberty, life, and property, the fundamental natural laws laid out by John Locke.

SOCIAL PROGRESS: Enlightenment thinkers believed strongly that social progress was possible. As a result, the writers of the Constitution built in a means for amending the Constitution, allowing it to progress with the nation it governed.

EXAMPLES

1) Which of the following aspects of the Constitution reflects the social contract philosophy?

   A. the presidential cabinet

   B. checks and balances

   C. judicial review

   D. direct election of representatives

   E. federalism

   Answers:

   A. Incorrect. The presidential cabinet strengthens the enforcement capabilities of the executive branch. It does not address the idea of the social contract in any way.

   B. Incorrect. Checks and balances most closely relates to Montesquieu's theory of separation of powers.

   C. Incorrect. The ability of the judicial branch to determine the constitutionality of laws reflects the Enlightenment ideas of the rule of law and separation of powers.

D. **Correct.** The Constitution provides for the direct election of representatives (to the House of Representatives) to establish the sovereignty of the people. By selecting their leaders, the people are endowing these individuals with the authority to make governing decisions.

E. Incorrect. Federalism balances power between the state and federal governments.

2) Which of the following best demonstrates the rule of law?

A. The president and members of Congress can be charged with crimes.

B. A government passes a law raising taxes, but later it does not require the wealthy to pay.

C. Congress passes a law declaring the Constitution null and void.

D. A king sentences his rival to death.

E. Courts make rulings based on what each judge thinks is fairest.

Answers:

A. **Correct.** In a government ruled by man, those who make and enforce the laws would be exempt from following them. However, in the United States, even those in authority are subject to punishment if they do not respect rule of law.

B. Incorrect. If the exemption for the wealthy were written into the original law, it might be unfair, but this would still be an example of the rule of law. However, by enforcing the law selectively, the government is arbitrarily governing; thus the people are subject to rule by man.

C. Incorrect. The Constitution is intended and written to be the highest law in the land; it is the basis for rule of law in the United States. If Congress were to declare it null and void, it would be violating the highest law in the land. Congress would be asserting its members' own power to govern (man's power) over that of the law.

D. Incorrect. A king sentencing someone who is a personal threat to death is a classic example of arbitrary use of power and of rule by man.

E. Incorrect. The rule of law requires judges to base their decisions on the law rather than personal beliefs.

The Constitution

A convention of the states was called to address problems in the young United States. At the **CONSTITUTIONAL CONVENTION** in 1787, a decision was made to completely throw out the old Articles and write a new governing document from scratch. There were five main goals for the new Constitution:

1. the protection of property
2. granting increased, but limited, power to the federal government
3. the protection of and limitations on majority rule
4. the protection of individual rights
5. the creation of a flexible framework for government

Each of these reflect the desire to balance authority and liberty. It is this balance that is at the core of the framework of the American government.

The crises of the 1780s made it clear that a stronger central government was needed. However, the states did not want a central government that was so strong that it would oppress the states or the people. The solution? Increase the power of the government, but prevent the concentration of power by dividing it.

The federal government was reorganized under the Constitution, shifting from a one-body political system to a three-branch system as conceived by Montesquieu. In addition to a now bicameral (two house) legislature, a legitimate executive branch was added as well as a judicial. Following Montesquieu's model of SEPARATION OF POWERS, the now-increased powers of the federal government were divided between these branches. In addition, each branch was given powers that would limit the power of the other branches in a system called CHECKS AND BALANCES. For example:

- the executive branch—via the role of president—has the power to veto (reject) laws passed by the legislature.
- the legislative branch can override the president's veto (with a two-thirds vote) and pass the law anyway.
- the judicial branch can determine the constitutionality of laws (JUDICIAL REVIEW).

The president has the power to appoint justices to the federal courts (including the Supreme Court), and the legislative branch—via the Senate—has the power to approve or reject presidential appointments.

The legislative branch also has the power to indict, try, and determine the guilt of a president. The indictment may only be for treason, bribery, and other "high crimes and misdemeanors." While not specifically defined in the Constitution, this is traditionally taken to mean crimes that are specific to office holders. These include perjury, abuse of power, misuse of funds, and dereliction of duty.

The separation of powers limited the powers within the federal government, but did not address the power relationship between the federal government and the states. Under the Articles, the federal government was completely beholden to the states for its very existence. However, it was clear that complete state sovereignty did not work. Instead, the Constitution created a FEDERAL relationship between the two levels of government. FEDERALISM is a system in which both the state government and federal government retain sovereignty by dividing up the areas for which they are responsible.

Under the Constitution, the federal government is charged with matters that concern the population at large: for example, handling federal lands, coining money, and maintaining an army and navy. It also handles conflicts between the states via the federal judiciary and by regulating interstate trade. Matters of regional or local concern are handled by state or local governments. This relationship is best codified in the Tenth Amendment, which states that any powers not explicitly given to the federal government are reserved for the states. However, according to the SUPREMACY CLAUSE (Article 6, Clause 2) the Constitution is the "supreme law of the land." Therefore, in cases of conflict between the states and the federal government, the federal government's authority generally supersedes that of the states.

The division of power has shifted over time with more power going to the federal government as its scope has expanded. The federal government also can exert influence over state governments through GRANT-IN-AID, money that is provided for a particular purpose. The federal government can attach stipulations to this funding. For example, grant-in-aid was given to the states in the late 1970s for highway improvement. However, states who accepted the money were required to set the drinking age at twenty-one years old in their state. This was a way for the government to influence law that was technically beyond their purview.

EXAMPLES

1) In the American federal system of government, the state governments' power derives from

   A. the Constitution
   B. the people of that state
   C. the state legislatures
   D. the people of the nation
   E. the national government

   Answers:

   A. Incorrect. The Constitution delineates the power and structure of the federal government, but does not address the nature of state governments.
   B. **Correct.** Each state government is a democratic republic in which authority is derived from the consent of the governed.
   C. Incorrect. State legislatures are one of the structures within the government—they do not give the government any of its power.
   D. Incorrect. A state government only has authority over citizens within its borders, so the population of the state endows the government with its power.
   E. Incorrect. In the United States, all power is derived from the people.

2) Which of the following best illustrates the system of checks and balances?

   A. state and federal government power to levy taxes
   B. a governor's right to send the National Guard in a crisis
   C. the Senate's power to approve treaties signed by the president
   D. Congress's power to censure its members
   E. the Supreme Court's power to choose its cases

   Answers:

   A. Incorrect. Levying taxes is a power held by both the federal and state governments. It is not a limitation on the power of any branch of government.
   B. Incorrect. This is an example of a power reserved to the states. Again, it is not a limitation on the power of any one branch.
   C. **Correct.** With the authority to approve treaties, the Senate can review and even restrain presidential foreign policy. One example of this was the Senate's rejection of the Treaty of Versailles, which ended World War I in 1919. Although President Wilson signed the treaty and was even one of

Structures and Powers of the Federal Government

In its original form—as described in the Constitution—the federal government was made up of the three branches. Almost immediately upon the ratification of the Constitution, it began to grow and now includes a massive bureaucracy made up of departments and agencies.

Types of Powers

Governmental powers in the Constitution can be divided into six types:

EXPRESSED POWERS: Also known as **ENUMERATED POWERS**, these are powers that are specifically granted to the federal government only. An example of an expressed power is the power to make treaties with foreign nations.

IMPLIED POWERS: These are powers the federal government has that are not in the Constitution. They derive from the elastic clause of the Constitution, Article I, Section 8. The **ELASTIC CLAUSE** gives Congress the right to "make all laws necessary and proper" for carrying out other powers. For example, over time as new technologies have emerged, such as radio and television, the commerce clause has been expanded to allow the federal government to regulate them.

The idea of implied powers was supported by the Supreme Court in *McCulloch v. Maryland* (1819). The state of Maryland tried to tax the Maryland branch of the Bank of the United States. When the bank refused to pay the tax, the case landed in the Maryland Court of Appeals; the court ruled that the Bank of the United States was unconstitutional, as the Constitution did not expressly give the federal government the power to operate a bank. Later, the Supreme Court overturned the ruling, citing the elastic clause.

RESERVED POWERS: These are powers that are held by the states through the Tenth Amendment, which states that all powers not expressly given to the federal government belong to the states. For example, the management of public education is a reserved power.

INHERENT POWERS: These are powers that derive specifically from US sovereignty and are inherent to its existence as a nation. For example, the powers to make treaties and to wage war are both inherent powers.

CONCURRENT POWERS: These are powers that are shared equally by both the national and state government. The power to tax and the power to establish courts are both concurrent powers.

PROHIBITED POWERS: These are powers that are denied to both the national government and the state governments. Passing bills of attainder (laws that declare someone guilty without a trial) is a prohibited power.

EXAMPLES

1) The power to coin money is an example of a(n)
   A. inherent power
   B. prohibited power
   C. concurrent power
   D. expressed power
   E. implied power

   Answers:
   A. Incorrect. While most national governments do have this power, not all do. For example, the national government did not have this power under the Articles of Confederation. This shows it is not a power that derives automatically from national sovereignty.
   B. Incorrect. Congress does have the power to coin money.
   C. Incorrect. Only the federal government may coin money in the United States.
   D. **Correct.** Article I of the Constitution states that Congress has the power to coin money.
   E. Incorrect. The power to coin money is directly stated in the Constitution.

2) The power to hold elections is an example of a(n)
   A. inherent power
   B. prohibited power
   C. concurrent power
   D. expressed power
   E. implied power

   Answers:
   A. Incorrect. Elections are inherent to a democratic government. However, the power to regulate those elections is not. For example, in the United States elections are primarily controlled by local and state governments.
   B. Incorrect. Elections are held by governments in the United States.
   C. **Correct.** Federal, state, and local governments all have the authority to hold elections.
   D. Incorrect. Because state and local governments also have this power, it is not an expressed power.
   E. Incorrect. The U.S. Constitution and state constitutions specifically give the power to hold elections.

The Legislative Branch

At the writing of the Constitution, the branch of the federal government endowed with the most power was the legislative branch. Simply called **CONGRESS**, this branch is composed of a bicameral legislature (two houses). Based on the British model, most colonies—and then states—had bicameral legislatures with an upper and lower house. While this structure was not originally adopted under the Articles of Confederation, the framers chose it when reorganizing the government. This was in large part due to a dispute at the convention over the structure of the legislative body—specifically the voting power of each state.

Small states advocated equal representation, with each state having the same number of representatives, each with one vote. Called the **New Jersey Plan**, this plan distributed decision-making power equally between the states, regardless of land mass or population. The more populous states found this system to be unfair. Instead, they argued for a plan called the **Virginia Plan**, based on **proportional representation**. Each state would be assigned a number of representatives based on its population (enslaved people deprived of their rights would even be counted among the population, benefiting those states with large slave populations). In the end, the **Great Compromise** was reached. There would be two houses: the **House of Representatives** (the lower house) would have proportional representation, and the **Senate** (the upper house) would have equal representation.

This system had two other advantages. The House of Representatives would also be directly elected by the people, and the Senate by the state legislatures. This supported the federal structure of the government: one house would serve the needs of the people directly, and the other would serve the needs of the states. Also, it curbed federal power by fragmenting it and slowing down the legislative process.

Powers of Congress

The structure and powers of Congress are outlined in Article I of the Constitution. As the most representative branch of government, the legislative branch was also designed to be the most powerful. Hence, it has the most expressed powers in the Constitution. Section Eight contains eighteen clauses listing specific powers which can be divided into peacetime powers and war powers:

Table 3.1. Powers of Congress

Clause	Peacetime Powers	Clause	Wartime Powers
1	To establish and collect taxes, duties, and excises	11	To declare war; to make laws regarding people captured on land and water
2	To borrow money	12	To raise and support armies
3	To regulate foreign and interstate commerce	13	To provide and maintain a navy
4	To create naturalization laws; to create bankruptcy laws	14	To make laws governing land and naval forces
5	To coin money and regulate its value; regulate weights and measures	15	To provide for summoning the militia to execute federal laws, suppress uprisings, and repel invasions
6	To punish counterfeiters of federal money	16	To provide for organizing, arming, and disciplining the militia and governing it when in the service of the Union
7	To establish post offices and roads		
8	To grant patents and copyrights		

Table 3.1. Powers of Congress (continued)

CLAUSE	PEACETIME POWERS	CLAUSE	WARTIME POWERS
9	To create federal courts below the Supreme Court		
10	To define and punish crimes at sea; define violations of international law		
17	To exercise exclusive jurisdiction over Washington, D.C. and other federal properties		
18	To make all laws necessary and proper to the execution of the other expressed powers (elastic clause)		

EXAMPLES

1) Congress was similar to the Congress of the Confederation in that

   A. both were designed to be slow-moving and deliberative.

   B. both represented the states only.

   C. both held very limited powers.

   D. both were unicameral.

   E. representation in both was based on population

   Answers:

   A. **Correct.** While Congress was designed to be more efficient and effective than the Congress of the Confederation, which was able to achieve very little, it was still divided into two houses with complicated structures in order to prevent a consolidation of power through quick legislation.

   B. Incorrect. While the Senate was originally designed to represent the states, the House of Representatives has always directly represented the people.

   C. Incorrect. The powers of Congress were greatly expanded beyond those of the Congress of the Confederation.

   D. Incorrect. Congress is a bicameral legislative body consisting of the House of Representatives and the Senate.

   E. Incorrect. In the Congress of the Confederation, representation was distributed equally among the states (each state had one vote). In the Constitutional Congress, only representation in the House of Representatives is determined by population.

2) Which of the following congressional powers was a direct response to the failings of the Articles of Confederation?

   A. the power to grant patents

   B. the power to make laws governing land forces

   C. the power to levy taxes

   D. the power to declare war

   E. the power to establish a post office

House of Representatives

The **HOUSE OF REPRESENTATIVES** is the house which was designed to directly represent the people, and it was originally the only part of the federal government that was directly elected by the citizens. It is the larger of the houses with the number of representatives from each state based on the states' population (**PROPORTIONAL REPRESENTATION**). Every state is guaranteed at least one representative. Apportionment of representatives is based on the census, so seats are reapportioned every ten years with the new census.

At the convention, Southern states argued that their (non-voting) slave population should count towards their overall population, therefore entitling them to more representatives. Northern states with few slaves disagreed. This issue was settled with the **THREE-FIFTHS COMPROMISE** which declared that each slave would be counted as three-fifths of a person for the purpose of the census. (Women, who could not vote until the ratification of the Nineteenth Amendment, were also counted in the census.)

The size of the House grew every ten years along with the population of the United States until 1929, when Congress set the number at 435 voting representatives where it has remained since. Today, each member of Congress represents approximately 700,000 people. Residents of Washington D.C. and territories held by the United States (Guam, American Samoa, and the US Virgin Islands) are represented by non-voting observers; Puerto Rico is represented by a resident commissioner.

Each state legislature divides its state into essentially equally populated congressional districts. This process can often become quite political, with political parties attempting to draw the lines to ensure the maximum number of seats for their party. This is called **GERRYMANDERING**. The Supreme Court has made several rulings to limit gerrymandering, including requiring each district to have equal population and contiguous or connected lines. It is also unconstitutional to draw lines based solely on race.

QUALIFICATIONS: Members of the House of Representatives are elected for two-year terms in an effort to keep them beholden to the people. The Constitution lays out basic requirements for membership to the House. In order to qualify, candidates must be at least twenty-five years old, have been a US citizen for at least seven years, and live in the state they are representing at the time of the election. The leader of the House is called the **SPEAKER OF THE HOUSE**. He or she is the leader of the majority party in the House.

SPECIFIC POWERS: Although it is technically considered the lower house, there are still powers that belong only to the House of Representatives:

- All revenue bills must start in the house. While the Senate may amend the bills, the framers wanted to keep the power of the purse in the hands of the house most beholden to the people.

- The House may bring charges of **IMPEACHMENT** against the president or a Supreme Court justice. Impeachment is the process by which a federal official can be officially charged with a crime. If found guilty, he or she is removed from office. This followed the British model in which the House of Commons (the lower house) had the power to impeach, and the House of Lords (upper house) heard arguments and decided. In order to impeach a president or justice, a simple majority is required. Only two presidents have ever been tried for impeachment: Andrew Johnson and Bill Clinton.

- The House must choose the president if there is no majority in the Electoral College. The House has only selected the president once: in 1824, Andrew Jackson, John Quincy Adams, and Henry Clay split the electoral vote. Jackson had the plurality (the greatest percentage), but did not win a majority. The vote went to the House, and, after some backroom politics, they voted for John Quincy Adams, much to Jackson's dismay.

THE SENATE

The Senate was designed to be the house of the states. To signify that no one state is more important than any other, representation in the Senate is apportioned equally, with two senators per state, making a total of 100 senators. The framers designed the Senate so that representatives were chosen by the state legislatures; there was no direct connection between the Senate and the people. However, as the power of the federal government grew, the people increasingly came to think of it as representing themselves rather than their states. Corrupt state legislatures sold Senate seats to the highest bidder rather than electing the most qualified individual. As a result, the Senate seemed disconnected from the democratic process, a millionaire's club rife with corruption.

The tension between the people's perception of their relationship to the federal government and the mechanism of Senate elections came to a head during the Progressive Era. Political machinations led to deadlocks in state legislatures over appointments, leaving Senate seats vacant for months at time. In 1913, the **SEVENTEENTH AMENDMENT** to the Constitution was ratified; it required the direct election of senators by the people of a state.

QUALIFICATIONS: As the upper house, the Senate was designed to have greater autonomy with stricter qualifications. Senators are elected for six year terms (rather than the two-year terms of members of the House) in order to allow them time to make decisions that might not be popular but that are best for the nation. They are staggered in three groups; one group is up for election every two years. This ensures that all senators do not face re-election at the same time, allowing for more consistent governance.

To be a senator, candidates must be at least thirty years old, have been a citizen of the United States for nine years, and—at the time of the election—live in the state they will represent. The president of the Senate is the US vice president. However, he or she only has the power to vote in case of a tie. The vice president is often absent from the Senate, in which case the **PRESIDENT PRO TEMPORE** presides. He or she is generally the longest-serving member of the Senate.

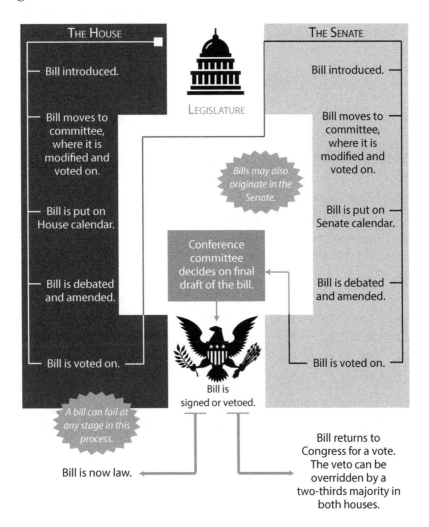

Figure 3.1. Bill to Law

SPECIFIC POWERS: Much like the House, the Senate has certain unique powers:

- Whereas the House has the power to impeach, the Senate acts as the jury in the impeachment of a president and determines his or her guilt. In order to remove, or oust, a president from office, the Senate must vote two-thirds in favor. This has never happened in American history; Andrew Johnson's removal failed by one vote.

- The Senate approves executive appointments and appointments to federal positions in the judicial system. These include, among others, members of the Supreme Court and other federal courts, the attorney general, cabinet members, and ambassadors. While the president may make appointments, no one may take one of these offices without the approval of the majority of the Senate.

The House of Representatives is the house of the people, and the Senate is the house of the states. In order to protect state sovereignty, the federal government was designed to serve the states, the states to serve the people. That is why the Senate is the upper house and has stricter requirements.

◆ The Senate approves (ratifies) all treaties signed by the president. The president is in charge of foreign relations and is responsible for negotiating all treaties; however, as part of the system of checks and balances, the president requires the Senate's approval before any treaty becomes a permanent agreement.

EXAMPLES

1) Why did the framers give the House of Representatives the power to start revenue bills?

   A. Based on their qualifications, members of the House would have more economic knowledge.

   B. Members of the House would be less influenced by outside forces and political parties than members of the Senate.

   C. The House was more truly a national legislature; therefore, it should be in charge of the national budget.

   D. The frequency of elections for House of Representatives would make them more responsive to the will of the people in terms of spending.

   E. Members of the House of Representatives would generally be less wealthy, and so more in line with the people.

   Answers:

   A. Incorrect. No educational or vocational experience is specified as a required qualification for congressional representatives.

   B. Incorrect. If anything, members of the House are more influenced by party and other forces because they face election so frequently.

   C. Incorrect. While the House is the house of the people, its representatives are actually more locally focused than those in the Senate; each congressperson represents a relatively small number of people.

   D. **Correct.** The framers thought it was important that those who spent the money be held most accountable to the people to avoid corruption and misuse.

   E. Incorrect. There are no wealth requirements for either house.

2) Which of the following is NOT an example of how the Senate represents the states?

   A. the power to approve treaties

   B. equal representation of each state in the Senate

   C. vice president serves as president of the Senate

   D. selection of senators by state legislatures (before 1913)

   E. term lengths of six years

   Answers:

   A. Incorrect. The Senate power to approve treaties ensures the states are not forced into a treaty detrimental to their interests.

   B. Incorrect. The Senate has equal representation to show that all states are equally important in the Union.

   C. **Correct.** The vice president's role in the Senate has nothing to do with the influence of states on the national government. Instead, it is a way for the executive branch to check the legislative.

LAWMAKING

The primary function of the legislature is to write and pass laws. The process by which this is done is intentionally cumbersome and complicated. The framers of the Constitution believed that the longer the process took, the more deliberation there would be, decreasing the risk of abuse of power.

Approximately 5,000 bills are introduced in Congress each year, only 2.5 percent of which become laws. There are no restrictions on who can write a bill. In fact, most are not written by Congress, but begin either in the executive branch or are written by special interest groups. A member of Congress is required, however, to introduce the bill. With the exception of revenue bills, bills can start in either house. Since the two houses have parallel processes, the same bill often starts in both houses at the same time.

Once it is placed in the "hopper," the bill is assigned a number and sent to the appropriate committee. Committees and their subcommittees are where most of the hard work of lawmaking is actually done. Here bills are read, debated, and revised. It is also where most bills die, by either being **TABLED** (put aside) in subcommittee or committee, or by being voted down. If a bill does get voted out of committee, it goes to the floor for debate. In the House of Representatives, the powerful **RULES COMMITTEE** not only determines which bills make it to the floor for debate, but also sets time limits for debate on each bill.

In the Senate, debate is unlimited. This allows for a unique tactic called the **FILIBUSTER**, in which a senator or group of senators continues debate indefinitely to delay the passage of a bill. Sixty votes are needed to end a filibuster, therefore senators often attempt to gather sixty or more votes for a bill before it comes to the floor to ensure it is not filibustered.

After debate has ended, the members of each house vote on the bill. If it passes out of both houses, it moves to the **CONFERENCE COMMITTEE** which must transform the two very different draft bills (as different revisions and amendments were made as the bill made its way through each house) into one. Once that is done, the unified bill returns to both houses for a final vote. If it passes, it then proceeds to the president for signature or veto. If the president does veto the bill, it returns to Congress where both houses can vote again. If two-thirds of each house vote in favor of the bill, Congress will override the veto and the bill will become law anyway. However, this rarely happens.

AMENDING THE CONSTITUTION

Congress is responsible for another significant legislative process: amending the Constitution. The framers understood that they could not possibly foresee every threat to state sovereignty and personal liberty nor every need that would require government management. So they added Article V to the Constitution, which lays out a procedure for amending it. This is one of the most significant aspects of the Constitution as it makes it a "living document."

Amendments to the Constitution can either come from Congress or from the state legislatures. For Congress to propose an amendment to the Constitution, two-thirds of each house must vote in favor of the amendment. Alternatively, an amendment can be proposed if two-thirds of the states call for a national constitutional convention. All amendments to date, however, have been proposed by Congress. Either way, once the amendment has been officially proposed, it is not ratified until three-quarters of state legislatures (or special conventions convened by each state) approve it. There are twenty-seven amendments to the Constitution, the first ten of which were passed immediately in 1791. These first ten amendments, now called THE BILL OF RIGHTS, were a condition for ratification imposed by those who thought the new government wielded too much power. These ANTI-FEDERALISTS argued that individual liberty had to be explicitly protected from federal intervention. According to the amendments, the government may not:

Two-thirds is a magic number in American government. Two-thirds of Congress is needed to 1) override a veto, 2) propose an amendment to the Constitution, or 3) remove a president, judge, or other civil official after impeachment (Senate only).

Amendment I: prohibit freedom of religion, speech, press, petition and assembly

Amendment II: prohibit the right to bear arms

Amendment III: quarter troops in citizens' homes

Amendment IV: conduct unlawful search and seizures

Amendment V: force anyone to testify against themselves or be tried for the same crime twice

Amendment VI: prohibit the right to a fair and speedy trial

Amendment VII: prohibit the right to a jury trial in civil cases (remember the original Constitution only guaranteed a jury in criminal cases)

Amendment VIII: force citizens to undergo cruel and unusual punishment

Amendment IX: violate rights that exist but are not explicitly mentioned in the Constitution

Amendment X: usurp any powers from the states not given to them in the Constitution (so all other powers not listed in the Constitution belong to the states)

These will be discussed in more depth later in the chapter.

UNOFFICIAL CHANGES TO THE CONSTITUTION

While the only official way to change the Constitution is through the amendment process, other loopholes for change exist within its framework. These include:

◆ CLARIFYING LEGISLATION: Using the ELASTIC CLAUSE, much legislation has been passed whose purpose is to clarify or expand the powers of the federal government. For example, the Constitution only provides directly for the

Supreme Court, but empowers Congress to create other courts. The Judiciary Act of 1789 created the federal judiciary.

- ◆ EXECUTIVE ACTIONS: Although Congress holds most lawmaking power, the president is able to issue executive actions which have the force of law without having to involve Congress. The most famous of these is Abraham Lincoln's Emancipation Proclamation.

- ◆ JUDICIAL DECISIONS: In *Marbury v. Madison* (1803) the Supreme Court established the precedent of JUDICIAL REVIEW, the power of the Supreme Court to determine the constitutionality of laws. *Marbury v. Madison* not only illustrated how judicial decisions can expand federal power in general, but it also broadened the power of the Supreme Court in particular, laying the groundwork for future decisions that would have a similar impact.

- ◆ POLITICAL PARTIES: The rise of political parties changed the political landscape as well. Some aspects of American politics—like how the Speaker of the House is chosen and nomination conventions for presidential candidates—have come from political parties rather than through a formal legislative process.

PROHIBITED POWERS

Although Congress was made much more powerful by the Constitution, a real fear of tyranny existed among the framers. While Section VIII of the Constitution lists the powers of Congress, Section IX lists what Congress cannot do. Most notable are:

1. NO SUSPENSION OF HABEAS CORPUS: A writ of habeas corpus is a legal demand a prisoner can make to appear in court in order to profess their innocence. Essentially a means of preventing unreasonable imprisonment, this was viewed as an essential element of a just government. The Constitution forbids its suspension except in cases of rebellion or invasion. (Note: Abraham Lincoln, during the Civil War, was the first president to suspend habeas corpus.)

2. NO BILLS OF ATTAINDER: A bill of attainder is a law that declares an individual or a group guilty of a crime without holding a trial. Much like with the writ of habeas corpus, this was seen as an essential protection in a fair society.

3. NO EX POST FACTO LAWS: An ex post facto law is a law which punishes an individual or group for breaking a law that was not a law when the act was committed. For example, slavery was abolished in 1865. If an ex post facto law was passed at that time, it would have punished anyone who had owned slaves before 1865.

4. NO TITLES OF NOBILITY: It was important to the framers to provide safeguards against a return to monarchy. Therefore, they prohibited an American nobility of any kind.

EXAMPLES

1) Which of the following is an example of the "unwritten" Constitution?

   A. the Senate's confirmation of a Supreme Court justice

   B. The passage of legislation organizing the federal court system

   C. Congress writing a law regulating interstate commerce

   D. the House of Representatives voting to impeach the president

   E. the nomination of a presidential candidate at a nominating convention

Answers:

   A. Incorrect. This is one of the powers of the Senate listed in Article II, Section 2 of the Constitution, also known as the advise and consent clause.

   B. Incorrect. The Constitution authorizes Congress to create a federal court system.

   C. Incorrect. This is one of the powers listed in Article I, Section 8 of the Constitution.

   D. Incorrect. Impeachment is a power granted to the House of Representatives by Article I, Section 2.

   E. Correct. This process for selecting a presidential nominee was created by the political parties and is not addressed at all in the Constitution.

2) The clause of the Constitution that prohibits the suspension of writs of habeas corpus except in cases of rebellion or invasion demonstrates that the framers believed that

   A. the people of the nation were likely to rebel.

   B. the president sometimes—like in cases of war—needs unlimited power.

   C. it is important to balance individual liberty with the security of the nation.

   D. the new laws would be resisted by most people.

   E. there were limits to the rule of law

Answers:

   A. Incorrect. While they knew that rebellion led to the birth of the nation, they believed they were creating a nation that would be unlikely to inspire one.

   B. Incorrect. The framers were greatly opposed to—and fearful of—unlimited executive authority.

   C. Correct. Under the Articles of Confederation, they had seen the danger of putting too high of a premium on individual liberty. While it was still one of the highest priorities for them, the needs of the nation had to come first.

   D. Incorrect. This section was not a reflection of their fears of rebellion, but rather an attempt to limit potential tyranny in a reasonable way that did not ultimately undermine the nation.

   E. Incorrect. This clause does not undermine the rule of law in anyway. It is clearly stated, applies to all and aims to be fair.

The Executive Branch

Defined by Article II of the Constitution, the executive branch enforces all federal law. Article II only provides for a president, vice president, and an unspecified number of executive departments. However, the federal government has expanded considerably over the past 225 years, in large part due to the expansion of the executive branch. Today, the executive branch is also responsible for administering a federal bureaucracy that spends $3 trillion a year and employs 2.7 million people.

Of the three mentioned, the president is the only executive role that is specifically defined in the Constitution. The president serves a term of four years, and may be re-elected up to two times. While the term length was set in the original Constitution, the term limit was added in the Twenty-Second Amendment in 1951, in response to Franklin Delano Roosevelt's four elections to the presidency (he was the first—and last—president to be elected to more than two terms). Many felt that allowing unlimited terms opened the door for a de facto dictator and threatened liberty.

QUALIFICATIONS: In order to qualify for the presidency, candidates must be natural-born American citizens, at least thirty-five years old, and have resided in the United States for at least fourteen years. While the Constitution does not specifically list requirements for the vice presidency, it does state that the vice president becomes the president in case of death, resignation, or impeachment. As a result, the vice president must meet the same qualifications as the president.

The CABINET consists of the heads of the executive departments and may advise the president on a variety of matters. It is not directly referred to at all in the Constitution. Instead, it was derived from one line in Section 2: "he may require the opinion, in writing, of the principal officer in each of the executive departments, upon any subject relating to the duties of their respective offices." However, the cabinet as we know it today was established immediately under George Washington. He established four executive departments, so the first cabinet consisted of four positions: the Secretary of State (Thomas Jefferson), the Secretary of the Treasury (Alexander Hamilton), the Secretary of War (Henry Knox; this position is now the Secretary of Defense) and the Attorney General, or head of the Justice Department (Edmund Randolph). Over time, eleven new executive departments were added, for a total of fifteen cabinet positions. The additional eleven are:

1. Department of Interior
2. Department of Agriculture
3. Department of Commerce
4. Department of Labor
5. Department of Energy
6. Department of Education
7. Department of Housing and Urban Development
8. Department of Transportation
9. Department of Veterans Affairs
10. Department of Health and Human Services
11. Department of Homeland Security

These fifteen departments employ more than two-thirds of all federal employees.

In addition to managing their departments, the members of the cabinet are also all in the line of presidential succession as established by the Presidential Succession Act (first passed in 1792 but most recently amended in 1947). The line of succession is as follows: following the vice president is the Speaker of the House, then the president pro tempore of the Senate, followed by each cabinet member in the order of the department's creation, beginning with the Secretary of State and ending with the Secretary of Homeland Security.

EXAMPLES

1) The cabinet is made up of
   A. the president's closest advisors.
   B. the heads of each executive department.
   C. the heads of each house of Congress and the chief justice of the Supreme Court.
   D. the secretaries of state, defense, the treasury, and the attorney general.
   E. a rotating group of state governors

   Answers:
   A. Incorrect. Presidential advisors are part of the White House staff and are separate from the cabinet.
   B. **Correct.** Based on Section 2 of Article II of the Constitution, the cabinet is the formalization of the president's right to seek advice from the heads of the executive departments.
   C. Incorrect. There is no official convening of the heads of each branch of government.
   D. Incorrect. These four secretaries made up the first cabinet under George Washington. However, the cabinet has expanded over the years to include the heads of new departments that were created.
   E. Incorrect. The cabinet is a part of the executive branch and is not related to the states.

2) Which of the following criteria must a vice president meet according to the original Constitution?
   A. She or he must be a natural-born citizen of the United States.
   B. She or he must be of the same party as the president.
   C. She or he must have previously served in the legislature.
   D. She or he must be at least 35 years old.
   E. There are no requirements specified.

   Answers:
   A. Incorrect. This is a de facto requirement of the vice presidency because it is a requirement for the presidency.
   B. Incorrect. While no president has ever run intentionally with a member of the opposing party, this is not a constitutional requirement. In 1797, Thomas Jefferson became John Adams' vice president although they were from different political factions (there were no formalized parties) because the Constitution then stipulated that the person with the second-most votes would become the vice president.
   C. Incorrect. Although the vice president serves as the president of the Senate, no previous legislative experience is required.

POWERS OF THE EXECUTIVE BRANCH

Article II is considerably shorter than Article I because the framers intended the role and powers of the president to be more limited than those of Congress. However, the president does have a number of expressed powers.

APPOINTMENT POWER: One of the most significant presidential powers is the power to appoint federal officials. The president's appointment power is far-ranging and includes cabinet members, heads of independent agencies, ambassadors, and federal judges. Through this power, the president not only controls the entirety of the executive branch as well as foreign policy, but also wields significant and long-term influence over the judicial branch. This power, however, is not unlimited. Based on the advise and consent clause of the Constitution, the Senate must approve all presidential appointments. The president does have the power to remove any of his or her appointees from office—with the exception of judges—without Senate approval.

COMMANDER IN CHIEF: The first line of section 2 of Article II declares the president commander in chief of the army and navy. In this role, the president is the supreme leader of US military forces. He or she can deploy troops and dictate military policy. However, this power is checked as well. While the president controls the military, Congress retains the power to declare war. Presidents have circumvented this check in the past, however, by deploying troops without requesting a formal declaration of war. In the twentieth century, this happened most notably in the Vietnam War, which was never officially declared. In 1964, Congress passed the Gulf of Tonkin Resolution in response to the perceived attack on an American ship in the Gulf of Tonkin. The resolution essentially gave the president a blank check for military action in Vietnam, which led to a rapid and massive escalation of US military spending and troops. Because of this, in 1974 Congress passed the War Powers Resolution; this resolution requires the president to inform Congress within forty-eight hours of a troop deployment and restricts deployment unsupported by congressional authorization to sixty days.

DIPLOMAT-IN-CHIEF: The president is also considered the chief diplomat of the United States. In this capacity, the president has the power to recognize other nations, receive ambassadors, and negotiate treaties. However, any treaties negotiated by the president must be approved by the Senate before taking effect.

Many of the president's diplomatic powers are informal. In the twentieth century, the US became a superpower, transforming the role of the president into that of a world leader as well as the leader of the nation. As a result, the president is now expected to manage international crises, negotiate executive agreements with other countries, and monitor and maintain confidential information related to the security of the nation and to the rest of the world.

JUDICIAL POWERS: While the executive and judicial branches are quite separate, the president has powers intended to check the power of the judicial branch. Primarily, this is the power to appoint federal judges. The president may also grant pardons and reprieves for individuals convicted of federal crimes. The purpose of this is to provide a final option for those who have been unfairly convicted. This is one of the president's more controversial powers, as pardons are often seen to be politically motivated or a tool for those with political or personal connections. The number of pardons granted by presidents has fluctuated over time with Woodrow Wilson granting the most: 2480. In recent years, presidents have issued fewer than one hundred pardons per president.

LEGISLATIVE POWERS: Like the judicial branch, the president is constitutionally accorded some legislative powers in order to limit the powers of the legislative branch. All laws that are passed end up on the president's desk. He or she has the choice to either sign the bill—in which case it becomes a law—or to **VETO** the bill. The president's veto prevents the bill from becoming law (unless Congress overrides the veto as discussed earlier). The president is required to either fully accept or fully reject a bill; he or she may not veto only sections of it. This is called a **LINE-ITEM VETO**, and the Supreme Court declared it unconstitutional in 1996. If the president does not wish to take such a clear stand on a bill, he or she can also simply ignore it. If the president does nothing for ten days, the bill automatically becomes law, even without a signature. If, however, there are less than ten days left in Congress's session, and the president does not sign the bill, it automatically dies. This is called a **POCKET VETO**.

The president also has the power to convene both houses of Congress to force them to consider matters requiring urgent attention.

While this is technically the extent of the president's legislative powers, in reality the position has a much greater legislative impact. The president sets the policy agenda both as the leader of his or her party and through the **STATE OF THE UNION** address. Section 3 of Article II states, "He [or she] shall from time to time give to the Congress information of the state of the union, and recommend to their consideration such measures as he [or she] shall judge necessary and expedient." This has evolved into an annual formalized address to Congress in which the president lays out executive legislative priorities.

Many bills originate in the executive branch, either from the president's office or from one of the executive departments. The president also often uses the power of the veto to influence legislation. By threatening to veto, the president can force changes to bills that align more with her or his political agenda.

ELECTION OF THE PRESIDENT

Almost half of Article II is dedicated to describing the process of electing the president. The framers wanted to ensure the president represented all of the states and was immune from the mob rule of democracy. As a result, they created the **ELECTORAL COLLEGE**. Over the years, the political parties have expanded the process into a nine-month series of elections by various groups of people.

PRIMARIES/CAUCUSES: The first step in choosing a president is selecting the candidates. Originally, this was done in smoke-filled back rooms; it then became the provenance of party caucuses and then conventions, eventually evolving into the current system of primaries and caucuses. In a PRIMARY election, members of a political party in a state vote at a polling place for whom they believe is the best candidate for their party. In ten states, a CAUCUS system is used, in which members of a party in a state gather together at party meetings and vote for the candidate using raised hands or by gathering in groups.

NATIONAL NOMINATING CONVENTION: Then, in July of the election year, the party holds a national nominating convention. Historically, this is where the candidate was chosen after days of heated debate and dealings. However, because of the primary and caucus systems, delegates at the convention arrive already knowing whom their state supports. The delegates vote for the candidate who won their primary or caucus. The candidate with the most votes becomes the party's nominee.

POPULAR VOTE: Presidential elections are held nationwide every four years on the Tuesday following the first Monday in November. Today, all American citizens over the age of eighteen are allowed to vote; however this was not always the case. The framers viewed the electorate as a small, select segment of the population. However, no voter qualifications are written into the Constitution; those were left to the states. In 1789, in every state, only propertied white men—one in fifteen white men—were allowed to vote. Starting with the removal of property qualifications during the Jacksonian era (1830s), views of democracy began to change, and the electorate expanded. Aside from property requirements, each expansion resulted from a new amendment to the Constitution.

Table 3.2. Constitutional Amendments Expanding Voting Rights

AMENDMENT	YEAR	PROVISION
Fifteenth	1870	All male citizens, regardless of race, are allowed to vote.
Nineteenth	1920	Women are allowed to vote.
Twenty-third	1961	Residents of the District of Columbia are allowed to vote in presidential elections.
Twenty-fourth	1964	Poll taxes, an indirect restriction of black voting rights, are prohibited.
Twenty-sixth	1971	All citizens over the age of eighteen are allowed to vote (in most states the voting age had previously been twenty-one years).

ELECTORAL COLLEGE: While the popular vote is tallied on Election Day, it does not determine the outcome of the presidential election. That is the job of the Electoral College. The Electoral College is composed of electors from each state who vote for the president. Electors are apportioned based on population; the number of a state's electors is the same as its number of representatives plus its number of senators (so each state has at least three electors). In its original conception, each state selected its electors by whatever means it chose. At first, most states allowed their state legislatures to choose their electors. By the end of the 1830s, almost every state allowed for the direct election of electors.

In the January following the election, electors gather in their states to cast their votes for president. Technically, electors are not bound to vote in line with their state's popular vote. However, rarely has an elector taken advantage of this, and it has never affected the outcome of an election. Today, most states are winner-take-all, meaning the electors are expected to all vote in line with the outcome of the state's popular vote. The president must win a majority—not a plurality—of the Electoral College in order to win. This is 270 votes.

The Electoral College was designed to elect a president for a nation that was scattered and had greater regional than national loyalty. It favors small states and minority groups, giving them greater influence on the election than they would have in a direct election system. Today many people feel that the Electoral College is outdated and ill-fitting. They argue it is undemocratic, and that it gives undue importance to certain states based on their number of electoral votes. Instead, they support a direct election system.

A state's number of electors is equal to its number of representatives plus its number of senators (which is two for every state). So, every state (and Washington D.C.) has at least 3 electoral votes. There are a total of 538 votes available.

EXAMPLES

1) Which of the following is an implied power of the president?
    A. granting pardons for federal crimes
    B. seeking ratification of a treaty from the Senate
    C. appointing a justice to the Supreme Court
    D. holding a regularly scheduled cabinet meeting
    E. meeting with foreign leaders

   Answers:
    A. Incorrect. The power to grant pardons is an expressed power of the president.
    B. Incorrect. The Constitution gives the president the power to negotiate treaties, but requires him or her to seek approval from the Senate.
    C. Incorrect. Appointing federal judges and Supreme Court justices is an expressed presidential power.
    D. **Correct.** While the Constitution does permit the president to seek the advice of executive department heads, it does not explicitly create a body like the cabinet which meets regularly with the president.
    E. Incorrect. The Constitution specifically states the president has this power.

2) Which of the following earns the president the unofficial title of "Chief Legislator"?
    A. He or she maintains US embassies abroad.
    B. He or she votes in Congress in case of a tie.
    C. He or she sets the agenda for much of what is debated in Congress.
    D. He or she chooses the Speaker of the House.
    E. He or she swears in all new members of Congress.

   Answers:
    A. Incorrect. The president is responsible for embassies (via the State Department), but this is an executive responsibility, not a legislative one.
    B. Incorrect. The vice president votes in the Senate in the case of a tie. The president never has a vote in either house.

C. **Correct.** Using legislation promoted through various executive departments, the presidential role as leader of his or her party, and the State of the Union address, the president leads public policy.

D. Incorrect. The Speaker of the House is the head of the party that holds the majority in the House. The president has no authority in selecting that person.

E. Incorrect. Each chamber of Congress is responsible for the swearing in of its new members.

3) The presidential action that best exemplifies his or her role as Chief Executive is:

A. appointment of a new Secretary of the Interior

B. vetoing a bill

C. negotiating a treaty with Russia

D. receiving the ambassador from Finland

E. issuing a pardon

Answers:

A. **Correct.** As Chief Executive, the president is responsible for the management of the federal bureaucracy and all of the federal departments.

B. Incorrect. Vetoing a bill is a legislative action.

C. Incorrect. Negotiating treaties is part of being Chief Diplomat, not Chief Executive.

D. Incorrect. Much like negotiating a treaty, receiving an ambassador is an example of the president functioning as the Chief Diplomat, not Chief Executive.

E. Incorrect. Issuing a pardon is a judicial action, not legislative.

4) The Electoral College represents which of the beliefs of the framers of the Constitution?

A. Government derives its authority from the consent of the people.

B. Concentration of power can lead to tyranny.

C. The federal government derives its authority from the states.

D. The federal government needs greater power to provide stability to the nation.

E. Power should be divided among different branches of government.

Answers:

A. Incorrect. The Electoral College, when created by the framers, excluded the people entirely from the selection of the president.

B. Incorrect. While the tyrannical potential of concentrated power concerned the framers, it did not relate to the development of the presidential election process.

C. **Correct.** The Electoral College is designed to balance the power of the states and to best represent their interests without allowing a single state to dominate.

D. Incorrect. While stabilizing the nation through federalism was the motivation for writing the Constitution, it was not a consideration when creating the Electoral College.

E. Incorrect. The other branches of government have no role in the Electoral College.

The Judicial Branch

The Constitution's framework for the judicial branch is the least detailed of the three branches. It is also a passive branch. Where the legislative branch creates laws, and the executive branch takes actions to enforce those laws, the judicial branch can only weigh in when an actual case is presented to it. It may not rule or make decisions based on hypotheticals. Yet this branch has grown to be at least as influential as the other two branches both in setting policy and molding the size and shape of the federal government.

The United States has a complex DUAL COURT SYSTEM; each state has its own multi-part judicial system in addition to the federal one. Even though federal district courts handle over 300,000 cases a year, ninety-seven percent of criminal cases are heard in state and local courts. While the federal courts hear more civil cases than criminal, the majority of these are still handled within the states. Because of the federal system, state courts have JURISDICTION—or the authority to hear a case—over most cases. Only cases that meet certain criteria (e.g. a dispute between two states, a case involving federal employees or agencies, or a violation of federal law) are heard in federal courts. Most cases also can only be APPEALED—or reviewed by a higher court—up to the state supreme court. For the federal Supreme Court to review a state supreme court's decision, there must be an issue involving the interpretation of the federal Constitution.

Article III, the article of the Constitution which discusses the judicial branch, only details the Supreme Court. It then empowers Congress to create the rest of the judiciary, which it did beginning with the Judiciary Act of 1789.

The federal court system is composed of three levels of courts. First are the district courts. There are ninety-four district courts in the country, served by 700 judges. They handle eighty percent of all federal cases. The next level of courts are the twelve circuit courts of appeal. These courts review district court decisions and the decisions of federal regulatory agencies.

At the top is the SUPREME COURT. Sometimes called the "court of last resort," the Supreme Court reviews cases from the circuit court and from state supreme courts, and is the final arbiter of constitutionality. Decisions made by the Supreme Court establish PRECEDENTS, rulings that guide future court decisions at all levels of the judicial system.

While the Constitution delineates which kinds of cases the Supreme Court may hear, its real power was established by the precedent of an early case, *Marbury v. Madison* (1803). In this case, William Marbury—citing the Judiciary Act of 1789—sought relief from the court when James Madison, Secretary of State to the newly inaugurated Thomas Jefferson, did not deliver the federal appointment Marbury was given under the previous president, John Adams. The court, under Chief Justice John Marshall, ruled that while Madison was in the wrong, the section of the Judiciary Act allowing Marbury to petition the Supreme Court was unconstitutional because it extended the jurisdiction of the court beyond the scope established in Article III. This established JUDICIAL REVIEW, the Supreme Court's power to determine the constitutionality of laws. This has become the most significant function of the court, and has it allowed it to shape public policy.

There are nine justices who serve on the Supreme Court. Appointed by the president and approved by the Senate, Supreme Court justices serve for life. Surprisingly, the Constitution does not provide any criteria for serving on the court. However, unofficial requirements do exist: justices must demonstrate competence through high level credentials or through prior experience. Today, all of the justices on the Supreme Court hold law degrees from major universities and first served in federal district or appellate courts. They also generally share policy preferences with the president who appointed them, although judicial inclinations do not always neatly align with political ones.

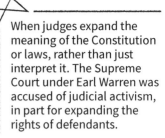

When judges expand the meaning of the Constitution or laws, rather than just interpret it. The Supreme Court under Earl Warren was accused of judicial activism, in part for expanding the rights of defendants.

It is very difficult to have a case heard by the Supreme Court. The court only has **ORIGINAL JURISDICTION** (first court to hear the case) in three situations: 1) if a case involves two or more states; 2) if a case involves the US government and state government; or 3) if a case involves the US government and foreign diplomats. All other cases come to the Supreme Court through the federal appellate courts or the state supreme courts. Appellants must request a **WRIT OF CERTIORARI**, an order to the lower court to send up their decision for review. The court determines its own caseload. It receives approximately 9000 requests for writs each year but typically only accepts eighty cases.

Once a case is accepted, each party must file a brief arguing its side of the case, specifically referencing the constitutional issue in question. Other interested parties may also file **AMICUS BRIEFS**, position papers supporting a particular side or argument. Once all briefs are read, both parties present **ORAL ARGUMENTS** in the Supreme Court. In the oral arguments, each lawyer presents an oral summary of his or her party's argument and then fields questions from the justices. Oral arguments are limited to thirty minutes per side. Next, the justices meet in private to discuss the case and to vote. The chief justice then assigns a justice to write the **MAJORITY OPINION**, a detailed explanation of the majority's decision and reasoning. Other justices who did not vote with the majority may write **DISSENTING OPINIONS**. While these have no force of law, they are a record of alternative reasoning which may be used in future cases. Sometimes justices also write **CONCURRING OPINIONS**, which agree with the majority's ruling, but provide different reasoning to support the decision. There are several significant Supreme Court cases to know, some of which are listed in Table 3.3.

Table 3.3. Supreme Court Cases

CASE NAME	RULING
Marbury v. Madison (1803)	This case established judicial review.
McCulloch v. Maryland (1819)	The court ruled that states could not tax the Bank of the United States; this ruling supported the implied powers of Congress.
Dred Scott v. Sandford (1857)	The Supreme Court ruled that enslaved persons were not citizens; it also found the Missouri Compromise unconstitutional, meaning Congress could not forbid expanding slavery to US territories.
Plessy v. Ferguson (1896)	This case established the precedent of separate but equal (segregation).
Korematsu v. US (1945)	This case determined that the internment of Japanese Americans during WWII was lawful.
Brown v. Board of Education (1954)	The Supreme Court overturned Plessy v. Ferguson; it ruled that separate but equal, or segregation, was unconstitutional.

Table 3.3. Supreme Court Cases (continued)

CASE NAME	RULING
Gideon v. Wainwright (1963)	The Supreme Court ruled that the court must provide legal counsel to poor defendants in felony cases.
Miranda v. Arizona (1966)	This ruling established that defendants must be read their due process rights before questioning.
Tinker v. Des Moines (1969)	This case established "symbolic speech" as a form of speech protected by the First Amendment.
Roe v. Wade (1973)	This case legalized abortion in the first trimester throughout the United States.
Bakke v. Regents of University of California (1978)	This case ruled that while affirmative action was constitutional, the university's quota system was not.
Citizens United v. Federal Elections Commission (2010)	The court ruled that restricting corporate donations to political campaigns was tantamount to restricting free speech; this ruling allowed the formation of influential super PACs, which can provide unlimited funding to candidates running for office.
Obergefell v. Hodges (2015)	The court ruled that same-sex marriage was legal throughout the United States.

EXAMPLES

1) Where did the Supreme Court's power of judicial review come from?
   A. the Judiciary Act of 1789
   B. an order by the president
   C. an amendment to the Constitution
   D. the court's own interpretation of the Constitution
   E. Article III of the Constitution

   Answers:
   A. Incorrect. The Judiciary Act was the first law to be subjected to judicial review; it did not empower the court to determine the constitutionality of law.
   B. Incorrect. The president does not have the power to change the powers of the Supreme Court.
   C. Incorrect. There is no amendment to the Constitution that concerns the Supreme Court.
   D. **Correct.** The court endowed itself with the power of judicial review in the case of *Marbury v. Madison*.
   E. Incorrect. Article III discusses the structure and jurisdiction of the Supreme Court, but does not mention judicial review.

2) Why are justices appointed for life?
   A. to insulate them from political pressure
   B. to prevent them from running for political office
   C. to ensure continuity of decisions
   D. to make the judicial branch the strongest branch of government
   E. to encourage careful consideration of appointments

Answers:

A. **Correct.** The framers were very concerned about judges making unfair decisions based on fears of job security or political allegiances.

B. Incorrect. While justices are appointed for life, they are not required to serve for life. They may resign at any time, and there is no law against them running for office. While it is rare, there have been a few justices who have left the court to serve in an elected office.

C. Incorrect. While the relative stability of the court is a benefit of life-long appointments, it was not the specific goal of the framers.

D. Incorrect. If the framers designed any one branch to be more powerful, it was the legislative, not the judicial. Regardless, their focus was on the separation of powers and ensuring checks on the powers of each branch.

E. Incorrect. The Framers expressed no concern about the selection of justices, as evidenced by the lack of requirements in the Constitution.

3) The Warren Court in the 1960s was accused of judicial activism, or legislating through court decisions. Whose rights were expanded under the Warren court?

A. blacks

B. women

C. defendants

D. youth

E. immigrants

Answers:

A. Incorrect. The case that most impacted the rights of blacks in the twentieth century was *Brown v. Board of Education*, which was decided in 1954.

B. Incorrect. The most significant decision affecting women in the second half of the twentieth century, *Roe v. Wade*, was decided in the Berger Court.

C. **Correct.** Several cases during the 1960s expanded the rights of defendants in court. Two of the most notable were *Miranda v. Arizona* and *Gideon v. Wainwright*.

D. Incorrect. Although youth activism was at an all-time high during this time, it did not have a significant impact on the court.

E. Incorrect. There were no landmark cases specific to immigrants during this time.

4) Which of the following would be written by a special interest to lobby the court?

A. writ of certiorari

B. amicus brief

C. bill of attainder

D. writ of habeas corpus

E. an executive order

Answers:

A. Incorrect. A writ of certiorari is an order sent from the Supreme Court to a lower court to send up a case for review.

B. **Correct.** Amicus briefs are written by organizations, agencies, or other groups who hope to influence to court to take a particular decision.

C. Incorrect. A bill of attainder is a law passed declaring someone guilty without a trial. These are prohibited.

D. Incorrect. A writ of habeas corpus is an order to bring someone before a court to allow them to challenge their detention.

E. Incorrect. An executive order is an order issued by the president that has the force of a law.

Civil Liberties and Rights

Influenced by the ideas of the Enlightenment and fresh from revolution, the framers of the Constitution valued CIVIL LIBERTIES. Civil liberties are rights—provided for either directly by the Constitution or through its historical interpretations—which protect individuals from arbitrary acts of the government. The framers protected some liberties explicitly in the Constitution via the prohibited powers, and expanded on them in the BILL OF RIGHTS (listed earlier in this chapter). Each of these amendments restricts the actions of the federal government rather than actually granting a freedom to the people.

THE FIRST AMENDMENT

SPEECH: The liberties most central to the American identity are articulated in the First Amendment: speech, press, petition, assembly, and religion. The first four are all closely related. No liberty is truly unlimited, however, and the court has imposed restrictions on speech over time. It has upheld laws banning libel, slander, obscenity, and symbolic speech that intends to incite illegal actions.

Figure 3.2. Checks and Balances

RELIGION: The freedom of religion comes from two clauses in the First Amendment: the **ESTABLISHMENT CLAUSE** and the **FREE EXERCISE CLAUSE**. The first prohibits the government from establishing a state religion or favoring one religion over another. The second prohibits the government from restricting religious belief or practice. Again, this is not unlimited. The court has found that religious practice can be banned if it requires engagement in otherwise illegal activity. There are also continuing debates on allowing prayer in schools and granting vouchers to students to attend parochial schools.

RIGHTS OF THE ACCUSED

Most of the civil liberties written into the body of the Constitution addressed the rights of the accused, including prohibitions on bills of attainder, ex post facto laws, and denials of writs of habeas corpus. Three of the amendments in the Bill of Rights address this as well.

The **FOURTH AMENDMENT** restricts unlawful searches and seizures. In *Mapp v. Ohio* (1961), the Supreme Court ruled that evidence obtained illegally—so in violation of the Fourth Amendment—could not be used in court. This **EXCLUSIONARY RULE** is very controversial, and the courts have struggled since to determine when and how to apply it.

The **FIFTH AMENDMENT** protects the accused from self-incrimination. Drawing on this amendment, the Supreme Court ruled in *Miranda v. Arizona* (1966) that arrestees must be informed of their due process rights before interrogation in order to protect them from self-incrimination. These rights, along with those in the Sixth Amendment, are now colloquially known as **MIRANDA RIGHTS**.

The **SIXTH AMENDMENT** guarantees the accused the right to a fair, speedy, and public trial, as well as the right to counsel in criminal cases. While originally this only applied at the federal level, in *Gideon v. Wainwright* (1963) the Supreme Court ruled that states must provide counsel to those who cannot afford it.

THE FOURTEENTH AMENDMENT

The Court's ruling in *Gideon v. Wainwright* was based on the Fourteenth Amendment's **EQUAL PROTECTION CLAUSE**. Ratified in 1868, the amendment's original purpose was to ensure the equal treatment of African Americans under the law after the abolition of slavery. However, its use has been expanded far beyond that original purpose. The equal protection clause has been used to protect the **CIVIL RIGHTS**—protections against discriminatory treatment by the government—of individuals of a variety of groups. Equality is a tricky concept for Americans. It is central to the American ideology, a guiding principle of the Declaration of Independence: "All men are created equal…"

The courts have regularly protected political and legal equality, as well as equality of opportunity (like the *Brown v. Board of Education* decision in 1954). However, the courts do not recognize a right to economic equality. The Supreme Court also recognizes the need for reasonable classifications of people, and allows discrimination along those lines. For example, age restrictions on alcohol consumption, driving, and voting are all considered constitutional.

The Supreme Court has also used the Fourteenth Amendment over time to extend federal civil liberties to the state level. Today, all states are held to the same standard as the federal government in terms of civil liberties.

DUE PROCESS: The second part of the Fourteenth Amendment extends the Fifth Amendment's due process guarantees to the state level. "No person shall be deprived of life, liberty, or property without the due process of law..." While this typically refers to the processes of the accused, as discussed above, it has also come to represent certain unnamed, or implied, rights. At the heart of most of these IMPLIED RIGHTS is the right to privacy, which is not specifically protected in the Constitution. However, the court has ruled that it is implied by the Fourth, Fifth, and Fourteenth Amendments. This was the basis for its decision to legalize abortion in *Roe v. Wade* (1973).

Give one example of a limitation on government power from Articles I, II, and III of the Constitution and the Bill of Rights.

EXAMPLES

1) Which of the following is NOT considered protected speech?
   A. burning the American flag
   B. writing an article criticizing the government
   C. publishing a false list of supposed KKK members
   D. protesting outside of an abortion clinic
   E. wearing a t-shirt with a target sign over the president's face

Answers:
   A. Incorrect. Although there have been attempts to make this illegal, including a failed constitutional amendment, burning an American flag is considered protected speech.
   B. Incorrect. Freedom to criticize the government was one of the primary reasons freedom of speech was included in the Bill of Rights.
   C. **Correct.** Incorrectly alleging that someone is a member of a white supremacist group is considered libel (if written) or slander (if spoken). This is not protected by the Constitution.
   D. Incorrect. As long as the protest remains peaceful, it is protected by the right to assemble as well as freedom of speech.
   E. Incorrect. An individual's dress is considered protected speech.

2) Which of the following does NOT address a due process issue?
   A. a law prohibiting marriage between cousins
   B. a law establishing grounds for termination of parental rights
   C. a law prohibiting airplane travel by convicted felons
   D. a law prohibiting indecent exposure
   E. a law requiring all children attend public schools

Answers:
   A. Incorrect. The right to marry—and privacy within marriage—was one of the first implied rights recognized by the court. This law, however, is constitutional because there is a rational explanation for the restriction.
   B. Incorrect. The right to parent is also considered a fundamental, implied right. The specifics of the grounds would determine the constitutionality of the law.

C.   Incorrect. The right to travel is also a recognized right by the court. This law would most likely be found unconstitutional, however, as the prohibition is too broad.

D.   Correct. There is no fundamental right to public nudity. Nudity generally falls under the right to privacy; however, when it becomes a public act, the individual's rights only extend as far as those of others in society.

E.   Incorrect. The right to determine the education of one's child is considered an implied right.

3)   Which of the following is an absolute right?

A.   freedom to hold any religious belief

B.   freedom of speech

C.   freedom from search and seizure

D.   freedom to bear arms

E.   freedom from cruel and unusual punishment

Answers:

A.   Correct. The government has no authority to restrict people's beliefs. They may, however, restrict religious activity if it violates other laws.

B.   Incorrect. Freedom of speech may be restricted if the speech is defamation, obscenity, or if it incites illegal activity.

C.   Incorrect. While there are restrictions on unreasonable search and seizure, searches that follow the law are allowed.

D.   Incorrect. There are many restrictions on the purchase, ownership, and use of guns.

E.   Incorrect. There are debates on the meaing of "cruel and unusual" and the meaning can change depending on circumstance.

4)   If the police search a home without a warrant, any evidence found could not be used based on:

A.   the equal protection clause

B.   the exclusionary rule

C.   the establishment clause

D.   Miranda rights

E.   the Fifth Amendment

Answers:

A.   Incorrect. The equal protection clause is the section of the Fourteenth Amendment that protects against arbitrary discrimination.

B.   Correct. The exclusionary rule prohibits any evidence obtained illegally from being used at trial.

C.   Incorrect. The establishment clause prevents the government from establishing a state religion or showing preference to a particular religion. It does not deal at all with searches.

D.   Incorrect. Miranda rights protect against self-incrimination, and inform the accused of his or her right to an attorney. They do not address searches.

E.   Incorrect. The Fifth Amendment protects an individual from self-incrimination.

American Political Systems

While the structure of the American government operates much as it is described in the original Constitution, a whole network of systems that support it has developed since it was written. These systems operate within the framework of the government, greatly impacting how the government functions. As the federal government has expanded and grown in power, so have these institutions.

One of the biggest influences on the American political system is **PUBLIC OPINION**, the public's attitude toward institutions, leaders, political issues, and events. Analysts use the extent to which individuals believe they can effect change in the political system, called **POLITICAL EFFICACY**, as a measure of the health of a political system. While faith in core political beliefs like liberty, equality, individualism, and democracy persists, Americans have become increasingly distrustful of government since the 1950s. As a result, there has been a steady decline in civic participation, which has led to a decline in the efficacy of government and its political systems.

Political Parties

Although the framers envisioned a political system without political parties, by the election of 1800, two official parties existed. A **POLITICAL PARTY** is a group of citizens who work together in order to: 1) win elections, 2) hold public office, 3) operate the government, and 4) determine public policy. Some countries have one-party systems; others have multiple parties. Although party names and platforms have shifted over the years, the United States has maintained a two-party system. Since 1854, our two major parties have been the **DEMOCRATIC PARTY** and the **REPUBLICAN PARTY**. Democrats generally follow a liberal political ideology, while Republicans espouse a conservative ideology. The parties operate at every level of government in every state. Although many members of a party serve in elected office, political parties have their own internal organization. Parties are hierarchical: they are comprised of national leaders, followed by state chairpersons, county chairpersons, and local activists.

The parties serve an important role in the American political system, fulfilling functions that aid government operations. These include:

- recruiting and nominating candidates for office
- running political campaigns
- articulating positions on various issues
- connecting individuals and the government

In Congress, parties have become integral to the organization of both houses. The leadership of each house is based on the leadership of whichever party has the majority. The majority party also holds all of the committee chairs, assigns bills to committees, holds a majority in each committee, controls the important Rules Committee, and sets the legislative agenda.

While still very important, the power of political parties has declined dramatically since the beginning of the twentieth century. In response to the dominance and corruption of political machines, many states implemented **DIRECT PRIMARIES** to circumvent the parties. Individual politicians can now build power without the party machinery.

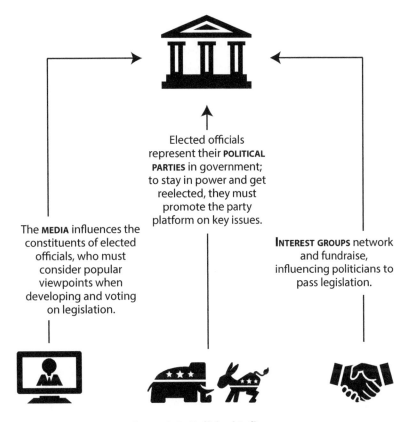

Figure 3.3. Political Influence

Although the United States has a two-party system, third parties still emerge from time to time. These parties are always relatively small and come in three types:

1. **CHARISMATIC LEADERSHIP**: These are parties that are dominated by an engaging and forceful leader. Examples include the Bull Moose Party (Teddy Roosevelt, 1912), the American Independent Party (George Wallace, 1972), and the Reform Party (Ross Perot, 1992 and 1996).

2. **SINGLE-ISSUE**: These are parties organized around one defining issue. Examples include the Free Soil Party and the Know Nothing Party in the 1840s, and the Right to Life Party in the 1970s and 1980s.

3. **IDEOLOGICAL**: These are parties that are organized around a particular non-mainstream ideology. Examples include the Socialist Party and the Libertarian Party.

Although they rarely succeed in gaining major political office, these third parties play an important role in American politics. The two main parties tend toward the middle in an attempt to garner the majority of votes. Third parties, on the other hand, target select populations and are thus able to express strong views on controversial issues. Because their views are usually shared by the most extreme elements of one of the major parties, their stances often push the major parties into more radical or progressive (or sometimes regressive) positions. They also can affect the outcome of an election, even without winning it. By siphoning off a segment

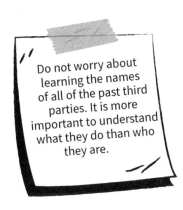

Do not worry about learning the names of all of the past third parties. It is more important to understand what they do than who they are.

of the vote from one of the dominant parties, they can "spoil" the election for that party. For example, in the 2000 presidential election, Ralph Nader, the Green Party candidate, did not win any electoral votes. However, he drew away votes that most likely otherwise would have gone to Al Gore, contributing to George W. Bush's election.

EXAMPLES

1) All of the following result from the two-party system EXCEPT
   A. how the Speaker of the House is selected.
   B. the lack of effective third parties.
   C. the lifetime appointment of Supreme Court justices.
   D. how members are assigned to committees.
   E. fewer instances of compromise in government

   Answers:

   A. Incorrect. The majority-minority split of the House is a direct result of the two-party system. The Speaker of the House is the Congressional leader of the majority party.

   B. Incorrect. The two parties dominate to such an extent that it is not possible for a third party to garner enough support or access to play a significant role in American politics. Furthermore, the agendas of the major parties are so broad that most citizens feel one or the other represents their interests and so do not seek out an alternative third party.

   C. **Correct.** While the appointment of Supreme Court justices can certainly be very political, their lifetime terms are constitutionally mandated and unrelated to political parties.

   D. Incorrect. Committee membership is a result of the majority-minority split in the House which is, in itself, the result of the two-party system.

   E. Incorrect. In multi-party systems, parties are required to form coalitions in order to have a majority to govern. In a two-party system there is no equivalent inducement to compromise.

2) Third parties primarily impact presidential elections by
   A. increasing voter turnout.
   B. preventing either party from winning a majority in the Electoral College.
   C. encouraging more voters to officially join a political party.
   D. bringing forward issues to be adopted by the major parties later.
   E. Increasing support for one of the candidates from a major party

   Answers:

   A. Incorrect. There are some voters who will come out to vote for a third party candidate who would not do the same for a candidate from one of the major parties. However, these numbers are not enough to significantly impact voter turnout.

   B. Incorrect. A third party candidate has never had such an impact on a presidential election. The closest was the three-way race among Henry Clay, Andrew Jackson, and John Quincy Adams. The three split the vote such that no one won a majority. However, none of these men represented a third party.

Interest Groups

An **INTEREST GROUP** is a private organization made up of individuals who share policy views on one or more issues. Organized together, the group then tries to influence public opinion to its own benefit. Interest groups play an important role in American politics. Much like political parties (and often even more directly than political parties), they connect citizens to the government. They act as a two-way street, both bringing their members' concerns and perspective to government officials and sharing information with their members about government policy. They wield more influence than the average citizen: they speak for many, and they raise money to influence policymakers, thereby influencing policy. Interest groups play an increasingly dominant role in American political life. The number of groups increased from 6000 in 1959 to 22,000 in 2010.

Most interest groups focus on one core issue or on a set of issues and draw their membership from people interested in those issues. For example, the National Rifle Association focuses on protecting the right to gun ownership. Other organizations focus on a specific group of people, and then determine their interests based on the interests of that group. The AARP (American Association of Retired Persons) is an example of this type of interest group. It determines which issues are most relevant to senior citizens (who make up their membership), and pursues those issues. In addition, large corporations, industry organizations, agricultural groups, professional associations, and unions act as interest groups.

Interest groups **LOBBY** lawmakers to try to effect the change they wish to see. To lobby means to attempt to persuade policymakers to make a certain decision. There are about 30,000 lobbyists in Washington D.C., making $2 billion a year. It is their full-time job to advance the agenda of their interest groups. They do this by testifying before congressional committees, meeting with aides, connecting influential constituents to lawmakers, drafting legislation, and providing relevant technical information to members of Congress. When all else fails, interest groups will turn to the courts to help them achieve their goals. They write amicus briefs in Supreme Court cases or initiate court cases to challenge existing laws. They also can play a significant role in determining who is nominated to the federal courts, including the Supreme Court.

Another tool interest groups use to influence policymakers is the **POLITICAL ACTION COMMITTEE**, also known as a PAC. These are committees that interest groups form with the purpose of raising money to support the campaigns of specific candidates who can further their interests. PACs are limited to contributions of $5000 per candidate per election (it is important to note that primary elections count as separate elections). In 2010, however, the Supreme Court ruled in *Citizens United v. Federal Elections Commission* that limiting corporate donations to candidates was tantamount to limiting free speech.

This controversial decision resulted in the creation of super PACs which have no limits on spending.

The role of lobbying, and most specifically PACs and super PACs, in American politics is a hotly debated one. Some political analysts are concerned that politics and money have become too closely tied together. Others argue that the sheer number of special interest groups is a benefit because they each balance each other out. In order to accomplish anything, politicians must bargain and compromise, creating solutions that are ultimately better for more people. Others still argue that rather than creating solutions, the number of competing interests leaves politicians scared to take any action for fear that they will anger one interest group or another.

Mass Media

Any means of communication—newspapers, magazines, radio, television, or blogs—that reaches a broad and far-reaching audience is considered part of the MASS MEDIA. Although certainly not a formal part of the political process, the mass media has a significant impact on American politics. It connects people to the government by providing them with inside information on its people and processes, through reports, interviews, and exposés. The media also can help set the political agenda by drawing attention to issues through its coverage. For example, the medical treatment of veterans became a significant political issue after two lengthy exposés in the *Washington Post* on the conditions at Walter Reed Medical Center in 2007.

Mass media has also reshaped American campaigns. Campaigns have become more candidate-centered rather than issue-centered, as candidates now must consider their image on television and other video sources. They also have to be media savvy, making

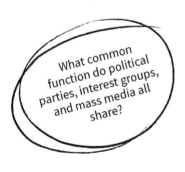

What common function do political parties, interest groups, and mass media all share?

appearances on popular nightly shows and radio programs. The need for a strong media presence is largely responsible for the increase in campaign spending, as candidates work to maintain an up-to-date web presence and spend millions of dollars on television advertising space. Candidates' lives and pasts are also more visible to the public as journalists research their backgrounds to a further extent than ever before. In the 1960 presidential campaign, John F. Kennedy and Richard Nixon engaged in the first televised presidential debate in American history. Those who listened to it on the radio declared Nixon—who was confident in speech, but sweaty and uncomfortable on camera—the winner, while those who watched it on television saw the suave and image-savvy Kennedy as the victor. Many credit this debate for Kennedy's eventual win, demonstrating the new importance of crafting a public image for politicians.

EXAMPLES

1) Which of the following is an example of an issues-driven organization?
   A. Americans for Tax Reform
   B. the American Medical Association (AMA)
   C. the AFL-CIO

D. the National Association for the Advancement of Colored People (NAACP)

E. American Association of Retired People

Answers:

A. **Correct.** This organization was formed around the issue of tax reform. People who are interested in this issue then join this group.

B. Incorrect. The American Medical Association is a membership-based organization for doctors. It determines which issues would be important to doctors and pursues those interests.

C. Incorrect. The AFL-CIO is a union; therefore it is a membership-based organization.

D. Incorrect. The NAACP's goal is to represent African Americans. Its agenda is based on the needs and wants of its membership.

E. Incorrect. The AARP represents Americans over 50 years old rather than a particular issue.

2) The most effective task for a lobbyist is

A. organizing protests

B. giving expert information to legislators

C. mobilizing letter-writing campaigns

D. leading politicians' campaigns for election

E. supporting Congressional leaders

Answers:

A. Incorrect. While some interest groups may engage in public protest, most do not. Moreover, such protests are rarely organized by lobbyists.

B. **Correct.** As a resource for legislators and their aides, a lobbyist can influence their thinking on a particular topic.

C. Incorrect. While letter-writing campaigns can be an effective grassroots strategy, they are beyond the purview of a lobbyist.

D. Incorrect. Lobbyists do not play a direct role in helping politicians get elected, although they can mobilize on behalf of certain politicians who support their issues.

E. Incorrect. Lobbyists have no direct responsibility to members of Congress.

3) Throughout the twentieth and twenty-first centuries, changes in politics have coincided with the emergence of new media or a change in the organization of media. This shows that:

A. New media develops in response to political changes.

B. Media has a greater impact on the functioning of government than other political systems.

C. There is no connection between the functioning of media and politics.

D. Politics is responsive to changes in how people communicate.

E. Government policy drives changes in media.

Answers:

A. Incorrect. Because media reaches beyond politics, it tends to lead political developments and trends.

B. Incorrect. While this statement shows the importance of media, it is only one player in the political system. It does not carry more weight than political parties or interest groups, both of which have had a tremendous impact on shaping American politics.

C. Incorrect. There is a clear connection between the two, as they are dependent on each other for functioning (although their relationship can be antagonistic at times).

D. **Correct.** Politicians are always trying to find the best way to connect to their constituencies; therefore they must be adaptable to new media as it emerges. Also, new media changes the way in which politics is reported, which then changes the way it functions.

E. Incorrect. New media typically emerges from private enterprise rather than government policy.

Comparative Politics and International Relations

All nations have governments; however, those governments come in very different forms. A government's structure is influenced by environmental factors like geography, population size, economic strength, industrial development, and cultural diversity. Significant changes to any of these categories can lead to a restructuring of the government itself.

Types of Governments

Categories of governments can be divided up in three different ways.

TYPE OF RULE

Governments are either ruled by man or ruled by law. In a government ruled by man, decisions are arbitrary and absolute. These tend to be AUTOCRACIES, meaning *rule by one person*. There are two types of autocracies. In a DICTATORSHIP, the ruler derives power from political control, military power, or a cult of personality. In a MONARCHY, authority is derived from a DIVINE RIGHT to rule given by God. Some governments ruled by man are OLIGARCHIES, ruled by a powerful group, or ARISTOCRACIES, ruled by an elite class. In both of these cases, the right to rule is based on wealth, social status, military position, or some level of achievement. In a THEOCRACY, authority is also held by a small group—the religious leadership—and is derived from divine right.

Governments ruled by law are governed according to a code of law. An early example of legal code is the Twelve Tables, developed in the fifth century in the Roman Empire. In the sixth century, these laws and others that had been developed across the breadth of the Eastern Roman Empire were organized into the Justinian Code by the Byzantine emperor. These became the basis of many modern legal systems, including that of the United States. In general, countries ruled by law are some form of republic or democracy. Most modern nations are—at least in theory—ruled by law.

Geographic Distribution of Authority

A second way to organize different types of governments is by how their authority is distributed across the territory of the state or nation. A **UNITARY GOVERNMENT** vests all of its power in the central government. This is the kind of the government used by most nations. For example, Great Britain, France, and China all have unitary governments. On the other end of the spectrum are **CONFEDERATE GOVERNMENTS**. The prime example of this is the first government of the United States under the Articles of Confederation. A confederate government is decentralized with power distributed among regional governments. Finally, power can be distributed through a **FEDERAL** system. As discussed earlier, in a federal government the power is shared between the central government and the regional governments.

Separation of Powers

Governments can be organized depending on the way power is divided within the government itself. In an **AUTHORITARIAN GOVERNMENT**, there is no division of power. All aspects of government are controlled by the same body, whether that is a single ruler or a council of some kind. North Korea is an example of an authoritarian government. In a **PARLIAMENTARIAN GOVERNMENT**, the legislative and executive functions of government are combined, with the judicial acting as a separate body. In this system, the head executive—the **PRIME MINISTER**—and his or her cabinet are chosen from the legislature. The prime minister maintains power as long as his or her party (or parties) maintain a majority in the legislature. Great Britain has a parliamentary government. The final type is the US-style, three-branch system which has been discussed at length in this text.

EXAMPLES

1) The British historian Lord Acton said, "Power corrupts; absolute power corrupts absolutely." Based on this, which of the following systems do you think he would have most likely supported?

    A. a monarchy

    B. a democratic republic

    C. a unitary government

    D. an aristocracy

    E. an oligarchy

    Answers:

    A. Incorrect. Because a monarchy is an autocratic government, power is concentrated in the hands of one person; this leads, according to Acton, to corruption.

    B. **Correct.** In a democratic republic, power is distributed across multiple branches of government.

    C. Incorrect. In a unitary government, only one branch of government holds all of the power. Acton would view this as a dangerous concentration.

    D. Incorrect. While power is less concentrated in an aristocracy than in a monarchy, control is still consolidated in the hands of a relative few.

    E. Incorrect. In an oligarchy, a few elite individuals hold all of the power.

2) In the Soviet Union, Joseph Stalin used secret police, purges, and censorship to rule. This type of government is called

- **A.** a monarchy.
- **B.** a democratic republic.
- **C.** a dictatorship.
- **D.** an oligarchy.
- **E.** a democracy.

Answers:

- A. Incorrect. While monarchies are also autocratic governments, the authority for rule comes from God.
- B. Incorrect. In a democratic republic, power is shared and power is derived from the consent of the governed.
- **C. Correct.** An autocratic government in which power is maintained by force is a dictatorship.
- D. Incorrect. In an oligarchy, power is concentrated in the hands of a few. While Stalin was supported by a massive bureaucracy, all of the true power resided with him alone.
- E. Incorrect. In a democracy the people hold the power and make all decisions.

Political Party Systems

Almost all modern governments are run by political parties. However, party systems come in three different types: single-party, two-party and multi-party.

The simplest party system is the ONE-PARTY SYSTEM. In a one-party system, only one party controls the entire government without opposition or challenge. Elections are still held, but their purpose is to allow citizens to show their support for the existing government. Autocratic governments are one-party systems. China, North Korea, and Cuba all have one-party systems.

In a TWO-PARTY SYSTEM, two major parties compete for control. In these systems, fewer differences divide the parties, and each party trends toward the middle in order to try to gain as much public support as possible. The parties generally split along the liberal-conservative line; neither one takes an extreme stance on an issue. The United States, Great Britain, and Australia all have two-party systems.

In MULTI-PARTY SYSTEMS, several different parties compete for government power. Unlike those in two-party systems, the parties in a multi-party system represent very different and often more radical ideologies. Because it is difficult for one party to win a true majority, parties seek PLURALITIES—the largest percentage of votes—rather than MAJORITIES—more than half of the votes. Consequently, the government is run by a coalition of different parties that form alliances. As a result, there must be some degree of consensus between at least some parties. France, Italy, and Israel all have multi-party systems.

In both two-party and multi-party systems, citizens use their votes in elections to support certain policies or agendas.

The framers of the Constitution intentionally tried to avoid political parties, yet a party system emerged anyway. But why was it a two-party system? Several factors make a nation more receptive to a two-party or a multi-party system.

A key structural factor affecting the development of a party system is the apportionment of power within the legislature. In the United States for example, power is distributed among **SINGLE-MEMBER DISTRICTS**. States are divided into districts, and each district elects one representative in a winner-take-all model. This discourages the growth of smaller parties, as they are unlikely to win a majority—the only way they can gain any power. Italy, on the other hand, uses **PROPORTIONAL REPRESENTATION**. In this system, the number of seats any one party gets is based on the percentage of the vote it wins overall. This encourages smaller parties as they can still win some seats with only a small percentage of votes.

Don't confuse this party-based proportional representation with the proportional representation of the House of Representatives. In that case, the "proportion" refers to how representatives are divided amongst the states. Even though a state like Texas may have a greater proportion of the representatives than Delaware, in both cases the actual representatives are still chosen in a single-member district, winner-take-all style.

In the United States, these natural tendencies have been strengthened by legislation passed by the two major parties which makes it more difficult for third parties to gain a foothold. For example, only Democratic and Republican candidates automatically appear on the ballot; all other parties must petition to gain access. Finally, in spite of its diversity, the United States generally has a high level of consensus on core issues. This is most likely a result of the fact that the nation was founded on a common ideology.

EXAMPLES

1) Autocratic governments typically have which kind of party system?

A. a single-party system

B. a two-party system

C. a multi-party system

D. no party system

E. all of the above

Answers:

A. **Correct.** Because autocratic governments are controlled by one person or a small group of people, challenges to their authority are unwelcome. However, party affiliation usually indicates members of the ruling group and gives a semblance of democracy.

B. Incorrect. Two-party systems require two opposing points of view, which is not conducive to autocracy.

C. Incorrect. Governance in a multi-party system emerges as a result of broad choice in determining leadership. This does not exist in an autocratic government.

D. Incorrect. It is true that most absolute monarchies operate without parties. However, the majority of autocracies today are not monarchies but are instead some form of dictatorship. In these cases, having some kind of political party helps create a common ideology.

E. Incorrect. In an autocratic government, because power is held by one or a few people, competition for leadership is not allowed.

2) Which of the following is NOT true of multi-party systems?

    A. They lead to coalition governments.

    B. They have parties with more radical views.

    C. They result from single-member districts.

    D. Parties seek to win a plurality of votes instead of a majority.

    E. There are more governments with multi-party systems than two-party systems.

Answers:

    A. Incorrect. Because it is difficult for one party to win a majority, governments in multi-party systems are formed through compromises and alliances between different parties.

    B. Incorrect. In a multi-party system, clearer and more extreme views are more effective in garnering a support base.

    C. **Correct.** Two-party systems result from single-member districts where there is a winner-takes-all race for each individual seat. In a multi-party system, seats are apportioned based on the percentage of the vote received by each party.

    D. Incorrect. Because representation is proportional, parties do not need a majority in order to be influential—or even represented—in government.

    E. Incorrect. Multi-party systems are the most common in the world's democratic governments.

Foreign Policy

FOREIGN POLICY describes how and why one nation interacts with the other nations of the world. As new technologies emerge and the world becomes more interdependent, foreign policy has become an increasingly important part of any nation's governance. The goals for international engagement vary from country to country and even from moment to moment; these goals influence how policy is defined and communicated. Foreign policy goals include:

- protecting and increasing a nation's independence
- improving national security
- furthering economic advancement
- spreading political values to other nations
- gaining respect and prestige from other nations
- promoting stability and international peace

Nations use a variety of tools—military, economic, and political—to further their foreign policy goals. They may build up their military resources or position troops in strategic locations. At the most extreme, they can deploy troops to engage hostile nations or to support allies. Economic tools can be either punitive or supportive. For example, a country may impose economic sanctions on another country to try to pressure it into changing an undesirable policy, or it may offer economic support in exchange for a favorable outcome. Countries may also use political pressure to influence the decisions of others by forming alliances or granting or withholding official recognition of another state.

While nations are the key players in foreign policy, they are not the only ones. Non-state ethnic minorities (like Basque separatists in Spain), world organizations, and multinational corporations all wield a great deal of influence. While often indirect, they use many of the same tools to influence political leaders to form policy friendly to their own objectives.

American foreign policy has grown increasingly complex as the United States has undergone extensive changes in its relationship to the rest of the world since the eighteenth century. In George Washington's Farewell Address, he warned against forming any "permanent alliances" with other nations. This call for ISOLATIONISM set the tone for American foreign policy until the end of the nineteenth century. While not always successful—or even consistent—American political leaders maneuvered to keep the United States out of major foreign entanglements and especially European affairs.

But as American economic interests and power increased, so did American engagement with the rest of the world. The first half of the twentieth century saw divisions between groups favoring INTERNATIONALISM (more engagement in global affairs) and others favoring a return to isolation. After World War II, the United States became a global superpower, taking responsibility for affairs in and among countries around the world. With the end of the Cold War and the fall of the Soviet Union, the political landscape shifted again. There were no longer two major superpowers dictating the world's foreign policy. As the world has become more globalized, the United States has responded with a shift in its foreign policy to one of INTERDEPENDENCE, mutual reliance with and on other countries.

The president, as commander in chief and head diplomat, is the primary foreign policy leader. He or she is supported from within the executive branch by the Secretary of State, the National Security Agency advisor, and the Secretary of Defense. Congress also plays a significant role as it controls the appropriation of money and declarations of war. The Senate also has the power to ratify treaties negotiated by the president and to control representation of the United States abroad by confirming diplomatic appointments.

EXAMPLES

1) The United States and the Cuban leader Fidel Castro were at odds following the Cuban Revolution. Which of the following is NOT an example of an attempt by the United States to influence Cuba during the twentieth century?

   A. encouraging emigration from Cuba to the United States

   B. placing severe economic sanctions on Cuba

   C. building a military base at Guantanamo Bay

   D. supporting the failed Bay of Pigs invasion

   E. prohibiting American travel to Cuba

   Answers:

   A. Incorrect. During the Cuban Revolution and later in the twentieth century, the United States facilitated the entry of Cubans escaping the Castro government.

   B. Incorrect. The United States placed severe economic restrictions on Cuba that persist to this day.

   C. Correct. The US military base at Guantanamo Bay was established before the Cuban Revolution.

D. Incorrect. The Kennedy administration supported this failed attempt at toppling the Castro government.

E. Incorrect. Between 1963 and 2015, American travel to Cuba was prohibited in an attempt to isolate Cuba politically and economically.

2) US involvement in Europe after World War II is an example of

A. internationalism

B. isolationism

C. interdependence

D. imperialism

E. none of the above

Answers:

A. **Correct.** Learning from worldwide depression and the rise of totalitarianism after World War I, the US took on the responsibility of aiding the quick rebuilding of Western Europe. This is a clear example of internationalist foreign policy.

B. Incorrect. The US invested in Europe financially and militarily after World War II, including through the Marshall Plan and the creation of NATO. An isolationist policy would have advocated no involvement at all.

C. Incorrect. The relationship between the United States and Western Europe was very one-sided after World War II. An interdependent foreign policy would have required give-and-take from both sides.

D. Incorrect. The US was not trying to assert political control over Europe.

E. Incorrect. US foreign policy, throughout history, has always fallen into one of these three categories.

Theories of International Relations

The study of INTERNATIONAL RELATIONS is based around the idea that states always act in their own national interest. In deciding how to interact with other nations, they are always seeking to promote the foreign policy goals listed in the previous section. However, theorists disagree on which of those goals is of utmost importance. There are two main schools of thought:

REALISM: First articulated by Hans J. Morgenthau, the theory of realism argues that a state's primary interest is self-preservation, which can only be achieved by maximizing power. As a result, nations are always working to acquire more power relative to the power of other states. This theory is a direct continuation of Machiavelli's political theory: morality has no place in policy. Realists believe war is inevitable. They also do not believe any kind of global policing (in the form of a supra-national law enforcement body) is truly possible, as its power would only extend as far as the world's nations allowed it. Furthermore, they would only allow it insofar as it did not diminish their own nation's individual power. If all states are acting in their own self-interest, there is no room for global interest. Realism guided Cold War politics from both the US and Soviet perspectives.

LIBERALISM: Liberal theorists argue that realism is outdated. Globalization and the growth of international trade have created too many ties among nations to allow for each to truly have a national interest separate from that of other nations. This theory emerged in the 1970s, as the clear lines of the early Cold War became muddled, and the consequences of military action—specifically in Vietnam—came to light. Liberals argue that the world is now a system of complex interdependence, greatly decreasing the usefulness of military power. In fact, the consequences of military force usually outweigh the benefits, as it is impossible to strike another nation without serious repercussions in one's own. Instead, economic and social power are much more effective tools. Liberals acknowledge that different states will have different primary interests, but international cooperation is actually in the best interest of every state. They also argue that international organizations and rules—policing and otherwise—help to foster that cooperation, build trust, and lead to prosperity for all.

Among liberals are a sub-group called **IDEALISTS** who move even further away from realism. They actually stand directly in opposition to Machiavelli, arguing that states must follow moral goals and act ethically in order to serve their best interest. The best example of an idealist is Woodrow Wilson. His Fourteen Points envisioned a world beyond war and conflict—peace and prosperity through moral foreign policy.

EXAMPLES

1) Which of the following actions follows a realist approach?
   A. creating the United Nations
   B. building the Berlin Wall
   C. imposing economic sanctions on Russia following conflict with Ukraine
   D. sending economic aid to Afghanistan
   E. sending peacekeeping troops to Cambodia

   Answers:
   A. Incorrect. With its goal of promoting world peace through cooperation among nations, the United Nations is a prime example of liberalism.
   B. **Correct.** East Germany built the Berlin Wall in order to prevent defections to the West. This is an example of self-preservation.
   C. Incorrect. The use of economic sanctions to influence a government's policy—in this case, Russian aggression against Ukraine—is a key liberal approach.
   D. Incorrect. Providing economic aid is an example of liberalist global cooperation.
   E. Incorrect. Helping maintain the peace in a country where the U.S. has no direct interest is a liberal, or even idealist, policy.

2) In 1994, over half a million people were killed in Rwanda during a genocide that lasted only a few weeks. An idealist response by the United States to this tragedy would have been to:
   A. take no action
   B. declare war on Rwanda
   C. insist that the UN or other international organizations take action
   D. impose economic sanctions on Rwanda
   E. seize control of the Rwandan government

Current Global Relations

Realism and liberalism describe how various theorists think nations should act, but have also dictated foreign policy over time. Realism guided policy in the eighteenth, nineteenth, and first half of the twentieth centuries. It resulted in the rise of the nation-state in the eighteenth century, widespread nationalism throughout the nineteenth, the rise of global colonialism, and the development of imperialism among Western European countries, Russia, and the United States. Although liberalism was not articulated as a theory until the 1970s, its guiding principles began to emerge at the end of the nineteenth century, with ideology and "isms" replacing the domineering policies of the previous centuries. From the second half of the twentieth century to this day, another shift is occurring. Technological advancement and globalization have reshaped global politics, led to increased interdependence, and given greater influence to non-government entities (like terrorist groups) and transnational organizations.

Today, INTERNATIONAL ORGANIZATIONS are as important as individual nations to global politics. There are two types of international organizations:

NONGOVERNMENTAL ORGANIZATIONS (NGOs): Funded primarily by individuals or foundations, NGOs provide services or advocate for certain policy positions within a particular nation or across national borders. NGOs vary widely in their missions, their ideologies, and their practices; however they all work outside of national governments. Some are highly religious or political in nature, while others intentionally avoid all such associations. They address issues such as healthcare, the environment, human rights, and development. Currently, there are approximately 1.5 million NGOs operating in the US alone, with millions more worldwide. Doctors without Borders and the Red Cross are both examples of NGOs.

INTERGOVERNMENTAL ORGANIZATIONS (IGOs): IGOs are organizations comprised of individual sovereign nations (they can also be made up of other IGOs). Whereas NGOs are entirely private, and therefore operate under a loose definition, IGOs are official governing bodies that must adhere to international legal guidelines. For an IGO to be created, all participating members must sign (and ratify) a treaty establishing the organization's existence and outlining its mission and functioning. Not all treaties create IGOs.

The North American Free Trade Agreement (NAFTA), for example, does not create an official organization, although the signatories may need to meet from time to time to ensure its proper implementation. Three examples of IGOs are:

- ◆ **THE NORTH ATLANTIC TREATY ORGANIZATION (NATO)**: Created after World War II, the NATO treaty was originally signed by ten Western European nations, the United States, and Canada. The treaty created an organization of countries that pledged to come to each other's defense in case of external aggression; this was mainly in response to the threat posed by the Soviet Union. Today, NATO has twenty-eight members.

- ◆ **THE UNITED NATIONS (UN)**: Also created after World War II, the United Nations was the second attempt at an international organization dedicated to promoting world peace. The UN addresses economic, health, social, cultural, and humanitarian issues throughout the world. The United Nations currently has 193 member states. While it is a significant player in world politics, its effectiveness is often questioned as it has very limited military power (its peacekeeping troops are not allowed to engage militarily without Security Council authorization, which is very difficult to obtain) and is subject to the consent of its members.

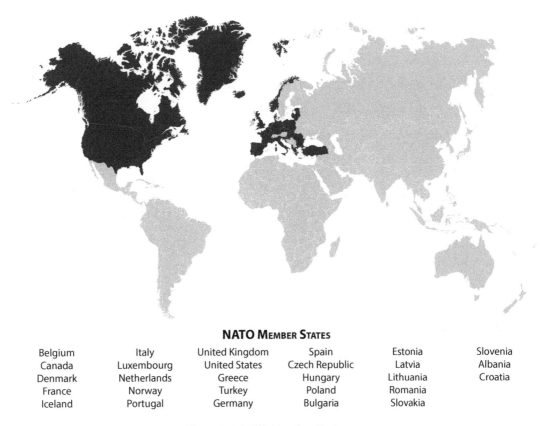

NATO MEMBER STATES

Belgium	Italy	United Kingdom	Spain	Estonia	Slovenia
Canada	Luxembourg	United States	Czech Republic	Latvia	Albania
Denmark	Netherlands	Greece	Hungary	Lithuania	Croatia
France	Norway	Turkey	Poland	Romania	
Iceland	Portugal	Germany	Bulgaria	Slovakia	

Figure 3.4. NATO Member States

The United Nations is made up of several components, each dedicated to one of the UN's focus areas. The most powerful is the **SECURITY COUNCIL**, which is tasked with the maintenance of international security and peace. The Security Council also must approve the application of any country seeking

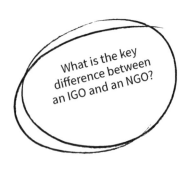

What is the key difference between an IGO and an NGO?

admission to the United Nations before it can be voted on by the General Assembly. The Security Council is composed of five permanent members—the United States, Great Britain, Russia, China, and France—and ten elected members who serve two-year terms. Each of the permanent members holds veto power and can single-handedly stop any Security Council resolution. The affirmative vote of each permanent member—as well as two-thirds of the General Assembly—is needed to amend the UN charter.

♦ **THE WORLD BANK**: Another organization created after World War II, the World Bank provides loans to developing nations for capital projects. Its primary purpose is to eliminate poverty in the world; however—a product of its time—it is also designed to support and encourage the growth of capitalism. Today, the World Bank has eight primary goals:

1. to eradicate extreme poverty and hunger

2. to achieve universal education

3. to promote gender equality

4. to reduce infant mortality

5. to improve maternal health

6. to combat highly infectious diseases like HIV/AIDS and malaria

7. to ensure environmental sustainability

8. to develop a global partnership for development

While an independent organization, the World Bank works closely with the United Nations.

EXAMPLES

1) Which of the following is NOT an example of an NGO?
   A. Amnesty International
   B. Wikimedia Foundation
   C. Oxfam
   D. the World Trade Organization
   E. the World Wildlife Fund

Answers:

A. Incorrect. Amnesty International is a private non-profit dedicated to the fair treatment and/or release of political prisoners.

B. Incorrect. Wikimedia Foundation is a non-profit organization that provides access to and encourages the development of free, multilingual content.

C. Incorrect. Oxfam is a private non-profit foundation focused on eliminating global poverty.

D. **Correct.** The World Trade Organization is an IGO that governs the rules of trade between nations.

E. Incorrect. The World Wildlife Fund is a private non-profit that raises money for the protection of endangered animals and their habitats.

2) Which of the following issues would be addressed by the United Nations?
A. the voting age in France
B. the election of the president of the United States
C. the national highway system in Canada
D. disarmament after civil war in Sierra Leone
E. the building of an oil pipeline between the United States and Canada

Answers:
A. Incorrect. The voting age in France is an internal matter that does not threaten global security, so it does not fall under the purview of the UN.
B. Incorrect. The election of a president in any country is considered an inherent power and an internal matter. As such, the UN has no authority to intervene. However, the UN can send in officials to monitor elections to ensure they are conducted fairly.
C. Incorrect. Internal infrastructure does not fall under the UN's purview either. However, a developing country (which Canada is not) may request financial assistance from the UN for development projects.
D. **Correct.** From 1999 to 2005, the UN stationed peacekeeping troops in Sierra Leone to disarm combatants after the country's civil war. Creating a stable and peaceful Sierra Leone was directly in line with the UN's mission to promote global peace. In this mission, the UN destroyed more than 42,000 weapons and 1.2 million rounds of ammunition.
E. Incorrect. The creation of a pipeline would only be the concern of the two countries.

four

GEOGRAPHY

What is Geography?

In its most basic form, geography is the study of space; more specifically, it studies the physical space of the earth and the ways in which it interacts with, shapes, and is shaped by its habitants. Geographers look at the world from a spatial perspective. This means that at the center of all geographic study is the question, *where?* For geographers, the *where* of any interaction, event, or development is a crucial element to understanding it.

This question of *where* can be asked in a variety of fields of study, so there are many sub-disciplines of geography. These can be organized into four main categories: 1) regional studies, which examine the characteristics of a particular place, 2) topical studies, which look at a single physical or human feature that impacts the whole world, 3) physical studies, which focus on the physical features of Earth, and 4) human studies, which examine the relationship between human activity and the environment.

The Five Themes of Geography

While *where?* is the most basic geographic question, it is simply the starting point. To engage in real study, geographers also ask, *why is it there?* and *what are the consequences of it being there?*

To answer these questions, geographers have developed five themes of geography: Location, Place, Region, Human-Environment Interaction, and Movement. Each of these addresses the basic geographic questions:

LOCATION addresses the question, *where is it specifically located?*

An example of location would be the address of someone's house or a description of where it is in the neighborhood.

Place and Region both address the question, *why is it there?*

PLACE asks, *what is it like there? What are its qualities and characteristics?*

REGION asks, *what do different areas have in common and why?*

While the address of a specific house is an example of location, a description of the neighborhood would be an example of *place*. Comparing that neighborhood to others in the area would be an example of *region*.

Human-Environment Interaction and Movement both address the question, *what are the consequences of it being there?* HUMAN-ENVIRONMENT INTERACTION asks, *how do humans shape the environment and how does the environment shape them?*

The development of cities illustrates human-environment interaction. For example, San Francisco is known for its steep streets, a result of the physical landscape on which it is built.

Chicago is an example of the human impact on the environment. In 1900, engineers successfully reversed the flow of the river so that it pulled water from Lake Michigan rather than feeding into it.

MOVEMENT asks, *how do places connect to and interact with one another?*

Blues music spreading from the South into the rest of the United States and beyond is an example of movement.

All of geography can be organized around these five themes.

EXAMPLES

1) Which of following is NOT an example of geographic study?
   A. patterns of volcanic eruptions
   B. climate change and global warming
   C. settlement patterns in Southern Europe
   D. the rise and fall of the American dollar
   E. a study of how Peru's leadership has changed over time

   Answers:
   A. Incorrect. A study of the pattern of volcanic eruptions is an example of physical geographic study.
   B. Incorrect. A study of climate change and global warming are examples of topical geographic study.
   C. Incorrect. A study of settlement patterns in Southern Europe is an example of human geographic study.
   D. **Correct.** A study of the rise and fall of the American dollar does not address the question of *Where?* It is solely an economic question, not a geographic one.
   E. Incorrect. Looking at Peru's past leaders does not answer the question of *Where?*. It is a political question, rather than a geographic one.

2) Migration patterns are an example of which geographic theme?
   A. location
   B. place
   C. human-environment interaction
   D. region
   E. movement

Location

Location is the most specific and concrete of the themes. It simply describes where something can be found on Earth. When location is RELATIVE, the object in question is positioned in relation to something else. For example, if someone says that his or her house is located two blocks north of the school, the person is providing a relative location for the house.

Relative location is most often used in informal settings. In formal geographic settings, ABSOLUTE LOCATION is generally used. A location is absolute when it is described by its position on Earth, without reference to other landmarks. For example, the tallest building in the world—the Burj Khalifa—is located at 25.2°N and 55.3°E.

Something's location can also be described by either its site or situation. When a place is described by its SITE, it is being described by its internal physical and cultural characteristics. For example, the site of a football stadium could be described by the number of seats, the field, the Jumbotron, the concession stands, and even the screaming fans. When a place is described by its SITUATION, its characteristics are described relative to those around it. So the football stadium might be described by its relative size as compared to the other buildings in the city, its accessibility, or the amount of foot traffic it receives. The more connected a place is to powerful places, the better its situation. So, the front row of seats in a stadium is better situated than the top row.

Maps

Because of the size of the Earth, it is difficult to articulate and visualize the absolute location of a place or thing. Instead, illustrations are used. To make the information more manageable, the scale can be adjusted; thus these illustrations can communicate more detailed and complete information more quickly and effectively. Globes and maps are illustrations used to show location.

GLOBES are spherical representations, or models, of the Earth. They show the correct size, shape, and location of land masses, and the accurate distance between places on Earth. However, because globes are models for the entire earth, it is impossible for them to provide much detail.

MAPS, on the other hand, are flat representations of the Earth or parts of the Earth. Because they are flat, maps can range in what they illustrate, from a single park to the entire planet. The more specific the area a map covers, the more detailed it can be. Maps do, however, have drawbacks which will be discussed later in this section.

Whether map or globe, both types of illustrations use the same system for identifying location. Called the GRID SYSTEM, the earth is divided by imaginary, equidistant lines running vertically and horizontally to create a grid. Each line is measured as a DEGREE (°), which can be subdivided into MINUTES (') and SECONDS (").

The lines that run horizontally around the Earth, parallel to the equator, are called lines of LATITUDE. Degrees of latitude are numbered 0° to 90° running north and south from the equator (the equator is 0°). In actuality, there are approximately 69 miles between each degree of latitude. This number shifts slightly because the Earth is not a true sphere, but is slightly egg-shaped.

The lines that run north and south from pole to pole are called lines of LONGITUDE, or MERIDIANS. Because there is no natural "center" of the Earth when measuring this way (like the equator), a 0° line was established by international agreement. Called the PRIME MERIDIAN, it is the line that runs through the Royal Observatory in Greenwich, England. Meridians are then numbered up to 180° running east and west of this line.

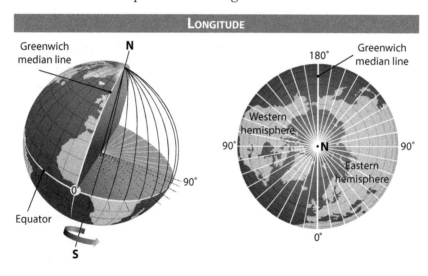

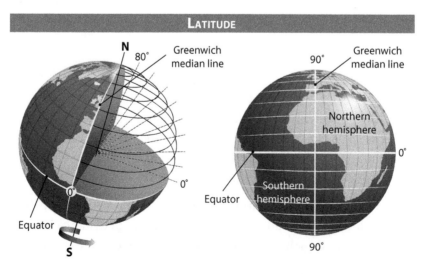

Figure 4.1. Longitude and Latitude

Time zones around the world have been organized based loosely on the meridians, with each time zone representing approximately 15 degrees, and time measured as an offset of Universal Coordinated Time (a system that measures time based on the rotation of the earth). This is a general rule, but there are many exceptions. For example, China uses one time zone for the entire country.

At approximately 180° opposite of the prime meridian is the International Date Line. This is where the date changes in order to allow the global time zone system to work.

While the flat nature of maps provides greater flexibility in terms of focus and scale, representing something spherical—the Earth—as flat inevitably leads to distortion. Every map is a **PROJECTION**, a representation of the Earth's features on a flat surface. There are different ways to do this, but every projection has four main properties: the size of areas, the shape of areas, consistency of scales, and straight line directions. No map is able to accurately depict all four of these properties: every projection must sacrifice accuracy in at least one. In general, mapmakers choose to maintain the accuracy of one property and distort the others as needed. Which property is maintained is determined by the perspective of the mapmaker and the purpose of the map.

Which is longitude and which is latitude? Here is an easy way to remember: Lines of longitude are "long" so they stretch from pole to pole. Lines of latitude lie "flat" ("flat-itude latitude"), and so run horizontally.

In an **EQUAL AREA MAP**, the accuracy of the size of areas is maintained. Each land mass is kept to scale in its size. The best example of this type of map is the **GALL-PETERS** projection. In order to preserve land mass size, the shape of land masses is distorted.

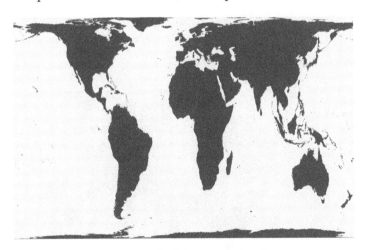

Figure 4.2. Gall-Peters Projection

CONFORMAL MAPS, conversely, maintain the shape of areas at the expense of accuracy in size. The most used conformal map is the **MERCATOR** projection. It uses straight lines for latitude and longitude, rather than curving them to indicate the curve of the Earth. It is made by wrapping the paper into a cylinder around a globe, called a **CYLINDRICAL PROJECTION**. On a Mercator projection map, the scale is accurate only at the equator or at two parallels equidistant from the equator. The farther from the equator, the more enlarged land masses appear. It is used primarily for marine navigation.

Figure 4.3. Mercator Projection

An **AZIMUTHAL EQUIDISTANT PROJECTION** maintains accuracy in scale for distances from one single point on the map to all other points on the map. This kind of projection is most often used in showing airplane routes from one city to multiple other cities, for example.

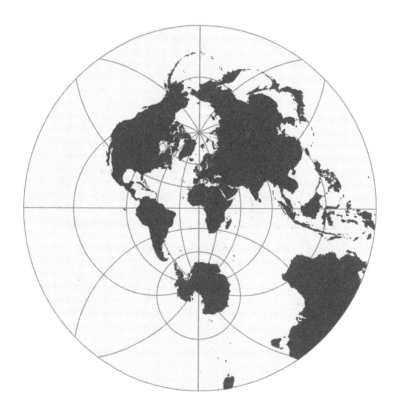

Figure 4.4. Azimuthal Equidistant Projection

A **Gnomonic projection** preserves the property of accuracy of distance. Every straight line on a gnomonic projection is the arc of a **great circle**, which represents the shortest distance between any two points on Earth. A great circle is any circle that bisects a sphere. In most projections, great circles are curved due to distortion resulting in the maintenance of one or more other properties. The Gnomonic projection is the exception. This projection is particularly useful, then, in navigation by sea or air where direction—for its own sake—is important. It is also often used to map the poles which are usually highly distorted in other map projections.

Figure 4.5. Gnomonic Projection

The most commonly used maps, however, are some sort of **compromise map**, meaning they distort all four properties to some degree in order to minimize distortion overall. The most popular of these are the Robinson projection and the Winkel tripel projection. From 1988 to 1998, the National Geographic Society used the Robinson projection for all of its

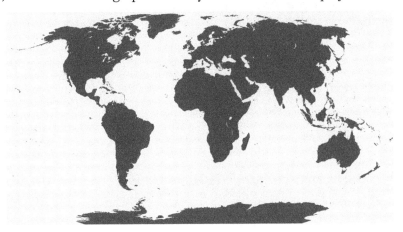

Figure 4.6. Robinson Projection and Winkel Projection

world maps. It was then replaced with the Winkel tripel, as it had less area distortion at the poles. Both projections balance size and shape, with minor distortions in each.

Most maps have four main tools to aid the reader in understanding:

The TITLE of the map provides a description of the purpose of the map as well as the area of focus. Without a title, the reader would not know what the map was depicting.

The SCALE of the map tells the reader the relationship between the unit of measurement used on the map and real distances on the earth. This information is particularly important when using a map for distance or navigation.

The GRID consists of lines placed on the map to aid in finding locations. The grid is often, but not necessarily, based on lines of longitude and latitude. In particular, maps of smaller areas will use different, more effective grid systems for their size.

Maps are first and foremost illustrations. They convey images through pictures, images, and symbols, with minimal use of words. In order to understand a map, the LEGEND explains the meaning of any symbols used. For example, a dot map showing population would have a legend explaining how many people are represented by each dot.

Finally, most maps are also equipped with a COMPASS ROSE that indicates the four directions: north, south, east and west. This allows the user to properly orient the map and accurately identify direction.

Use a map to determine which city is at 41.9°N, 12.5°E.

Some maps are designed to illustrate information other than absolute location, direction, land mass, and shape. CONTOUR MAPS illustrate varying levels of elevation in an area. Rather than having the standard markings of latitude and longitude lines, the lines on the map connect points of equal elevation, with the provided scale indicating the distance between the lines. RELIEF MAPS also depict elevation, but through shading to create a three-dimensional effect, rather than the drawing of lines.

An ISOTHERMAL MAP is used to illustrate ranges of temperature. Much like with contour maps, the lines are used to show areas of equal or constant temperature.

EXAMPLES

1) In a conformal map, areas are represented accurately in terms of which of the following?
   A. shape
   B. size
   C. direction
   D. Shape, size and direction are distorted.
   E. A, B, and C

Answers:

A. **Correct.** Conformal maps are designed to ensure the shape of all land masses are correct. In order to do this, they distort the other properties of the map: specifically, size.

B. Incorrect. Conformal maps distort the size of land masses and bodies of water in order to preserve their correct shape.

C. Incorrect. On a conformal map, straight line directions are distorted. This is to allow for the shape of land masses to be correct.

D. Incorrect. Compromise maps distort all aspects slightly to achieve greatest overall accuracy.

E. Incorrect. There is no map that is able to accurately represent all four map properties.

2) Which of the following is an advantage of globes over maps?

   A. Globes provide more detailed information.

   B. Globes can be used to show a variety of sizes of areas.

   C. Globes are accurate models of the Earth without distortion.

   D. Globes show elevation levels in addition to size, shape, and location of areas.

   E. Globes more accurately depict distance than maps.

Answers:

   A. Incorrect. Maps can reveal more detail than globes as they can focus on one specific area. Globes are always representations of the whole earth, and so display less detail.

   B. Incorrect. Globes are exact models of the earth in its entirety. Maps can be made of specific regions or areas; globes cannot.

   C. Correct. A globe is a model replica of the earth. It is precisely scaled to reflect the dimensions of the planet, accurately preserving size, shape, direction, and distance.

   D. Incorrect. While some globes do display mountain ranges in relief, they are rarely to scale. Maps, specifically contour or relief maps, are a much better tool for illustrating elevation.

   E. Incorrect. While some maps distort distance, others show distance with equal accuracy to globes.

3) To determine the distance between Tokyo and Shanghai on a map of Asia, which of the following parts of the map would be used?

   A. compass rose

   B. scale

   C. legend

   D. grid

   E. Distance cannot be accurately measured using a map.

Answers:

   A. Incorrect. The compass rose points to the four directions: North, South, East and West. It would be the right choice for determining that Tokyo is east of Shanghai, but not for determining the distance between the two cities.

   B. Correct. The scale shows the ratio between distance on the map and true distance.

   C. Incorrect. The legend decodes specific symbols used on the map. These symbols usually give more physical or human information about specific regions or places; they do not address distance.

D. Incorrect. The grid is used to help find specific locations on a map. It would be used to locate both Tokyo and Shanghai, but would not help in terms of determining distance.

E. Incorrect. Maps are used to measure distance as long as distance is represented accurately, and a scale is included.

4) A scientist exploring Antarctica would most likely use which type of map?

A. Equal Area projection

B. Azimuthal Equidistant projection

C. Conformal projection

D. Gnomonic projection

E. Robinson projection

Answers:

A. Incorrect. Equal Area projection maps ensure the accuracy of land mass size at the expense of the other properties. Distortion is particularly extreme at the poles, making it essentially useless for navigating Antarctica.

B. Incorrect. Since it accurately indicates distances from one point to all others, an Azimuthal Equidistant map would be most useful when both the starting and ending points are known. In an exploration expedition, this map does not provide sufficient accuracy in distance or direction.

C. Incorrect. Conformal projections accurately illustrate accurate land mass shape. In order to do so, they must distort distance and direction. In the lower latitudes, the distortion is minimal, but it is more extreme at the poles, making it a poor choice for navigation in Antarctica.

D. **Correct.** The Gnomonic projection map allows for great circles and accurate straight-line directions. It is often used for mapping the poles; it would be an excellent choice for an explorer of Antarctica.

E. Incorrect. The Robinson map distorts all aspects slightly, and so would not be reliable for navigation.

Mental Maps

While most maps are illustrations, some maps exist inside an individual's mind. These are called MENTAL MAPS. They are an individual's internal representation of the physical and human aspects of the earth.

Some mental maps are very much localized: for instance, an individual may have a mental map of his or her bedroom or house. Others are regional or even global. For example, one's understanding of the location of oceans or the continents would constitute a mental map.

Mental maps are constructed from both direct experiences—like actually being in a place—and indirect experiences—like reading about a place in a magazine or looking at a friend's vacation pictures. As a result, they have elements that are both objective and subjective. Take, for example, a four-story building in a residential neighborhood. Its presence is an objective fact. However, a local resident's perception of the distance between the building and his or her home, or the resident's understanding of how the building is accessed, could be subjective elements.

Mental maps are gateways into understanding perspectives not only of individuals, but of entire cultures. When examining mental maps, it is important to consider both what the map indicates and what the map does not indicate (in other words, what the individual or group does *not* account for).

EXAMPLES

1) Which of the following is NOT an accurate description of a mental map?

 A. Mental maps always reflect a personal location.

 B. Mental maps can be based in both fact and perception.

 C. Mental maps are studied in order to understand different cultures.

 D. Mental maps can be based on both direct and indirect understandings of a place.

 E. Mental maps are drawn on paper based on the idea in someone's mind.

Answers:

 A. **Correct.** Mental maps can reflect locations personal to the individual, but people also develop mental maps of entire cities, regions, and the world.

 B. Incorrect. Because they are individualized and internal, mental maps incorporate elements that are both objective and subjective.

 C. Incorrect. In geography, understanding an individual's or a group's spatial understanding of their area and the world at large provides great cultural insight. Mental maps help geographers develop this understanding.

 D. Incorrect. People build mental maps based on their direct experiences as well as on reading, hearing, or seeing the experiences of others.

 E. Incorrect. A mental map only exists in the individual's head.

8) A teacher asks two students in her class to describe the school's gymnasium. Student A—a basketball player—describes it as being in the middle of the school, with bleachers, high ceilings, bright lights, two basketball hoops, and markings on the floor. Student B—a soccer player—describes it as down the hall from the main office, small and stuffy, and poorly lit. What conclusion may be drawn about the mental maps of these two students?

 A. Student A has a more accurate mental map of the gymnasium than Student B.

 B. Student B's mental map is clouded by his or her dislike of basketball.

 C. Neither Student A nor Student B has constructed a useful mental map of the gymnasium.

 D. Both Students A and B have constructed mental maps influenced by their relationship to the gym and their respective sports.

 E. Student A's mental map exaggerates the positive features of the gymnasium.

Answers:

 A. Incorrect. While the two descriptions are very different, there is no way to know from the information given whether one mental map is more accurate than the other.

 B. Incorrect. While Student B's mental map paints the gymnasium in a more negative light, there is nothing to indicate that he or she dislikes basketball.

It is important not to make unfounded assumptions when analyzing mental maps.

C. **Incorrect.** Both students' maps could be used to give someone else an improved understanding of the gym's location. They also help each student spatially locate the gym.

D. Correct. The two mental maps are very different, but not necessarily contradictory. Instead, both are possible descriptions of the same place. Each student, however, has a different relationship to the gym. We can assume, as a basketball player, Student A spends more time in the gym than Student B. The stuffiness and poor lighting noted by Student B could simply be a reflection of the fact that, as a soccer player, Student B is used to playing sports outside in an open field. Student A may have located the gymnasium at the center of the school because of the central importance it plays in that student's school experience.

E. **Incorrect.** There is no evidence that student A is misrepresenting aspects of the gynmnasium.

Place

The second theme of geography—place—is directly related to location. If location answers the question, *where?*, place answers the question, *what?* To describe a geographic place is to describe all of the characteristics—both human and physical—of a location. Physical attributes include climate, terrain, and natural resources, while human attributes include language, religion, art, political organization, and customs. Different geographers focus on different aspects of place, but understanding place is at the core of any geographic study.

PHYSICAL CHARACTERISTICS OF PLACE

In order to describe a place physically, five main categories must be addressed: LAND, WATER, CLIMATE, VEGETATION, and ANIMAL LIFE, with the latter two dependent on the first three.

Land forms categorize areas by elevation, like MOUNTAINS, HILLS, FOOTHILLS, and PLATEAUS on one hand and PLAINS and VALLEYS on the other. It also describes areas created by water: DELTAS—the flat plains created by deposits from diverging branches of a river; BASINS—the bowl-like land that catches water and directs it toward a river; MARSHES—wetlands that are frequently inundated with water; and SWAMPS—any wetland primarily covered in woody plants. Geographers also look at SOIL: how fertile it is, the kind of life it can support, and how it easily it is shaped by wind and water.

Bodies of water can be subdivided into several categories as well. The biggest bodies of water are the Earth's five oceans:

◆ The ATLANTIC OCEAN separates North and South America from Europe and Africa.

◆ The PACIFIC OCEAN—covering almost one-third of the Earth—separates North and South America from Asia and Australia.

◆ The INDIAN OCEAN touches Africa, Asia, and Australia.

◆ The ARCTIC OCEAN extends from the northern edge of North America and Europe to the North Pole and is composed primarily of ice for much of the year.

◆ The SOUTHERN, or ANTARCTIC, OCEAN extends from the southern tips of South America and Africa to Antarctica.

In addition to these, there are other bodies of salinated water called SEAS, which are smaller than oceans and are surrounded—in part or wholly—by land. The largest sea is the MEDITERRANEAN SEA. The largest fully enclosed sea (or salted lake) is the CASPIAN SEA. Land-bound freshwater bodies of water are called lakes and can be found in varying sizes throughout the world, with a particular concentration in Canada, where more than 60 percent can be found.

Finally, and most important for the development of civilization, are RIVERS, bodies of water that flow towards the ocean. The world's major river systems: the NILE, the TIGRIS and EUPHRATES, the INDUS, the GANGES, the HUANG HE (YELLOW RIVER) and the YANGTZE, the AMAZON, and the MISSISSIPPI all gave birth to early and complex civilizations.

In conjunction with land masses and water sources, the other major defining physical characteristic of a place is its CLIMATE. Climate is the average weather for a specific location or region. It is based on monthly and yearly temperatures, as well as the length of the GROWING SEASON (which then has a direct impact on human characteristics of a place). Climate is shaped by the latitude of a location, the amount of moisture it receives, and the temperatures of both land and water. Varying climates create different ECOSYSTEMS, the communities of living organisms and nonliving elements of an area. These are discussed more in depth later in this chapter.

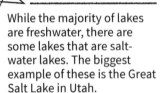

While the majority of lakes are freshwater, there are some lakes that are salt-water lakes. The biggest example of these is the Great Salt Lake in Utah.

EXAMPLES

1) Which of the following is NOT a physical characteristic of Switzerland?
   A. mountain chains on both the northern and southern sides of the country
   B. three river valleys
   C. It shares borders with Germany, France, Italy, Austria, and Lichtenstein.
   D. over 1400 lakes
   E. Its highest point is over 1500 feet high.

   Answers:
   A. Incorrect. The dominant land masses—like mountains—are one of the major physical characteristics of a place.
   B. Incorrect. River valleys describe both the land and water of Switzerland, both of which are significant physical characteristics.
   C. **Correct.** Political borders are man-made, and therefore are considered human characteristics of a place.
   D. Incorrect. Like rivers, lakes are key characteristics of a place. The fact that Switzerland has so many is certainly a defining quality of the place.
   E. Incorrect. The highest peak in Switzerland describes it land.

2) Which of the following statements best illustrates the geographic theme of place?

A. Northern Mali is primarily composed of desert.

B. St. Louis is approximately 300 miles from Chicago.

C. Beijing is located at approximately 40°N and 116°E.

D. English is the dominant language in North America as well as Australia.

E. When British individuals migrated to Australia they brought the English language with them.

Answers:

A. **Correct.** "Place" answers the questions: What is an area like? What are its defining features? This identifies the primary physical characteristic of a specific area.

B. Incorrect. This is an example of relative location because it describes where something is relative to another location, not place.

C. Incorrect. This is an example of absolute location because it provides the specific latitude and longitude coordinates of Beijing.

D. Incorrect. Comparing two regions, like North America and Australia, is an example of the geographic theme of region.

E. Incorrect. The impact of migration relates to the theme of movement.

Region

A REGION is a group of places that share common characteristics, whether human or physical. Regions can be large—incorporating multiple continents—or quite small.

There are three types of regions. In a FORMAL REGION the shared characteristics define the region. For example, the Middle East is a formal region, as the area has common physical and cultural traits. A FUNCTIONAL REGION is an area defined by common movement or function. Functional regions have a focal point, called a node, around which they are organized, related to their function. For example, a school district is a functional region organized around a school (or set of schools). The third type of regions are PERCEPTUAL REGIONS. These are areas grouped not by actual commonalities, but by perceived ones. For example, Africa is often addressed as a single region, even though the continent has a large number of differing cultural systems and physical characteristics.

To analyze global phenomena, geographers divide the world into REALMS, the largest logical regions possible. Realms are based on clusters of human population, economic, political, cultural, and physical traits.

There are twelve widely accepted realms: Sub Saharan Africa, North Africa and South West Asia, Europe, Russia, South Asia, East Asia, South East Asia, North America, Middle America, South America, the Austral Realm, and the Pacific Realms.

Regions are not static, and can change over time. The borders of regions are also often not sharply defined, but instead gradually shift from one region to the next. The areas between regions, then, are called TRANSITION ZONES. Transition zones are marked by a greater diversity of cultural traits; furthermore, they more often experience conflict.

Human geographers study regions the way they study place, applying the same concepts on a larger scale. While regions are defined primarily by their commonalities, geographers often study them in order to create comparisons. For example they might look at economic development, the growth of religions, or gender roles in different regions. The various theories and models apply as well. Geographers can use the Demographic Transition Model to understand demographic growth in a region as a whole, not just a specific place.

In physical geography, one of the key ways regions are organized is by climate. These regions are called ECOSYSTEMS. The Earth's ecosystems can be divided by latitude, with different latitudes having different climates.

The LOW LATITUDES, from the equator to latitudes 23.5° north and south, have three distinct climates. TROPICAL RAINFORESTS can be found in the equatorial lowlands. They experience intense sun and rain every day. Although temperatures in the rainforest rarely go above 90° Fahrenheit, the combination of sun and rain creates high humidity levels, leading to extreme heat.

North and south of the rainforest is the SAVANNAH. The savannah is dry in the winter and wet in the summer, experiencing an average of ten to thirty inches of rain. Temperatures generally stay below 90° Fahrenheit with lower temperatures (under 80° Fahrenheit) in the winter.

The DESERT lies beyond the savannah to the north and south. Deserts are the hottest and driest parts of the Earth. Deserts receive fewer than ten inches of rainfall a year. Temperatures swing widely from extreme heat during the day to extreme cold at night. The best known deserts in the world are the Sahara Desert, the Australian Outback, and the Arabian Desert.

The MIDDLE LATITUDES, from latitudes 23.5° to 66.5° north and south, have a greater variety of climates, determined more by proximity to water than by the exact latitude. While none of these climates are as wet as those in the low latitudes, three climates in the middle latitudes receive the most rain and therefore are the most fertile. The first is the MEDITERRANEAN CLIMATE. This climate can be found in lands between latitudes 30° and 40° north and south that lie along the western coast. These territories include land bordering the Mediterranean Sea, a small part of Southwestern Africa, southern and Southwestern Australia, a small part of the Ukraine near the Black Sea, central Chile, and southern California.

The Mediterranean climate features hot summers and mild winters. Unlike the savannah, the winters receive the most rain, and the summers are generally dry. This climate allows a year-round growing season.

The HUMID SUBTROPICAL CLIMATE is located on coastal areas north and south of the tropics. This climate receives warm ocean currents and warm winds year round, leading to a climate that is warm and moist. The summers are long and wet, and the winters are short and mild. This creates a long growing season. This is also the climate that supports the greatest percentage of the world's population. Japan, southeastern China, northeastern India, southeastern South Africa, the southeastern United States, and parts of South America all have subtropical climates.

Areas that are near or surrounded by water experience the MARINE CLIMATE. This climate has very temperate weather, with winters that rarely go below freezing and summers that stay below 70° Fahrenheit. Marine climates are warm and rainy, resulting in part from the warm ocean winds. This climate can be found in Western Europe, the British Isles, the Pacific Northwest, southern Chile, southern New Zealand, southeastern Australia, and on the western coast of Canada.

The climate best for farming is the HUMID CONTINENTAL CLIMATE, the true four-season climate. Average temperatures vary based on an area's distance from the ocean, but regions with this climate all feature fertile land. Summers are warm to hot and usually humid. Winters range from cold to extremely cold, and precipitation is distributed evenly throughout the year. This climate can be found in the northern and central United States, south-central and south-eastern Canada, northern China, and the western and southeastern parts of the former Soviet bloc.

Those areas of continents far from the ocean are called STEPPES, or prairie. These are dry flatlands with minimal rainfall (ten to twenty inches annually). Steppes can even become deserts if rainfall consistently dips below ten inches per year. Summers are hot and winters are often very cold. Steppes can be found in the interiors of North America and Asia, as these continents are so large that their interiors are not subject to the ocean winds.

The HIGH LATITUDES, from latitudes 66.5° north and south to the poles, are home to two climates: TUNDRA and taiga. The tundra features extremely cold and long winters. *Tundra* means *marshy plain* in Russian; while the ground is frozen for most of the year, during the short summer the ground becomes mushy. The tundra has low precipitation and actually receives less snow than the eastern United States. With no arable land, it is home to few people. There is, in fact, abundant plant life mostly growing close to the ground, which supports a vibrant animal life; however this is insufficient to support a human population.

The TAIGA can be found south of the tundra in Northern Russia, Sweden, Norway, Finland, Canada, and Alaska. Another Russian word, *taiga* means *northern forest*, and this area is home to the world's largest forestlands. It also contains many swamps and marshes. The taiga has more extreme temperatures than the tundra because it is farther from the ocean. While there is a growing season, it is so short that meaningful agriculture is impossible; thus, the taiga is sparsely populated. However, this region features distinctive and extreme mineral wealth.

In the low and high latitudes, the farther north, the drier the climate. In the middle latitudes, distance from the ocean determines how wet or dry the climate is.

EXAMPLES

1) Which ecosystem experiences extreme temperatures—both hot and cold—in a single day?

   A. tundra

   B. rainforest

   C. desert

   D. savannah

   E. taiga

   Answers:

   A. Incorrect. Temperatures on the tundra remain relatively steady. While they can get very cold in the winter (down to -30° F) there is not a significant difference between night and day.

B. Incorrect. Rainforests have high temperatures daily, but do not experience extreme low temperatures at night.

C. **Correct.** The desert has extreme heat during the day and extreme cold at night.

D. Incorrect. The savannah can get very warm during the summer, but does not experience major fluctuations in temperature.

E. Incorrect. The taiga is just south of the tundra and experiences cold temperatures for most of the year.

2) A congressional district is an example of which kind of region?

   A. a functional region

   B. a formal region

   C. a perceptual region

   D. a node region

   E. a general region

   Answers:

   A. **Correct.** A congressional district is a region with a common purpose—representation in Congress.

   B. Incorrect. A formal region is a region created through shared cultural or physical traits. While many congressional districts will have these, this is not how the region is determined.

   C. Incorrect. A perceptual region is a region based on perceived commonalities. Again, congressional districts might have perceived commonalities, also, but this is not how they are created.

   D. Incorrect. There is no such thing as a node region. A node is the focal element of a functional region.

   E. Incorrect. This is not a geographic term. All regions can be identified as either formal, functional or perceptual.

3) According to the map below, if Biome 1 is tundra, which type of ecosystem is represented by Biome 2?

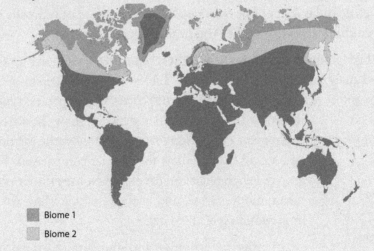

Biome 1
Biome 2

   A. marine

   B. taiga

   C. desert

   D. steppe

   E. savannah

Answers:

A. Incorrect. Marine climates are found in the middle latitudes in areas that are near or surrounded by water.

B. Correct. Taiga is found just south of the tundra primarily in Sweden, Norway, Finland, northern Russia, Canada, and Alaska.

C. Incorrect. Deserts are found in low latitudes.

D. Incorrect. Steppes are found in the middle latitudes and located far from the ocean.

E. Incorrect. The savannah can be found in the low latitudes.

Human Characteristics of Place

The human characteristics of a place make up its CULTURE. These include the shared values, language, and religion of the people living in a location or region. It also includes the ways in which they feed, clothe, and shelter themselves. Cultures can be very specific or regional, like FOLK CULTURES, or they can be diffuse and widespread, like POPULAR CULTURE.

The Study of Culture

A folk culture is the sum of cultural traits of a localized, traditional group. Folk culture is often threatened by the spread of popular culture.

CULTURAL GEOGRAPHERS study the ways in which each of these characteristics is shaped by the physical characteristics of a place. One key area of study for cultural geographers is the MATERIAL COMPONENTS of a culture—the physical artifacts that can be left behind, like a bowl or a religious icon. They also look at the NON-MATERIAL COMPONENTS of a culture—the thoughts, ideas, and beliefs of a people, like their code of law or their religion. They also study a place's CULTURAL LANDSCAPE. Also called a *built landscape*, this is the impact a culture has on its environment: what kind of buildings or infrastructure did it create? For example, the development of railroads is an important part of the cultural landscape of the American West.

Cultural geographers (also known as HUMAN GEOGRAPHERS) use a variety of tools to interpret and analyze geographic information. Tables and graphs help geographers organize information and reveal trends over time. A HISTOGRAM is a specific type of graph that illustrates the distribution of data and shows how frequently various phenomena occur. SCATTER PLOTS show the relationship between two sets of data to allow for broader comparison. From tables and graphs, geographers can develop DESCRIPTIVE STATISTICS, like the mean, mode, range, and average, which allow for more detailed understanding of the data.

Interpreting graphs and tables is an important part of the Praxis Social Studies exam. Knowing and understanding various types of geographic tables, charts, and graphs will give you a leg up!

In order to recognize and understand spatial patterns, geographers use GEOGRAPHIC MODELS. For example, a CONCENTRIC ZONE PLOT shows urban social structures, and the DEMOGRAPHIC TRANSITION MODEL explains the population patterns (this will be discussed later in this section).

But where does the data come from to use in these various graphs, tables, and models? Geographers use both PRIMARY GEOGRAPHIC DATA and SECONDARY GEOGRAPHIC DATA to build models and interpret information. Primary data comes from the researcher's own observations in the field; secondary data is taken from sources that have already collected and aggregated useful data. The US Census Bureau, CIA World Factbook, the Population Reference Bureau, the National Institutes of Health, and the United Nations are all good sources for secondary data. Geographers also use GEOGRAPHIC INFORMATION SYSTEMS (GIS), which are any computer systems that store, manage, manipulate, or analyze spatial data.

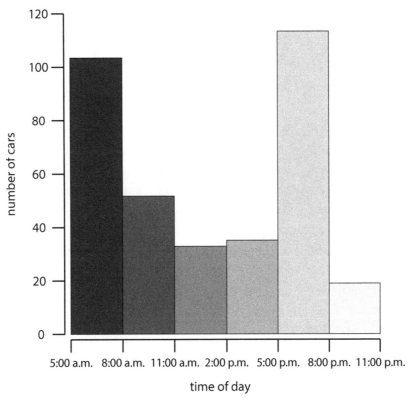

Cars Through Tollbooth by Time of Day

Figure 4.7. Sample Scatter Plot

B. **Correct.** While Aristotle's physical writings would be material components, his actual teachings—what he believed and said—are nonmaterial.

C. Incorrect. A newspaper from the day of the stock market crash that launched the Great Depression would be a material component.

D. Incorrect. A medieval sword, which is an example of a military tool as well as of how medieval objects were made, would be a material component.

E. Incorrect. A segment of a neolithic tool is a material component. It is an example of tool use developed in early cultures.

2) A geographer visits a village along the Amazon River and collects information about the role the river plays in the culture of the village. This is an example of

A. a descriptive statistic.

B. a geographic information system.

C. primary geographic data.

D. secondary geographic data.

E. a geographic model

Answers:

A. Incorrect. A descriptive statistic is a way of analyzing raw data—not collecting it—to provide meaningful information.

B. Incorrect. A geographic information system is a computer system that stores, analyzes, or manages geographic data. It is not the data itself, nor its collection.

C. **Correct.** Because the geographer is collecting the data on the river him- or herself, this is primary geographic data.

D. Incorrect. Secondary geographic data is data that is gleaned from elsewhere, such as the research of other geographers, geographic resources, or geographic information systems.

E. Incorrect. A geographic model is a depiction that helps geographers understand patterns.

Structures of Cultures

Each culture is made up of countless, specific CULTURE TRAITS, single aspects of a culture, like shaking hands in greeting, or eating with a fork. A culture trait is not necessarily unique to one culture, nor does it—in and of itself—define a culture. For example, Eastern Orthodox nuns and conservative Jewish women cover their hair, but these are clearly two distinct cultures. This is because while the two cultures might have this one distinct trait in common, the combination of all of their culture traits—their CULTURE COMPLEXES—are quite different.

In fact, no two cultures have the exact same complex. Therefore, wherever a difference in trait can be identified, two separate culture complexes exist. If, though, two culture complexes have many overlapping traits, they will form a CULTURE SYSTEM. For example, after the fall of the Berlin Wall there were distinct differences between East and West Germany, based on physical characteristics and differing histories. East Germans had a greater collective sense due to the socialist political and economic system they had experienced, while West Germans were more individualistic, having lived in a more capitalist society. The West had more access to technology; therefore television, movies, popular music, and video games were all a bigger part of West German culture. Even in terms of language there were differences: as a second language, the majority of West Germans spoke English, while the majority of East Germans spoke Russian. The East and the West made up distinct culture complexes.

However, they also had enough traits in common—a common language, a common government after reunification, and a shared history—to be a single culture system. And that culture system had linguistic and historical connections with the Netherlands, Norway, Denmark, and Sweden; these countries all, in turn, share history and have similar music and arts with France, Italy, Spain, and other neighboring countries. As such, they all make up a common CULTURE REGION (Western Europe). That cultural region also has a shared history with Eastern Europe, as well as similarities in art and music. Together, they comprise a CULTURE REALM.

Development of Cultures

While cultures exist today in a multitude of forms across the Earth, there are eight locations where formal culture—meaning the development of agriculture, government, and urbanization—began. These locations are known as CULTURE HEARTHS.

In the Americas, culture began in Andean America and Mesoamerica. In Africa, the culture hearths were in West Africa and the Nile River Valley. In the Middle East, culture began in Mesopotamia, and in Asia, hearths existed in the Indus River Valley, the Ganges River delta, and along the Wei and Huang Rivers in China. In each of these hearths, similar innovations—the seeds of culture—developed completely independently of one another.

Once the seeds sprouted, they spread across the Earth in a process called CULTURAL DIFFUSION, moving outward from the hearths in a variety of ways. Sometimes this occurred through inheritance, when one culture left an imprint on a place that was then used by the next culture to inhabit the same place. This is called SEQUENT OCCUPANCY. New Orleans was founded by the French; it then switched between French and Spanish control several times, all the while attracting immigrants from Europe and importing slaves from West Africa and the Caribbean. The influence of each of these various cultures can be seen in New Orleans' hybrid culture today.

Other times, cultures change by coming into contact with each other, called TRANS-CULTURATION. This can be symbiotic as in CULTURAL CONVERGENCE, when two cultures adopt traits of each other and become increasingly similar. For example, with the advent of national television programming, broadcasters and actors developed neutral accents and dialects which could be understood throughout the United States. These then diffused into the public, reducing regional language differences. Or it can be less balanced: for example, a weaker culture may take on the qualities of a more powerful culture. Called ACCULTURATION, examples of this throughout history abound, particularly anywhere that was subjected to colonization. In extreme cases, the weaker culture fully ASSIMILATES, losing all aspects of its own original culture.

Cultures can also DIVERGE, or change from being one culture complex into two, if they begin to develop differing traits. For example, as American mainstream culture modernized, the Amish diverged into a separate culture maintaining traditional ways.

Settlement Patterns

For cultures to grow, an area must first be settled. SETTLEMENTS are the cradles of culture. They allow for the development of political structures, the management of resources, and the transfer of information to future generations. While settlements differed greatly, they did all share some commonalities. Settlements all began near natural resources that can support life, namely water and a reliable food source. The success and growth of a settlement was based on its proximity to these natural resources and its ability to collect and move raw materials. As each of these characteristics reached a new level of sophistication, population in that area began to concentrate near the point of resource allocation and production.

The spatial layout of these settlements, then, was determined by the environment and the primary function of the settlement. For example, European villages were clustered on hillsides to more easily protect against invaders and to leave the flat areas for farming. Settlements that rose up around trade, like those on the outskirts of the Saharan desert, concentrated around access to the trade routes and were generally more dispersed.

Later in history, successful settlements also needed an ample work force, and the ability to produce and deliver finished products elsewhere. Once transportation methods were developed, the populations of these settlements became mobile, allowing for a faster diffusion of culture, and—eventually—the development of industrial centers. These industrial centers became cities. A CITY is a major hub of human settlement with a high population density and a concentration of resource creation or allocation. Today, almost half of the world's population lives in cities. In more developed regions the percentages are even higher. With the development of cities, three types of areas emerged: URBAN (in the city itself), SUBURBAN (near the city), and rural (AWAY FROM THE CITY). In some cases today, urban and suburban areas or multiple urban areas merge into a MEGALOPOLIS, or super-city.

EXAMPLES

1) Which of the following statements is an example of cultural diffusion?
   A. Russia has the most lumber in the world.
   B. There is a Starbucks at the Mall of the Emirates in Dubai.
   C. Chopsticks are a key utensil in China.
   D. Spanish is the official language of Spain.
   E. American builders often use Chinese steel in construction.

Answers:
A. Incorrect. This is a physical characteristic of Russia, not a culture trait that has been adopted.
B. **Correct.** Starbucks began in the United States, and is distinctly American. Its existence—and popularity—in Dubai is an example of cultural diffusion.
C. Incorrect. The use of chopsticks is an example of a cultural trait of China. However, it is a trait original to the area.
D. Incorrect. The language spoken in Spain is a cultural trait which developed over time. It was not adopted from another place.
E. Incorrect. This is an example of globalization. However the steel is an economic resource, not a cultural component.

2) The adoption of French as an official language throughout most of West Africa is an example of

    A. sequent occupancy.

    B. cultural convergence.

    C. cultural divergence.

    D. acculturation.

    E. a cultural hearth.

Answers:

    A. Incorrect. Sequent occupancy refers to the inheritance of the traits of a previous culture by the current culture existing in an area. In the case of West Africa, the new language trait of French was brought into the existing culture.

    B. Incorrect. Cultural convergence describes the process of two cultures growing together to become one. Rather than two equally situated cultures becoming increasingly similar, the adoption of French in West Africa was the result of colonization.

    C. Incorrect. Cultural divergence describes the process of one culture growing into two separate cultures. That does not apply in this situation.

    D. **Correct.** The adoption of French in West Africa as an official language is a classic example of a local culture overcome by a powerful force and taking on the traits of what would thus become the dominant culture. This occurred wherever colonization took place.

    E. Incorrect. A cultural hearth is a place where culture began.

3) The majority of people in the world today live in

    A. urban areas.

    B. suburban areas.

    C. rural areas.

    D. megalopolises.

    E. an approximately equal divide between urban and rural areas.

Answers:

    A. **Correct.** More than half of the world's population lives in cities.

    B. Incorrect. While more widespread in area than cities, suburban areas are not home to as many people as cities.

    C. Incorrect. For most of human history, the majority of people have lived in rural areas. The shift to an urban-based populace is a recent change.

    D. Incorrect. Megalopolises are growing and do hold significant populations. However, most cities still do not fall into this category.

    E. Incorrect. Rural populations are steadily declining around the world.

4) Settlements developed near rivers would most likely

    A. be designed in a circular fashion a few miles away from the river.

    B. be built into nearby hills.

    C. be long and narrow to follow the shape of the river.

    D. have clear access to land trade routes.

    E. remain small as a result of limited access by land

Answers:

A. Incorrect. Access to the water would be the most important concern in developing the settlement. Therefore, the settlement would be as close to the water as possible.

B. Incorrect. Again, access to the water is paramount, so building the settlement back and away into the hills would not be ideal.

C. **Correct.** In order to maximize the residents' access to the water, the settlement would grow along the bank of the river.

D. Incorrect. For a settlement near a river, the river itself would be the most likely avenue for trade.

E. Incorrect. The first major civilizations developed along rivers.

Demographic Patterns

DEMOGRAPHY is the study of human population. It is a major branch of human geography, as the DISTRIBUTION of people (how people are spread across the Earth), and the DENSITY (the number of people in a particular area) are closely tied to other factors in both human and physical geography. As discussed earlier, more than half of the world's population today lives in cities. While this is a relatively recent change, the population has always been unevenly distributed based on resources. So, as cities have become better at obtaining and allocating resources, they have attracted more people. This uneven distribution can be seen in other ways as well. Seventy-five percent of all people live on only 5 percent of the earth's land. While much of the world's wealth is concentrated in North America and Western Europe, 80 percent of people live in poor, developing countries in South America, Asia, and Africa. The most populated area in the world is East Asia, which is home to 25 percent of the world's population. In terms of population, East Asia is followed by Southeast Asia, and then Europe, from the Atlantic Ocean to the Ural Mountains.

Demographers use POPULATION EQUATIONS to analyze changes in population. GLOBAL EQUATIONS look at the total population of the Earth, including the number of births and deaths that occur. SUB-GLOBAL EQUATIONS look at total population in a given area and also include immigration and emigration as factors.

Over the last 300 years, the population of Earth has exploded; population has been growing at an exponential rate, meaning the more people are added to the population, the faster it grows. In 1765, the global population was 300 million people. Today it is six billion. This increase has raised concerns for many demographers, particularly in the areas with a higher population concentration. To determine if an area is at risk, demographers determine its CARRYING CAPACITY, the number of people the area can support.

Name one way a country can increase its carrying capacity.

The carrying capacity of various areas can differ greatly depending on technology, wealth, climate, available habitable space, access, and INFRASTRUCTURE, or institutions that support the needs of the people. When a country exceeds its carrying capacity, it suffers from OVERPOPULATION. Countries in danger of overpopulation may attempt to restrict their growth, like China did through its one-child policy. Conversely, they may attempt to increase their carrying capacity by increasing their resources using technology such as irrigation or desalination, or increasing their access to trade.

For example, Japan greatly increased its carrying capacity by importing significant quantities of food. As a result, it is able to maintain a much larger population than it would otherwise be able to.

In spite of the population boom, some countries actually suffer from UNDER-POPULATION. They have a much greater carrying capacity—due to their high levels of production, amount of land, or abundance of natural resources—than their population uses.

DEMOGRAPHIC TRANSITION MODEL

In order to understand how populations will change, demographers use the DEMOGRAPHIC TRANSITION MODEL. This is a geographic tool which predicts changes in population using the CRUDE BIRTH RATE (CBR), CRUDE DEATH RATE (CDR), and the RATE OF NATURAL INCREASE (RNI), or how much the population is increasing based on the first two factors. The model ties the changes in population to economic development by making two major assumptions: 1) all population growth is based on economic status, and 2) all countries pass through the same economic stages. While both of these assumptions have been challenged, the Demographic Transition Model is still the best indicator of population change.

The Demographic Transition Model outlines four states of economic and population growth (and one theoretical one):

- **STAGE ONE:** This is a low growth stage. Both the CBR and CDR are high, making the RNI low or stationary. Some fluctuation will occur at this stage based on disease, war, and famine, all of which are somewhat common in Stage One economic development. Most of the population consists of subsistence farmers. Today, there are no countries that are still considered Stage One because of advances in medical technology which have eventually permeated down to every country. The prevention of disease—and death from it—decreases CDR, allowing RNI to increase.

- **STAGE TWO:** Because CDR has declined, but CBR remains high, this is a high growth stage. Medical advances can have an immediate impact on CDR, but CBR tends to be a deeply-rooted cultural tradition and is much more difficult to change. In Stage Two countries, the majority of the population still engages in subsistence farming. Many developing countries today are Stage Two countries.

- **STAGE THREE:** As countries move from only subsistence farming into industrialization, CBR begins to slow. Women have more choices in work and this, in conjunction with urbanization—and the reduced living space that goes along with it—leads to a decline in the birth rate. Most Latin American and Asian countries today are Stage Three countries.

- **STAGE FOUR:** Industrialization leads to modernization. Once countries become fully industrialized and begin to develop more complex service economies, as well as advanced healthcare and education systems, CBR and CDR are once again equal but at a much lower rate, leading to a low RNI. This is a low growth stage. Stage Four is considered to be the ideal stage for population growth as the country is stable and prosperous, and population growth is slow and steady. The United States, Argentina, and Singapore are all Stage Four countries.

◆ STAGE FIVE: The last stage of the Demographic Transition Model is mostly a theoretical one, although several countries are moving towards it. In Stage Five, medical advances not only succeed in limiting early deaths, but also in extending the life of the elderly. The decline in CBR continues, leading eventually to a negative RNI. Many countries in Western Europe and Japan are facing such graying populations.

UNITED STATES POPULATION (2015)

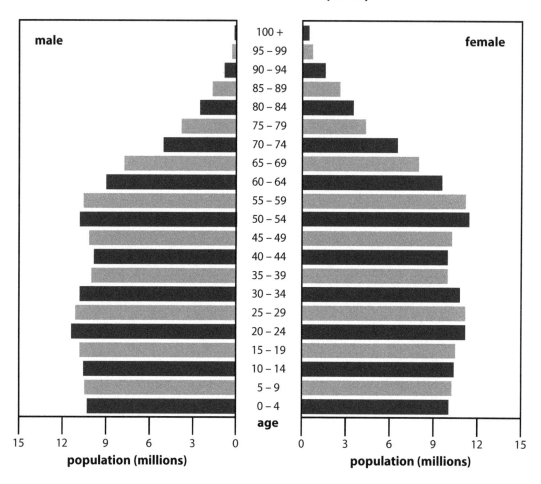

Figure 4.8. Population Pyramid

EXAMPLES

1) Overpopulation is most likely to occur in which stage of the Demographic Transition Model?

   A. Stage One

   B. Stage Two

   C. Stage Three

   D. Stage Four

   E. Overpopulation can occur at any stage.

Answers:

A. Incorrect. In Stage One, population growth is low. While the crude birth rate is high in this stage, so is the crude death rate, leading to little population growth.

B. **Correct.** In Stage Two, the crude death rate declines (as a result of medical advancements), but the crude birth rate remains high. This leads to high population growth, putting the country at risk of overpopulation.

C. Incorrect. In Stage Three, population growth is moderate as the crude death rate declines while the crude birth rate remains relatively high. However, the crude birth rate is lower than in Stage Two, making overpopulation less likely.

D. Incorrect. Stage Four, like Stage One, is a low population growth stage. The crude birth rate and crude death rate are both low.

E. Incorrect. Overpopulation only occurs when birth rates substantially outpace death rates.

2) Which of the following areas has the highest population density?

A. India

B. United States

C. Germany

D. Belgium

E. Brazil

Answers:

A. **Correct.** The second biggest population center in the world is Southeast Asia (the first is East Asia).

B. Incorrect. The United States, as a Stage Four country, has a large and stable population well within its carrying capacity.

C. Incorrect. Germany is a country that is entering into Stage Five, with a graying population. Its population density is decreasing.

D. Incorrect. Belgium is an example of an underpopulated area. The resources of the country outpace the population.

E. Incorrect. While Brazil is home to a megalopolis (Rio de Janiero), its overall population is significantly lower than India's.

3) Canada produces more resources than its population can consume. This is an example of

A. overpopulation

B. carrying capacity

C. under-population

D. graying population

E. high density

Answers:

A. Incorrect. This is the opposite of overpopulation. Overpopulation occurs when a country does not have enough resources to support its population.

B. Incorrect. Carrying capacity refers to the number of people an area can sustain with its resources. An example of Canada's carrying capacity, then, would be the number of people it could reasonably hold.

Economic Patterns

A country or area's ECONOMY is the system by which it produces, consumes, and distributes resources and goods. The various parts of the economy are classified into five sectors:

♦ The PRIMARY SECTOR focuses on the extraction of raw materials. This includes mining, farming, and fishing. In an industrialized economy, this is the smallest part of the economy.

♦ The SECONDARY SECTOR processes the raw materials extracted by the first sector. This sector is made up primarily of factories. Things like steel, canned tuna, and rubber are all secondary sector products.

♦ The TERTIARY SECTOR moves, sells, and trades the products created by the secondary sector; it is also known as the service economy. Transportation companies, merchants, and stores are all parts of the tertiary sector.

♦ The QUATERNARY SECTOR does not deal in physical products, but instead creates and transfers information. University researchers, journalists, and information technology specialists are members of the quaternary sector. This sector only exists in highly developed countries with well-established, complex industrial economies.

♦ The QUINARY SECTOR involves those that at the highest levels of decision-making and focuses on managing the overall functioning of the economy. In most countries, the quinary sector is made up almost exclusively of government agencies and officials.

Most economies also have an informal sector which encompasses all business transactions that are not reported to the government. The range of this sector includes everything from unregistered street vendors to neighborhood babysitters to illegal sales of drugs.

Industrialization

As areas develop and economies grow, manufacturing becomes increasingly important to the functioning of the economy. This is called INDUSTRIALIZATION. Because industrialization requires a shift in the labor force, it pairs with a decline in subsistence farming.

Industrialization is a relatively recent phenomenon. The INDUSTRIAL REVOLUTION began in Great Britain in the 1760s, then diffused to Western Europe and North America by 1825. The discovery of new energy sources like coal (which was later replaced by oil) and technological advancements which allowed machine labor to replace human labor led to the emergence of manufacturing centers and a shift in the functioning of the economy.

Industrialization had significant spatial implications. The extraction of resources and building of factories changed the physical landscape of places. As transportation infrastructure improved and labor was commodified, migration—from rural to urban areas—increased. Also, population settlements grew up around energy sources (like the coal deposits in Pennsylvania, the Ukraine, and Ruhr Valley in Germany) and around factories (like Manchester and Liverpool in England). Called AGGLOMERATION, related industries often are developed near each other in order to share resource costs. Modern examples of agglomeration are high-tech corridors or TECHNOPOLES, areas of high-tech production like Silicon Valley in California.

Throughout the 1990s, technology firms *agglomerated* in San Francisco, creating a *technopole*. However, in 1999 the bubble burst, and many companies lost much of their value. This resulted in *deglomeration*: many companies moved out of San Francisco because of the high rent and operational costs.

In some cases, an area can become over-agglomerated and pollution, traffic, restricted labor pools, and over-taxed resources can lead to the spreading out of industries, called DEGLOMERATION. Increasingly, industries also are moving their operations to places with lower labor costs, even though it may incur higher transportation costs.

EXAMPLES

1) An owner of a grocery store is part of which sector of the economy?

   A. primary

   B. secondary

   C. tertiary

   D. quaternary

   E. It depends on the average quantity of produce sold.

Answers:

   A. Incorrect. The primary sector deals with the extraction of raw materials, which is not under the purview of a grocery store.

   B. Incorrect. The secondary sector processes raw materials, also not under the purview of a grocery store.

   C. Correct. The tertiary sector sells and trades processed goods. Any store is part of the tertiary sector.

   D. Incorrect. The quaternary sector creates and disseminates information, also not in the range of activities performed by a grocery store.

   E. Incorrect. The sector of the economy is based on what the business sells, not how much.

2) Which of the following is NOT a consequence of industrialization noted by geographers?

   A. significant changes to the physical characteristics of the area in which industrialization takes place

   B. decrease in subsistence farming

   C. migration to suburban areas

D. increasing importance of energy sources like coal and oil

E. increasing rates of resource consumption

Answers:

A. Incorrect. The impact on physical characteristics is of particular concern to geographers. Changes in water and air quality and the impact on soil are all effects of industrialization.

B. Incorrect. The decrease in subsistence farming is one of the key factors geographers look at when examining the industrialization of a society.

C. **Correct.** With industrialization, geographers note a rise in the migration of people from rural to urban areas, not suburban.

D. Incorrect. As a result of industrialization, the extraction of energy sources becomes an increasingly important part of the economy, and the location of these sources impacts migration and economic centers.

E. Incorrect. As populations concentrate, resource consumption increases.

Economic Development

The growth of economies is strongly connected to DEVELOPMENT, the use of technology and knowledge to improve the living conditions of people in a country. While economic in its foundation, development focuses on a range of quality of life issues like access to basic goods and services, education, and healthcare. Countries on the wealthier side of the spectrum are called MORE DEVELOPED COUNTRIES (MDCs), while those on the poorer side are called LESS DEVELOPED COUNTRIES (LDCs). MDCs are concentrated primarily in the Northern Hemisphere. Their primary economic concern is maintaining growth. LDCs, found mostly in the Southern Hemisphere, face the challenge of improving their economic conditions by stimulating significant and sustainable economic growth.

There are several different measures used for development. The most common is a country's GROSS DOMESTIC PRODUCT (GDP). It is the value of the total outputs of goods and services produced in a country in a given period of time, typically a year. The GDP is usually calculated per capita. In MDCs the per capita GDP is more than $20,000. In LDCs it is less than $1000. GDP should not be confused with another measure of development, the GROSS NATIONAL PRODUCT, which is the value of goods and services owned and produced by citizens of a country, regardless of where those goods and services are produced.

Neither of these, however, take into account the distribution of wealth in a country or non-monetary factors in quality of life. They also exclude the informal sector. Therefore, both of these are considered ineffective measures of development. Instead, two other measures provide a better understanding.

PURCHASING POWER PARITY (PPP) is an exchange rate that determines how much currency it would take to buy the equal amounts of goods in two different countries. For example, a Big Mac in South Africa costs 19.45 rand, 9.50 real in Brazil, and $4.07 in the United States (as of 2011). So which is actually the most expensive? By looking only at the numbers, it seems that it is significantly harder to buy a Big Mac in South Africa; therefore, it would seem that quality of life is lower in general for South Africans. However, once the purchasing power parity is determined (by dividing the numeric cost of each Big Mac), and then adjusted using the currency exchange rate, a Big Mac in South Africa actually costs US $2.87 and a Big Mac in Brazil costs US $6.17. Therefore, Big Macs are actually significantly less expensive in South Africa and significantly more expensive in Brazil. So, the perceived disparity between South African development and American development is less than it originally seemed (when measured by a Big Mac!).

The second measure is the **UNITED NATIONS HUMAN DEVELOPMENT INDEX (HDI)**. Rather than purely an economic measure, the HDI is based on the idea that development is actually best measured by the choices available to the population of a country. The HDI focuses on quality of life measures like education, healthcare, and general welfare. It does use GDP, but only as one measure among others including life expectancy, level of education attainment, and literacy rates. It then creates a ranking system of the world's countries with the highest score being 1.000 and the lowest 0.000.

Rostow Modernization Model

In the 1950s, sociologist Walt Rostow created a model to explain the economic development of countries. He argued that each country goes through five stages.

- Stage One is the ***TRADITIONAL SOCIETY***. This is when an economy consists mostly of subsistence farming with little trade or industry.

- Stage Two he called ***PRECONDITIONS FOR TAKEOFF***. In this stage, small groups of individuals initiate "takeoff" economic activities. They begin to develop small industries in certain pockets of a country.

The Demographic Transition Model (DTM) is based off of Rostow's Modernization Model. The five stages of each model align. This can help you with questions that ask you to analyze the relationship between population and development.

- In Stage three, called ***TAKEOFF***, those small industries begin to grow very quickly and become an increasingly significant part of the economy. This is when the shift from subsistence farming to industry begins.

- Stage Four is the ***DRIVE TO MATURITY***. During this phase, advanced technology and development spread beyond the takeoff areas to the rest of the country. A skilled and educated workforce emerges and becomes sustainable. Other industries begin to grow rapidly.

- Finally, Stage Five is ***HIGH MASS CONSUMPTION***. In this stage the majority of the populatiovn is employed in service, rather than factory, jobs. The level of education of the populace is higher overall as a result. Economic development reaches new levels, leading to increased consumption.

LDCs are all in Rostow's Stages One, Two, and three, while MDCs are in Stages Four and Five. Rostow's model has many critics who argue that is too Anglo-centric. They also point out that it unrealistically assumes countries develop independently of one another, and so it does not take into account the impact of colonization (discussed in the next section).

Critics also take issue with Rostow's fifth stage, arguing that increased consumption is not a necessary consequence of economic growth. Instead, they argue that the surplus wealth could lead to increased social welfare programs or sustainable activities. Northern Europe more closely models this version of a fifth developmental stage.

Development Gap

By any measure, the gap between MDCs and LDCs is widening. In the last ten years, the GDP of MDCs has tripled while the GDP of LDCs has only doubled. RNI in MDCs has dropped by 85 percent in the same time period, while it has only decreased by 5 percent in LDCs. Several theories attempt to explain this trend.

DEPENDENCY THEORY argues that the root of the problem can be traced back to colonization and imperialism. Dependency theory is built on the idea that the decisions and actions of one country directly impact those of others.

The majority of MDCs today were colonizers, while the majority of LDCs were colonized. The goal of the colonizing countries was to increase their wealth by using the colonized area as both a source of natural resources and as a market for the sale of their finished goods. So industrialization was suppressed in the colonies. Even after colonization, MDCs need LDCs in order to maintain their economic growth and dominance. LDCs rely on MDCs for aid and support. Therefore, LDCs are kept in a cycle of underdevelopment by the structure of the global economic system.

The **CORE-PERIPHERY MODEL** presents a similar perspective. It divides the countries of the world into three groups: the core, semi-periphery, and periphery. The *core* consists of industrialized countries, those with the highest per capita income and standard of living (the United States, Canada, Australia, New Zealand, Japan, and Western Europe). The *semi-periphery* is composed of newly industrialized countries like India, Brazil, South Africa, and China. These countries usually have significant inequities between the haves and have-nots in their population. The *periphery* consists of countries with very low levels of industrialization, infrastructure, and per capita income and standards of living. Essentially, these are LDCs, and include most of Africa (not South Africa as noted above), parts of Asia, and parts of South America.

Most semi-periphery countries are spatially located between core and peripheral countries, and between two competing core areas. They also, typically, have larger land masses (like India, China, and Brazil); however there are exceptions to this (Poland, Greece, and Israel).

To explain this structure, sociologist Immanuel Wallerstein posited his **WORLD SYSTEMS ANALYSIS THEORY** which states that the global system is a capitalist system interlocked by competition, both political and economic. This competition made the exploitation of some countries by others inevitable. Those that did the exploiting became the core, and those that were exploited became those on the periphery and semi-periphery (based on location and, to a degree, size).

Improving Economic Development

There are three main approaches for improving the economic development of LDCs. The first is the **SELF-SUFFICIENCY APPROACH**. This is based on the idea that a country can only develop if the country provides for its people itself, rather than relying on outside aid and support. In order for this to happen, countries cannot concentrate on just one industry (which is more typical for LDCs based on the colonization model), but must promote development across all sectors and all regions. The self-sufficiency approach requires a closed economic state with minimum imports and high tariffs to limit international trade.

However, critics of this model argue that, while it may allow native industries to grow, it stifles competition which will ultimately inhibit growth.

The opposite approach is the **INTERNATIONAL TRADE APPROACH**. In this export-oriented approach, a country focuses on products that it can provide to the rest of the world. By doing this, a country develops a **COMPARATIVE ADVANTAGE** in that industry, meaning it becomes better than the rest of the world in that industry.

For example, Japan chose to focus on developing a comparative advantage in high-tech products rather than food production. Instead, it imports much of its food. Critics of this approach argue it only works if a country is able to actually develop a comparative advantage. If a country invests in developing a comparative advantage in one industry, but is unable to become the "best," it has wasted its resources and crippled the rest of its economy. Also, even if it does develop a comparative advantage, this can still leave the country open to exploitation, particularly if its chosen market is an export-based product. This can best be seen in many African countries that export raw materials like gold, diamonds, rubber, and cocoa. While exportation levels might be high, development remains low, as the push to produce more leads to severe mistreatment of labor with limited opportunities for small business growth, market competition, or upward mobility.

Finally, inter-governmental organizations attempt to improve the development of LDCs through **STRUCTURAL ADJUSTMENTS**. Organizations like the **WORLD BANK** or the **INTERNATIONAL MONETARY FUND** offer loans in exchange for changes to a country's economic structure. These usually involve increasing privatization, which negatively impacts families reliant on resources previously provided by the government. However, advocates argue this is only a short-term negative impact that is necessary for longer-term gain.

EXAMPLES

1) The countries of West Africa remain LDCs because of their dependence on Western MDCs developed during French colonization of the area. This statement most reflects which of the following?

A. Rostow's Modernization Model

B. World Systems Analysis Theory

C. International Trade Approach

D. Dependency Theory

E. Self-sufficiency Approach

Answers:

A. Incorrect. Rostow's Modernization Model assumes countries develop independently of one another.

B. Incorrect. While positing a similar argument, colonization is not an overt part of the World Systems Analysis Theory which draws on the Core-Periphery model.

C. Incorrect. The International Trade Approach is a method of trying to help LDCs increase their economic development. It does not explain why countries develop the way they do.

D. Correct. Dependency Theory argues that colonization created a dependent relationship between LDCs and MDCs that cannot be broken due the global economic structure.

E.   Incorrect. The self-sufficiency approach is a method for addressing the development gap, rather than identifying its cause.

2)   Which of the following is true of MDCs?
    A.   They have GDP per capita in excess of $20,000.
    B.   They are concentrated in Western Europe and North America.
    C.   They rely heavily on LDCs for processed goods.
    D.   both A and B
    E.   none of the above

    Answers:
    A.   Incorrect. While this statement is true, it is not the best answer because it is not the most complete option.
    B.   Incorrect. Again, while the statement is true, it is not the most complete answer.
    C.   Incorrect. MDCs primarily obtain raw materials from LDCs.
    D.   **Correct.** Both A and B are accurate descriptors.
    E.   Incorrect. All MDCs do have a GDP per capita over $20,000 and the majority of them are in Western Europe. The United States and Canada are also MDCs.

3)   Purchasing Power Parity is a better measure of economic development than Gross Domestic Product because
    A.   PPP allows for direct comparisons of what money can acquire in different countries.
    B.   It is based on more accurate numbers than GDP.
    C.   GDP is only calculated every ten years, whereas PPP is annual.
    D.   PPP takes into account class differences in quality of life.
    E.   GDP is based on an outdated understanding of economics.

    Answers:
    A.   **Correct.** By looking at the ratio of the cost of certain items (or groups of items) in different countries, PPP gives a more accurate comparative measure of development.
    B.   Incorrect. Both PPP and GDP are based on detailed empirical data.
    C.   Incorrect. Neither GDP nor PPP have requirements or standards about when information is collected.
    D.   Incorrect. While PPP can better show internal economic inequalities, neither is focused on that, nor does either look at non-monetary quality of life issues.
    E.   Incorrect. The economics behind GDP is valid, it just does not provide as useful of a comparison.

4)   How does the UN Human Development Index differ from other measures of economic development?
    A.   It focuses on the gap between the wealthy and the poor in a country.
    B.   It differentiates between private and public sources of economic growth.
    C.   It only examines the top fifty and bottom fifty nations in the world.
    D.   It is the only measure focused on comparative economic growth.
    E.   It considers non-monetary factors like healthcare, literacy rates, and education.

Globalization

GLOBALIZATION is the trend of increasing interdependence and spatial interaction between disparate areas of the world economically, politically, and culturally. At its core, globalization is an economic trend; however it has significant cultural and political impacts as well. For example, the exportation of American fast food restaurants, like McDonald's, to other parts of the world reflects the capitalist drive to find new markets. Furthermore, the introduction of this type of food has a significant impact on one of the major distinguishing cultural traits of other countries—their cuisine.

The primary driving force of globalization is MULTINATIONAL CORPORATIONS (MNCs) or TRANSNATIONAL CORPORATIONS (TNCs). Often made up of several smaller companies that all contribute to the same production process, these are companies whose headquarters are located in one country (usually an MDC) and whose production is located in one or more different countries (usually an LDC). The process of moving production to a different country is called OUTSOURCING, and it allows for several financial advantages for the MNC including reduced labor costs, lower tax rates, and cheaper land prices. The new country also often has more lax safety and labor standards. Although outsourcing increases transportation costs, this increase is offset by a lower cost in labor. This is called the SUBSTITUTION PRINCIPLE.

Some countries create SPECIAL ECONOMIC ZONES (SEZs) to encourage outsourcing. In these zones, companies are held to lower environmental and labor standards and can receive special tax breaks and other incentives. SEZs also encourage companies to invest directly in the economy of the hosting country to help maintain the government that is supporting their business. Both China and Mexico have created several SEZs (although Mexico's should be phasing out under NAFTA).

Similar to SEZs are EXPORT PROCESSING ZONES, also known as free trade zones, in which duties and tariffs are waived, and restrictions on labor practices are significantly loosened. Again, the goal is to attract the factories of MNCs.

The globalization of the manufacturing process has created a NEW INTERNATIONAL DIVISION OF LABOR in which different parts of a product are manufactured in different places of the world, then sent to yet another location to be assembled. Essentially, this is a globalization of the Fordist assembly line. The problem with this model is that LDCs become very dependent on MNCs. Furthermore, MNCs may engage in DIRECT INVEST-

MENT in the country as part of their activities there, investing directly into its economy. In the long run, local involvement allows MNCs to gain disproportionate influence over governmental affairs as they advocate for governmental policies favorable to their own financial goals, especially FREE TRADE, or no regulations, on outsourcing.

NICs are countries that are not yet developed, but are developing faster than other less developed countries. They have strong manufacturing export economies, a great deal of foreign investment, strong political leadership, and increasing rights for citizens.

Free trade allows the global market to run its course because the market always maximizes efficiency, sometimes to the detriment of workers and the environment. However, advocates argue that outsourcing allows for economic growth in otherwise struggling economies. They point to the Four Asian Tigers (Singapore, Hong Kong, South Korea, and Taiwan) as examples of countries that began as sources of production for MNCs, and then became NEWLY INDUSTRIALIZED COUNTRIES (NICs), experiencing unprecedented economic growth. As a result, today many argue that these countries should now be considered MDCs.

Critics, however, argue that free trade only benefits MNCs because it does not protect local workers, local environments, or ensure an appropriate quality of life in the countries that provide the labor. They argue that the Asian Tigers succeeded not because of outsourcing, but because they shifted their focus from production for MNCs to developing a comparative advantage in service industries, namely high-end technology and financial management. These critics argue for FAIR TRADE in which governments oversee and regulate outsourcing to ensure all workers receive a living wage.

EXAMPLES

1) Special Economic Zones attract multinational corporations by doing all of the following EXCEPT
   A. offering them tax breaks.
   B. providing them space for their headquarters.
   C. lessening environmental standards.
   D. loosening labor laws.
   E. offering direct investment opportunities in the host government.

   Answers:
   A. Incorrect. One of the key ways in which countries attract MNCs is by offering them tax breaks to increase their profit margin.
   B. **Correct.** Most MNCs headquarter their companies in MDCs, and only use the LDC's SEZ for production purposes.
   C. Incorrect. Adhering to environmental standards can greatly increase the cost of production. By lowering them, SEZs offer a significant incentive to companies.
   D. Incorrect. Labor is often the most expensive cost of doing business. The loosening of laws about pay and length of workday allows companies to make more economically efficient use of labor.
   E. Incorrect. Host countries encourage direct investment to allow the companies greater influence (and increase their investment in the country's health).

2) The Substitution Principle states that:

A. Corporations headquarter their company in one country and produce their goods in another.

B. Companies can invest money directly into a country's economy.

C. Companies will accept increased transportation costs in exchange for decreased labor costs.

D. New industrialized countries switch from hosting production to focusing on new cutting edge industries.

E. Local industries and businesses are replaced by those imported from abroad.

Answers:

A. Incorrect. The practice of having headquarters in one country and production in another is called outsourcing.

B. Incorrect. When a corporation invests directly into the economy of a country, it is called direct investment.

C. Correct. Although outsourcing leads to higher transportation costs as companies have to pay to get finished goods back to their markets, the reduced cost of labor is enough to offset it. This is called the Substitution Principle.

D. Incorrect. This process, best exemplified by the four Asian Tigers, is based off of the International Trade Approach to development. The four Tigers focused on developing a comparative advantage in their respective industries.

E. Incorrect. The replacement of local business by transnational corporations is part of globalization.

Political Geography

The study of political organization—another human characteristic of place—is called **POLITICAL GEOGRAPHY**. Political structures emerged over time in response to ongoing competition for control over territory, resources, trade routes, and people. In order to strengthen their positions, groups often cooperate with each other through alliances and agreements. For example, today the world is mostly divided into various state sovereignties as different groups came together in order to access different resources, solidify their power, or control strategic positions. In fact, the only unorganized area left in the world is Antarctica. Cooperation exists on the **SUPRANATIONAL SCALE** as well in the form of multi-national organizations like the United Nations.

However, more often competition between groups leads to conflict. Those same agreements and alliances that allow for cooperation may also determine the sides of a conflict. These sides are often based on culture traits: religion, political ideology, national origin, language, or race. They can be local, regional, national, or global. For example, within a state different regions might compete for a greater share of government funds, or two towns might fight over access to roads or rivers. In the nineteenth-century United States, the North and South engaged in an ideologically and economically based armed conflict during the Civil War. In the twentieth century, the nations of the world divided into two sides—the fascist Axis and the western, democratic capitalist Allies (in an uneasy alliance with the Soviet Union)—during World War II.

Humans desire to establish ownership of their own specific, personal space. This HUMAN TERRITORIALITY has manifested differently over time from tribes, clans, and villages to kingdoms and empires. In Europe, for example, city-states then emerged in Greece and Rome, followed by the rise of feudal society after the fall of these empires. Feudal society led into monarchy, which eventually transformed into nation-states (which has become the global organizing political principle since World War II). At the center of each of these political forms, though, was the concept of SOVEREIGNTY, the public recognition of an individual or group's control over a place, its people, and its institutions.

States

In political geography, there is a distinction between the physical area and the people of a place. A STATE refers to the physical place: it is any area with defined borders, a permanent population, and a relatively effective government and economy.

The borders, or POLITICAL BOUNDARIES, of a state can be drawn in three different ways. PHYSICAL BOUNDARIES are based on natural features like rivers or mountains, whereas CULTURAL POLITICAL BOUNDARIES are based on religion or language (or rarely another cultural trait). For example, Pakistan and India were separated into two countries based on religion: Pakistan became home to Muslims, India to Hindus primarily (despite an ongoing large population of Muslims). The third type of boundary, GEOMETRIC POLITICAL BOUNDARIES, are drawn as straight lines without regard to natural or cultural features. When Korea was divided after World War II, a geometric political boundary was drawn between North and South at the thirty-eighth parallel.

Most modern boundaries are the result of negotiation between states, or human settlement or interaction. These are called SUBSEQUENT BOUNDARIES. Others either pre-dated human cultures—ANTECEDENT BOUNDARIES—or were imposed by an outside force—SUPERIMPOSED BOUNDARIES. For example, after World War I and following the collapse of the Ottoman Empire, the Middle East was organized into states by Britain and France using superimposed boundaries. RELICT BOUNDARIES are boundaries that are no longer functioning, but serve as a reminder that the boundary used to exist. For example, the Great Wall of China is a relict boundary.

In order to create a legal political boundary, four steps must be followed.

- ◆ DEFINITION: The boundary must be legally described. This is where most of the negotiation between states takes place.
- ◆ DELIMITATION: The boundary must be drawn onto a map.
- ◆ DEMARCATION: The boundary must be marked, in some way, on the physical landscape.
- ◆ ADMINISTRATION: The boundary must be policed and enforced.

In this process, there are many opportunities for disagreement and conflict. Disputes over borders can arise over the borders actual location, how that location is defined, how the border is administered, and how resources are distributed near and across the border. Disputes also arise in FRONTIERS, areas where boundaries are either not well-established or not maintained well.

On land, boundary negotiations can be tricky, but they become significantly more complicated in the oceans. States have agreed that each state has an EXCLUSIVE ECONOMIC ZONE up to 200 miles from its shore. If there is less than 200 miles between two countries, the ocean area is divided equally in half. This is called the MEDIAN LINE PRINCIPLE.

Boundaries determine the outer edges of a state. From the inside, states are organized around a CORE, the location of the concentration of power. The core is essential in determining the functionality of a state. If the core is well-integrated into the rest of the state, development is more likely to spread evenly. In this case, CENTRIPETAL FORCES pull the state and the people together to create a unified identity. If however, the state has several cores—a MULTICORE STATE—development can occur unevenly and in pockets. South Africa, for example, has divided its political core into three different cities: the executive capital is Pretoria, the legislative capital is Capetown and the judicial capital is in Bloemfontein. CENTRIFUGAL FORCES then can divide the state and its people. Infrastructure is often underdeveloped and inefficient, and internal conflict is likely. This can lead to BALKANIZATION, the disintegration of a state into smaller pieces.

In some countries, there may be a single core, but it is not well-integrated, and development is not evenly distributed. Instead, the core is located in a PRIMATE CITY. This is a city in which all of the resources are concentrated, with smaller cities serving as support for the primate city. As a result, it serves as the political center for the country and holds greater economic power than any other city in the state.

Name one centripetal force and one centrifugal force at work in the United States.

Primate cities are common in less developed countries. For example Lagos, with a population of 13.4 million, is a primate city in Nigeria. The second biggest city in the country, Kano, has a population of only 3.6 million. They also can be found in very old nation-states, like Hungary (Budapest) and Great Britain (London). In these cases, the primate city not only has a concentration of political and economic power, but is the cultural center of the country as well.

Some states, in an attempt to disperse the concentration of power and resources, attempt to remove political power from the primate city by creating a FORWARD CAPITAL which better serves national goals. So, while Lagos is Nigeria's primate city, Abuja is its capital. Abuja was built in the 1980s specifically to reduce the power of Lagos and shift political power to a neutral location that would neither help nor hinder any of Nigeria's various religious and ethnic groups. Pakistan did the same thing in the 1960s when it built Islamabad to replace its primate city of Karachi as the nation's capital.

Territorial Morphology

Different boundaries lead to states with different shapes which then create different political situations for each country. This TERRITORIAL MORPHOLOGY—the relationship between a state's size, shape and location and its political situation—is critical to political geography. The ideal (politically) state structure is a COMPACT STATE, a state which is relatively small and nearly square or circular in shape. In these states, the center of power is always close, no matter where a group or individual is within the state. Switzerland is a compact state.

However, most states are not compact, and instead fall into one of three major categories. **FRAGMENTED STATES**—like Indonesia, which is comprised of 16,000 islands—exist in several pieces. **ELONGATED STATES**, like Vietnam and Chile, are long and thin, and **PRORUPTED STATES**, like Thailand, have a piece that protrudes. In each of these cases, political administration is more challenging because it is difficult to maintain control over the areas that are far from the center of power.

States that are **LANDLOCKED** face economic challenges because they have no direct access to the ocean for trade. They also have a greater potential for boundary disputes since they have more borders to administer. These states must rely more on their neighbors which can lead to political problems. Many small, landlocked states end up serving as **BUFFER STATES**, independent states that are sandwiched between two (usually larger) conflicting countries. Jordan is a buffer state between Israel and Iraq.

While most landlocked countries are simply surrounded by multiple other countries (again, Switzerland is a good example), others are actually **PERFORATED STATES** and make a hole in the middle of another country. Lesotho is a good example; it is a perforated state within South Africa.

While sovereignty is a defining character of a state, not all states enjoy the same level of sovereignty. **SATELLITE STATES** are states that are technically independent, but are heavily controlled by another, more powerful state. Belarus is a satellite state of the Russian Federation.

Sometimes, states are divided. A **POLITICAL ENCLAVE** is a state—or part of a state—that is surrounded by another. In contrast a **POLITICAL EXCLAVE**, is part of a state that is separated from the rest of the state. During the Cold War, West Berlin was a political exclave of West Germany and a political enclave within East Germany. Alaska and Hawaii are also both examples of exclaves.

EXAMPLES

1) The country of Panama is an example of which of the following kinds of states?
   A. landlocked state
   B. compact state
   C. fragmented state
   D. elongated state
   E. none of the above

Answers:
   A. Incorrect. Landlocked states are surrounded by land on all sides. Panama is an isthmus and has ocean on two sides.
   B. Incorrect. A compact state is nearly circular or square in shape. Panama is long and thin.
   C. Incorrect. A fragmented state exists in multiple pieces. Panama is made up of one contiguous stretch of land.
   D. Correct. Panama is an elongated state because it is long and thin.
   E. Incorrect. Panama's shape makes it an elongated state.

2) The mountains surrounding Switzerland create which kind of boundaries?

  A. physical boundaries

  B. relict boundaries

  C. geometric political boundaries

  D. superimposed boundaries

  E. subsequent boundaries

Answers:

  A. **Correct.** Mountains are an example of physical boundaries because they are part of the landscape.

  B. Incorrect. A relict boundary no longer functions. Switzerland's mountains still serve as an active border.

  C. Incorrect. Geometric political boundaries are drawn in a straight line. Switzerland's mountains create an uneven border based on land, not politics.

  D. Incorrect. Superimposed borders are imposed from the outside. Switzerland's mountains create a natural boundary and required no outside imposition.

  E. Incorrect. Subsequent boundaries are those resulting from human interaction or settlement.

3) What is a disadvantage that results from a primate city?

  A. The primate city has limited access to political power.

  B. A primate city creates a multi-core state.

  C. A primate city has a disproportionate share of a state's resources.

  D. A primate city is particularly vulnerable to invasion and conflict.

  E. A primate city lags behind the rest of the state developmentally.

Answers:

  A. Incorrect. Political power is concentrated in a primate city, giving it greater access than anywhere else in the country.

  B. Incorrect. Multi-core states result from multiple sources of concentrations of power. Primate cities have essentially all of the power within a country, not allowing for the development of other sources.

  C. **Correct.** Because of its concentration of power, primate cities also have a much greater share of a country's resources.

  D. Incorrect. Primate cities have the greatest power and so are generally more protected from outside attack. However, because the resources are concentrated in them, parts of the country that are far from the primate city are more at risk.

  E. Incorrect. A primate city tends to outpace the development of the rest of the state because of its increased access to resources and power.

4) Poland is considered a buffer state because of its location

  A. sharing a border with seven other states.

  B. between Germany and the Soviet Union during World War II.

  C. on the Baltic Sea.

  D. in Eastern Europe.

  E. north of the Sudeten and Carpathian mountain ranges.

Nations

A NATION, on the other hand, is a group of people who identify as a group and share a culture. In most cases, a state is composed of one nation (and so called a nation-state). However, in some cases, like the former Soviet Union, states can be multinational. There are also STATELESS NATIONS, like the Romani people throughout Europe, who exist as a nation but do not have their own territory.

Conflict can often arise between stateless nations and the states in which they reside. For example, the stateless nation may be a minority within a state and at odds with that state in terms of cultural traits or political beliefs. In these cases, members of a stateless nation become ETHNONATIONALISTIC, maintaining allegiance for their nation over the state.

If a nation is dispersed across multiple states—as is often the case—that nation may strive to reunite its various parts. Called IRREDENTISM, this was Hitler's goal in occupying Czechoslovakia in 1939. He believed the German nation needed to be brought together under one administration. Today, the Kurds are primarily based in northern Iraq, having achieved a degree of autonomy in that unstable country. However, Kurdish people are dispersed throughout Turkey, Syria, Iran, and Azerbaijan, and are alternatively perceived as a threat and a potential ally among the states of the Middle East depending on the geopolitical situation in the region.

Geopolitics

The study of the interaction between states—politically and territorially—is called GEO-POLITICS. Geopolitical theory has been very important in shaping the major global conflicts in history.

For example, Adolf Hitler used Friedrich Ratzel's ORGANIC THEORY to justify his aggressive actions toward neighboring countries. In the late nineteenth century, Ratzel posited that states are essentially living organisms that feed on land. So, in order to grow (as all living things must), they must obtain more land. Ratzel argued this process was the root of all state decision-making and conflict.

The Soviet Union's foreign policy was based on Halford John Mackinder's HEARTLAND THEORY, first published in 1904. Mackinder stated that the world was made up of the World-Island (Europe, Asia, and Africa), outlying islands (Great Britain and Japan) and offshore islands (North America, South America, and Australia). Therefore, in order to control the world, one needed to control Eurasia (the World-Island). In order to do that, a country needed to control Eastern Europe—the heartland of Eurasia. This theory not only motivated Soviet aggression in Eastern Europe, but US attempts to curb it as well. Mackinder's Heartland Theory was the basis for the American concept of **DOMINO THEORY**, the idea that if one country fell to communism, the whole region would fall.

Taking Mackinder's theories further, Nicholas Spykman developed the **RIMLAND THEORY**, which argued for a balance of power in the periphery of Eurasia in order to prevent the emergence of a global power there (namely, a Soviet or Chinese global power). As a result, the United States developed **CONTAINMENT**, a policy to keep communism *contained* to the areas where it already existed. This policy, rooted in Domino Theory, drove both the Korean and Vietnam Wars.

EXAMPLES

1) The Basque people in Spain are an example of

   A. a nation-state.

   B. a stateless nation.

   C. a multinational state.

   D. a divided nation.

   E. a satellite state

   Answers:

   A. Incorrect. A nation-state is a state which is composed of a unified nation. The Basque are a minority group within Spain.

   B. **Correct.** Having a distinct culture complex from the rest of Spain, the Basque people make up a separate nation. However, as they do not have their own state, they are considered a stateless nation.

   C. Incorrect. Because the Basque are a separate nation within Spain, Spain could be considered a multinational state. However, the Basque people themselves are neither a state nor multinational.

   D. Incorrect. *Divided nation* is not a geographic term. A nation can be divided or dispersed if its members are in several different states. However, the Basque people reside as a group in Spain, and are therefore not divided.

   E. Incorrect. Satellite states are technically independent states. The Basque people have no recognized sovereignty.

2) The United States became involved in what was essentially a Korean civil war (resulting in the Korean War), primarily because of which geopolitical theory?

   A. Organic Theory

   B. Heartland Theory

   C. Domino Theory

   D. Irredentism

   E. Rimland Theory

Answers:

A. Incorrect. The organic theory argued that all countries needed to physically expand to survive. This was not the concern in Korea.

B. Incorrect. The Heartland Theory argued that Eastern Europe was the lynchpin to world domination. Korea's location is not strategically significant based on this theory.

C. **Correct.** The domino theory states that if one country falls to communism, the rest around it will as well. Once communist forces began to gain power in the north, US officials became concerned that all of the peninsula—and then the rest of Asia—would become communist.

D. Incorrect. Irredentism is not a geopolitical theory, but the practice of trying to reunite disparate parts of a nation. Korea was not trying to reunite itself, nor was the United States.

E. Incorrect. Rimland theory focused on creating geopolitical balance. US involvement in Korea was an active movement against the spread of communism.

Human-Environment Interaction

The relationship between humans and their environment—the ways in which cultural traits impact physical traits and vice versa—is of utmost importance to geographers. Humans have always modified the environment to suit their needs. For example, with the advent of agriculture, humans began loosening the topsoil to make planting easier. A looser topsoil is more susceptible to erosion from wind and rain, allowing greater changes to the physical landscape. Cities are also a prime example. Cities significantly reduce the amount of exposed ground in an area and lead to a concentration of fuel and resource consumption.

The environment has also shaped human activity. For example, the main economic activities of a place—farming, fishing, trade—have historically been determined, in large part, by the physical characteristics of the place. People living in deserts have traditionally been nomadic because the restricted access to food and water sources requires them to continually move around. Climate impacts clothing, housing, and work and leisure patterns. For example, a period of rest in the middle of the day is common in cultures in hot climates.

Theories of Human-Environment Interaction

Theorists continually debate the cause and effect nature of the relationship between humans and their environment. There are four main schools of thought. ENVIRONMENTAL DETERMINISM, dating back to ancient Greece, argues that human behavior is controlled by the physical environment. For example, when Europeans first arrived in Hawaii, they concluded that the natives were lazy because they did not see them toiling over crops. They believed that the ideal climate and abundant natural food sources had created a slothful people, even though the Hawaiians used systems of resource management not based on plantation agriculture.

POSSIBILISM posits an opposing theory: while the environment does replace restrictions on the options available to a group of people, it is still ultimately the people who make the choice. Possibilists would point to European and Americans who settled in Hawaii and built large and productive plantations, rather than becoming "lazy." (It is important to note that Hawaiians were engaged in their own agricultural endeavors, despite the European perspective.)

Beyond possibilism is CULTURAL DETERMINISM, which reflected the changing ideology of the nineteenth and early twentieth century. Cultural determinists argue that the environment, in fact, places no restrictions on the development of culture, and that the only restrictions come from human limitations. For example, cultural determinists would point out that both the Philippines and Japan are islands with limited resources. However, Japan was not limited by its location because it chose to colonize other areas and create trade agreements to gain access to other resources.

Finally, POLITICAL ECOLOGY argues that the government of a region affects the environment which, in turn, affects the choices available to the people. For example, mountains theoretically blocked the building of a transcontinental railroad. However, government policies in the nineteenth century United States allowed railroad companies complete discretion in engineering infrastructure, so they chose to use dynamite to create tunnels in the mountains, ultimately leading to the successful creation of a transcontinental railroad.

The First Agricultural Revolution

The primary way humans have affected the Earth is through the development of agriculture. With the domestication of plants and animals, humans transitioned from a nomadic existence to a sedentary one. They learned not just to locate food, but to cultivate it themselves. Early domestication consisted of cutting a stem off of a plant and planting that stem or dividing a plant by the roots. This process diffused from multiple hearths: Southeast Asia, northwestern South America, and West Africa.

Approximately 12,000 years ago, humans began to collect and plant seeds and to raise animals for their own use. This was the start of the FIRST AGRICULTURAL REVOLUTION. Like the advent of agriculture itself, this revolution diffused from several hearths: Western India, Southwest Asia, Northern China, Ethiopia, Southern Mexico, and Northern Peru. Humans became stationary and self-supporting. Large communities—a hindrance for nomads—became an asset for farmers. As communities grew, civilization emerged. Of course, not all people became farmers; many still continued to live a nomadic existence. However, those numbers dropped dramatically with each wave of agricultural innovation. Today, there are fewer than 250,000 hunter/gatherers in the world.

Not only did the advent of seed agriculture and animal domestication change the way people lived, it also increased the carrying capacity of the Earth. Attempts to increase yield led to the development of more advanced tools. For example, the plow emerged in Mesopotamia around 6000 years ago. With specialized tools came specialized skills which more added value. People began to use their skills to benefit the larger community rather than just themselves.

Increased agricultural efficiency eventually led to surplus that could be traded for other goods. As a result, markets and trade systems developed; so did the notion of WEALTH as the accumulation of goods.

The revolution did not bring about only positive change, however. Farmers were vulnerable to the weather in ways nomads were not, and had to depend on specific planting and harvesting times. Also, those who had acquired goods were vulnerable to theft of their wealth. Consequently, humans developed secure storage methods (as they no longer carried everything around with them) and began to construct fortifications to protect their communities.

Success in seed agriculture led to SUBSISTENCE FARMING in which the farmer grows only enough food to feed his own family. This type of farming is still very common today, especially in less developed countries. Subsistence farming takes three main forms:

EXTENSIVE SUBSISTENCE FARMING uses a large amount of land to farm food for a family. It is found mostly in areas with low populations, but a great deal of land. The land, however, tends to have a thin topsoil, and therefore is limited in its production capacity. Large amounts of land are needed because farmers practice SHIFTING CULTIVATION, meaning they rotate which types of crops are grown in each field in order to maintain healthy soil. Once the soil becomes too worn out, fields are left fallow for several years to rebuild nutrients.

In some cases, the farmers will use SLASH-AND-BURN to clear the land. They will cut down the plants, then burn the remaining stalks, stumps, and roots to create new farmland (called making it SWIDDEN). Most farmers who use this technique also practice INTER-TILLAGE, planting different crops in the same area to reduce the risk of crop failure and promote a healthier diet.

Today, extensive subsistence farming can be found mostly in tropical areas, especially in the rainforests of Africa, near the Amazon, and throughout Southeast Asia.

Extensive subsistence farming has serious environmental ramifications. As populations have grown and the land available for agriculture has decreased, farmers need to replant fields too soon, leading to permanent soil damage. The desire for more land has led to the destruction of other types of areas—like rainforests—to allow for the creation of new farmland.

INTENSIVE SUBSISTENCE FARMING uses a small amount of land as efficiently as possible to feed a family. This type of farming can be found in areas with high populations and very fertile soil. Intensive subsistence farming is marked by innovative farming techniques like terrace-farming pyramids, which make use of vertical *and* horizontal space for farming. Another technique used is DOUBLE-CROPPING, when farmers plant two subsequent crops in the same field in a single year.

For thousands of years, this type of farming has been most dominant in Asia, especially in China, India, and Southeast Asia. Rice is commonly grown using intensive-subsistence farming; however wheat, corn, and millet are also grown using this method in areas that are too cold for rice.

PASTORALISM is a type of farming that emerged with the domestication of animals. Rather than raising crops, pastoralists breed and herd animals (primarily goats, camels, sheep, and cattle) for food, clothing, and shelter. Pastoralism is dominant in areas with very limited growing capabilities such as grasslands, deserts, and steppes like North Africa, central and southern Africa, the Middle East, and Central Asia. Pastoralists can be sedentary or nomadic, moving their herds in search of new food sources or improved climate depending on the season. However, the land used by pastoralists is shrinking as governments take control of it to use for other economic purposes like drilling and mining.

EXAMPLES

1) All of the following are accurate descriptors of the First Agricultural Revolution EXCEPT:

   A. Humans began to settle in stationary communities.

   B. Humans began to use technology to increase production of food.

   C. It led to the development of a more stable food supply.

   D. It allowed for significant population growth.

   E. Humans developed the notion of wealth.

   Answers:

   A. Incorrect. Stable communities are one of the hallmarks of the First Agricultural Revolution as people transitioned from nomadic to sedentary living.

   B. **Correct.** The First Agricultural Revolution resulted from humans learning how to gather and replant seeds to grow crops. Technology did not play a significant role.

   C. Incorrect. By being able to grow their own food, people were no longer reliant on trying to find it—which was precarious at best. However, the food supply did become more dependent on weather and season.

   D. Incorrect. The stable food supply and safety of stable communities led to a major population boom.

   E. Incorrect. The increased efficiency in farming led to surplus, which led to the accumulation of goods and then wealth.

2) Which of the following farming techniques would most likely be used in a Vietnamese rice field?

   A. intertillage

   B. slash-and-burn

   C. double-cropping

   D. shifting cultivation

   E. swidden

   Answers:

   A. Incorrect. Intertillage, the practice of sowing different crops together, is a technique used in extensive subsistence farming, not the intensive subsistence farming used in Vietnam.

   B. Incorrect. Slash-and-burn is used in places with large amounts of land, and the ability to leave many fields fallow at a time. Vietnam has limited space for farming and cannot do this.

   C. **Correct.** Double-cropping is the intensive subsistence farming practice of planting subsequent crops within the same year. Vietnam's climate is ideal for this type of farming.

   D. Incorrect. Shifting cultivation, or crop rotation, is used primarily where the topsoil is thin and the soil is somewhat lacking in nutrients. The climate of Vietnam creates particularly fertile soil so crop rotation would not be needed.

The Second Agricultural Revolution

The SECOND AGRICULTURAL REVOLUTION began around 500 C.E., was centered in Europe, and was marked by an increase in agricultural technology. This revolution occurred in two major bursts. The first was right after the fall of Rome, when the feudal village structure emerged. During this time, agricultural production was organized by the OPEN-LOT SYSTEM in which there was one plot of land for the community, and all members worked in it to provide for themselves and their families. Refinement of tools like the plow and the introduction of other, more complex tools like water mills increased production.

The second burst came about 1200 years later. The growth of capitalism shifted the way people farmed, and individuals began fencing off their land in what was called the enclosure movement. This coincided with the Industrial Revolution and the decline of the feudal system. As people began to migrate in increasing numbers to the cities, the demand for food to be shipped to these areas of population concentration skyrocketed. New innovations in farming like the steel plow and the mechanical reaper led to higher outputs, and eventually, a population boom that kept the entire cycle continuing.

As the demand for food increased—and has continued to increase—subsistence farming was replaced in industrialized countries by COMMERCIAL FARMING, growing food to be sold on the market rather than to feed one's own family. There are several forms of commercial farming. However they all have one thing in common—they are designed to maximize profit.

MIXED CROP AND LIVESTOCK FARMING is commercial farming that involves both crops and animals. This was the first type of commercial farming to emerge in the Second Industrial Revolution and evolved from subsistence farming. It differs from subsistence farming in two notable exceptions: 1) these farms are generally much bigger than the average subsistence farm, and 2) most crops are raised to feed the animals, not for human consumption. The income from the farm, then, comes from the sale of animal products: wool, eggs, and meat. Thus these types of farms are not as dependent on the seasons as crop-only farms.

Other types of commercial agriculture focus on one animal byproduct. For example, RANCHING, the commercial grazing of animals, also became a profitable form of farming. The textile mills of Europe's Industrial Revolution demanded high quantities of wool, greatly increasing the value of sheep worldwide. In the United States, the advent of refrigerated railcars allowed for the transport of meat over long distances. The demand from the burgeoning cities led to a ranching boom—mostly cattle—in the second half of the nineteenth century. Ranching was, and remains, especially popular in areas where the climate is too dry to support crops but where land is abundant: the western United States, northern Mexico, Argentina, southern Brazil, Uruguay, the west coast of Latin America, and some areas of Spain and Portugal. Ranching has had a significant negative impact on the environment, destroying grasslands through overgrazing.

Today, ranching is on the decline. Government standards for beef show a preference for fattier meat rather than the tough, stringier meat from cattle that roam far to graze. Instead, more and more cattle are raised on "fattening farms" where they are kept in a closed lot and fed large amounts to fatten them for slaughter. Furthermore, low grain prices make it unnecessary to allow the animals to roam in order to feed them.

Another type of specialized commercial farming is DAIRYING, farming which focuses solely on bringing milk-based products to market. Because milk is so perishable, the distance from the market became very important for determining what a farm could produce. Originally, farms within the MILKSHED, the area surrounding the market in which fresh milk could be safely transported, usually focused their efforts on milk and other fluid products because these are more perishable. Those outside of the milkshed focused mostly on more sustainable products like butter and cheese. Over time, the milkshed has grown as a result of technological advances in transportation and refrigeration.

Dairy farms differ from other farms in that they are particularly CAPITAL INTENSIVE, meaning they require a great deal of machinery over manual labor. Dairy farmers must invest a great deal of money into their equipment, so these farms tend to be small.

The most common type of commercial farm is the LARGE-SCALE GRAIN PRODUCTION FARM. These are farms that focus solely on the production of one to two key grain crops. These farms were important for increasing the food supply because they not only provided grain for people, but they also provide the food for those animals used for consumption. In fact, more large-scale grain production is dedicated to animal feed than to food for humans to eat. These are found primarily (but not solely) in humid continental climates, specifically Canada, the United States, Argentina, Australia, France, England, and the Ukraine. Wheat is the most common crop, most of which is grown in the United States and Canada; these two countries are responsible for over half of the world's wheat. Like dairy farming, large-scale grain production is capital-intensive. However, the farms tend to be much bigger to allow for the growth of a profitable quantity of grain.

Similar to large-scale grain production are PLANTATION FARMS, which focus on producing only one or two crops. These farms are also large-scale; however—unlike grain farms—they are labor intensive rather than capital intensive. Plantation farms rely on large numbers of seasonal workers and are most used for crops that cannot be easily mechanized: bananas, cotton, and tea, for example. They also must be located near ports (and so are generally coastal) to allow for easy export of crops. The location of plantation farms reflects the global power structure: they are located primarily in less developed countries—mostly low-latitude Africa, Asia, and Latin America, but are owned by and produce crops primarily for export to more developed countries. They monopolize the high-quality land in these areas, leaving little for local farmers and impeding development within the host country.

How does climate affect the type of farming that develops in a location?

Both the development of new technology and the growth of factories led to a globalization and industrialization of agriculture. It became increasingly cost effective to grow food in one place and process it in another. For example, Great Britain and the northeastern United States dominated the textile industry. However, the cotton they used was grown primarily in the American South, India, and Egypt. The methods being used to improve the efficiency and profit of industry were applied to agriculture as well. Developing seeds, fertilizing fields, farming, processing, packaging, distributing, and advertising all became part of a larger **AGRIBUSINESS**. As a result, the number of people involved in agribusiness has increased, while the number of actual farmers has steadily declined. In 1950, 12 percent of the American workforce was farmers, today they compose less than 1 percent.

In the 1820s, Johann Heinrich von Thünen developed the first spatial economic theory, called **AGRICULTURAL LOCATION THEORY**. Writing before the Industrial Revolution was in full swing, von Thünen created a theoretical model to determine how distance impacted human location decisions. In order to do this, he had to treat all other factors as constants in order to isolate distance. He assumed there was one city with one market in which all farmers sold their goods, and that there was only one type of transportation. Therefore the only factor impacting price of transportation was distance. He also assumed that all land was equally farmable; therefore the only thing affecting rent was distance from the market. Based on this model, he predicted that the city would be surrounded by rings of agricultural activity moving from the most intensive, like dairy—which requires less land and carries a higher risk of spoilage, to the most extensive, like large-scale grain production or ranching—which requires much more land and can be transported farther without reducing quality. This was the first model to look at economics through a geographic lens.

EXAMPLES

1) The Industrial Revolution impacted agriculture in all of the following ways EXCEPT:
   A. The emergence of the feudal system created more labor-intensive farming.
   B. Increased technological innovations led to more efficient farming and greater production.
   C. The rise of capitalism led to the individualization of farmland.
   D. The demand for food made growing crops for the market more profitable.
   E. Farms began to specialize in one aspect of farming.

   Answers:
   A. **Correct.** The feudal system was ending as the Industrial Revolution got underway, and farming actually became less labor-intensive with the introduction of new machinery.
   B. Incorrect. Technological innovations like the mechanical reaper, steel plow, and the cotton gin revolutionized farming during the Industrial Revolution.
   C. Incorrect. As market forces became a factor in farming, the enclosure movement led to farmland changing from being community-owned to individually-owned.
   D. Incorrect. The growth of cities led to population centers unable to produce their own food. Hence, an increased demand for commercial farming allowed farm products to be primarily sold at market rather than fed to the farmer's family.
   E. Incorrect. Farms moved toward commercialization, and farmers began to focus primarily dairy or a single crop.

2) Which of the following types of commercial farming are most capital intensive?

  A. dairy and ranching

  B. ranching and plantation farms

  C. large-scale grain production and dairy

  D. plantation farms and large-scale grain production

  E. ranching and large-scale grain production

Answers:

  A. Incorrect. While dairy farms are very capital intensive, ranching farms require little to no mechanical equipment.

  B. Incorrect. Plantation farms are particularly labor intensive, not capital intensive as they focus on plants that are not easily picked or planted by a machine.

  C. **Correct.** Both large-scale grain production and dairy are highly mechanized, requiring significant capital investment.

  D. Incorrect. While similar in their production of only one to two crops, large-scale grain production farms and plantation farms are opposite in the source of their work. Plantations draw primarily from cheap, local labor while large-scale grain production farms require a great deal of machinery.

  E. Incorrect. While ranching requires a lot of land, it does not have high machinery costs.

3) According to Agricultural Location Theory, what is the relative location to the city of a dairy farm and a mixed crop-livestock farm that specializes in cheese and butter?

  A. The dairy farm will be closer to the city.

  B. The mixed crop-livestock farm will be closer to the city.

  C. They will be equidistant from the city.

  D. The two farms will be located near each other.

  E. Their distance from the city cannot be determined with the information given.

Answers:

  A. **Correct.** Because the dairy farm is a more intensive farming practice that requires less land, it will be located closer to the city. It also carries a greater risk of spoilage (milk vs. butter and cheese), so it requires a shorter distance to market.

  B. Incorrect. The mixed crop-livestock farm will need more land for both its crops and livestock, which will be more expensive the closer it is to the city. There is no quality advantage for them to be as close as possible to the market because their products can be transported some distance without negative effect.

  C. Incorrect. Agricultural Location Theory predicts that distance from the city will impact these types of farms differently based on the relative importance of amount of land and acceptable transportation distance.

  D. Incorrect. Agricultural Location Theory does not address the location of farms in relation to each other.

  E. Incorrect. In Agricultural Location Theory, all other factors are held constant, so this is all the information that is needed.

The Third Agricultural Revolution

The THIRD AGRICULTURAL REVOLUTION, also known as the GREEN REVOLUTION, centered on a dramatic increase in crop yields based on BIOTECHNOLOGY, scientific modifications to seeds and fertilizers. In response to the burgeoning global population, scientists looked to find ways to improve grain production capabilities. As a result of their efforts, from 1945 – 1990, grain production increased by 45 percent in Mexico, where this work began. In Asia, rice production increased by 66 percent by 1985. By the 1980s, India no longer needed to import rice and wheat to feed its growing population; the country was self-sufficient in production of these crops. NORMAN BORLAUG, seen as the father of the Green Revolution, won a Nobel Prize for his work in 1970. The world's food supply was no longer an issue in terms of quantity.

Unfortunately, however, this does not mean that hunger no longer exists. The world's food supply, while large, is unevenly distributed, and hunger persists as a global problem due to social and transportation issues. Yield was increased for many crops, but not all, and most Green Revolution crops are not arable in Africa. The base crops of Africa—sorghum and millet—have received very little attention. As a result, less than 5 percent of African farmers use Green Revolution seeds for farming.

Moreover, other problems emerged as a result of the Green Revolution. Farming jobs decreased dramatically as less labor was required to produce the same amount—or even more—food. In addition, the higher yield crops are more susceptible to disease and pests, making crop failure more common. Green Revolution technology had a significant environmental impact as well. Overall, farming high-yield crops requires more technology and machinery, which requires more fuel, thereby increasing pollution and consumption. These crops also require more water, straining water supplies. The pesticides which were developed to protect the crops cause pollution and soil contamination; they have even led to health problems in those workers who experience prolonged exposure to the chemicals. Finally, global genetic diversity in plant life has been reduced as local strains of various crops are phased out to make room for high-yield crops. While this has led to a growth of the food supply, it has also greatly increased its vulnerability.

Renewable and Nonrenewable Resources

One of the most significant ways humans impact their environment is through the use of natural resources. Some resources are RENEWABLE RESOURCES, meaning they are virtually unlimited or can be grown and regrown. Wind, sun, and plants are all examples of renewable resources. Other resources are NONRENEWABLE RESOURCES because they cannot be replaced once they are consumed. Iron ore, coal, and petroleum are three of the most important nonrenewable resources. Trees can be considered both renewable and nonrenewable, depending on how they are used. If managed properly, they can be replanted and grown again. However, the rapid consumption of old growth forests uses up a resource that essentially cannot be replaced. Also, the land trees are on is often repurposed for farm land, urbanization, or mining once the trees are removed, resulting in a permanent loss of the resource.

Consuming nonrenewable resources—and consuming renewable resources too quickly—is a growing concern as industrialization has greatly increased overall consumption. Many countries are searching for ways to promote SUSTAINABLE DEVELOPMENT, the use of natural resources and the growth of new ones at a rate that can be maintained from one generation to the next. The UNITED NATIONS COMMISSION ON SUSTAINABLE DEVELOPMENT defines several criteria for global sustainable development: caring for the soil, avoiding overfishing, preserving the forest, protecting species from extinction, and reducing air pollution.

Other sustainability efforts focus on indirect factors impacting the Earth's natural resources. For example, efforts to reduce fuel consumption are both motivated by the finite quantity of oil in the world, and also by the GREENHOUSE EFFECT caused by industrialization. Industrial production unleashes carbon dioxide, methane, and other gases. These create a vapor that transforms radiation into heat, which leads to GLOBAL WARMING, an overall rise in the Earth's temperature. As a result, the ice caps are melting prematurely, leading to rising sea levels and changes in oceanic patterns.

EXAMPLES

1) In Asia, the Green Revolution resulted in
   A. the introduction of new crops like wheat and barley.
   B. new farming techniques like terrace farming.
   C. an increase in the importation of grain.
   D. a dramatic increase in rice production.
   E. increased exportation of grain to India

   Answers:
   A. Incorrect. While some new crops were introduced in Asia during the Second Agricultural Revolution, rice remains the dominant grain crop.
   B. Incorrect. Terrace farming is a traditional farming technique that has been used for thousands of years in places in Asia with limited land availability.
   C. Incorrect. The Green Revolution allowed countries in Asia to increase their crop yields, decreasing their reliance on foreign food sources.
   D. **Correct.** As a result of high-yield rice developed during the Green Revolution, rice production increased by 66 percent in the 1980s.
   E. Incorrect. As a result of the Green Revolution, India became self-sufficient in terms of grain.

2) Which region of the world shared least in the benefits of the Green Revolution?
   A. Southeast Asia
   B. Africa
   C. Central America
   D. Western Europe
   E. Eastern Europe

   Answers:
   A. Incorrect. Southeast Asia increased production of rice and wheat as a result of the Green Revolution.

B. **Correct.** Most Green Revolution crops cannot be grown in Africa, and little research was done on millet and sorghum, the most common grains used in African countries.

C. Incorrect. Many Green Revolution plants and fertilizers are used throughout Central America.

D. Incorrect. The Green Revolution dramatically increased Europe's grain production.

E. Incorrect. As previously stated, grain production increased significantly throughout Europe.

3) Which of the following statements is true about sustainable development?

A. Sustainable development requires a prohibition on the use of nonrenewable resources.

B. Sustainable development only applies to energy resources like wind, sun, oil, and coal.

C. Sustainable development is championed by non-profits, but unsupported by governments.

D. Sustainable development contributes to the greenhouse effect and increases global warming.

E. Sustainable development requires the proper management of renewable resources like trees and fish.

Answers:

A. Incorrect. Sustainable development programs focus on proper management, not prohibitions. So they will require a reduction in the use of nonrenewable resources, but still allow them to be used.

B. Incorrect. Sustainable development focuses on all natural resources: mineral, plant, animal, water, and air.

C. Incorrect. Many governments are finding ways to increase their sustainability efforts.

D. Incorrect. Sustainable development aims to reduce the greenhouse effect and global warming; it does not contribute to them.

E. **Correct.** The goal of sustainable development is to ensure resources are available to the next generation. Therefore, renewable resources must be managed to make sure consumption does not outpace the rate of replacement.

Movement

Geography is the study of spatial patterns, and movement includes many important spatial patterns. All types of movement—of people, of things, of phenomena—are important to the study of geography. Geographers examine SPATIAL INTERACTION, the ways in which different places interact with one another through the flow of people, goods, or ideas. The ways in which farmers move their goods to market, the movement of labor from rural areas to urban areas, and the diffusion of culture are all examples of spatial interaction.

Distance is an important factor in the study of movement. Geographers examine the FRICTION OF DISTANCE in movement, or the extent to which distance interferes with the spatial interaction. The level of energy—and money—required to overcome distance increases with the distance itself. So there is less friction of distance—and greater spatial interaction—between Boston and New York than between Boston and Shanghai.

Distance also impacts the intensity of phenomena that travel between places. This DISTANCE DECAY can be seen in the impact of an earthquake. Those closest to the earthquake will see the biggest changes to the physical characteristics of their place, as well as the most cultural, political, and economic ramifications. Those hundreds or thousands of miles away may feel little to no impact at all. However, the impact of distance decay has been decreasing over time. SPACE-TIME COMPRESSION—the feeling that the world is getting smaller—resulting from globalization means that the 2011 earthquake and tsunami in Japan, for instance, had significant consequences as far away as Chicago. Markets were affected, trips were cancelled to and from Japan, and sadly, people around the world lost family and friends in the disaster.

Diffusion

The type of movement most commonly studied in geography is SPATIAL DIFFUSION, the spread, or movement, of people, things, and ideas across space. Cultural diffusion (discussed earlier in this chapter) is a major subset of spatial diffusion. There are two main types of spatial diffusion.

The first, EXPANSION DIFFUSION, describes the process of a phenomenon remaining strong at its hearth while expanding outward to new places. As it spreads to a new place, the new adopters may modify the idea. This is called STIMULUS EXPANSION DIFFUSION. For example, the sport of tennis began in the royal courts of France and England, and was played on grass. As the game diffused to new areas—and new groups of people—different playing surfaces (clay and hardcourts) were adopted.

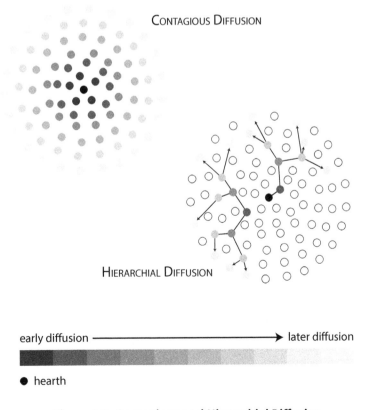

Figure 4.9. Contagious and Hierarchial Diffusion

In other cases, when the phenomenon spreads to a new area, it starts with a person or place in a position of power or influence and then spreads to others in a leveled pattern. This is called HIERARCHICAL DIFFUSION. For example, sushi arrived in the United States from Japan as a result of stimulus expansion diffusion. It began in New York City, a city of significant cultural power, and then followed a hierarchical diffusion pattern by spreading to other large cities, then mid-size and smaller cities, and finally suburbs and some towns.

The final method of expansion diffusion is CONTAGIOUS DIFFUSION. In this case, multiple places near the hearth become adopters, rather than the phenomenon spreading in a sequential manner. As the name implies, the classic example of contagious diffusion is a disease. For example, during the flu epidemic of 1919 when people in one town became ill, the disease then spread to all of the surrounding towns, and so on. This is the most widespread type of diffusion.

DIFFUSION S CURVE

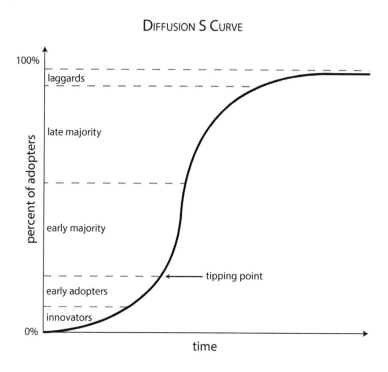

Figure 4.10. Diffusion S Curve

Diffusion does not always occur in an expansive manner. Sometimes, the original adopters move from the hearth to a new place, taking their ideas with them. This is called RELOCATION DIFFUSION. For example, in the 1850s, Mormons moved west from New York State to Illinois and then to what would become Utah. As they moved, the hearth of Mormonism moved with them as well. A variant on this is MIGRATION DIFFUSION, when the original adopters move but the idea or trait lasts only a short while in the new place. This is called migration diffusion because it occurs most often among immigrants, who move to a new place originally carrying the traits of their home culture. However, in a relatively short time (a generation or two) they shed their original cultural traits and adopt the traits of the new culture. This is a common story among immigrants to the United States who begin in ethnic enclaves and then, over time, diffuse into the general pop-

Which type of diffusion is most closely associated with the spread of disease?

ulation. In this type of diffusion it is often hard to pinpoint the epicenter because the phenomenon fades so quickly.

In reality most diffusions follow more than one of these patterns. However, all diffusions follow an S-curve pattern when the number of users over time are plotted on a graph. For example, when the MP3 player—or any new technology—was first introduced, only a small group of early adopters used it. As time passed, those early adopters introduced it to more people, advertising became more effective, and an early majority were downloading music on these devices. The more people who bought and used MP3 players, the more common they became, and the more they seemed like a cultural norm, prompting other adopters to join. During this time, the adoption rate was high and continued until the majority of people abandoned their CD players for an MP3 player. Then, adoption tapered off, and then only the last few stragglers were left.

EXAMPLES

1) The diffusion of smartphones within the United States is an example of which kind of diffusion?

A. stimulus diffusion

B. relocation diffusion

C. hierarchical diffusion

D. contagious diffusion

E. expansion diffusion

Answers:

A. Incorrect. In a stimulus diffusion the phenomenon changes with each new group of adopters. Smartphones remained the same as they were adopted throughout the country.

B. Incorrect. Smartphones did not spread as a result of the original adopters moving, so it was not relocation diffusion.

C. **Correct.** Smartphones were first adopted by those who could afford them (because the price point was prohibitive for others) and who were in a position of power. They then diffused through economic levels as the prices changed and companies provided opportunities to make them more affordable.

D. Incorrect. In a contagious diffusion, all areas surrounding the hearth adopt the phenomenon simultaneously. Smartphones were not adopted in this pattern, but moved first between urban centers, and then out into other areas.

E. Incorrect. In expansion diffusion the phenomenon begins at a specified hearth and expands outwards. The spread of cell phones in the U.S. was not geographically based.

2) Based on the S-curve graph above, the least number of new users occur at which point in the diffusion process?

A. the very beginning only

B. the middle only

C. the end only

D. both the beginning and end

E. the number of new users remained consistent

Migration Patterns

MIGRATION is the permanent relocation of an individual or group from one home region to another region. As globalization and space-time compression have increased, global mobility has increased as well, both in frequency and length of migrations. Some migration is internal—people moving from one place to another within the same region, like urbanization. Other migration involves people moving from one region of the world to another. Many immigrants have migrated to the United States from other countries around the world.

Geographers study migration to understand *how* people move through space as well as *why* they move through space. To answer the question of *how*—the manner and numbers of people moving—geographers examine MIGRATION STREAMS, the specific spatial movement from the starting location to the destination. These are mapped using arrows of differing thickness to indicate the number of migrants. Migration streams are usually paired with MIGRATION COUNTER-STREAMS of people returning home.

Migration rate per 1,000 people in 2011

- < –10
- –9.9 to –5
- –4.9 to –0.1
- 0 to 5
- 5.1 to 10
- > 10.1

Figure 4.11. Migration Streams

To answer the question *why?* geographers look at both PUSH FACTORS—negative aspects of the home region that make someone want to leave it—and PULL FACTORS—positive aspects of the new region that make someone want to move there. Push factors include high taxes, high crime rates, resource depletion, and corrupt governments. Migrants who cross international borders fleeing persecution, governmental abuse, war, or natural disaster are called REFUGEES. People who migrate intra-nationally by moving from one part of a country to another are called INTERNALLY DISPLACED PERSONS. According to the UN, at least 40 percent of Syria's population was internally displaced in 2014, fleeing violence in that country's civil war. In 2015, millions of refugees from Syria and elsewhere in the Middle East, Asia, and North Africa began migrating to Europe, seeking safety from violent conflict.

Examples of pull factors include new, better-paying jobs, schools, abundant resources, and greater protection of individual rights. A common pull factor for new immigrants are previous immigrants to a place. This is called CHAIN MIGRATION. For example, in the late 1990s Eritreans began to immigrate to the United States as the result of the Eritrean-Ethiopian War (a push factor). They settled primarily in Washington D.C. and Los Angeles, prompting other Eritreans to move to these two cities as well (a pull factor).

If a location attracts more IMMIGRANTS (people moving into a place) than it has EMIGRANTS (people moving out of a place), it has NET IN-MIGRATION, and is considered to have HIGH PLACE DESIRABILITY. Western Europe, the United States, and Canada all have net in-migration. On the other hand, if a place has more emigrants than immigrants, it has NET OUT-MIGRATION. Today that includes most of Asia, Africa, and Latin America.

Geographers determine how likely someone is to migrate using MIGRATION SELECTIVITY. While personal, social, and economic factors all play a role, age is actually the most important factor in migration. Most Americans, for example, typically migrate to a new town, city, or state between eighteen and thirty years of age. Research has also shown that greater education leads to greater mobility.

Not all migration is voluntary. History has many examples of FORCED MIGRATION, when a group of people is forcibly removed from their home and brought to a new region. The African slave trade and the removal of Native American tribes from the Southeastern United States are both examples of forced migration.

Migration patterns tend to be predictable and can be determined using three key theories:

RAVENSTEIN'S LAWS OF MIGRATION: In the 1880s, geographer Ernst Georg Ravenstein developed his laws of migration which remain the basis for migration theory today. These include:

1. Most migrants travel only short distances. Even when they do travel longer distances, they often use STEP MIGRATION, traveling in short steps to ultimately achieve a longer distance.

2. People living in rural areas are more likely to migrate, especially in areas that are industrializing.

3. Migrants who do travel farther tend to choose big cities as their destination.

4. Large towns grow by migration instead of by natural growth.

5. Mostly adults migrate.

6. Young adults are more likely to cross borders than families who tend to migrate internally.

7. Every migration stream has a counter-stream.

The DTM, Rostow's Modernization Model, and Zelinsky's Model of Migration Transition are all closely related. If you master one—probably Rostow's—you can use it as a tool to help you recall the others.

GRAVITATIONAL MODEL: The gravitational model of migration estimates the size and direction of migration between two places. It is based on the assumption that the migrational "gravity" of a place is determined by its size and its distance. So places that are larger and/or closer attract more migrants. The limitation of this model is that it only considers location and does not include migration selectivity factors.

ZELINSKY'S MODEL OF MIGRATION TRANSITION: Geographer Wilbur Zelinsky developed a model of migration based on the development stage of a country, using the Demographic Transition Model. So, countries in Stage One of the DTM migrate locally to search for food and shelter materials. In Stage Two, the high RNI overstresses resources resulting in emigration out of the country. There is also a high rate of rural-to-urban migration. In Stage Three, rural-to-urban migration is surpassed by urban-to-urban migration, and immigration exceeds emigration. In Stage Four, urban-to-suburban migration (and vice versa) emerges as the dominant form of migration, stabilizing in Stage Five.

EXAMPLES

1) Which of the following events would be considered a pull factor for migration?
   A. the opening of a new factory in a different town
   B. a drought in the home region
   C. an increase in terrorist activity in the home region
   D. the construction of a high-speed train between the hometown and the nearest city
   E. a sudden population increase in the home region

Answers:

A. **Correct.** A new factory would provide jobs and encourage migration into the area.

B. Incorrect. A drought would reduce resources and push people out of a region.

C. Incorrect. Terrorist activity would threaten the safety of individuals as well as reduce economic opportunity, therefore pushing people out of a region.

D. Incorrect. A high speed train is not a typical push or pull factor. However, if it had an impact, it would most likely keep people in the town as they could easily commute out for work.

E. Incorrect. A population increase might reduce resources and push people out. It is not a pull factor.

2) During the late 1990s, Ireland had such a strong economy it was known as the "Celtic Tiger," attracting migration and investment. Recent Irish immigrants to the United States and even some Irish Americans began returning to their homeland with their families. This phenomenon is best explained by which of the following?

A. the US' stage of development (Stage Four) based on Zelinsky's Model of Migration Transition

B. the size of Ireland, based on the gravitational model of migration

C. Ravenstein's law that young adults are more likely to cross borders than families

D. Ravenstein's law that for every migration stream, there is a counter-stream

E. the increased migration of people in rural areas, based on Ravenstein's third law of migration

Answers:

A. Incorrect. In Zelinsky's model, Stage Four development focuses on suburban-urban migration.

B. Incorrect. The United States is bigger than Ireland, so the gravitational model would not address migration from the former to the latter.

C. Incorrect. Both individuals and families migrated to Ireland from the United States.

D. **Correct.** Historically, the Irish fled poverty and oppression in Ireland, many settling in North America. The migration of Irish to Ireland from the United States constitutes a counter-stream to the migration stream of the Irish diaspora.

E. Incorrect. Most Irish immigrants to the US settled in cities, not rural areas.

five

ECONOMICS

Fundamental Economic Concepts

Scarcity

There are some basic concepts that are part of all branches of economics. Scarcity, choice, and opportunity costs all figure in day to day living for everyone. In economics, there is an assumption that all people have unlimited wants; however, there are limited resources to satisfy those wants. This concept is called SCARCITY. Scarcity forces individuals to make a CHOICE, to select one want over another. In making choices, people seek to maximize their UTILITY, the point of greatest happiness.

For example, a student wants to go to the movies with her friends, but also wants to do well on her exams the next day. Her resource—in this case, time—is limited, so she must choose between the options. She will weigh the cost, or value lost, of not studying for her exam, against the benefit, or value attained, of seeing the movie, and vice versa. The value of the option not selected is called the OPPORTUNITY COST. So, the opportunity cost of staying home to study is the lost fun of seeing the movie and strengthening of bonds with friends.

Resources, also called FACTORS OF PRODUCTION, fall into four basic categories: labor, land or natural resources, physical capacity, and entrepreneurial ability, or know-how.

Each of the four factors of production is necessary to the process of producing anything in the marketplace and they are considered some of the most basic parts of the business equation.

Law of Diminishing Marginal Utility

TOTAL UTILITY is the sum of an individual's happiness or the extent to which an individual's needs are met. MARGINAL UTILITY is the increase in happiness one gains from a product. For example, a child desires a treat. She receives an ice cream cone, thereby increasing her utility. Then, she receives a cupcake which further increases her utility. That increase is her marginal utility.

While needs are unlimited, an individual's need for a specific product can be met. In fact, the LAW OF DIMINISHING MARGINAL UTILITY states that the more units of a product one has, the less one needs. Think of a very hungry person. His need for food seems unlimited. However, with each bite he takes, his need—and the amount of additional utility a bite brings—is shrinking or diminishing, until he is finally sated.

Marginal Analysis

People tend to make decisions AT THE MARGIN, meaning as an addition to the status quo. Looking back at our student, she has already studied for an hour (and she has already spent time with her friends and seen movies on previous days), so her choice is a marginal one; she is considering the MARGINAL BENEFIT (the additional benefit) and MARGINAL COST (the additional cost) of studying for another hour or the marginal benefit and cost of going to the movies.

MARGINAL ANALYSIS is used in many economic decisions, including production, consumption, and hiring. For example, when a company looks at the extra costs of producing a good or service in regard to the benefit of producing that good, it uses marginal analysis. Marginal analysis is most helpful in company decision-making in regards to production. Changes in marginal costs and benefits can also affect decision-making in both the short and long term. If consumers are happy with an item and they buy it in quantity, then businesses flourish. A company would use marginal analysis to determine if the benefit of offering more of the item outweighed the cost of increasing production. Similarly, a new company would use marginal analysis to decide if the benefit of selling a popular item outweighed the cost of heavy competition from many similar companies on the market, or if the cost of a lower price was overshadowed by the benefit of potentially selling more units than the competitor.

EXAMPLES

1) Which of the following is NOT an example of the principle of scarcity?
   A. overfishing in key coastal waters
   B. a pharmaceutical company lowers the price of a commonly used generic drug
   C. drought reduces the amount of pumpkins sold in fall farmer's markets
   D. flu season ramps up and flu vaccines are hard to find
   E. an embargo on oil decreases the availability of gas

   Answers:
   A. Incorrect. In this case, the natural resource (fish) is in limited supply while the wants or needs of the fishermen remain high, an example of scarcity.
   B. **Correct.** The lowered price in and of itself does not create scarcity, as the supply of the drug is not impacted.
   C. Incorrect. The drought has reduced the pumpkin supply, yet nothing seems to have impacted the want for pumpkins. Thus, there is a scarcity of pumpkins.
   D. Incorrect. The resource in this case is the flu vaccine, whose supply is limited. However, the need for the vaccine is high, generating scarcity.

E.   Incorrect. An embargo on oil means less can be imported. Therefore it is a scarce resource.

2) A company is looking to hire a new website designer to refresh its website. The first candidate is fresh out of college and this would be his first job. The second candidate has worked as a website designer for ten years; however, the company would have to pay him twice as much as the first candidate. Which of the following illustrates how the company uses marginal analysis to decide which candidate to hire?

A.   weigh the cost of hiring a web designer against the benefit of having customers

B.   weigh the cost of increased pay for the second against the benefit of more experience

C.   weigh the cost of the first candidate's lack of experience against the cost of the second candidate's high price

D.   weigh the benefit of the first candidate's price against the benefit of the second candidate's experience

E.   weigh the cost of an expensive website against the benefit earned from selling its products.

Answers:

A.   Incorrect. Here, the company uses marginal analysis to decide whether to hire anyone to do the website, not which candidate to hire.

B.   **Correct.** Here, the additional cost of the second candidate's higher salary is weighed against the extra ten years of experience he brings.

C.   Incorrect. Marginal analysis requires comparing cost and benefit, not cost and cost.

D.   Incorrect. While determining the relative value of each candidate's benefits would be part of the decision-making process, marginal analysis looks at the comparison between the added benefit and the added cost.

E.   Incorrect. The cost-benefit analysis should focus on the two candidates only.

3) At an amusement park, a child takes her first rollercoaster ride. She loves it so much, she wants to go again. According to the law of diminishing marginal utility, which of the following is most likely to happen after the child's tenth ride?

A.   The child will have a greater desire to ride the rollercoaster than on her first ride.

B.   The child will never want to ride any rollercoaster again.

C.   The child will experience the same level of excitement as after her first ride.

D.   The child will be less interested—or uninterested entirely—in riding the rollercoaster again that day.

E.   The child will become interested in new aspects of the rollercoaster.

Answers:

A.   Incorrect. If the child had a greater desire to ride, her marginal utility would be increasing, not diminishing.

B.   Incorrect. While the repeated rides will impact her immediate interest, there is no economic reason for them to have a long-term effect on her appreciation of rollercoasters.

Production Possibilities Curve

A PRODUCTION POSSIBILITIES CURVE determines if an individual, company, or nation is producing at its most efficient level and what product will likely make the highest profit. The curve assumes that there are two choices for production. A production possibilities curve demonstrates opportunity costs, economic efficiency, economic growth, and scarcity.

For example, a company that produces soccer balls is looking to diversify and produce basketballs as well. However, for each basketball the company produces, there is an opportunity cost in soccer balls. Perhaps it takes a worker twice as long and costs twice as much money to make a basketball as a soccer ball. The opportunity cost of making a basketball is two soccer balls. The production possibility curve plots the relationship between the number of soccer and basketballs produced to help the company find the most efficient combination of production. This curve is also called the PRODUCTION POSSIBILITY FRONTIER because it represents the maximum level of production. It is not possible for a company to produce soccer balls and basketballs beyond the curve. The scarcity of resources (materials for soccer balls and labor) creates this upper bound. At the points under the curve, the company is not using its resources to their maximum potential.

Economists believe that the frontier expands over time, a process called ECONOMIC GROWTH. This results from one or more of the following: an increase in the quantity of resources, an increase in the quality of existing resources, or technological advancements in production. The reflection in the production possibility curve, however, is not proportional, as an increase in resources or new technology does not impact all sectors of the economy in the same way. A classic historical example is the invention of the cotton gin. The cotton gin was a technological advancement allowing cotton seeds to be separated from harvested cotton by machine rather than by hand. This dramatically expanded the production possibility of cotton, shifting the curve. However, it had no impact on the actual production of cotton plants.

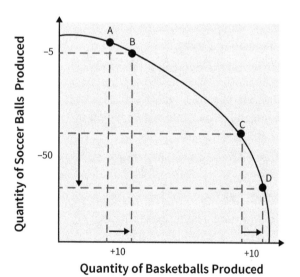

Figure 5.1. Production Possibilities Curve

Opportunity cost can be determined by calculating the slope of the curve: the slope represents the opportunity cost on the *x*-axis; the inverse of the slope represents the opportunity cost on the *y*-axis. The production possibility frontier is curved because opportunity costs increase as the quantity produced increases. This is called the LAW OF INCREASING COSTS.

Economic efficiency is as necessary for consumers as it is for business entities. For consumers, setting a budget for monthly expenses is part of running a household. At the same time, businesses must continually analyze production possibilities curves to determine more efficient production processes, cost-cutting measures, and ways to boost profits.

Market Efficiency

As discussed, an economy is working inefficiently if it is producing below the production possibility curve. This is called PRODUCTIVE INEFFICIENCY. An economy's efficiency is not only measured by its use of resources, but by the benefit it provides to society, called its ALLOCATIVE EFFICIENCY. For example, a country could direct all of its resources to the production of hats. This economy might have high productive efficiency, maximizing its output, but it is providing little benefit to its citizens, and so has low allocative efficiency.

To offer a real world example, Equatorial Guinea is rich in petroleum; however, only the elite have profited from it, and the standard of living for most of the country remains extremely low. Equatorial Guinea therefore exhibits low allocative efficiency.

Absolute and Comparative Advantage

When deciding between producing two different products, a company must also consider its production capabilities for each item relative to the rest of the market. If a company (or nation) can produce a good more efficiently than all competitors, it has an ABSOLUTE ADVANTAGE in that market. Consider, again, the soccer ball company. If that company can produce soccer balls more efficiently than all other soccer ball companies, it has an absolute advantage in soccer ball production. A company can have an absolute advantage in more than one product (if the company also produced basketballs most efficiently, for example).

It may then seem that the company should produce both products. However, that is not necessarily the case. For example, the ball company may be able to produce both soccer balls and basketballs more efficiently than its competitor. But, if the company has workers specifically trained in stitching high quality soccer balls very quickly, the opportunity cost of producing basketballs instead will be high. Their competitor, on the other hand, may have workers who may stitch quality soccer balls at a much slower rate, leading to a lower opportunity cost for producing basketballs (but the first company's opportunity cost for producing soccer balls will be lower). In this case, the competitor actually has a COMPARATIVE ADVANTAGE in producing basketballs, and the original company has one in producing soccer balls. Comparative advantage compares the opportunity cost of producing an item between companies. It would then be in the best interest of the original company to specialize in soccer balls and the competitor to specialize in basketballs, even though the original company can produce both more efficiently.

Specialization and Interdependence

SPECIALIZATION occurs when an individual, company, or nation focuses on producing one thing, typically because it has a comparative advantage. For example, a doctor may also be the fastest wood chopper in a town. However, the doctor does not both chop the town's wood and tend to its patients; the opportunity cost of chopping wood is too high. So, he specializes in being a doctor, leaving the wood chopping to someone else (even though they are not as fast as he is). Specialization leads to increased profits and lower prices for consumers.

INTERDEPENDENCE is part of a larger global or regional economy. When countries or businesses are interdependent, goods from one are necessary to the economy of another and both must function together for both to work. Colonization is a classic example of interdependence. The mother country relied on the colony both for raw materials and as a market for its finished goods. On the other hand, the colony relied on the mother country as a market for its raw materials, and as a source for finished goods.

Both globalization and specialization lead to increased interdependence. Countries depend on treaties and business partnerships to provide goods necessary for production. One country provides lithium to another for cell phone battery production while the lithium-providing country is permitted to buy stockpiles of seed corn for its agricultural concerns. That means that both sides gain from this trading equation.

EXAMPLES

1) Company A can produce 900 pencils at the cost of producing 300 pens. For the same cost, Company B can produce either 200 pens or 1000 pencils. Which company has the comparative advantage and which company has the absolute advantage in producing pencils?

   A. Company A has the comparative advantage; Company B has the absolute advantage.

   B. Company A has both the comparative and absolute advantages.

   C. Company A has the absolute advantage; Company B has the comparative advantage.

   D. Company B has both the comparative and absolute advantages.

   E. There is not enough information given to determine advantage.

   Answers:

   A. Incorrect. Company A has a higher opportunity cost in pencil production than Company B does. As a result, it does not have a comparative advantage.

   B. Incorrect. For the same cost as Company B, Company A is able to produce fewer pencils at a higher opportunity cost.

   C. Incorrect. Company A can produce only 900 pencils at the cost of Company B producing 1000 pencils, putting it at an absolute disadvantage in pencil production. However, it can produce 300 pens to Company B's 200, giving Company A an absolute advantage in pen production.

   D. **Correct.** Company B can produce 100 more pencils than Company A at the same cost, giving it an absolute advantage. Its opportunity cost for producing pencils is .2 (200/1000), whereas Company A's is .33 (300/900), giving Company B a comparative advantage as well.

E.   Incorrect. Comparative advantage is based on what a company must give up in order to produce an item. Absolute advantage is a measure of overall production capabilities. Both of these can be determined simply with the information given.

2)   At point A on the production possibility graph below, which of the following is true about the economy?

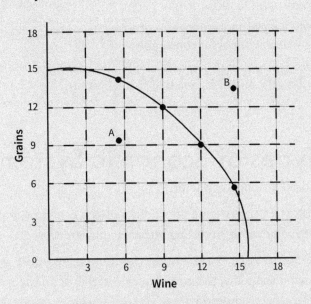

A.   The economy should increase wine production and decrease grain production.

B.   New resources are required before production can increase.

C.   Some resources are being underutilized or wasted.

D.   The economy is producing at its greatest efficiency.

E.   The economy should decrease win production and increase grain production.

Answers:

A.   Incorrect. The location of point A does not indicate that grain production is inhibiting wine production to a degree that is harmful to the economy.

B.   Incorrect. To reach a point beyond the production possibility curve (like point B), new resources must be obtained, but point A is below the curve.

C.   **Correct.** Point A is below the production possibility frontier, indicating that the use of resources is not being maximized.

D.   Incorrect. The production possibility curve (or frontier) indicates where the economy is producing at maximum efficiency. Point A is below that curve.

E.   Incorrect. The curve does not show a negative impact of wine production on grain production.

3)   Which of the following is NOT a consequence of specialization?

A.   lower wages

B.   higher quality goods

C.   higher profits

D.   lower prices

E.   more efficient use of resources

Answers:

A. **Correct.** Specialization does not cause low wages. Sometimes, specialization in the workforce, or the division of labor, can lead to lower wages because the skills required of a worker are reduced. However, specialization can also lead to higher wages because it may require a higher level of skill from a worker.

B. Incorrect. When production is focused on one item, workers become more skilled at making that item, leading to higher quality goods.

C. Incorrect. By focusing their efforts on one area of the market and allowing other companies to focus on other areas, all companies increase their profits.

D. Incorrect. Specialization allows a company to use its resources more efficiently, leading to lower prices for consumers.

E. Incorrect. Because each segment of labor focuses on its "best" task, all work is done more efficiently as a result of specialization.

Types of Economic Systems

There are four kinds of economic systems.

A TRADITIONAL ECONOMY is a pre-industrialized economy, guided by tradition, and often using bartering rather than currency.

A PURE COMMAND ECONOMY is usually found in communist societies. In a pure command economy, the government—rather than the market—determines all aspects of production. Today, they are very rare; North Korea is an example.

A PURE MARKET ECONOMY, also known as capitalism, is governed by the laws of supply and demand with no outside interference.

A MIXED ECONOMY is governed by both the market and the government. The people may decide what is produced by what they are willing to buy, but the government regulates different aspects of the economy with regards to the safety of the population. Most modern economies are mixed economies.

Functions of the Market

There are several defining principles of a market economy.

A pure market economy is a self-running entity; its internal forces govern its functioning, and it does not require outside intervention. Therefore, government has no place in a pure market economy. This leads to two key principles:

PRIVATE PROPERTY: The market favors private ownership of most economic resources. Private ownership leads to innovation and investment, which in turn lead to growth. It also allows for trade (of services and goods). Economists often point to the inefficiency of the United States Postal Service (USPS) as compared to private carriers like FedEx or UPS to illustrate this point. The owners of FedEx and UPS have an incentive to provide better service, in order to stay in business and grow. USPS, as a publicly owned entity, is guaranteed survival by the government.

FREEDOM OF CHOICE: In a market economy, all individuals are free to acquire, use, and sell resources without restriction or regulation. This allows market forces to function properly. Two important elements in the market are supply and demand (discussed more in-depth later). If there was a restriction on buying large cars, for example, this would artificially alter demand, and throw off the functioning of the automobile market.

Private property and freedom of choice create the two primary driving forces of the market:

SELF-INTEREST: Market theory assumes that people are motivated by self-interest in their use of their own resources. The seller in the market wants to maximize resources (or profit). The buyer wants to maximize utility (or happiness). As a result, the seller offers goods that will maximize the happiness of buyers in order to attract sales. Self-interest, then, leads to innovation and quality, as it creates a market where the best products are available to buyers. For example, Apple has noted that technological integration brings buyers a great deal of happiness, so the company works to continually innovate new ways of integrating technology (like the Apple watch) in its quest for profit.

COMPETITION: Because all individuals are motivated by self-interest, new sellers will enter the market when they determine that there is a possibility for profit. And, because all individuals have freedom of choice, buyers will buy from the sellers whose products maximize their happiness (either through prices or quality usually). Therefore, sellers compete with each other to attract buyers by appealing to their maximum happiness. Competition leads to lower prices and higher quality.

Consequently, the primary communication tool of the market is **PRICE**. Because of competition, prices are set by the market rather than by individuals. As a result, price signals buyers and sellers who, in turn, use it to make decisions about how to use their resources. Prices communicate the relative value of products in the market and deliver to both sellers and buyers what they seek through their own self-interest: profit and happiness, respectively.

EXAMPLES

1) In the 1870s in the United States, Americans favored laissez-faire economics, minimizing government regulations and controls on business. This most closely resembles which type of economy?

A. traditional

B. command

C. market

D. mixed

E. private

Answers:

A.   Incorrect. A traditional economy is based primarily on subsistence, through farming, fishing and hunting, and bartering (rather than currency). Business is not an element of a traditional economy.

B. Incorrect. A command economy is one in which the government holds complete control over all aspects of production—the opposite of the US economy in the 1870s.

C. **Correct.** Laissez-faire economics essentially means to leave the market alone to function. The United States came close to having a pure market economy in the 1870s.

D. Incorrect. A mixed economy balances elements of a market economy and a command economy. Mixed economies are marked by significant government regulation and oversight, as well as a mix of public and private ownership.

E. Incorrect. *Private economy* is not an economic term.

2) A buyer decides to switch to a new brand of detergent that promises to leave clothes cleaner. Which of the following market principles is NOT involved in this decision?

A. self-interest

B. freedom of choice

C. competition

D. price

E. All four market principles are involved.

Answers:

A. Incorrect. By seeking out a detergent that leaves clothes cleaner, the buyer wants to maximize his own happiness with both the quality of detergent and the cleanliness of his clothes.

B. Incorrect. The buyer is able to switch between detergents because he has freedom of choice in how and where to spend his money.

C. Incorrect. The seller of the new detergent was driven by competition to create a formula (or at least advertise one) that was more effective than other brands.

D. **Correct.** The buyer makes his decision based on the effectiveness of the product rather than its price. Price does not come into play.

E. Incorrect. The buyer is only using three market principles to make their decision.

Supply and Demand

If price is the communication tool of the economy—determining the allocation of resources by both buyers and sellers—then what determines price? Price is the result of the interplay between two important economic forces: demand and supply.

Law of Demand

The LAW OF DEMAND is simple. As the price for a good or service increases, the demand for it will decrease, if all other factors are held constant. In other words, if the price goes up, purchases usually go down. For example, a coffee shop sells coffee for $1 a cup and sales skyrocket. The coffee shop then quadruples the price to $4 a cup, and sales plummet. It is important to note that only RELATIVE (REAL) PRICE affects demand. The relative price of a good is its value in relation to other items of similar value (what else could you buy for $4?). For example, perhaps the same shop sells donuts for $2. Yesterday, the buyer could have gotten two cups of coffee for the price of one donut. Now two donuts are equivalent to the price of one cup of coffee. This is called the SUBSTITUTION EFFECT. Relative price is also determined by the percentage of one's income the price demands (if the buyer makes $16 an hour, the cup of coffee is 25% of her hourly income versus the 6.25% that the $1 price was). This is called the INCOME EFFECT. The actual number of $4—the ABSOLUTE price—does not impact demand.

Demand Curve

A DEMAND CURVE shows how demand changes as prices increase. The curve actually measures QUANTITY DEMANDED in relation to price. In economics, this is different from simple demand.

Once again, a demand curve assumes all other factors remain constant. This is an assumption often made in economics to allow for the creation of models. If multiple factors were taken into consideration (e.g. price and weather and income), it would be impossible to determine causation. These other factors are called DETERMINANTS OF DEMAND and include:

- Consumer income (buyer's ability to pay)
- Price of a substitute good (in the example above, tea)
- Price of a complementary good (in the example above, donuts)
- Consumer preferences
- Consumer expectations about future pricing (Do consumers anticipate the price will go down in the future?)
- Number of buyers in the market

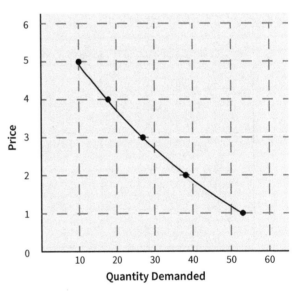

Figure 5.2. Demand Curve

While changes in price affect the quantity demanded, changes in determinants of demand lead to changes in demand overall—regardless of price—which are shown by a shift in the entire demand curve. For example, consider a fruit stand selling raspberries. As the end of the season approaches, buyers anticipate that prices will increase when less fruit is available. So, fruit buyers increase their demand for raspberries. This is translated into a rightward shift in the demand curve. This shift is unrelated to the current price, and—in fact—would be seen regardless of the price of raspberries. So, whether raspberries are $2 per pint or $4 per pint, there will be an increase in demand a week or two before the end of the season. A decrease in demand, conversely, is shown by a leftward shift in the curve.

Law of Supply

Whereas demand addresses the behavior of buyers, supply deals with the behavior of sellers. The LAW OF SUPPLY states that as the price of a good increases, suppliers will increase the quantity of the good they supply, if all other factors are held constant. This is because of INCREASING MARGINAL COSTS: as suppliers increase the amount they are supplying, the marginal costs of production increase as well. Therefore, they will only increase supply if price is high enough to offset that cost. For example, at the holidays, a toy company decides to double its supply of its most popular toy. In order to do this, they must hire more workers, keep the factory open longer, run the machines longer, pay more in electricity, and pay more in packing materials and shipping costs to get the toys to the stores. If they decided to triple the supply, these costs would only increase. So, the price of the toy would need to be at a point that it could generate enough revenue to offset these additional costs.

Supply Curve

A SUPPLY CURVE shows the relationship between what something costs and how much a business is willing to supply for sale. In the graph below, the vertical line on the left indicates price while the horizontal line shows quantity produced for sale. The higher the price, the higher the supply (holding all other factors constant).

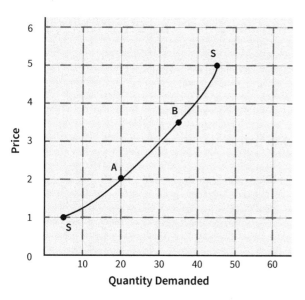

Figure 5.3. Supply Curve

Just like with the demand curve, points on the supply curve represent the QUANTITY SUPPLIED rather than the overall supply. Changes in the overall supply result from DETERMINANTS OF SUPPLY which shift the curve either rightward or leftward. These include:

- the cost of an input
- technology and productivity
- taxes or subsidies
- producer expectations about future prices
- the price of alternative goods that could be produced
- the number of similar companies in the industry

For example, the price of flour drops. Because it now costs less to make baked goods, bakeries across the industry will increase their production of muffins and cakes. This is an overall increase in supply, shifting the curve rightward. In the same way, if flour suddenly became more expensive, bakeries would produce less (as cost of production increased), and the curve would shift leftward.

Supply and Demand

The interplay of supply, demand, and price is used to describe the state of the market. When the quantity demanded equals the quantity supplied at a given price, the market is in a state of **EQUILIBRIUM**. Essentially, this means that both suppliers and buyers are satisfied with the price. In a graph, equilibrium is located where the supply and demand curves intersect. The other areas of the graph, where the supply and demand curves do not meet, are states of **DISEQUILIBRIUM**.

When the quantity demanded exceeds the quantity supplied, a **SHORTAGE**, or **EXCESS DEMAND**, exists. Shortages occur when prices are low because low prices lead to high demand but low supply. For example, if the market price of a television is $20, demand for these inexpensive TVs will be high, but the marginal cost of increasing supply at that price would quickly outweigh the revenue from sales, keeping the supply low.

When the quantity supplied exceeds the quantity demanded, a **SURPLUS**, or **EXCESS SUPPLY**, exists. Again, this is caused by the supply and demand's opposing relationships to price. If the TVs are now $2000 each, fewer buyers will be willing to purchase one. However, the high price allows the supplier to clearly outstrip her marginal costs.

The market always tends toward equilibrium. So, in the case of a shortage, buyers will offer to pay more—say $50—for the television, and suppliers will begin to increase supply. This trend will continue until they reach equilibrium. On the flip side, when a surplus exists, suppliers will lower prices in order to attract buyers, thereby increasing demand until equilibrium is reached.

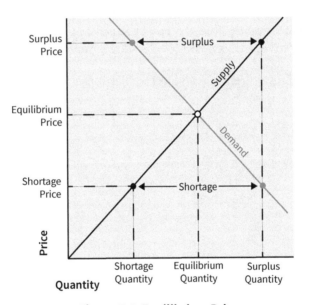

Figure 5.4. Equilibrium Price

Changes in overall supply and demand impact equilibrium as well. For example, the ability to stream television shows on a tablet or phone created an equivalent product. If the cost of a tablet dropped below the cost of a television, there would be a decreased overall demand, shifting the demand curve to the left. This would, in turn, shift the equilibrium price, also called **MARKET CLEARING**.

If both supply and demand are changed (e.g. the price of tablets drop and a tornado destroys half of the television factories), the relative degree of each change must be gauged before a new equilibrium can be determined.

EXAMPLES

1) At the price of $15 a manufacturer of bowls expects to sell 10,000 bowls. If the bowls are instead offered at a price of $20 per bowl, how many can the manufacturer anticipate selling?

   A. fewer than 10,000 bowls

   B. exactly 10,000 bowls

   C. more than 10,000 bowls

   D. The price increase is too much. No bowls will be sold.

   E. More information is needed to make the prediction.

   Answers:

   A. **Correct.** The law of demand states that when price increases, demand drops. This means the manufacturer will make fewer sales.

   B. Incorrect. Changes in price affect demand, so the manufacturer cannot expect to sell the same number of bowls if he changes the price.

   C. Incorrect. Price and demand are inversely related: when one goes up, the other goes down. Therefore, the manufacturer cannot anticipate selling more bowls at the higher price.

   D. Incorrect. There is no reason to believe the price increase is dramatic enough to end all sales.

   E. Incorrect. It is not possible to predict a specific number with the information provided; however, it is possible to predict a trend.

2) Which of the points below is the original equilibrium?

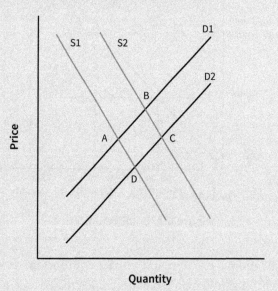

   A. A

   B. B

   C. C

   D. D

   E. The graph does not indicate the original equilibrium point.

Answers:

A. **Correct.** The original equilibrium can be found at the intersection between the original demand curve (D1) and the original supply curve (S1).

B. Incorrect. Point B shows the equilibrium when supply changes but demand stays the same. The supply increases, shifting the curve to the right.

C. Incorrect. Point C shows the equilibrium when both supply and demand have shifted.

D. Incorrect. Point D shows the equilibrium when demand changes but supply remains the same.

E. Incorrect. Equilibrium exists where the supply and demand lines cross.

3) Workers at pen factories earn minimum wage. When the state raises the minimum wage, what impact will that have on the market supply of pens?

   A. The supply curve will shift to the right.

   B. The supply curve will remain unchanged, but the quantity supplied will increase.

   C. The supply curve will shift to the left.

   D. The supply curve will remain unchanged, but the quantity supplied will decrease.

   E. Supply is unaffected by wage changes.

Answers:

A. Incorrect. In order for the curve to shift to the right, a determinant factor must trigger an increase in supply. An increase in the minimum wage is an increase in cost.

B. Incorrect. State minimum wage law is a determinant factor, and so affects overall supply, not quantity supplied.

C. **Correct.** An increase in the minimum wage increases the cost of producing pens, which in turn reduces supply (as pen manufacturers do not want to invest when their margins of profit are reduced).

D. Incorrect. There is not enough information to determine the quantity supplied. However, because the graph shifted leftward, it will take more quantity to reach the same prices as before.

E. Incorrect. A change in wages increases cost to the producer, which then changes amount supplied.

Elasticity

Price Elasticity of Demand

The law of demand states that demand increases when price decreases. It does not, however, provide a means for determining the magnitude of decrease. ELASTICITY, in general, is the measure of sensitivity to change. PRICE ELASTICITY OF DEMAND measures the extent to which changes in price alter demand. For example, if the price of bread were to increase, price elasticity of demand would indicate the extent to which people would stop buying bread.

In a perfect world, the elasticity of the price will find equilibrium between price and demand (as in the diagram below). The upper line represents elasticity with demand at the same level. The mathematical equation for this is below:

$$E_D = \frac{\% \text{ OF CHANGE IN QUANTITY DEMANDED}}{\% \text{ OF CHANGE IN PRICE}}$$

The greater this ratio is, the more responsive buyers are to the change in price. When the change in demand is greater than the change in price (so Ed > 1), demand is called **PRICE ELASTIC**. For example, the price of a car increases by 5% and there is a 20% decrease in quantity demanded (Ed = $\frac{20}{5}$ = 4).This shows that the change in price greatly affected quantity demanded.

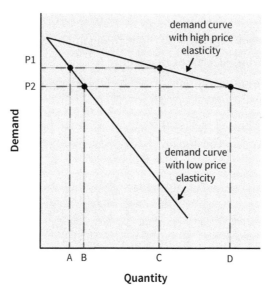

Figure 5.5. Price Elasticity of Demand

When change in price is greater than the change in demand (so Ed < 1), demand is called **PRICE INELASTIC**. Reverse the previous example. If the price of a car increased by 20% and there was a 5% increase in quantity demanded (Ed = $\frac{5}{20}$ = .25), it is clear the change in price had only a small effect on consumer demand.

If any change in price will lead to unlimited demand, demand is **PERFECTLY ELASTIC**.

What are some perfectly elastic and perfectly inelastic goods?

This usually occurs in cases where there are many substitutes of the product. A coffee shop surrounded by other coffee shops might have perfectly elastic demand. If there is no change in quantity demanded based on a change in price, demand for that good is considered **PERFECTLY INELASTIC**. For example, a life-saving drug for a rare disease might have perfectly inelastic demand: it does not change regardless of how expensive the drug becomes. A perfectly elastic demand curve is horizontal, whereas a perfectly inelastic curve is vertical. So, the steeper a demand curve, the less elasticity it has.

Finally, if the change in price equals the change in demand (Ed = 1), demand is **UNIT ELASTIC**. For example, the price for chewing gum decreased by 7% and the quantity of chewing gum demanded increased by 7%.

There are several factors that impact elasticity, including:

- proportion of income
- number of good substitutes
- time

EXAMPLES

1) The price elasticity of demand measures which of the following?

    A. The extent to which changes in demand impact price.

    B. The extent to which changes in price impact demand.

    C. Whether demand will decrease based on price.

    D. Whether demand will increase based on price.

    E. The point at which both price and demand are maximized.

Answers:

    A. Incorrect. Price elasticity of demand is a measure of demand, not of price.

    B. **Correct.** Price elasticity of demand measures how much demand will change based on changes in price.

    C. Incorrect. The law of demand addresses the reaction demand will have to changes in price. Price elasticity of demand addresses the question of "how much."

    D. Incorrect. All else being equal, demand will always increase when price decreases and vice versa. Price elasticity of demand works from this assumption to determine just how much demand will increase or decrease.

    E. Incorrect. Price elasticity of demand does not measure a single point but a rate of change.

2) If the supply curve for a product shifted to the right, creating a 5 percent decrease in price and a 4 percent increase in demand, the price elasticity of demand would be which of the following?

    A. 1.25

    B. 1

    C. 0.8

    D. The demand would be perfectly inelastic.

    E. The demand would be perfectly elastic.

Answers:

    A. Incorrect. This number would be derived from dividing the decrease in price by the increase in demand, which is not the proper formula for elasticity of demand.

    B. Incorrect. An elasticity of 1, or unit elasticity, can only be achieved if the change in price equals the change in demand. In this case, the percent change in price is greater than the percent change in demand.

    C. **Correct.** When the change in demand (4) is divided by the change in price (5), the elasticity is 0.8.

    D. Incorrect. Demand for a product is perfectly inelastic when demand will not change, regardless of change in price.

Factors of Production

Labor

Just like production, labor is also subject to the market forces of supply and demand. A **SUPPLY CURVE OF LABOR** shows the number of hours labor workers are willing to work at a given wage rate. Because engaging in labor is an individual economic decision, opportunity cost plays a role. As wages increase, workers are willing to forgo leisure activities in order to increase their labor and thereby increase their earnings. This is called the **SUBSTITUTION EFFECT**. The demand for leisure, however, also increases as income increases. Therefore, when wages reach a certain amount, the number of hours workers are willing to work decreases as they increasingly choose leisure over labor. This is called the **INCOME EFFECT**. As a result, labor supply curves that extend to these high wages can take a backward-bending shape.

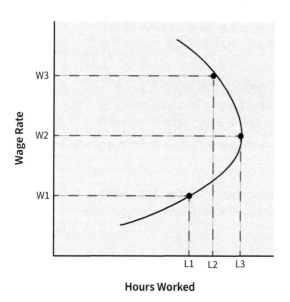

Figure 5.6. Supply Curve of Labor

The labor supply curve can shift overall based on the following factors:

- population growth or increased immigration
- changing worker attitudes
- changes in alternative opportunities

Labor demand is more complicated to calculate as it is a function of wage, desired quantity of production, and price of unit sold. Generally speaking, whereas labor supply curves are upward sloping overall, labor demand curves are downward sloping.

The **EQUILIBRIUM WAGE RATE** and quantity occurs where the quantity of demanded labor equals the quantity supply of labor.

The Basic Categories of Financial Assets

STOCKS AND BONDS are securities, monetary units that can be exchanged. Public and private interests and individuals may invest in stocks as stockholders, or in bonds as lenders. Stocks and bonds are traded on the stock market, a venue where private individuals, businesses, government agencies, and even foreign investors and foreign countries can invest.

Stocks are essentially shares of any given company or corporation that has "gone public" or offered its stock for sale to the highest bidder, whomever that may be. In the last century, the value of the stock market has come to reflect the state of the American economy as never before.

Dow Jones Industrial Average

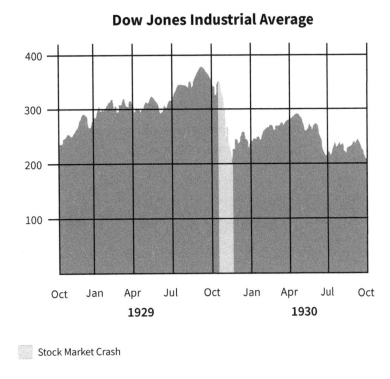

Figure 5.7. Stock Market Crash and Consequences

In 1929, the stock market was the precursor to an economic downturn that history has called the Great Depression. It was not just an American economic downturn. There were few nations unaffected by the stock market crash in 1929 and the decade of Depression that followed. The graph below shows the pitfalls of more than a decade of questionable buying practices by investors of all economic demographics.

Stock Market Trends

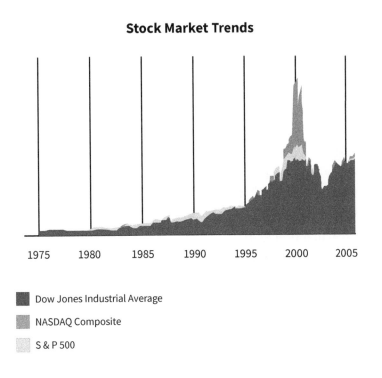

Figure 5.8. Stock Measures

The American economy is still more or less a mirror reflection of the American stock market. Its movement, both up and down, is the fodder of presidential campaigns and Congressional debate. For smaller investors, it's often boom or bust, bear or bull markets. There are fortunes to be made and lost for anyone who wants to take the risk. The graph below explores the three different stock measures over a period of several years.

MONEY MARKET FUNDS invest in short term investments like treasury bonds. These are considered safe and solid investments much like bank deposits, but encompass a broader scope for large scale investors.

The Allocation of Resources

ALLOCATION OF RESOURCES, or how resources are distributed across an economy, can fall to either the government or the market, depending on the type of economy. Within a specific firm, the allocation of resources is determined by profit maximization: how can the resources be used most efficiently?

One of the best ways to explain government control of the allocation of resources is to look at rationing during the Second World War in the United States. Rather than allow the public to hoard goods and create shortages, the federal government decided to control the flow of goods to civilians by allocating only a small amount of goods to the public on a weekly and monthly basis. Most resources are limited. In this case, economists determine the best way to allocate resources that does the least harm to all parties.

PUBLIC GOODS are products that an individual can consume without reducing their availability to other individuals. Public goods are also equally available to all. Basic television, plumbing infrastructure, and sewage systems are all examples of public goods. Some people now argue that internet access should be a public good. In a pure market economy, the market would provide for all public goods. However, in reality, often private markets fail to provide the allocatively efficient level of public goods and providing falls to the government.

EXAMPLES

1) When a new factory paying higher wages opens two towns over from Smallville, what will happen to Smallville's labor supply curve?

   A. It will begin to slope upwards.

   B. It will begin to bend backwards.

   C. It will shift to the right.

   D. It will shift to the left.

   E. The new factory will have no direct impact on Smallville's labor supply.

   Answers:

   A. Incorrect. Labor supply curves always slope upwards; generally, as wages increase, the labor supply increases.

   B. Incorrect. Labor supply curves only bend backwards when wages become so high that the income effect outweighs the substitution effect and workers begin to choose leisure over labor.

C.   Incorrect. A rightward shift in the labor supply curve would indicate an overall increase in the labor supply. This would be seen in the labor supply curve of the town with the new factory, as it will most likely experience an influx of workers.

D.   Correct. Smallville's labor pool will shrink as workers leave Smallville to work higher-paying jobs at the new factory. A reduction of the labor pool results in a leftward shift of the graph.

E.   Incorrect. A better wage opportunity will pull workers out of Smallville's labor force.

2)   Which of the following is NOT an example of a public good?

A.   air travel

B.   streetlights

C.   public parks

D.   radio broadcasts

E.   clean air

Answers:

A.   Correct. Air travel is not available to everyone; it is restricted by price. Also, once one person "consumes" air travel by taking up a seat on a plane, the passenger prevents someone else from "consuming" that good.

B.   Incorrect. Everyone can experience the benefits of streetlights—there is no fee to pay in order to benefit from the light they emit.

C.   Incorrect. Although funded by taxes (like many public goods), public parks are open to all, whether people paid their taxes or not. Also, one person's use of the park does not prevent someone else's use of the park.

D.   Incorrect. Radios have unrestricted access to broadcasts. When one person listens to the radio, this listener does not prevent someone else from listening to the radio (even on a different station).

E.   Incorrect. Clean air is available to everyone without a fee. Also someone can breathe the air without preventing anyone else from doing so.

Behavior of Firms

In economics, any organization that uses factors of production to produce a good or service which it intends to sell for profit is called a FIRM. Firms can range from a child's lemonade stand to a multinational corporation like Walmart. While individuals make economic decisions to maximize their utility, firms make economic decisions to maximize their profit. ECONOMIC PROFIT is different from simple accounting profit (subtracting costs from revenue). Economic profit also takes into consideration non-priced, or IMPLICIT COSTS. For example, a young entrepreneur starts a bicycle sandwich delivery business. She charges $4 per sandwich plus a $1 delivery fee. In her first month, she sells 200 sandwiches, which equals revenue of $1000. She spent $300 on bread, meat, and fixings, $50 on packaging and paid $50 for her bike and basket. These are her EXPLICIT COSTS. Her accounting profit for the month then was $600. However, economic profit takes into account other non-priced factors, including opportunity costs, like wages not earned from another job or interest not earned on money that has been liquidated. In this case, she passed up a job working at a coffee shop for $700 a month. Taking that into account, her economic loss would actually be $100.

Types of Firms

A SOLE PROPRIETORSHIP is a business belonging to a single individual. Either as the sole owner or the inventor, a sole proprietorship is dependent on the skills and income of a single individual.

A PARTNERSHIP is a joint venture between two individuals or two business entities. Some might say that a partnership is the next step in business ownership. A sole proprietor has too much business or too much inventory to manage alone, so he or she has the option to hire more help or bring in a partner to share both the risk and the profits.

A CORPORATION is a group of individuals or businesses working together to share the business risk and the business profit. Of all the economic terms listed here, the corporation is the newest. It originated during the nineteenth century in the second phase of the Industrial Revolution, but it took off with the availability of credit at the end of the century and in the beginning of the twentieth century. Credit meant that the financial risk of the corporation was spread out among a larger pool of business leaders and therefore even more attractive than before.

Short Run Loss and Long Run Equilibrium

Firms make decisions in both the short and long term. The SHORT TERM, in economics, is a period in which at least one production input is fixed and cannot be changed. For example, a store experiences a major increase in foot traffic and sales during the holiday season. It can respond by increasing staff and extending hours. It may even be able to order more merchandise. It cannot, however, increase the size of the store during that time. The LONG TERM refers to a period of time in which all production inputs are changeable. While that same store could not change its size for the few months of the holiday season, it could do so over the course of a year or two if high foot traffic continued.

Firms operating at a loss will continue to produce in the short run if money coming in—revenue—exceeds variable costs. Loss of profit in the short run is unimportant as long as there is a long term profit. If there is no long term profit, then the item will likely be discontinued and replaced with more cost-effective, profitable merchandise.

Of course, loss is not sustainable beyond the short run. If an industry is perfectly competitive, it will reach equilibrium (or LONG RUN EQUILIBRIUM) when price is the same as the average total costs. This point is called ZERO ECONOMIC PROFIT; it is the amount of income that a business needs to break even in the marketplace.

Fixed and Variable Inputs

FIXED INPUTS are any production inputs that cannot be changed in the short run. These are the costs that do not change and must be paid monthly or bimonthly, such as wages, rent, or materials costs.

VARIABLE INPUTS are production inputs that can be changed in the short term, like the cost of labor (if the number of employees is increased or decreased). In the diagram below, fixed inputs or fixed costs appear as the stable bottom of the graph, while variable inputs or variable costs appear as an ever-changing line going up in terms of price.

MARGINAL COSTS are the costs of producing one more unit. Changes in any of the above costs can affect the final cost of production. Of all the costs in the productivity of a business, the ones most likely to change would be VC or variable costs.

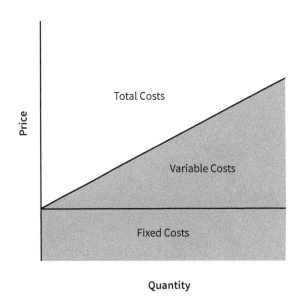

Figure 5.9. Fixed and Variable Inputs

Labor Analysis of Production

Economic analysis of production is based on production measures:

- Total Product of Labor (TPL) is best defined as the total amount of product at each quantity of labor.
- Marginal Product of Labor (MPL) is defined as the change in amount of product resulting from a change of labor.
- Average Product of Labor (APL) is the total product divided by the amount of labor which gives the average productivity of a market's labor.

For example, the sandwich entrepreneur's total product of labor is based on the variable inputs of the labor she put into her sandwich-making and her time on her bike. In her first month, she used 1 unit of labor, creating a TPL of 200 sandwiches. Her APL is calculated by dividing her TPL by her units of labor: 200/1 = 200.

Her business takes off and she decides to hire someone else to help her deliver sandwiches. The unit of labor increases to 2 and her TPL increases to 275. Her MPL is her change in TPL for the additional unit of labor. In this case, then, the MPL would be 75. Her new APL will then be 137.5.

Fixed and Variable Costs

FIXED COSTS are business costs that remain stable while VARIABLE COSTS change with the markets. As discussed earlier, fixed costs represent rent, wages, or insurance costs. Variable costs are the items needed for production or the cost of utilities that might change from month to month.

TOTAL COSTS include all of the costs to reach a certain level of production. Total costs are the bottom line in a new business and will include both fixed costs and variable costs with a hope of profit at the end of the fiscal year.

What are some variable costs a firm might have?

AVERAGE COSTS include all of the costs to produce items divided by the number of items produced. This is the cost per item that a business must consider and hope to lower. Lower average costs of production means higher profits.

MARGINAL COST is the difference in price when production is increased by one unit. Marginal costs can either increase or decrease the overall price of the item produced. It depends on a whole variety of different factors and the market at the time.

Long Run Average Costs

How do firms determine how and when to expand? By examining long-run average cost (LRAC). A firm can calculate its LRAC by combining snapshots of its short-term average costs (SRAC) at various production points. For example, our entrepreneur could calculate her SRAC based on selling 0–100 sandwiches. She could then calculate her costs at 75–250, and so on. Her LRAC would combine these graphs to indicate when she should prepare to expand.

An LRAC graph would show a decrease in price with increasing quantity, followed by a leveling out, and then an increase in price with increasing quantity. The first section of the graph, in which price decreases, is called ECONOMIES OF SCALE. This shows the advantages (in decreased costs) of greater production and expansion. Labor and management are able to specialize. Our entrepreneur now focuses on assembling the prettiest sandwiches and hires others—who are faster and more efficient—to organize sandwich supplies, wrap the sandwiches, and make deliveries.

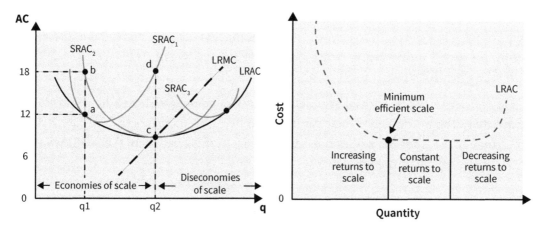

Figure 5.10. Long Run Average Costs

However, she will eventually reach a point where adding more workers will bring fewer and fewer advantages. This is called the LAW OF DIMINISHING RETURNS. For example, if she hires more riders than she needs at one time, she will not see the same benefit as she did when each new rider allowed deliveries to happen faster. This stage is called CONSTANT RETURNS TO SCALE.

Finally, a firm reaches a point where expansion hurts profit rather than helps. This is called DISECONOMIES OF SCALE. The increase in production becomes more costly. So our entrepreneur now has hired too many people to help in the sandwich preparation process, and they are bumping into each other and working inefficiently.

EXAMPLES

1) If a long run average cost curve is falling left to right, this indicates that a firm should do which of the following in that price range and quantity range?

   A. expand its operation

   B. maintain its operation at its current size

   C. decrease the size of its operation

   D. diversify its products

   E. There is insufficient information to make a determination.

   Answers:

   A. **Correct.** A LRAC that falls left to right shows decreasing cost with increasing quantity, or economies of scale. In this situation, it is beneficial for a company to expand.

   B. Incorrect. If the LRAC was flat, indicating constant returns to scale, then the firm should maintain its current size.

   C. Incorrect. If the LRAC was rising left to right, indicating diseconomies of scale, the firm should reduce its size

   D. Incorrect. Because the increased efficiency is the result of economies of scale, the firm will not necessarily benefit from the introduction of new products.

   E. Incorrect. While the information provided does not permit specific numerical predictions, it does show that it is a good time for the firm to expand.

2) If a firm wanted to know the impact that hiring 100 new workers would have on production, it would examine which of the following?

   A. Total Product of Labor

   B. variable costs

   C. Average Product of Labor

   D. fixed costs

   E. Marginal Product of Labor

   Answers:

   A. Incorrect. Total Product of Labor is the total output at a particular quantity of labor. It does not show how that output changes at different levels.

   B. Incorrect. Variable costs are a type of input, not a measurement tool. Variable costs are the production inputs that can be changed in the short run. Labor is a variable cost.

   C. Incorrect. Average Product of Labor indicates, on average, the amount of production per unit of labor.

   D. Incorrect. Fixed costs are costs that cannot be changed in the short run. They do not relate to the relationship between labor and production.

   E. **Correct.** In economics, the term marginal always means "additional." In this case, the Marginal Product of Labor is a measurement tool used to determine the additional output resulting from an increase in labor.

3) Which of the following is an example of a variable input?

    A. a contractor's work crew

    B. money obtained from a bank loan

    C. a caterer's kitchen

    D. a magazine's printing press

    E. a dry cleaner's machinery

Answers:

    A. **Correct.** A contractor can hire or cut employees in response to changes in the short term. That makes his crew a variable input.

    B. Incorrect. Capital of any kind, including a bank loan, is a fixed input because the quantity of that capital cannot be increased in the short term (by either taking out more money or paying a large sum of it back).

    C. Incorrect. A caterer cannot quickly increase the size of his kitchen, making this a fixed variable.

    D. Incorrect. Printing presses are large and expensive and not easily replaced. Major investments like heavy machinery are considered fixed inputs.

    E. Incorrect. The dry cleaning machinery is very expensive and cannot be changed out without considerable expense.

4) Which of the following is an example of an implicit cost?

    A. the money an entrepreneur anticipates spending in the next six months to grow her business

    B. ad space purchased in a local newspaper to advertise an entrepreneur's new business

    C. money spent on certification courses to achieve a license in a field

    D. the time an entrepreneur spent researching information to launch a new business

    E. the registration fee for a networking conference

Answers:

    A. Incorrect. While the money is not currently being spent, anticipated spending is still an explicit cost planned for another day.

    B. Incorrect. Payment for ad space is an explicit cost for the growth of a business.

    C. Incorrect. While certification courses are not a direct cost of a business, they are still considered explicit costs because they constitute money spent to increase profit.

    D. **Correct.** Time spent researching information is a non-priced cost. There are many other things the entrepreneur could have been doing but did not do. Therefore, this is an implicit cost.

    E. Incorrect. Because the individual spent money on the conference, it is an explicit cost even though it is not a direct cost of the business.

Types of Markets
Perfect Competition

There are four main characteristics of **PERFECT COMPETITION**: there are many small and independent buyers and sellers; everybody produces the same product; there are no barriers to the entry of new or exit of old firms; and all firms must accept the price where it is and produce as much as they want at that price (because they cannot change it).

Put simply, perfect or pure competition occurs when there is no one business that controls the entire marketplace because no one business is big enough to do so. For example, three pizza restaurants compete against each other in a small college town. Price wars and showmanship may establish one of the restaurants as a leader for a time, but none of the three restaurants dominates the market because they all produce the same product for roughly the same price.

Monopoly

Not all markets are perfectly competitive markets. When one corporation or business controls one entire area or product of a given market, it is called a **MONOPOLY**. In addition, monopolies are marked by a lack of close substitutes for the product, barriers to entry for new firms, and market power. Barriers can include legal barriers, like licensing restrictions or copyright laws. The advantages of producing large quantities (discussed later) also can edge newcomers out of the market. For example, big box stores like Walmart can purchase or produce products on a large scale. This allows them to decrease their costs and lower their prices. A small family-owned store in the same town—buying a small fraction of the same products—cannot compete. Finally, if a firm controls all of the resources needed in production, it can prevent others from entering the market. Andrew Carnegie used this technique at the end of the nineteenth century with his company, US Steel. He purchased every layer of production, allowing him to streamline costs and prevent competitors from accessing the resources.

In response to Carnegie and others like him, the United States government legislated the breakup of monopolies across the country and even inspired a board game of the same name during the Great Depression.

Monopolies function best in a new market where competition is either too expensive or not possible because of legal roadblocks like patents.

Oligopoly

An **OLIGOPOLY** occurs when a few businesses control one market. As a result, they become interdependent; the action of one affects the others. For example, when one airline started to require payment for checked luggage, the others quickly followed suit. In an oligopoly, the product can be standardized as in a perfectly competitive market, or may be differentiated. For example, telephone service is essentially a standardized product, whereas the car industry is an oligopoly with differentiated products. Like monopolies, oligopolies have entry barriers.

EXAMPLES

1) If a market has perfect competition, which of the following is true?
   A. There are many buyers, but only a few sellers.
   B. There are many sellers, but only a few buyers.
   C. There are many sellers and buyers.
   D. There is an equal number of buyers and sellers.
   E. Either one buyer or one seller dominates the market.

   Answers:
   A. Incorrect. In a market with only a few sellers, each of those sellers would be able to set price rather than follow the price set by the market.
   B. Incorrect. If there are only a few buyers in the market, each buyer would have disproportionate power over demand, and therefore would be able to control price.
   C. **Correct.** A perfectly competitive market has a large number of small buyers and sellers, which prevents any one (or two) entities from controlling price.
   D. Incorrect. An equal number of buyers and sellers is not necessary; more important is that there is a large number of each to prevent interference with the market.
   E. Incorrect. A perfectly competitive market means that no single person or entity can control the market.

2) Which of the following types of markets have barriers to entry for new firms?
   A. monopolies and perfect competition markets
   B. oligopolies and perfect competition markets
   C. monopolies only
   D. monopolies and oligopolies
   E. perfect competition markets only

   Answers:
   A. Incorrect. While monopolies do have entry barriers, perfect competition markets have no barriers for entry or exit, allowing the market to determine the need for more or fewer firms.
   B. Incorrect. Oligopolies have entry barriers, protecting the few firms who control the market. True competition cannot exist with these barriers, which is why they do not exist in a perfectly competitive market.
   C. Incorrect. While monopolies do have entry barriers, oligopolies do as well.
   D. **Correct.** Both monopolies and oligopolies are markets in which a very small number of firms—one or a few, respectively—control the market. In order to maintain control, they must stifle competition from new firms. This is done by maximizing the benefits of large-scale operations or controlling relevant resources.
   E. Incorrect. Perfectly competitive markets have no barriers.

Government Intervention

Price Floors and Price Ceilings

A **PRICE FLOOR** is the lowest price established by the government. Governments use price floors to aid producers in unfair markets with depressed prices. If the price floor instituted by the government is lower than the price the market will support, the price floor is ineffective as demonstrated by the figure below, line F being the price floor set by the government. When set above the market price, they can lead to a surplus. Price floors lead to overall inefficiency in the market as neither producers nor consumers are maximizing the available resources. They also can price people out of the market.

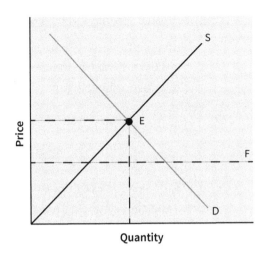

Figure 5.11. Ineffective Price Floor

A **PRICE CEILING** is the highest price allowed by government. Often the price ceiling dictated by the government is higher than the market actually allows as demonstrated by the diagram below where the government set price ceiling is indicated by line F. If the price ceiling is set below the market price, then demand will outstrip supply, leading to a shortage.

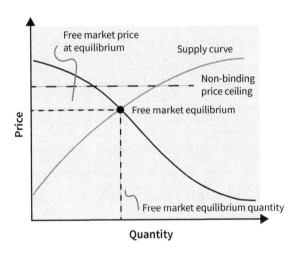

Figures 5.12. Price Ceiling

Antitrust Laws

ANTITRUST LAWS are used to promote a competitive market environment. Antitrust laws exist to protect consumers from illegal mergers and other unfair business practices. Antitrust laws emerged out of the Progressive movement of the nineteenth century in response to the monopolies and trusts dominated by banking and heavy industry in the Second Industrial Revolution.

The richest businessmen of the nineteenth century were called **ROBBER BARONS** because they controlled vast amounts of money and property. For the robber barons, controlling all aspects of one given industry was simply good business practice. For example, a steel magnate might control the steel industry of a given region of the United States. That means he controls the mines where raw ingredients are mined from the earth as well as the miners, even providing company houses and a company store. Furthermore, the magnate controls the railroad that hauls raw ingredients to his steel foundries and the railroads that carry the finished product to its destination.

Competition is key to a market economy and a capitalist system. Establishing a TRUST—control over the entire industrial process—defeats that purpose. It was for that reason that the US government set out to break the trusts of the late nineteenth and early twentieth centuries.

Types of Taxes

PROGRESSIVE TAXES tax the income of the wealthy more than other groups in society, or so the theory goes. These taxes increase gradually as income rises for an individual, but, in a free market economy, taxes are adjusted to account for income losses in business, charitable contributions, and other circumstances. Therefore, in reality, tax rates may vary considerably across income levels.

Other forms of taxation include PROPORTIONAL and REGRESSIVE TAXES. Proportional taxes are similar to flat rate taxes in that all taxpayers are taxed at the same rate or at the same proportion of their incomes. Regressive taxes affect everyone at the same rate without a sliding proportional scale, making life more expensive for the lower classes.

EXAMPLE

Which of the following statements is true of antitrust laws?

A. They are designed to increase the power of the seller over the buyer in perfect competition markets.

B. They are designed to protect controlling firms in oligopolies.

C. They are designed to shift perfect competition markets towards monopolies.

D. They are designed to increase the power of the buyer over the seller in perfect competition markets.

E. They are designed to decrease the power of monopolists.

Answers:

A. Incorrect. Antitrust laws are designed to prevent sellers from controlling a market.

B. Incorrect. Antitrust laws diminish the power of controlling firms by ensuring that they do not work together to control prices or means of production.

C. Incorrect. Antitrust laws were designed to do just the opposite. They were created in response to the increase in monopolies at the end of the nineteenth century and were an attempt to shift the economy back towards perfect competition.

D. Incorrect. Antitrust laws focus on the practices of business, not the relationship between sellers and buyers.

Macroeconomics

Circular Flow Models

A CIRCULAR FLOW MODEL shows where money goes in any given economy. The circular flow model follows money as it enters the marketplace to be spent by consumers and to be invested by businesses. The model also reveals places in the economy where money is being wasted. In a CLOSED ECONOMY model (as in the image below), households provide factors of production to firms, which the firms then transform into goods and services. The firms pay the households competitive compensation for those factors of production, providing income for the household. The household then uses that income to buy the goods and services created by the firms.

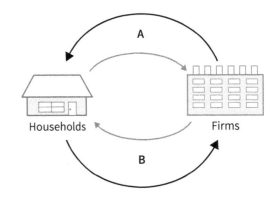

Governments also play a role in the circular flow, acting as both recipients of factors of production (in the form of tax collection) and creators of goods and services.

Figure 5.13. Circular Flow Model

The study of macroeconomics focuses on how to keep this flow moving at a strong and steady pace, primarily through the use of measurement tools.

Gross Domestic Product (GDP)

The **GDP,** THE GROSS DOMESTIC PRODUCT, is the total value of domestic production: the market value of all of the FINAL GOODS AND SERVICES produced within a nation in one year. Final goods are those that are ready for consumption. INTERMEDIATE GOODS, goods that still require more processing, are not counted. Tomatoes are intermediate goods; jarred tomato sauce is a final good. Also, to avoid DOUBLE COUNTING, the count takes place at the final sale.

GDP focuses on what was actually produced within a country, regardless of where it is headquartered. For example, if a shoe company has its headquarters in California, but all of its production takes place in Vietnam, the total production of shoes would contribute to Vietnam's GDP, not that of the United States.

The higher the GDP is for the nation, the better the economy for both business and individual citizens.

Second hand sales, nonmarket transactions, and underground economies are all excluded from GDP. This means that a country (usually developing countries) in which these play a stronger role have relatively weak GDPs.

Nominal GDP in Billion U.S. Dollars in 2014

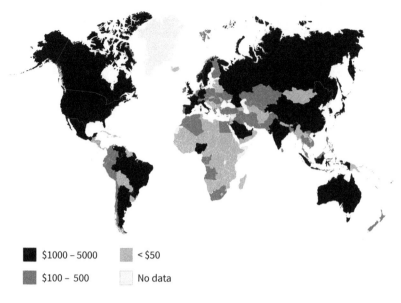

■ $1000 – 5000	■ < $50
■ $100 – 500	☐ No data

Figure 5.14. 2014 World Economies Map

Inflation and the Consumer Price Index

To measure the health of an economy based on consumer spending, economists use the **Consumer Price Index (CPI).**

The **CPI** measures prices of goods and services as they change over time. It does this by selecting a base year and compiling a market "basket" of 400 consumer goods and services that year, ranging from gas to candy to refrigerators. A price index is created for subsequent years by measuring the change in prices. Here is an example:

Table 5.1. CPI Example

Items in the basket	Quantity Purchased (2010)	2010 Price	2010 Spending	2015 Price	2015 Spending (based on 2010 quantities)
Candy Bar	12	1.50	18	1.75	21
Books	10	12	120	14	140
Movie Tickets	6	10	60	12	72
Total Spending			= 198		= 233

$$\text{Current Year Price Index} = 100 \times \frac{\text{Spending Current Year}}{\text{Spending Base Year}}$$
$$\text{2015 Price Index} = 100 \times \frac{233}{198} = 117.68$$

This shows a 17.68 percent increase in price. To calculate the official CPI, the average price level of consumer goods is taken for the base year and the current year. The percent change from year to year is called **inflation.** Sudden or unexpected inflation—particularly inflation that does not keep up with wages—causes problems within an economy.

The graph below shows a sample of the CPI for the United States between 1913 and 2014, just over a century. The dark line shows the average CPI for each year with 1982 –

1984 as the "base year" (when CPI = 100). The graph shows that there has been an overall increase in CPI over time. The light line shows the percent change in average CPI from year to year. This is the measure that shows inflation within the economy. Inflation peaked in the 1970s, but there has been very little since. In the 1970s inflation reached an all-time high, and economists struggled to figure out how to bring it back down. Eventually, the Federal Reserve stopped issuing new money, leading to a sharp rise in unemployment but eventually curbing inflation.

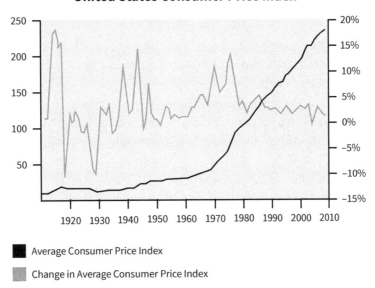

United States Consumer Price Index

■ Average Consumer Price Index

▨ Change in Average Consumer Price Index

Figure 5.15. US Consumer Price Index

EXAMPLES

1) Which of the following transactions would be used in a calculation of GDP?

 A. compensation a teenager receives for raking a neighbor's leaves

 B. the resale of a coffee table on eBay

 C. the sale of strawberries to a jam manufacturer

 D. the sale of five pounds of carrots at a grocery store

 E. the sale of bottles to a flavored water company

Answers:

 A. Incorrect. This is an example of a nonmarket transaction, as the income is not reported nor are taxes paid on it.

 B. Incorrect. Resale transactions are not included in GDP, as this would constitute double-counting an item.

 C. Incorrect. In this case, the strawberries are an intermediate good; the jam will be the final good. If the strawberries were sold at the grocery store or a farmer's market to a consumer, they would be included in GDP.

 D. **Correct.** Because the carrots are going directly to a consumer, and not being used to create another item for sale, they are considered a final good.

E. Incorrect. Although the bottles do not require more processing, their cost will be included in the cost of the bottled water.

2) When is inflation an economic problem?
   A. when it continues over a long period of time
   B. when it occurs unexpectedly
   C. when it is lower than wage increases
   D. when it is paired with a shift in goods produced
   E. It is always a problem.

Answers:

A. Incorrect. The money supply gradually inflates over time. The graph above showed a general increase in CPI over time, during times of both economic growth and recession.

B. **Correct.** Unexpected and sudden inflation causes problems because people do not have time to prepare for it, and wages do not have time to catch up. This kind of inflation leads to the sudden loss of value of money, investments, and capital.

C. Incorrect. If inflation stays below wage increases, it has little impact on the economy as the real income of individuals is unaffected.

D. Incorrect. There is no economic evidence of a shift in goods produced interacting negatively with inflation

E. Incorrect. Inflation is an economic fact—neither good nor bad in and of itself. When it occurs in circumstances that negatively impact the real value of individuals' earnings and savings, it becomes a problem.

Economic Growth

In its simplest form, economic growth is the outward movement of the production possibility frontier over time, which in turn results from an increase in PRODUCTIVITY. In economics, productivity is defined as the quantity of output that can be produced per worker in a prescribed amount of time. There are four main DETERMINANTS OF PRODUCTIVITY.

PHYSICAL CAPITAL: When the physical capital, or tools of production, are increased, productivity increases. For example, a bottle maker has a machine that can produce 100 bottles an hour. The company upgrades to a more efficient machine and can now produce 200 bottles an hour. On a macroeconomics level, governments should craft policies that encourage investment in capital.

HUMAN CAPITAL: Human capital refers to the knowledge and skills of the labor force. The more skilled its labor, the more productive the economy. This is reflected in the rapid economic growth of the four Asian Tigers: South Korea, Singapore, Hong Kong, and Taiwan. Each economy began to grow thanks to factory jobs requiring unskilled workers. However, economic growth really took off when their skilled labor forces allowed them to dominate international banking and manufacturing information technology. Increasing human capital does not simply mean encouraging education (although that is part of it). Health initiatives (like vaccination drives) that create a healthier workforce also increase human capital and productivity.

NATURAL RESOURCES: Minerals, soil, timber, and waterways all constitute productivity resources that are provided by nature. Government policies that provide for sustainable consumption of renewable resources and protection of nonrenewable resources can foster economic growth.

TECHNOLOGY: Technology does not just mean computers and machines. Technology refers to a nation's knowledge and ability to efficiently produce goods. In this way, discovering how to make fire was a technological advancement on par with smartphones. Governments should create policies to encourage and incentivize innovation.

Social and cultural changes can impact economic growth as well. For example, significant economic reforms introduced market principles to the Chinese economy beginning in the early 1980s. Since then, China has experienced rapid economic growth fueled by government policies that capitalize on the country's huge labor pool.

The following chart looks at economic growth between the years of 1990 and 2006 in the United States and different countries. It gives a glimpse of the economic highs and lows of the last two decades and it also reveals the peaks and valleys that accompany not only the economic, but social, cultural, and historic events as well.

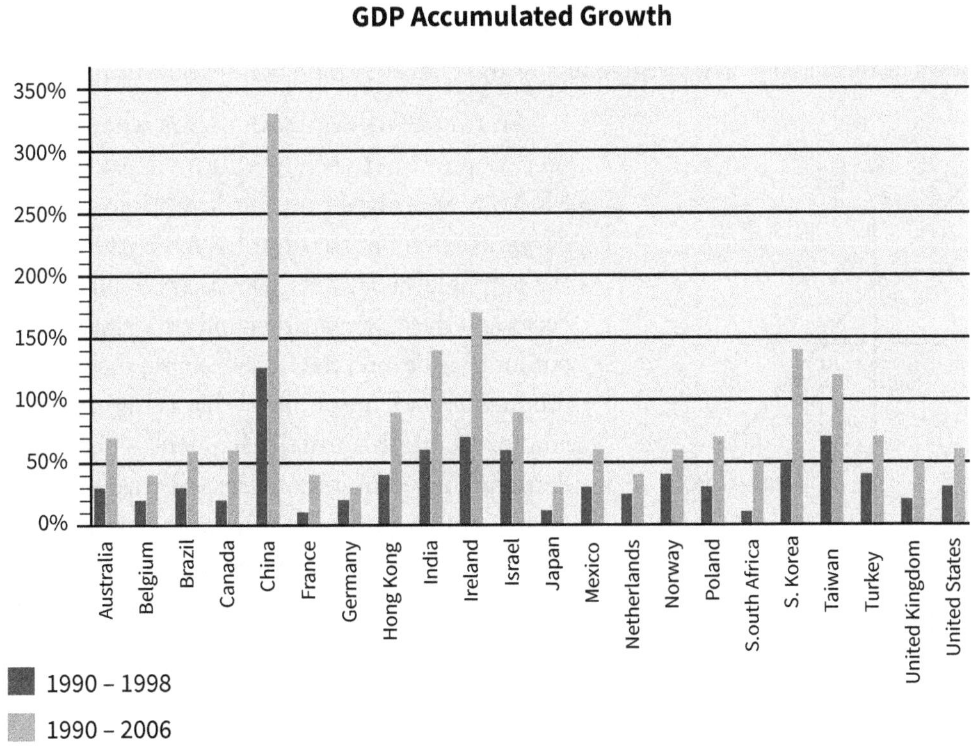

GDP Accumulated Growth

Figure 5.16. Global Economic Growth (1990 – 2016)

Aggregate Supply

AGGREGATE SUPPLY (AS) is the relationship between the total of all domestic output produced and the average price level. Essentially, it is the sum of all of the microeconomic supply curves in an economy. The LONG RUN AGGREGATE SUPPLY (LRAS) assumes that input prices have had enough time to adjust to changes in the various product markets. All markets—product and input—are at equilibrium, and there is full employment. This means that output does not change, regardless of price, creating a vertical curve.

SHORT RUN AGGREGATE SUPPLY (SRAS) curves fluctuate without impacting employment; however, if the long-run AS curve shifts, there must be a change in the output level at full employment. These changes result from a change in the availability of resources or changes in technology and productivity, both of which could alter a nation's output when working at full employment. In this way LRAS can be used as a measure of economic growth.

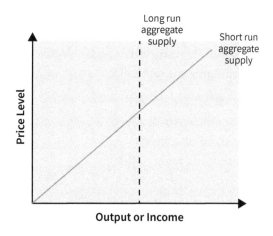

Figure 5.17. Aggregate Supply

Inflationary and Recessionary Gaps

An economy is in MACROECONOMIC EQUILIBRIUM when the quantity of output demanded in an economy (as shown by AGGREGATE DEMAND, the sum of all demand curves in an economy), is equal to the quantity of output supplied. This equilibrium does not always occur at full employment, though. If it does not, the economy is either experiencing inflation or recession—an aggregate supply and demand graph will reveal this information.

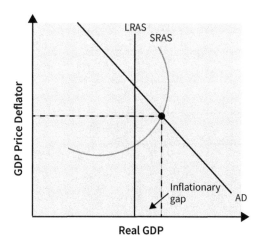

Figure 5.18. Inflationary Gap

An INFLATIONARY GAP occurs when the intersection point between AGGREGATE DEMAND and SRAS is at a higher output level than the LRAS curve. Remember that the LRAS curve represents the output level of full employment. So, if the SRAS curve and the aggregate demand curve intersect at an output level beyond the LRAS curve, the economy is producing at an output level that is higher than full employment. This usually happens when quantity demanded is suddenly increased through foreign or government spending, or even just very active consumers. When demand increases like this, factories stay open longer and pay their workers more overtime, thus exceeding full employment output.

On the other hand, if the equilibrium point is lower than LRAS, a RECESSIONARY GAP exists. This indicates that the nation is experiencing high levels of unemployment.

EXAMPLES

1) In the New Deal, the government created new jobs for people in an attempt to counteract the recession (the Great Depression). Which of the following best describes the economic theory guiding that policy?

   A. Government-created jobs shift the SRAS curve to the right which shifts the equilibrium point closer to the LRAS curve.

   B. Government-created jobs shift the LRAS curve to the left to bring it closer to the equilibrium point between short term aggregate supply and aggregate demand.

   C. Government-created jobs increase the nation's productivity, which eliminates recession.

   D. Government-created jobs increase aggregate supply, which shifts the intersection between SRAS and long-term aggregate supply.

   E. Government-created jobs increase aggregate demand, which shifts the equilibrium point closer to the LRAS curve.

   Answers:

   A. Incorrect. When the SRAS curve changes, it does not impact employment.

   B. Incorrect. The LRAS is based on full employment and can only be shifted by changes in resources or productivity, not demand.

   C. Incorrect. As productivity is a per-worker measure, increasing productivity would not affect unemployment. In fact, increasing productivity would actually shift the LRAS further to the right, increasing the recessionary gap.

   D. Incorrect. The creation of new jobs impacts demand, not supply. In addition, the intersection between SRAS and LRAS is not relevant to a recessionary gap.

   E. Correct. The jobs generated by the New Deal created new demand for labor, increasing aggregate demand and shifting the equilibrium point closer to LRAS (which is at full employment). The danger is in going too far the other way and creating an inflationary gap.

2) Which of the following policies would be least likely to increase a nation's productivity?

   A. a law providing free post-secondary education

   B. a national immunization campaign against malaria

   C. government funding for research into high-yield crops

   D. a government-mandated minimum wage

   E. a law regulating the cutting of old growth forests

   Answers:

   A. Incorrect. Providing free post-secondary education to all citizens will increase the nation's human capital, which could then increase its productivity.

   B. Incorrect. A national immunization campaign would improve the overall health of the labor pool, improving its human capital and increasing productivity.

   C. Incorrect. Bioengineering, such as the creation and improvement of high-yield crops, is a technological advancement. If farmers plant high-yield crops, the output per worker would increase dramatically.

   D. Correct. Mandating a minimum wage does not affect productivity; it simply improve wages for labor and impacts the cost of production.

The Federal Reserve

THE FEDERAL RESERVE behaves as a central bank of the United States and ensures the safety of the American monetary system. In the century since its inception, the role of the Fed has expanded tremendously, but the Fed's primary role at the end of the day is to maximize employment and stabilize prices in the United States.

The Federal Reserve was created in 1913 to help thwart the rising numbers of so-called "panics" that seized the nation every few years. The Fed was created to stabilize the US money supply and to moderate interest rates. As mentioned earlier, the Fed's duties have also expanded to include monitoring and maintaining reserves for US banks. With its own seal and flag, the Federal Reserve is among the most important components of the US federal government.

The Federal Reserve is the arbiter of interest rates for mortgages, the stock market, and any other monetary policy involving interest (such as money markets). EQUILIBRIUM INTEREST rates, regulated by the Fed, occur only when interest rates and the money supply are roughly equivalent.

As of 2016, interest rates established by the Federal Reserve are at an all-time low. While the low interest rates can be a boon for borrowers, lenders also can take advantage of low interest rates to offer loans, sometimes questionable ones, to borrowers who historically were not eligible for loans in the past. This contributed heavily to a recent housing crisis that is still being felt throughout the housing industry.

The interest rate set by the Federal Reserve is established by a number of factors, including the federal funds rate, the interest that the Federal Reserve charges banks. The chart below shows the fluctuating interest rates that banks have paid in recent decades and how they ultimately trickled down to consumers.

The Federal Reserve also monitors MONETARY STABILIZATION: efforts to keep prices, unemployment, and the money supply, among other fiscal indicators, relatively stable. Monetary stabilization helps to prevent the economy from oscillating between inflation and recession.

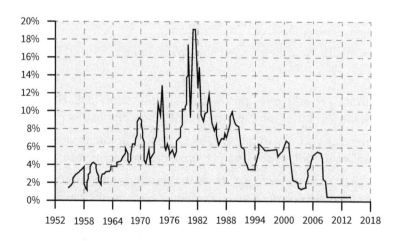

Figure 5.19. Federal Funds Rate

Fiscal Policy

FISCAL POLICY is an approach to economic management in which the government is deeply involved in managing the economy. When an individual or firm spends or saves money, those choices impact that individual's or firm's own finances. When the government makes similar choices, the government's decisions impact the economy as a whole. These economic decisions are called MULTIPLIERS.

In EXPANSIONARY FISCAL POLICY, the government either increases spending or decreases taxes in order to increase the AD curve to counteract a recession. When the economy experiences inflation, the government uses CONTRACTIONARY FISCAL POLICY: reducing government spending or increasing taxes.

A TARIFF is a tax or duty paid on anything imported or exported into or from a given country. Low tariffs encourage foreign goods to enter the market. Countries may do this to stimulate trade or in exchange for other trade agreements. For example, the North American Free Trade Agreement (NAFTA) essentially eliminated tariffs among Canada, the United States, and Mexico.

High tariffs protect domestic industry by making foreign goods more expensive. However, they also risk slowing trade. For example, between World War I and World War II, the United States passed a very high protectionist tariff. In response, other countries instituted retaliatory tariffs to block American trade as Americans had blocked foreign trade. Consequently, world trade ground to a halt.

When governments make changes to spending and taxes, it affects the government's budget. When revenue (primarily money from taxes) exceeds spending, the government has a SURPLUS. When spending exceeds revenues, the government has a DEFICIT. A deficit is not the same thing as a debt. A deficit is simply the gap between what the government has spent and what it has earned. In order to cover that deficit, it must borrow money, generating government debt. National debt develops over years of deficits.

Changes in CURRENCY are caused by and impact the strength of a nation's economy. CURRENCY APPRECIATION occurs when a country's money gains value in national and international markets. This increases foreign investment, as other countries are able to gain more value for their money. However, a strong currency makes that nation's exports more expensive, which can affect trade.

CURRENCY DEPRECIATION occurs when a country's money loses value in national and international markets. Currency depreciation may point to instabilities in the nation's economy (such as high rates of inflation). However, when carried out in an intentional and orderly manner, it can increase a nation's global competiveness by lowering the cost of its exports. For example, China has used intentional currency depreciation to build a strong export-based economy and foster economic growth.

GO ON

EXAMPLES

1) Which of the following would NOT be an example of contractionary fiscal policy?

A. freezing annual cost of living increases on the salaries of government employees

B. reducing the operating hours of national parks

C. increasing property taxes

D. financing a new dam

E. increasing the interest rate on loans

Answers:

A. Incorrect. By denying federal employees a scheduled pay increase, the government is decreasing spending (or preventing an increase in spending).

B. Incorrect. By reducing the hours that national parks are open, the government can reduce spending on labor and operating expenses.

C. Incorrect. An increase in property taxes removes money from the circular flow of the economy. People must pay money in taxes instead of spending on goods and services.

D. **Correct.** If the government builds a new dam, it injects new spending into the economy, thereby expanding the economy.

E. Incorrect. Increasing the interest rate will make it less likely that people will borrow money, reducing the supply of money in circulation.

2) Which of the following is NOT a responsibility of the Federal Reserve?

A. to set interest rates

B. to determine government spending

C. to maximize employment

D. to stabilize prices

E. monitoring reserves in US banks

Answers:

A. Incorrect. Monitoring and adjusting interest rates is one of the primary ways the Federal Reserve influences the economy.

B. **Correct.** Although the Federal Reserve plays an important role in fiscal policy, it has no control over government spending.

C. Incorrect. One of the primary tasks of the Federal Reserve is to maximize employment. This was established at its founding in 1913.

D. Incorrect. The primary focus of the Federal Reserve is to prevent excessive inflation or recession. It does this by using fiscal tools to stabilize prices.

E. Incorrect. While not one of the original responsibilities of the Fed, it now is responsible for maintaining reserves in American banks.

six

PRACTICE TEST

United States History

Directions: Read the question carefully and choose the best answer.

1) All of the following contributed to the destruction of Native American populations in North America except

    A. mass exportation of Native Americans to plantations in the Caribbean

    B. unintentional transfer of smallpox from Europeans to Native Americans.

    C. violent conflict over land and resources between Europeans and Native Americans.

    D. geographical displacement by colonists.

    E. introduction of guns by colonists

2) What was a consequence of the Kansas-Nebraska Act?

    A. the Fugitive Slave Act

    B. the Compromise of 1850

    C. violence between pro- and anti-slavery advocates in Kansas over the legalization of slavery ("Bleeding Kansas")

    D. the Missouri Compromise

    E. a balance in the Senate between free and slave states

3) The early Democratic Party (the Democratic-Republicans) was mainly concerned with which of the following?

    A. agrarian issues, small landowners, and maintaining a weaker federal government

    B. fiscal policy in support of urban areas and big businesses

    C. limitations on federal oversight of business and banks

    D. maintaining a strong federal government

    E. limiting the power of large states like Virginia

4) Which of the following best describes the conditions faced by Latinos and Latinas who had remained in western territories won by the US in the Mexican-American War?

   A. They were treated with derision; many lost land and wealth they had held under Mexico, and did not enjoy the same rights under the law as citizens, even though they had been promised American citizenship in the Treaty of Guadalupe Hidalgo.

   B. While many had lost land and wealth they had held under Mexico, they were entitled to and received restitution from the government of the United States.

   C. They were treated equally in social and political situations under the United States.

   D. Most Latinos and Latinas left the western territories for Mexico following the Mexican-American War, due to discriminatory conditions they faced under the United States government.

   E. Although they suffered economically, the American citizenship granted under the Treaty of Guadalupe Hidalgo gave them political equality.

5) How did the colonies in New England differ from southern ones like Virginia, the Carolinas, and Georgia?

   A. Farms tended to be larger in the southern colonies and produce cash crops like tobacco, using slave labor; in the north, smaller family farms predominated and early urbanization was more widespread.

   B. Farms tended to be larger in the northern colonies and produce cash crops like tobacco, using slave labor; in the south, smaller family farms predominated and early urbanization was more widespread.

   C. The southern colonies were wealthier than the northern colonies, with a more educated population.

   D. The northern colonies had fewer immigrants and a more homogenous population than southern colonies.

   E. There were no major differences between the northern and southern colonies before independence.

6) How did the views of the Federalists and the Anti-Federalists differ during the Constitutional Convention?

   A. The views of the Federalists and Anti-Federalists did not significantly differ at the Constitutional Convention.

   B. The Anti-Federalists did not believe in a Constitution at all, while the Federalists insisted on including the Bill of Rights.

   C. The Anti-Federalists favored a stronger Constitution and federal government, while Federalists were concerned that states would risk losing their autonomy.

   D. The Federalists favored a stronger Constitution and federal government, while Anti-Federalists were concerned that states would risk losing their autonomy.

   E. The Federalists did not believe in a Constitution at all, while the anti-Federalists insisted on including the Bill of Rights.

7) What advantage did the colonists have in the American Revolution?

    A. vast financial wealth

    B. superior weaponry

    C. strong leadership and knowledge of the terrain

    D. a professional military and access to mercenaries

    E. early international support

8) What did the Compromise of 1850 accomplish?

    A. It admitted California and Maine as free states and strengthened the Fugitive Slave Act.

    B. It admitted California as a free state, Utah and New Mexico with slavery to be decided by popular sovereignty, and strengthened the Fugitive Slave Act.

    C. It admitted California, Utah, and New Mexico as free states, and strengthened the Fugitive Slave Act.

    D. It admitted California, Utah, and New Mexico as states with slavery to be decided by popular sovereignty, and strengthened the Fugitive Slave Act.

    E. It admitted California as a state with slavery to be decided by popular sovereignty, Utah as a free state and New Mexico as a slave state.

9) How did the Lincoln-Douglas Debates impact the nation before the 1860 presidential election?

    A. They reflected the national mood: that the country was deeply divided over the question of slavery and whether states had the right to determine its legality.

    B. They reflected the national mood: that the country was deeply divided over the question of slavery—Lincoln called for abolition, while Douglas favored the practice.

    C. They reinvigorated the debate over slavery, which had been overshadowed by debate over states' rights.

    D. They reinvigorated the debate over states' rights, which had been overshadowed by debate over slavery.

    E. They highlighted the increasing influence of abolitionists as neither man wanted to publicly support slavery.

10) What did the Missouri Compromise accomplish?

    A. It admitted Missouri as a free state.

    B. It admitted California as a free state.

    C. It allowed slavery in New Mexico and Utah to be decided by popular sovereignty.

    D. It banned slavery north of the thirty-sixth parallel, so that new states formed in northern territories would be free.

    E. It overturned the Compromise of 1850.

11) The New Deal was intended to

    A. provide immediate economic relief to those suffering from the Great Depression.

    B. stimulate longer-term economic and social recovery for US society through various targeted programs.

    C. implement permanent reforms in banking and finance to prevent a reoccurrence of the failures that led to the Great Depression.

    D. only A and B

    E. A, B, and C

12) Following the Civil War, the United States ratified the Thirteenth, Fourteenth, and Fifteenth Amendments to the Constitution. What did these amendments guarantee?

    A. an end to slavery, equal rights for all Americans, and voting rights for all Americans, respectively

    B. an end to slavery, equal rights for all Americans, and voting rights for all African Americans, respectively

    C. an end to slavery, equal rights for all American men, and voting rights for all African American men, respectively

    D. an end to slavery, equal rights for Americans, and voting rights for African American men, respectively

    E. an end to slavery, equal rights for all American men, and voting rights for all American men

13) A major consequence of the Civil War was

    A. the rise of the Federalist Party.

    B. the destruction of the South's economy and the growth of the North's economy.

    C. the emergence of the Republican Party.

    D. the growth of the South's economy and the destruction of the North's economy.

    E. The dissolution of the Democratic Party.

14) Even after the end of slavery, African Americans in the rural South still suffered due to

    A. discriminatory property laws which explicitly prohibited African Americans from buying or owning land

    B. the Colored Farmers' Alliance, which was organized to limit their efforts to become independent farmers.

    C. the Reconstruction Acts, which specifically punished Southern blacks who did not join the Union army.

    D. labor unions, which advocated for white workers' rights in factories in urban areas and ignored rural issues.

    E. sharecropping, which kept them in heavy debt, often to their former "masters."

15) During FDR's terms in office, which of the following was created?

    A. Medicare

    B. Social Security

    C. the Federal Reserve

    D. the Department of Veterans' Affairs

    E. all of the above

16) The Spanish-American War

    A. brought the United States territories in Asia, the Pacific Ocean, and the Caribbean.

    B. received limited public support because of journalism biased against the revolutionaries

    C. was the first military action directed by Roosevelt's Corollary to the Monroe Doctrine.

    D. was a protracted war that lasted much longer than the government anticipated

    E. all of the above

17) The Cuban Missile Crisis ultimately resulted in

    A. the installation of the Castro regime.

    B. the fall of the Castro regime.

    C. a new opening of dialogue between the United States and the Soviet Union.

    D. the end of a period of détente between the United States and the Soviet Union.

    E. international embarrassment for the United States.

18) During periods of high tension between the United States and the Soviet Union in the 1950s, how was the US affected?

    A. Fear of communism was pervasive, and during the McCarthy era, accusations were made against public figures.

    B. Fearing Soviet communism, the United States supported Maoism in China as a counterweight to Leninism.

    C. During the McCarthy hearings, several members of Congress were found to be communist and so were removed from office.

    D. The US decreased government spending in Central America, Africa, and Asia in order to increase spending on defense.

    E. The United States supported the installation of pro-US leaders in Eastern Europe to provide a buffer against Soviet aggression.

World History

Directions: Read the question carefully and choose the best answer.

1) An important tenet of Judaism held that

    A. There is only one God and Muhammad is God's Prophet.

    B. A harmonious society is the ideal society.

    C. The moral codes provided by God in the Ten Commandments apply to all, even slaves.

    D. The son of God is both human and divine.

    E. Some individuals are pre-destined by God to ascend to heaven.

2) Which of the following best describes the Caste system in India?

    A. It is a defined, unchangeable social and religious hierarchy, determined by birth.

    B. It is a changeable social hierarchy.

    C. It is a hierarchy determined by skills and education wherein one's position can be changed.

    D. It is a defined, unchangeable social hierarchy, determined by birth.

    E. It is a religious hierarchy separate from social life.

3) During the Peloponnesian War,

    A. the dominant Hellenic powers, Crete and Sparta, went to war with each other.

    B. the dominant Hellenic powers, Athens and Sparta, went to war with the Ionian Greeks in Anatolia.

    C. Greece was able to unite as the dominant powers, Athens and Sparta, fought against Persia and the Ionian Greeks.

    D. the dominant Hellenic powers formed an alliance to conquer the weaker states.

    E. the dominant Hellenic powers, Athens and Sparta, went to war with each other.

4) The Hittites were able to expand from Anatolia due to

    A. superior seafaring technology, allowing expansion into the Mediterranean.

    B. superior military technology, including chariots and weaponry.

    C. advanced technology imported from Greece.

    D. their development of bronze metallurgy.

    E. Better social organization allowing for a large, highly disciplined and well-trained army.

5) How did the Neolithic Era mark a major development in human evolution?

    A. the development of agriculture and beginning of settled societies

    B. the early use of the wheel

    C. the use of bronze to develop basic tools

    D. early medical treatment

    E. the advent of trade among groups

6) Despite the period of relative stability enjoyed by Europe during the High Middle Ages, the Black Death resulted in which of the following outcomes?

    A. European powers were made vulnerable to attacks by the Magyars, who toppled the disorganized Holy Roman Empire.

    B. Instability in Europe led to military conflict, division within the Catholic Church, and weakening of the Holy Roman Empire.

    C. The Mongols were able to expand their empire into Eastern Europe.

    D. Islamic powers were able to completely conquer the Iberian Peninsula as a result of instability there.

    E. England took advantage of the continent's instability and extended its authority over France and Spain.

7) One reason the Muslim Arabs were able to take over Byzantine- and Persian-controlled areas was

    A. Muslims were ambivalent towards Christian minorities who may have opposed the Greek Orthodox Byzantines or the Zoroastrian Persians; these groups therefore preferred Arab-Muslim rule to more oppressive power structures.

    B. Arabic-speaking people in the region were more responsive toward Arabic-speaking rulers.

    C. Muslims already living in the Byzantine and Persian empires welcomed Islamic rule.

    D. A and B only

    E. A, B, and C

8) Many scholars argue that modern banking began in Venice in the fifteenth century. Which of the following strengthens this argument?

    A. Venice was the first major colonial power, developing mercantilism.

    B. Venice was a center of intellectual and cultural development.

    C. Venice was a commercial center, ideally situated to profit from goods imported on the Silk Road and from Africa.

    D. Venice was not badly affected by the plague.

    E. Venice, politically, was one of the strongest city-states and exerted great iinfluence over its neighbors.

9) The Qur'an

    A. contains the legal teachings of Islam.

    B. contains the legal teachings of Judaism.

    C. is believed to have been transmitted from Allah and is the holy book of Islam.

    D. was written by Muhammad and is the holy book of Islam.

    E. was the first holy book of a monotheistic religion.

GO ON

10) Which of the following best describes the motivation for Protestant reformers?

    A. Protestants, including Martin Luther, originally sought to develop a new form of Christianity separate from the Catholic Church.

    B. Protestants like Martin Luther were unhappy with the teachings of the Church, including Papal indulgences and corruption in the Church, and originally sought reform.

    C. Protestants were initially influenced by European political leaders, who used them to limit the power of the Church.

    D. Protestants, including Martin Luther, originally sought to topple the Catholic Church, believing it to have become too corrupt.

    E. Protestants like Martin Luther wanted to shift political control of the church from the clergy to lay people.

11) The Hundred Years' War

    A. is an example of European unity against an outside, non-European invading force.

    B. showed the technological dominance of the powers aligned with the Catholic Church, whose resources were massive.

    C. indicated a shift in European politics from allegiance to one's ethnicity or nation to allegiance to the empire.

    D. was a series of battles fought by Spain to regain control of the Iberian Peninsula from Muslim rulers.

    E. described ongoing ethnic conflict in Europe.

12) Which of the following best describes the consequences of the Opium Wars?

    A. British occupation of China

    B. Chinese victory over Britain

    C. unequal trade treaties favoring China

    D. unequal trade treaties favoring Britain

    E. The delay of further imperialist efforts in China

13) How were European empires affected by nationalism in the eighteenth and nineteenth centuries?

    A. European empires like the Austro-Hungarian Empire benefitted from nationalism, as Austrians and Hungarians were more loyal to the imperial government.

    B. The Austro-Hungarian Empire lost its Balkan territories to the Ottoman Empire, which was perceived to be more tolerant of Muslim minorities.

    C. Given the nature of empire—consolidated rule over an extended region home to diverse peoples—nationalism threatened empire as ethnic groups began to advocate for representation in imperial government.

    D. Given the nature of empire—consolidated rule over an extended region home to diverse peoples—nationalism threatened empire as ethnic groups began to advocate for their own independent states.

    E. Nationalist movements led to consolidation of empires as nations with similar majority ethnicities combined.

14) How was Europe affected by the Civil War in the United States?

    A. European powers were inspired to make slavery illegal following the American Civil War.

    B. Industrializing European powers relied on Southern cotton, but were encouraged not to trade with the Confederacy so as not to support slavery, which had already been abolished in Europe and most European empires.

    C. Industrializing European powers relied on Southern cotton, and traded with the Confederacy, supplying them with needed income during the Civil War.

    D. Conflict between governments and the people over which side to support led to instability in Europe.

    E. all of the above

15) Following the collapse of the Ottoman Empire after the First World War, European countries took control of the Middle East, establishing protectorates according to arbitrary boundaries and installing rulers in accordance with European strategic interests. What effect has this had on the Middle East in the twentieth and twenty-first centuries?

    A. The Middle East has not been greatly affected.

    B. Illegitimate national borders and rulers have led to instability in the region.

    C. Improved governance, thanks to the protectorates, improved stability following the decline of the Ottoman Empire in the region.

    D. European investment in strategic resources supported long-term political stability in the Middle East.

    E. Increased regional stability as state-based identity replaced ethnic or religious identity.

16) Which of the following best explains the economic impact on Germany following the First World War?

    A. Overspeculation on German farmland caused the market to crash.

    B. Wartime reparations mandated by the Treaty of Versailles and the worldwide Great Depression caused inflation to skyrocket, plunging the German economy into crisis.

    C. Germans were forced to pay extra taxes to cover reparations, and due to high prices, many could not afford to do so.

    D. The Reichsmark was removed from circulation and replaced with the dollar as a means of punishment, forcing many Germans into poverty.

    E. Trade embargoes imposed on Germany by the victors severely depressed its economy.

17) Choose the best description for the Russian strategy of empire-building.

    A. Russia focused on colonizing overseas, strengthening its navy to build a trans-oceanic empire.

    B. Russia focused on overland expansion, moving eastward into northern Asia across Siberia and westward into Eastern Europe.

    C. Russia remained isolated, avoiding expansion and focusing on industrialization instead.

    D. Russia lacked the resources to build an empire and struggled to maintain its agrarian-based society.

    E. Russia focused on areas strategic to trade, claiming territory in Asia and Africa.

18) The Treaty of Westphalia

   A. marked the end of the Thirty Years' War.

   B. was indicative of a shift in European politics, towards international relations based on non-interference and emerging concepts of independent states, rather than empires dominated by the Catholic Church and other forces.

   C. is often viewed as the foundation of modern European relations.

   D. involved almost of all of Europe's leaders, either as signers or guarantors.

   E. all of the above

Government

Directions: Read the question carefully and choose the best answer.

1) The framers instituted a system of checks and balances because they were concerned about

    A. one branch of government gaining too much power.

    B. mob rule.

    C. the military taking over the government.

    D. the states overpowering the national government.

    E. foreign leaders seizing control of the government

2) If no presidential candidate wins a majority in the Electoral College, how is the president chosen?

    A. The Electoral College votes based only on the top two candidates.

    B. The state legislatures select the president.

    C. Whichever candidate had a plurality of the popular vote wins.

    D. The Supreme Court selects the president.

    E. The House of Representatives selects the president.

3) Which of the following is currently true about the Supreme Court's interpretation of the right to free speech?

    A. The expression of ideas or opinions even without words is protected.

    B. Citizens who believe certain laws are unjust are constitutionally allowed to disobey them.

    C. Newspapers are protected even if they knowingly print a false story about someone.

    D. It cannot be restricted.

    E. It can only be restricted in times of war.

4) What can Congress do if the Supreme Court declares a law unconstitutional?

    A. override the decision with a two-thirds vote

    B. pass the law again

    C. amend the Constitution

    D. request a veto from the president

    E. request a review by the state Supreme Courts

5) Which of the following is the best example of federalism?

    A. The president sends troops to Iraq.

    B. Congress rejects the Treaty of Versailles.

    C. The Department of Agriculture is created.

    D. State legislatures elect senators.

    E. Supreme Court nominees are approved by the Senate

6) If a person believes they can effect positive change in their government, they have a high level of

    A. political aptitude.

    B. political allegiance.

    C. political efficacy.

    D. political insight.

    E. political confidence

7) Which of the following is true about political action committees (PACs)?

    A. They are managed by political parties.

    B. They are prohibited in state elections.

    C. The amount of money they can contribute in each election is restricted.

    D. They must work closely with the candidate that they support.

    E. They can only use their money on media supporting their candidate.

8) Which of the following differentiates district courts from appellate courts?

    A. An appellate court has original jurisdiction.

    B. A district court only hears criminal cases.

    C. An appellate court reviews previous court decisions.

    D. A district court is beholden to the state government.

    E. An appellate court is presided over by only one judge.

9) According to the original Constitution, who is eligible to vote?

    A. all citizens

    B. all property owners

    C. all white men

    D. The states have the power to determine voter eligibility.

    E. Congress has the power to determine voter eligibility.

10) Which of the following describes the means by which a president can be removed from office?

    A. The Senate votes by a majority to impeach the president; the House delivers a guilty verdict with a two-thirds vote.

    B. The House votes by a majority to impeach the president; the Senate delivers a guilty verdict with a two-thirds vote.

    C. The Senate votes to impeach the president with a two-thirds vote; the House delivers a guilty verdict through a simple majority.

    D. The House votes to impeach the president with a two-thirds vote; the Senate delivers a guilty verdict through a simple majority.

    E. The House and Senate both must vote to impeach the president with a two-thirds majority and to deliver a guilty verdict with a two-thirds majority.

11) If a developing nation needed help funding a new network of state-run hospitals, which of the following IGOs would it most likely ask for financial help?

   A. The World Health Organization

   B. NATO

   C. The World Bank

   D. The World Trade Organization

   E. the United Nations

12) Which of the following is an accurate example of checks and balances?

   A. The president signs treaties, and the Senate ratifies them.

   B. A bill becomes a law when Congress votes on it and the Supreme Court declares it constitutional.

   C. The Senate appoints justices to the Supreme Court, and the House of Representatives approves them.

   D. Congress has the power to remove the president, and the Supreme Court has the power to remove members of Congress.

   E. The Supreme Court can override a presidential pardon

13) How do the two major parties officially select their nominees for the presidency?

   A. through public opinion polls

   B. through a discussion among the party's national leadership

   C. at nominating conventions

   D. through party votes in each state

   E. from the party leadership in each house of Congress

14) To which of the following does the Supreme Court's power of judicial review NOT apply?

   A. laws passed by Congress

   B. laws passed by state legislatures

   C. executive orders

   D. lower-court decisions

   E. none of the above

15) Which of the following is an example of a legislative check on another branch?

   A. a visit to Israel by a congressional delegation

   B. Congress passing the Crime Bill after revisions in conference committee

   C. the 2002 expulsion of Representative Jim Traficant after he was convicted of bribery

   D. the 1999 Senate rejection of the Nuclear Test Ban Treaty

   E. Provisions for monitoring elections in states listed in the Voting Rights Act of 1965

16) John Locke's theory of a social contract is best reflected in which section of the Constitution?

    A. the Bill of Rights

    B. Article V, which refers to amending the Constitution

    C. Article IV which addresses the powers of the states

    D. Article VII, which refers to ratification

    E. the Preamble

17) Which clause of the Constitution best supports the idea of the rule of law?

    A. the supremacy clause

    B. the elastic clause

    C. the advise and consent clause

    D. the due process clause

    E. the full faith and credit clause

18) Which of the following constitutional provisions was NOT a change from the Articles of Confederation?

    A. a bicameral legislature

    B. the possibility of amending the Constitution

    C. a three-branch government

    D. the creation of a standing army

    E. the creation of a judicial branch

Geography

Directions: Read the question carefully and choose the best answer.

1) The International Date Line is

    A. the same as the Prime Meridian.

    B. the same as the Equator.

    C. 180° from the Prime Meridian.

    D. 90° north of the Equator.

    E. 90° south of the Equator.

2) A farmer in Maine who grows fruits and vegetables only to feed his family is practicing

    A. swidden farming

    B. subsistence farming

    C. intensive farming

    D. traditional farming

    E. commercial farming

3) Ireland has a "right to return" law granting Irish citizenship to anyone with at least one Irish grandparent. This type of law is an example of

    A. irredentism

    B. balkanization

    C. ethnonationalism

    D. centrifugal force

    E. out-migration

4) Which of the following statements is true about the political geography of Antarctica?

    A. Antarctica is governed by the United Nations.

    B. Antarctica is governed jointly by the United States, Great Britain, and Russia.

    C. Antarctica is the only unorganized territory left in the world.

    D. Antarctica is governed jointly by its four nearest neighbors: Argentina, Chile, South Africa, and Australia.

    E. Governance is disputed among several states including Argentina, South Africa and Great Britain.

5) Which of the following factors most greatly contributes to a country's transition from Stage Two to Stage Three of the Demographic Transition Model (DTM)?

    A. the changing roles of women

    B. advances in agricultural technology

    C. advances in medicine

    D. increased industrialization

    E. greater mobility within a country

6) The Robinson map (which slightly distorts shape, size, and straight line direction) is an example of which kind of map?

   A. gnomonic projection

   B. azimuthal equidistant projection

   C. equal area projection

   D. compromise projection

   E. conformal projection

7) Which of the following would be considered a push factor for migration?

   A. the discovery of oil in a new region

   B. increased political freedoms offered in the home region

   C. a new law in the home country requiring the practice of Catholicism

   D. the relocation of a major company to the home region

   E. the outbreak of civil war in a new region

8) Silicon Valley is an example of which economic pattern?

   A. deglomeration

   B. agglomeration

   C. industrialization

   D. modernization

   E. globalization

9) Boston, New York, Philadelphia, Baltimore, and Washington D.C., as geographically close urban areas, form a(n)

   A. urban realm

   B. world city

   C. megalopolis

   D. transition zone

   E. primary zone

10) According to dependency theory, Senegal's low development is a result of which of the following?

   A. its dependence on funding from the World Bank

   B. its status as a Stage Two country based on the DTM

   C. its status as a peripheral country

   D. French colonization of West Africa

   E. its dependency on one major export

11) In the nineteenth century, Scotch-Irish families moved to Chicago, aided by glowing letters from family and friends who had migrated earlier. This is an example of which kind of migration?

    A. stream migration

    B. internal migration

    C. step migration

    D. net migration

    E. chain migration

12) Looking at the map below, what kind of boundary separates the United States and Canada?

    A. physical

    B. cultural political

    C. relict

    D. geometric political

    E. natural

13) Based on the core-periphery model, the majority of periphery countries are in

    A. Africa, parts of Asia, and parts of South America.

    B. Asia, parts of Eastern Europe, and parts of South America.

    C. North America, Africa, and parts of Asia.

    D. South America, parts of North America, and parts of Eastern Europe.

    E. Eastern Europe, the Middle East, and parts of Africa.

Economics

Directions: Read the question carefully and choose the best answer.

1) Paul decides that, having already completed two revisions of his resume, he should read through and revise it one more time. Which of the following is most likely true?

    A. The marginal benefit of the third revision is less than the marginal cost of the third revision.

    B. The marginal benefit of the third revision is at least as great as the marginal cost of the third revision.

    C. Without knowing Paul's opportunity cost of revising his resume, there is no way to determine if the marginal benefits outweigh the marginal costs.

    D. The second revision's marginal benefit was most likely less than its marginal cost.

    E. The marginal benefit of each revision is more than the marginal benefit of the previous revision.

2) Max and Karen can both make desserts and peel carrots for the restaurant's evening service. For every dessert made, Max can peel thirty carrots and Karen can peel sixty carrots. Based on this information, which of the following is true?

    A. Max peels carrots since he has absolute advantage in making desserts.

    B. Karen peels carrots since she has absolute advantage in making desserts.

    C. Karen makes desserts since she has comparative advantage in dessert making.

    D. Max makes desserts since he has comparative advantage in dessert-making.

    E. There is insufficient information to determine the best use of Max and Karen's labor resources.

3) The market for wool sweaters is in equilibrium. The price of hooded sweatshirts, a substitute good, rises. What impact will this have on the wool sweaters market?

    A. Supply will rise, increasing price and decreasing the quantity.

    B. Supply will fall, increasing the price and increasing the quantity.

    C. Demand will fall, increasing the price and decreasing the quantity.

    D. Demand will rise, increasing the price and increasing the quantity.

    E. Supply and demand will rise, increasing the price and increasing the quantity

4) According to the law of demand, when the price of cucumbers increases, which of the following should happen?

    A. The quantity of cucumbers demanded increases.

    B. The quantity of cucumbers demanded falls.

    C. The demand for cucumbers falls.

    D. The demand for cucumbers increases.

    E. Price does not directly impact quantity demanded nor demand.

5) In the production possibility curve below, economic growth would be indicated if the curve moved

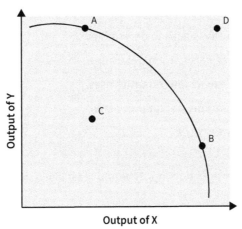

Output of Y

Output of X

A. from point C to point A

B. from point A to point B

C. from point B to point D

D. from point D to point C

E. from point A to point D

6) A startup software company determines that price elasticity for their software is 4.2. They wish to raise their total revenue. Which of the following will help them do that?

A. decrease price as demand is inelastic

B. increase price as demand is inelastic

C. decrease price as demand is elastic

D. increase price as demand is elastic

E. No change in price will affect demand.

7) When is a price floor put into place?

A. The equilibrium price is perceived as being too high.

B. The equilibrium price is perceived as being too low.

C. There is a surplus of a good.

D. There is a shortage of a good.

E. The equilibrium price is in danger of shifting downward.

8) What is the price elasticity of the demand for salt (E_d). if the price of salt rises 4 percent and the quantity demanded for salt falls 2 percent?

A. $E_d = 0$

B. $E_d = 4$

C. $E_d = 2$

D. $E_d = 1$

E. $E_d = 0.5$

9) The price of the type of tomatoes used in ketchup drops dramatically. At the same time, the price of mustard, a substitute for ketchup, increases. What impact will these two events have on the supply and price of ketchup?

   A. Price falls, but quantity is hard to determine.

   B. Price rises, but quantity is hard to determine.

   C. Price is hard to determine, but quantity rises.

   D. Price is hard to determine, but quantity falls.

   E. Price falls, but quantity rises.

10) Which of the following production inputs would least likely be able to be changed in the short run?

   A. the number of cashiers at a grocery store

   B. number of chocolate chips in a cookie

   C. the size of a restaurant's dining room

   D. the amount of electricity used at a high school

   E. the number of hours worked by carpenters at a construction site

11) All of the following are basic factors of production except

   A. labor

   B. land

   C. consumers

   D. capital

   E. infrastructure

12) Choosing among scarce items demonstrates the relationship between choice and

   A. opportunity cost.

   B. product cost.

   C. marginal cost.

   D. total cost.

   E. fixed cost.

13) Which of the following is NOT true of a production possibility curve?

   A. It depicts maximum output possibilities.

   B. It requires two goods.

   C. It is based on a particular set of production inputs.

   D. It maximizes utility.

   E. It demonstrates economic efficiency and growth.

ANSWER KEY

United States History

1)

A. **Correct.** The English settlers were not interested in trading the Native Americans as slaves.

B. Incorrect. Smallpox decimated Native American populations, which had never been exposed to the disease.

C. Incorrect. Ongoing violent conflict between European colonizers and Native Americans over hundreds of years caused thousands of deaths and led to social breakdown among some Native American societies.

D. Incorrect. Colonization and related conflict forced tribes to move from their traditional lands; for example, the Lenape were forced to move from Delaware west to the Great Lakes region. Later, many tribes were forced from their land during the Trail of Tears to Indian Territory (later, Oklahoma).

E. Incorrect. Guns dramatically changed the nature of warfare in North America. When tribes did come into conflict, the death tolls were significantly higher, which also made post-conflict resolution more difficult (leading to more conflict and death).

2)

A. Incorrect. The Fugitive Slave Act was already in existence.

B. Incorrect. The Compromise of 1850 had already taken place.

C. **Correct.** Violence broke out over the question of legalizing slavery in Kansas, where it had previously been prohibited.

D. Incorrect. The Missouri Compromise had taken place decades before and was essentially undone by the Kansas-Nebraska Act.

E. Incorrect. The conflict in Kansas was not resolved until the end of the Civil War. Also, there were more free states at this point in time.

3)

A. **Correct.** The Democratic-Republicans, descended from the Anti-Federalists, opposed a strong federal government and urban business interests, focusing on agrarian issues.

B. Incorrect. The Democratic-Republicans focused on rural constituents.

C. Incorrect. While the Democratic-Republicans surely did not favor a strong federal government, their priority was not supporting big business or banking.

D. Incorrect. The Democratic-Republicans were against federalism.

E. Incorrect. Many of the Democratic-Republicans were from large states, namely Virginia.

4)

A. **Correct.** Hispanic residents of the land the United States gained in the Treaty of Guadalupe Hidalgo did not obtain all they were promised; in fact, many lost their property and were not treated equally under the law or in society.

B. Incorrect. Those Hispanic residents of Mexico who were living on territory ceded to the United States did not receive restitution for losses suffered in violation of the Treaty of Guadalupe Hidalgo.

C. Incorrect. Latinos and Latinas living in United States territory often experienced unequal treatment under the law and in social situations.

D. Incorrect. Many people of Mexican descent stayed in what became the United States following the Mexican-American War.

E. Incorrect. The government did not honor the promise of American citizenship included in the treaty.

5)

A. **Correct.** Southern geography and climate lent itself to labor-intensive plantation agriculture, for which the colonists exploited slave labor. Natural harbors in the north fostered urban development, while the land was more appropriate for smaller farms.

B. Incorrect. The reverse was true.

C. Incorrect. All the colonies had wealthy, elite classes, in addition to working classes, indentured servants, and slaves.

D. Incorrect. With more ports and trade, and more readily available parcels of land, the north attracted a greater variety of immigrants from throughout Europe.

E. Incorrect. Economic and cultural differences developed among the colonies.

6)

A. Incorrect. The views of the Federalists and Anti-Federalists differed a great deal.

B. Incorrect. The Bill of Rights was a compromise measure; it was not originally a Federalist contribution.

C. Incorrect. The reverse was true.

D. **Correct.** The Federalists were the driving force behind a stronger Constitution that would empower the United States federal government; the Anti-Federalists worked to protect state sovereignty and ensured the passage of the Bill of Rights to protect certain rights not explicitly guaranteed in the Constitution itself.

E. Incorrect. The Federalists were strong proponents of the Constitution. The anti-Federalists were the greatest supporters of the Bill of Rights.

7)

A. Incorrect. While some colonists were quite wealthy, colonial wealth paled in the face of British wealth.

B. Incorrect. The colonists did not have superior weaponry.

C. **Correct.** The colonial military did have strong leaders, and an intimate knowledge of the terrain, many having been born there.

D. Incorrect. Britain had an experienced military with substantial experience fighting in Europe and elsewhere. In addition, King George III hired Hessian mercenaries from Germany to supplement British troops.

E. Incorrect. Spain and France did not support the colonists' efforts until after the Battle of Saratoga.

8)

A. Incorrect. Maine was admitted as a free state in the Missouri Compromise.

B. **Correct.** The Compromise of 1850 admitted California as a free state; however it strengthened the Fugitive Slave Act. The legalization of slavery in Utah and New Mexico would be decided by the voters.

C. Incorrect. Slavery in New Mexico and Utah would be decided by popular sovereignty.

D. Incorrect. Slavery would never be permitted in California.

E. The Compromise of 1850 sought to avoid the issue of slavery and so granted Utah and New Mexico the right of popular sovereignty.

9)

A. **Correct.** The Lincoln-Douglas Debates showed how divided the country was over slavery.

B. Incorrect. Douglas was not so much in favor of slavery as he was a proponent of states' rights.

C. Incorrect. Slavery and states' rights were intertwined.

D. Incorrect. The question of slavery was at the root of the debate over states' rights.

E. Incorrect. The country was already very aware of the growing divide and the increasingly radical abolitionists.

10)

A. Incorrect. The Missouri Compromise allowed slavery in Missouri.

B. Incorrect. California was not admitted as a state until 1850.

C. Incorrect. This was a feature of the Compromise of 1850.

D. **Correct.** The Missouri Compromise prohibited slavery north of the thirty-sixth parallel in new US territories, permitting slavery in Missouri.

E. Incorrect. The Missouri Compromise was passed in 1820, before the Compromise of 1850.

11)

A. Incorrect. While many New Deal programs targeted impoverished Americans, the New Deal had a wider scope than short-term poverty alleviation.

B. Incorrect. Several New Deal programs and projects sustained economic and social development in the United States, but this does not describe the breadth of the New Deal.

C. Incorrect. New Deal legislation did indeed address needed banking reform; however, the New Deal had other components as well.

D. Incorrect. FDR prioritized long term banking and finance reforms like the FDIC.

E. **Correct.** The New Deal encompassed programs providing immediate relief for impoverished Americans, long-term development projects, and financial

reforms to prevent a repeat of the Great Depression.

12)

A. Incorrect. The Fifteenth Amendment only enabled African American men to vote. No American women could vote in national elections until the ratification of the Nineteenth Amendment in 1920.

B. Incorrect. African American women were still unable to vote, even though the Fifteenth Amendment allowed African American men to exercise that right. African American women would not be able to vote until 1920.

C. Incorrect. The Fourteenth Amendment ensures equal protection under the law to all Americans, regardless of race, gender, or other categories.

D. **Correct.** The Thirteenth Amendment abolished slavery; the Fourteenth Amendment promised equal protection under the law to all US citizens; the Fifteenth Amendment ensured that (male) African Americans and former slaves could vote.

E. Incorrect. While voting rights were restricted to men, equal rights were granted to all citizens.

13)

A. Incorrect. The Federalist Party had declined in the early nineteenth century and never returned to the political scene.

B. **Correct.** The Civil War devastated the South's economy due to infrastructural damage and international isolation.

C. Incorrect. The Republican Party appeared before the Civil War.

D. Incorrect. The Southern economy suffered from the Civil War.

E. Incorrect. The Democratic Party remained strong in the South and dominated politics there following Reconstruction.

14)

A. Incorrect. While laws were put in place to inhibit black ownership of land, it was not explicitly prohibited.

B. Incorrect. The Colored Farmers' Alliance assisted African American farmers.

C.   Incorrect. The Reconstruction Acts did not include this provision.

D.   Incorrect. While labor unions championed urban workers, most of whom were white, this was not in direct opposition to efforts to advance African Americans in the South; indeed, the Progressive Movement brought together activists for these and many diverse causes.

E.   Correct. Sharecropping perpetuated racial inequality in the South.

15)

A.   Incorrect. The Medicare Act was passed under the Johnson administration.

B.   Correct. The Social Security Act was part of the New Deal.

C.   Incorrect. The Federal Reserve Act was passed in 1913 following the Panic of 1907.

D.   Incorrect. The Department of Veterans' Affairs was made a Cabinet-level department in 1989.

E.   Incorrect. Only answer choice B is correct.

16)

A.   Correct. The US greatly increased its overseas holdings and became a true empire.

B.   Incorrect. Yellow journalism fanned the flames of public support for the war.

C.   Incorrect. Roosevelt did not become president until 1901, after the war was over.

D.   Incorrect. The war was very brief, lasting less than a year.

E.   Incorrect. Only answer A is correct.

17)

A.   Incorrect. Castro was already in power at the time of the Cuban Missile Crisis.

B.   Incorrect. Fidel Castro has remained in power, at least in name, through 2015; his brother Raul controls Cuba and despite many reforms, the same government is in place.

C.   Correct. Following the extreme tensions between the two countries, the United States and the Soviet Union improved dialogue in the early 1960s, leading to a period of détente.

D.   Incorrect. The Cuban Missile Crisis led to a period of détente; it did not end one.

E.   Incorrect. The United States ultimately came out victorious in the Crisis, agreeing to move outdated missiles in Turkey, just to let the Soviet Union save face.

18)

A.   Correct. Public paranoia over communism was widespread, and many public figures were accused of being communist.

B.   Incorrect. The United States never supported Maoism.

C.   Incorrect. No members of Congress were removed from office due to the McCarthy hearings.

D.   Incorrect. The US increased its foreign spending in an attempt to counteract the influence of the Soviet Union.

E.   Incorrect. The Soviet Union extended its sphere of influence over Eastern Europe to create a buffer between them and the rest of Europe.

World History

1)

A.   Incorrect. This is an important tenet of Islam.

B.   Incorrect. This is a core belief of Confucianism.

C.   **Correct.** This was a teaching of Judaism.

D.   Incorrect. This was a major teaching of Christianity.

E.   Incorrect. The concept of predestination was a tenet of early Protestantism (namely Puritanism).

2)

A.   **Correct.** The caste system is a social hierarchy rooted in religious tradition. It is not possible to change the caste into which one is born.

B.   Incorrect. While the caste system is a social hierarchy, and while there is more social and economic flexibility within it than before, it is not possible to move from one caste to another.

C.   Incorrect. One's position in the hierarchy is determined by birth; a person is born into his or her caste, and that position is permanent.

D.   Incorrect. While this definition is true, it leaves out the traditionally religious nature of the caste system.

E.   Incorrect. While based in religion, the caste system determined social rank, position, and profession.

3)

A.   Incorrect. The Peloponnesian War was between Sparta and Athens, not Sparta and Crete.

B.   Incorrect. The Peloponnesian War was fought between Greeks in Peloponnesus and Central Greece, not in Anatolia.

C.   Incorrect. The Peloponnesian War did not involve Persia.

D.   Incorrect. Athens and Sparta did not form an alliance during this time.

E.   **Correct.** The Peloponnesian War was between the major Greek powers.

4)

A.   Incorrect. The Hittites expanded overland.

B.   **Correct.** The Hittites were skilled charioteers and were early pioneers of iron weaponry.

C.   Incorrect. The Hittites created their own weapons; furthermore, they preceded ancient Greek development.

D.   Incorrect. The Hittites worked with iron.

E.   Incorrect. The military superiority of the Hittites came primarily from their weaponry.

5)

A.   **Correct.** Developing agricultural practices in the Neolithic Era allowed humans to establish settled societies sustained by reliable food sources.

B.   Incorrect. While the wheel was an important development in the Neolithic Era, it was just one part of the major change in human behavior exhibited in that era: the development of settled societies.

C.   Incorrect. The use of bronze was a defining characteristic of the eponymous Bronze Age, which followed the Neolithic Era.

D.   Incorrect. While it is likely that early medical treatment developed in the Neolithic Era, again, this was not a defining characteristic of this period; furthermore it was made possible by the development of settled societies.

E.   Incorrect. While some trade likely took place during this period, it was a consequence of the development of settled societies.

6)

A.   Incorrect. The Magyars did not topple the Holy Roman Empire; furthermore, their incursions into Europe had been several hundred years prior.

B.   **Correct.** The continental—indeed, global—impact of the Black Death destabilized much of Europe.

C.   Incorrect. The Black Death actually destabilized the Mongol Empire.

D.   Incorrect. The Umayyads reached Iberia long before the Black Death.

E.   Incorrect. While England did rule for France for periods during the plague, it never controlled Spain.

7)

A.   Incorrect. While this is true, it is not the complete answer given the other options presented.

B.   Incorrect. Again, while this is true, it is not the complete answer.

C.   Incorrect. Islam had not yet spread to these areas.

D.   Correct. Even though the peoples living under Byzantine and Persian rule were not Muslim or Arab, the Islamic tradition of tolerance toward the "People of the Book" and, to an extent, Zoroastrians, made them more acceptable rulers than the oppressive and disorganized collapsing regimes; furthermore, many people in the region spoke Arabic, which made it easier to accept Arab rule.

E.   Incorrect. Answer choice C is incorrect.

8)

A.   Incorrect. Venice was not a major global colonial power, nor did it develop mercantilism.

B.   Incorrect. While Venice was a center of intellectual and cultural development, this was not a major reason for development of modern banking there.

C.   Correct. As a commercial center and well-situated to handle goods arriving in Europe from the Silk Road and from Africa, Venice developed banking institutions that influenced modern banking.

D.   Incorrect. As a center of international trade, Venice was strongly affected by the plague.

E.   Incorrect. While Venice did wield substantial regional power, this does not relate to the establishment of banks.

9)

A.   Incorrect. While the Qur'an is a major source for Muslim legal scholars, Islamic law draws primarily from the Hadith.

B.   Incorrect. The Qur'an is not a holy book in Judaism; Jewish law relies on the Talmud.

C.   Correct. The Qur'an is the holy book of Islam and it is believed that the book was transmitted directly from God to Muhammad.

D.   Incorrect. While the Qur'an is the holy book of Islam, it is not believed that Muhammad himself wrote it.

E.   Incorrect. Both the Torah and Bible pre-date the Qur'an.

10)

A.   Incorrect. Martin Luther was a Catholic monk; he originally sought reform within the Catholic Church.

B.   Correct. Martin Luther and his followers opposed corruption in the Church and wanted changes.

C.   Incorrect. The Reformation was not originally a political movement.

D.   Incorrect. Again, Martin Luther wanted reform, not to overthrow the papacy or the Church.

E.   Incorrect. The focus of the movement was not on leadership but on the actions of the church.

11)

A.   Incorrect. The Hundred Years' War was an intra-European war.

B.   Incorrect. The Hundred Years' War occurred before the Reformation and was a conflict mainly between England and France; the Church was not a major figure.

C.   Incorrect. This was not a factor of the Hundred Years' War.

D.   Incorrect. The conflict over the Iberian Peninsula is called the Reconquista.

E.   Correct. The Hundred Years' War was really an ongoing conflict between different European ethnic groups (mainly, the French and the English).

12)

A.   Incorrect. Britain did not occupy China, although it did control Hong Kong, which remained a colony until 1997.

B.   Incorrect. China was not successful in the Opium Wars.

C.   Incorrect. Trade treaties at the time did not favor China.

D.   **Correct.** Britain gained economic and commercial privileges in China it had previously not had, including gaining Hong Kong, freedom of movement in China, and access to ports.

E.   Incorrect. The destabilization of China by the Opium Wars made it a prime target of imperialist forces.

13)

A.   Incorrect. Nationalism did not benefit the Austro-Hungarian Empire: smaller ethnic groups living in territory controlled by the empire wanted their independence due to nationalism.

B.   Incorrect. The Austro-Hungarian Empire began losing control over its Balkan territories due to nationalism and due to interference from Russia, which supported Slavic minorities in the Balkans.

C.   Incorrect. Nationalism drove ethnic groups to seek self-rule and independence, not representation in government.

D.   **Correct.** Nationalism triggered independence movements and advocacy.

E.   Incorrect. Nationalism led to a fracturing of the European states.

14)

A.   Incorrect. Some European powers had already made slavery illegal (legally, if not in practice).

B.   **Correct.** Abolitionist European powers were unwilling to support the South economically, due to the Confederacy's stance on slavery.

C.   Incorrect. While rapidly industrializing Europe needed cotton, many European countries ceased trade with the states that seceded from the Union and developed sources of cotton elsewhere (in Egypt and India, for example).

D.   Incorrect. B is the correct answer choice.

E.   Incorrect. While the people and the governments did often disagree over the Civil War, there was no resulting governmental upset in Europe.

15)

A.   Incorrect. Many of the boundaries are the modern borders of Middle Eastern countries today, so the region has been greatly affected.

B.   **Correct.** Borders did not take into account history or ethnic groups; installed rulers did not necessarily have legitimacy in the eyes of the people, leading to political instability and violence.

C.   Incorrect. The protectorates did not improve governance or stabilize the region following the decline of the Ottoman Empire.

D.   Incorrect. Outside investment in strategic resources (like oil) has contributed to instability in the region by providing support to illegitimate rulers and contributing to income inequality and conflict.

E.   Incorrect. Ethnic and religious identity remained strong creating significant conflict within and between states.

16)

A.   Incorrect. This explanation is insufficient.

B.   **Correct.** The main factors in post-WWI German economic collapse are all addressed here.

C.   Incorrect. This explanation does not account for global economic depression.

D.   Incorrect. This is untrue.

E.   Incorrect. The winners of the war imposed reparations on Germany, not a trade embargo.

17)

A.   Incorrect. Russia's strategy was land-based expansion; it did not have a strong navy until the twentieth century.

B.   **Correct.** Russia expanded to the east, taking control of Siberia. Russia also extended westward to an extent, controlling part of Eastern Europe.

C.   Incorrect. Russia expanded and employed developmental strategies under a number of czars, including Catherine the Great and Peter the Great. In terms of industrialization, some efforts were made under the Romanovs; however, industrialization accelerated under the Soviets.

D.   Incorrect. Russia engaged in empire building throughout Eurasia well into the twentieth century; some argue that it has continued to do so in Crimea and Ukraine today.

E.   Incorrect. Russia was more concerned with expanding its empire than establishing strong trade relationships.

18)

A.   Incorrect. While the Treaty of Westphalia did end the Thirty Years' War, this answer choice is incomplete given the other possibilities offered.

B.   Incorrect. Again, while this is true, it is incorrect due to the other options presented.

C.   Incorrect. The Treaty of Westphalia is considered the foundation of modern international relations as it is based on the idea of state sovereignty; however, the due to the other answer choices this one is incorrect.

D.   Incorrect. While all countries with the exception of England, Russia and Poland were directly involved in the treaty, this answer is not complete.

E.   Correct. All of these answer choices are correct.

Government

1)

A. **Correct.** The purpose of checks and balances was to prevent tyranny in any branch of the government.

B. Incorrect. While there was some concern among the founders about the dangers of a pure democracy, checks and balances do not address the relationship between the government and the people.

C. Incorrect. Separation of powers kept the military in check. Also, with a civilian commander in chief, the military remains accountable to civilian authority.

D. Incorrect. Checks and balances do not refer to the relationship between the state and national governments.

E. Incorrect. Checks and balances do not address the relationship between the United States and foreign governments.

2)

A. Incorrect. The Electoral College only votes once on the initial candidates.

B. Incorrect. The state legislatures do not choose the president.

C. Incorrect. The national popular vote has no bearing on presidential elections. However, today members of the Electoral College vote based on the popular vote within their state.

D. Incorrect. The Supreme Court has no role in presidential elections.

E. **Correct.** The House of Representatives selects the president from the candidates by a majority vote of its state delegations.

3)

A. **Correct.** Symbolic speech—the expression of ideas through actions—is protected speech.

B. Incorrect. The rule of law is still paramount. There is no justifiable reason for breaking the law under the Constitution.

C. Incorrect. This is called defamation and is not protected under the First Amendment.

D. Incorrect. There are restrictions on freedom of speech; specifically, speech

that defames someone, is considered obscene by the courts, or is designed to incite violence is prohibited.

E. Incorrect. There is no exception for wartime.

4)

A. Incorrect. The two-thirds override only applies to presidential vetoes.

B. Incorrect. Once declared unconstitutional, a law remains unconstitutional.

C. **Correct.** Once a law has been declared unconstitutional, the only way to make it constitutional is to change the Constitution. This can only be done through a formal amendment.

D. Incorrect. The president cannot veto Supreme Court decisions.

E. Incorrect. The Supreme Court is the final authority in issues of constitutionality.

5)

A. Incorrect. Presidential troop deployment is an example of an expressed executive power, not of the relationship between the central government and the states.

B. Incorrect. Congressional rejection of a treaty is part of the system of checks and balances.

C. Incorrect. Creating an executive department through an Act of Congress is an expressed legislative power.

D. **Correct.** State election of senators demonstrates how the Senate was originally beholden to the states.

E. Incorrect. This is an example of a legislative check on executive power, not federalism.

6)

A. Incorrect. Aptitude refers to how well one can perform an action.

B. Incorrect. Allegiance refers to one's level of loyalty.

C. **Correct.** Political efficacy is a measure of an individual's belief in the importance of his or her role in the political system.

D.   Incorrect. Insight is a strong understanding of the inner workings of a system.

E.   Incorrect. Political confidence would imply the individual has a lot of faith in his or her government.

7)

A.   Incorrect. PACs are separate from the parties and are run by special interest groups, organizations, or corporations that are trying to advance a particular cause or candidate.

B.   Incorrect. PACs operate at every level of government; there are no restrictions on whom PACs can support.

C.   Correct. PACs may only contribute up to $5000 per election. Super PACs may provide unlimited funding.

D.   Incorrect. PACs are not allowed to collaborate with the candidate that they support; they must remain independent.

E.   Incorrect. There are no restrictions on how PAC money is used in a campaign.

8)

A.   Incorrect. In most federal cases, district courts have original jurisdiction. In cases between two states, cases involving an ambassador, or cases in which a citizen is suing his or her state, the Supreme Court has original jurisdiction. The appellate courts never do.

B.   Incorrect. There are both criminal and civil district courts. Appellate courts hear both kinds of cases.

C.   Correct. The purpose of the appellate court is to review the decisions of the district courts in order to determine if an error of law has been made.

D.   Incorrect. Both district and appellate courts are federal courts. The states have no authority over them.

E.   Incorrect. District courts are presided over by a single judge. Appellate courts typically have a panel of three judges.

9)

A.   Incorrect. The Constitution does not provide for voter eligibility. The pool of eligible voters increased over time; now, the majority of the population may vote.

However, there are still restrictions based on age and criminal record.

B.   Incorrect. The Constitution lists no property qualifications for voting.

C.   Incorrect. Again, the Constitution does not provide for voter eligibility. And, for the first fifty years, only propertied white men were eligible to vote.

D.   Correct. Because it is not an expressed power, voter eligibility was left up to individual states. However, the Fifteenth, Nineteenth, and Twenty-Sixth Amendments all expanded the right to vote under the Constitution.

E.   Incorrect. Determining voter eligibility is not an expressed power.

10)

A.   Incorrect. The House is responsible for impeachment, the Senate for removal.

B.   Correct. The House has the power to impeach, and it only requires a simple majority to do so. The Senate acts as a jury and delivers the verdict. Two-thirds of the Senate must vote guilty for the president to be removed.

C.   Incorrect. While the Senate does require a two-thirds majority, that is to remove the president, not to impeach him or her.

D.   Incorrect. The House is responsible for bringing formal charges against the president, but it is in the Senate that two-thirds of the members must vote for impeachment.

E.   Incorrect. The powers to impeach and oust the president are divided between the House of Representatives and the Senate, respectively.

11)

A.   Incorrect. The World Health Organization focuses on research and investment in the eradication of disease rather than developing healthcare infrastructure.

B.   Incorrect. NATO—or the North Atlantic Treaty Organization—is a defense agreement among the United States, Canada, and several countries in Europe.

C.   Correct. The World Bank promotes development and capitalism in developing countries around the world by providing loans for infrastructure and internal development.

D. Incorrect. The World Trade Organization determines the rules of trade between nations.

E. Incorrect. The United Nations is political organization, primarily, not a financial one.

12)

A. Correct. The Constitution empowers the president to make treaties with the advice and consent of the Senate.

B. Incorrect. In order for a bill to become a law, Congress votes on it, and the president must sign it. The Supreme Court rules on it only if a relevant case comes before the court.

C. Incorrect. The president appoints justices to the Supreme Court and the Senate approves them.

D. Incorrect. Congress does have the power to impeach and remove the president, but members of Congress can only be removed by the House or the voters.

E. Incorrect. A presidential pardon cannot be overturned by anyone.

13)

A. Incorrect. Opinion polls play no official role in the election process.

B. Incorrect. Candidates were chosen this way before the 1820s but no longer are today.

C. Correct. Each party holds a nominating convention the summer before the election. Delegates from each state cast votes for the candidate they support.

D. Incorrect. Each party does hold primaries and caucuses, which are elections at the state level. However, these determine how delegates at the convention should vote and technically do not determine the candidate.

E. Incorrect. Parties select candidates with a wide variety of history in and out of politics.

14)

A. Incorrect. The Supreme Court may determine the constitutionality of laws passed by Congress. In fact, the case

that created the power of judicial review, *Marbury v. Madison*, dealt with a law passed by Congress (the Judiciary Act of 1789).

B. Incorrect. While laws passed by state legislatures are primarily reviewed by the state's supreme court, laws that violate the protections provided in the U.S. Constitution can be struck down by the Supreme Court.

C. Incorrect. As acts of the federal government, executive orders are subject to judicial review.

D. Incorrect. Using a writ of certiorari, the Supreme Court has the power to demand any case within its jurisdiction be sent up for review.

E. Correct. The Supreme Court can review all of the types of laws listed here.

15)

A. Incorrect. The visit of a congressional delegation to another country is an unofficial diplomatic function of Congress. It does not limit the power of any other branch.

B. Incorrect. Passing a bill after committee revisions only involves the legislative branch. The complex nature of the process is designed to limit chances for abuse of power, but only limits the legislative branch itself.

C. Incorrect. The House of Representatives' power to expel one of its members is a check of abuse on itself, not on another branch of government.

D. Correct. The rejection of the treaty shows the Senate checking the power of the executive branch, as the president had negotiated the treaty.

E. Incorrect. This is an example of the federal government asserting authority over the state governments, not a check on one branch's power.

16)

A. Incorrect. The Bill of Rights is an example of Locke's theory of natural rights: it lists rights protected from government interference.

B. Incorrect. Article V is an example of the rule of law: it states that the only way to override the provisions of the Constitution is to legally change it.

C. Incorrect. This section of the Constitution reflects federalism.

D. Incorrect. Article VII is an example of federalism: the federal government could not exist without the approval of the states.

E. **Correct.** The Preamble states, "We the People," supporting the idea that the government exists with the consent of the governed.

17)

A. **Correct.** The supremacy clause declares the Constitution the highest law in the land. The only way to change the Constitution is through the amendment process; no individual has authority higher than the Constitution.

B. Incorrect. The elastic clause, also known as "necessary and proper," provides room for Congress to utilize powers not specifically listed in the Constitution. It does not assert the law's authority over individuals.

C. Incorrect. The advise and consent clause gives the Senate the power to approve presidential appointees. This is a prime example of a check on executive authority.

D. Incorrect. The due process clause is one of the clauses of the Fourteenth Amendment. It guarantees all citizens fair treatment under the law. While it does deal with the relationship between individuals and the law, it does not explicitly restrict any individual's authority from superseding the law.

E. Incorrect. The full faith and credit clause states that all states must respect the proceedings and procedures of the other states.

18)

A. Incorrect. Under the Articles of Confederation, the legislature was unicameral. It became bicameral under the Constitution.

B. **Correct.** The Articles of Confederation could also be amended. However, amendment required a unanimous vote in the legislature, making it extremely difficult.

C. Incorrect. The Articles of Confederation provided for no judicial or executive branches, only a legislative one.

D. Incorrect. The Congress of the Confederation was not empowered to maintain an army. Under the Constitution, Congress is empowered to do so.

E. Incorrect. There was no federal judicial branch under the Articles of Confederation.

Geography

1)

A. Incorrect. The Prime Meridian is the internationally accepted 0° longitudinal line.

B. Incorrect. The International Date Line is a longitudinal line. The equator is at latitude 0°.

C. Correct. The International Date Line is where the date changes when following time zones around the world. This location was selected primarily because it was located almost entirely in open ocean and so would disrupt the fewest number of people.

D. Incorrect. Like with answer B, the International Date Line is a longitudinal line.

E. Incorrect. The International Date Line runs from pole to pole.

2)

A. Incorrect. "Swidden" is the term used for a field that has been prepared for planting by burning the remaining crops.

B. Correct. Subsistence farming is the process of growing crops primarily in order to feed one's own family. No extra crops are grown for sale.

C. Incorrect. Intensive farming is a type of subsistence farming. There is nothing in the question to indicate which type of subsistence farming the farmer uses.

D. Incorrect. Traditional farming would refer to the techniques used by the farmer, which are not discussed in the question.

E. Incorrect. Commercial farming is the raising of produce or livestock for sale on the market.

3)

A. Incorrect. Irredentism is the process by which a state tries to reunite its various pieces that were previously divided. It applies to land, not people.

B. Incorrect. Balkanization is the process by which a state is broken into smaller pieces. The "right to return" law aims to bring people of Irish descent together.

C. Correct. Ethnonationalism is when an individual or group identifies with its ethnicity, in this case Irish, over its state affiliation. Ireland's right to return law places ethnic heritage before political affiliation or location in terms of determining membership to the nation.

D. Incorrect. Centrifugal forces are those that divide the people of the state. A right to return law, for the most part, has the opposite effect.

E. Incorrect. Out-migration describes the process of moving from one place to another.

4)

A. Incorrect. The United Nations does not govern Antarctica.

B. Incorrect. While several different countries have research stations in Antarctica, no country or group of countries has authority over it.

C. Correct. In 1961, a treaty was signed banning any individual claims on Antarctica and preserving it for scientific research. It is the only land in the world not claimed by a state.

D. Incorrect. While each of these countries has a research station in Antarctica, none of them has any claim on the territory.

E. Incorrect. None of these countries have laid claim to Antarctica.

5)

A. Correct. The biggest difference between Stage Two and Stage Three is the slowing of the birth rate. This occurs as women are given more opportunities and societal views about their purpose shift.

B. Incorrect. Changes in agricultural practices do not have a direct impact on the birth rate of a country.

C. Incorrect. Advances in medicine transition countries from Stage One to Stage Two.

D. Incorrect. While industrialization does help open up new opportunities for women, it alone does not decrease the birth rate.

E. Incorrect. Mobility is not a measure of development.

6)

A. Incorrect. A gnomonic projection distorts size and area in order to maintain accurate straight-line directions.

B. Incorrect. An azimuthal equidistant projection distorts shape, size, and overall straight-line direction in order to maintain accuracy of direction from a single point to all other points.

C. Incorrect. Equal area projections preserve the size of land masses by distorting shape and direction.

D. **Correct.** The Robinson map distorts all map characteristics in order to minimize overall distortion.

E. Incorrect. Conformal maps maintain accuracy in land shape.

7)

A. Incorrect. The discovery of oil would lead to new job opportunities and act as a pull factor in migration.

B. Incorrect. If the outbreak of civil war was in the home region, then it would be a push factor. However, because it is in a new region, it would not impact migration in the home region.

C. Incorrect. Increased political freedoms would encourage people to stay, thereby discouraging migration.

D. Incorrect. The relocation would likely provide new job opportunities in the home region, discouraging migration out.

E. **Correct.** This new law would push out any individuals who did not wish to practice Catholicism.

8)

A. Incorrect. Deglomeration is the process by which industries spread out due to the over-exploitation of a place's resources. This is the opposite of what has happened in Silicon Valley.

B. **Correct.** Agglomeration is the bunching together of like industries in order to reduce costs by sharing resources. Tech companies have come together in Silicon Valley for just this reason.

C. Incorrect. Industrialization is the process by which a country moves from an economy based on sustainable agriculture to one based on manufacturing. Silicon Valley is the product of a post-industrial society.

D. Incorrect. Modernization is the process by which a society's economy develops according to Rostow's model. This is unrelated to Silicon Valley.

E. Incorrect. Globalization describes the increasing interconnectedness of countries and markets.

9)

A. Incorrect. An "urban realm" is not a geographic term. A realm is the largest unit the world can be divided into, and includes multiple regions.

B. Incorrect. A world city is a locus of global economic, cultural, or political power. While New York City is a world city, these five cities do not make up one.

C. **Correct.** A megalopolis is a large urban area formed by the close proximity of multiple urban centers. These five cities are sometimes called the "BosWash megalopolis."

D. Incorrect. A transition zone is an area between culture regions where traits from both regions exist. It does not relate to urban zones.

E. Incorrect. Globalization describes the increasing interconnectedness of countries and markets.

10)

A. Incorrect. While Senegal does receive a great deal of funding from the World Bank, dependency theory argues that development is based upon a country's history.

B. Incorrect. Dependency theory does not address population growth.

C. Incorrect. The core-periphery model is a separate model of economic development linked to the World Systems Analysis Theory.

D. **Correct.** Dependency theory argues that past colonization crippled the colonized countries, preventing them from being able to develop economically.

E.   Incorrect. The dependency theory argues that low development is a result of dependency created by colonization.

11)

A.   Incorrect. Stream migration is not a geographical term. A migration stream is the flow of migration from one place to another.

B.   Incorrect. Internal migration describes the process of moving from one place to another within the same country.

C.   Incorrect. Step migration is the process of moving a long distance in short intervals.

D.   Incorrect. Net migration is used to describe the total migration (in and out) for a particular region or place.

E.   Correct. Chain migration describes the movement of people from their home region to another region, following earlier migrants.

12)

A.   Incorrect. Physical boundaries are borders created by natural aspects of the landscape like hills, mountains, or rivers. The map shows that the US-Canada border mostly does not follow a natural physical boundary.

B.   Incorrect. Cultural political boundaries are based on religion, language, or other cultural traits. The culture on either immediate side of the US-Canadian border is very similar. The border is not based on any cultural difference.

C.   Incorrect. A relict boundary is one that is no longer functional, which is clearly not the case with the US-Canadian border.

D.   Correct. The border is drawn essentially as a straight line with little to no regard for physical features, making it a geometric political boundary.

E.   Incorrect. A natural border is based on natural features such as rivers or mountains.

13)

A.   Correct. Periphery countries are essentially LDCs, all of which can be found in Africa (with the exception of South Africa), parts of Asia, and parts of South America.

B.   Incorrect. While some periphery countries are in Asia, not all of Asia is considered part of the periphery. Eastern Europe mostly belongs to the semi-periphery.

C.   Incorrect. North America is not considered part of the periphery.

D.   Incorrect. Some countries in South America like Brazil and Argentina are part of the semi-periphery. North America (specifically the United States and Canada) are part of the core.

E.   Incorrect. The Middle East is considered part of the semi-periphery, not the periphery.

Economics

1)

A. Incorrect. Because we do not what Paul could be doing instead of the third revision or how much he improved his resume during the second revision, this cannot be said with any certainty.

B. Incorrect. It may seem this way because Paul has decided to complete a third revision. However, there is no information to support or refute this statement.

C. **Correct.** There is not enough information here to determine the opportunity cost of revising his resume. So, it is impossible to know the marginal cost or the marginal benefit of a third revision.

D. Incorrect. Since Paul has decided to complete a third revision, it would seem likely that the marginal benefit of the second revision was greater than the marginal cost. However, there is not enough information to determine either way.

E. Incorrect. Without knowing the opportunity cost of each revision, it is not possible to compare their marginal benefits.

2)

A. Incorrect. We do not know if Max has an absolute advantage in making desserts. In addition, the decision should be made based on comparative advantage, not absolute advantage.

B. Incorrect. Much like above, we do not know whether Max or Karen has an absolute advantage in dessert-making. Instead, we need to look at who has the comparative advantage in each task.

C. Incorrect. Karen's opportunity cost of making desserts is sixty carrots, compared to Max's opportunity cost of thirty carrots. This means that Karen should peel carrots, because she will "lose" more by making dessert.

D. **Correct.** Because Max's opportunity cost of making dessert is less than Karen's, he should make dessert. He has the comparative advantage in dessert-making.

E. Incorrect. The most efficient use of resources is determined by knowing the opportunity cost for each person producing each resource. This information is given.

3)

A. Incorrect. A change in a substitute good is a determinant of demand, not supply. Supply will not change in this situation.

B. Incorrect. The increase in price of hooded sweatshirts will not affect the wool sweater market.

C. Incorrect. If demand were to fall, price would increase. However, an increase in a substitute good does not lead to a decrease in demand of a product.

D. **Correct.** When the price of a substitute good increases, the demand for a product also increases, as people are more interested in buying what is now a less expensive alternative. When demand rises, price rises as well and the entire production possibility curve shifts rightward, demonstrating an increase in quantity as well.

E. Incorrect. Supply and demand are impacted inversely by changes in the price of substitute goods.

4)

A. Incorrect. Price and quantity demanded have an inverse relationship. When prices rise, consumers are less willing to buy the product.

B. **Correct.** The law of demand states that, holding all else constant, an increase in price causes a fall in demand.

C. Incorrect. Demand—rather than quantity demanded—is affected by changes in determinants of demand, including consumer income and prices of substitute or complimentary goods.

D. Incorrect. Demand only increases when consumer income increases or there is a change to another determinant of demand. Changes in price impact quantity demanded.

E. Incorrect. Price shifts quantity demanded, although it does not impact demand.

5)

A. Incorrect. Point C represents under-utilization of resources. Movement from C to A simply demonstrates that resources are now being used at their full potential.

B. Incorrect. Movement along the production possibility frontier indicates a shift in the ratio of output for the two products. This is not economic growth but simply a reallocation of resources.

C. Incorrect. A leftward shift of the curve indicates an inefficient use of resources.

D. Incorrect. Movement from D to C would indicate an inefficient use of resources, not a shift in overall economic growth.

E. Correct. Economic growth is shown by an overall outward shift in the production possibility curve, as would happen if A moved to D.

6)

A. Incorrect. With Ed > 1 (4.2), the demand for the software is certainly elastic.

B. Incorrect. If the demand was inelastic (which it is not since Ed > 1), changing the price would not impact demand, and so would not increase revenue.

C. Correct. Because Ed > 1, demand is elastic and changes at a faster rate than price. Decreasing the price by even a small amount will increase demand, thereby increasing revenue.

D. Incorrect. Although demand is elastic in this case, increasing the price would decrease demand and negatively impact revenue because price and demand are inversely related.

E. Incorrect. 4.2 shows a high degree of elasticity, meaning a change in price would have a big impact on demand.

7)

A. Incorrect. A price ceiling is set when the equilibrium price is perceived as being too high. The ceiling prevents the price from rising above a certain point.

B. Correct. Price floors set a minimum price below which the market is not allowed to fall. This is done when the equilibrium price is seen as too low to allow producers to profit.

C. Incorrect. Price floors create a surplus because the price is above the equilibrium price, which decreases quantity demanded and increases quantity supplied.

D. Incorrect. Shortages result from price ceilings. A price ceiling is below the equilibrium price, which increases quantity demanded and decreases the quantity supplied.

E. Incorrect. A price floor is used to improve a market in which equilibrium is already at an unacceptably low point.

8)

A. Incorrect. Price elasticity of 0 would mean that a percent change in price caused no change in demand.

B. Incorrect. For Ed = 4, the change in demand would need to be much larger at 16 percent, or the change in price would need to be much smaller at 0.5 percent.

C. Incorrect. If the demand changed by 4 percent and price by 2 percent, then Ed = 2.

D. Incorrect. Ed = 1 when the change in price is the same as the change in demand (the demand is then unit elastic).

E. Correct. Elasticity of demand is calculated by dividing the change in demand (2) by the change in price (4). This yields 0.5.

9)

A. Incorrect. With two opposing forces on the ketchup market, it is impossible to tell the impact on price without knowing which force is stronger. The hypothetical does not give us that information.

B. Incorrect. There are too many factors in this situation to determine the impact on price without more specific information.

C. Correct. Price cannot be determined from the information given; however, the lowered tomato price will increase the supply of ketchup, and the higher mustard price will increase the demand for ketchup. Together, these will increase the overall supply of ketchup.

D. Incorrect. If tomatoes became more expensive or mustard less expensive, the supply of ketchup would fall because both would act as deterrents to ketchup production. However, that is not the case in this situation.

E.   Incorrect. While it can be determined that supply will increase overall, there is insufficient information to determine the impact on price.

10)

A.   Incorrect. A grocery store can quickly hire more people in order to increase production.

B.   Incorrect. The number of chips in a cookie is a flexible production input.

C.   **Correct.** It is very difficult to change the plant size of a firm. In this case, the restaurant would have to wait until its lease term was up or embark on an expensive remodeling campaign, both of which would be possible in the long run, but not the short run.

D.   Incorrect. Electricity usage at the high school most likely already has some variability; the amount used could be easily reduced through basic conservation efforts.

E.   Incorrect. A contractor can easily reduce or increase the number of hours his employees work.

11)

A.   Incorrect. Labor is an essential factor of production, involved in all economic activity.

B.   Incorrect. While some industries may no longer require physical land, most do. Land is stil considered a basic factor of production.

C.   **Correct.** Consumers provide the demand for products. They do not play a role in production.

D.   Incorrect. All businesses require capital to start and to maintain production. This is an essential factor of production.

E.   Incorrect. A company's infrastructure—its physical space—affects how much it can produce.

12)

A.   **Correct.** Opportunity cost is the idea that whenever an individual makes a choice, he or she is giving up something else.

B.   Incorrect. Product cost is simply the cost of purchasing a product. This often factors into determining opportunity cost.

C.   Incorrect. Marginal cost is the change in cost to produce an additional unit of the product. Marginal cost is considered in cost-benefit analysis, but relates to choosing something again, rather than simply choosing between scarce items.

D.   Incorrect. Total cost is the total amount including explicit and implicit costs (including opportunity costs).

E.   Incorrect. Fixed costs are costs that cannot be easily adjusted to change production or overall cost. For example, a company's rent would be a fixed cost.

13)

A.   Incorrect. The curve itself does show all possible maximum outputs. It is important to remember it only shows possibilities, not actual production levels.

B.   Incorrect. A production possibility curve has one product on the x-axis and the other product on the y-axis. The curve shows the relationship between the production of each.

C.   Incorrect. A production possibility curve holds all else the same, meaning it assumes no variability exists in production inputs.

D.   **Correct.** A product's utility is the amount of happiness it brings to the consumer. A production possibility curve does not measure the impact of products on consumers, but rather an entity's production capacity.

E.   Incorrect. By illustrating maximum out possibilities, a production possibility curve shows economic efficiency. The shift of the curve shows economic growth.

Follow the link below to take your CLEP Social Sciences and History practice test and to access other online study resources:

www.acceptedinc.com/clep-social-studies-online-resources

CPSIA information can be obtained
at www.ICGtesting.com
Printed in the USA
LVHW06s0041110418
573041LV00030B/347/P

9 781635 302554